Acclaim for *Star Shrines and*

t

"Gary David's efforts at capturing the astronomical ethos of ancient Hopi traditions have enthused me from the moment I began reading. He has laid the crucial groundwork for grasping Native concepts of uniting earth and heaven. David convincingly demonstrates the Hopi as remarkably skilled surveyors gifted with the knowledge of establishing power centers that store and release subtle energies in precision alignment across the landscape. Readers will also be astonished to learn the vast scale and accomplishment of the irrigation canal system of ancient Hohokam engineers.

"David's special attention to detail as well as long overdue assertions equating ancient Arizona's skill-sets to those of Mayan, Egyptian, and other highly touted cultures are delightfully groundbreaking and a little breathtaking. Gary David is a visiting *kachina* on special mission for the traditional Pueblo People. *Star Shrines and Earthworks of the Desert Southwest* is a must-read for pre-Columbian aficionados and aspiring anthropologists alike."

Ross Hamilton, author of *Star Mounds: Legacy of a Native American Mystery*

"Gary David's work is a treasure of enormous importance. He draws us deep into the mystery of Arizona and deeper still into the lost secrets of ancient cosmology. The truth behind the myths and symbols he's uncovering has the power to unify us, just as the Hopi prophesied."

William Henry, author of *Starwalkers and the Dimension of the Blessed*

"As above, so below. The parallels Gary David has found between the ancient Egyptian sky-ground system involving the pyramids of Giza and the constellation of Orion, and a similar project to build heaven on earth by the Hopi of Arizona, are eerie, compelling and deeply thought-provoking."

Graham Hancock, author of *Fingerprints of the Gods*

Star Shrines and Earthworks

of the Desert Southwest

Gary A. David

Adventures Unlimited Press

Adventures Unlimited Press
P.O. Box 74
Kempton, Illinois 60946 USA
www.AdventuresUnlimitedPress.com

ISBN: 978-1-935487-84-5

Cover art and design: Jack Andrews
www.reverbnation.com/jackandrews
Photographs and illustrations: by Gary A. David
or non-copyrighted Internet sources unless otherwise noted.

Acknowledgments

I would like to thank the following people for inspiring, supporting, and in various ways facilitating the writing of this book:

Rob Milne, T. L. Subash Chandira Bose, Mark Borcherding, Jamie Hunter, J. Christine Tegler-Del Campo, Roberta Ruth Hill, Steven Blonder, Susan Seymour Hedke, Gary Osborn, Ross Hamilton, Jack Andrews, Dr. Amanda Laoupi, Jeff Nisbet, Michael Seabrook, Glenn Kreisberg, Michael Bourne, Andrew Gough, Patrick Chouinard, Alexander Giannakos, Walter Cruttenden, Adriano Forgione, Christopher O'Brien, Thomas O. Mills, Hugo Kennes, Brian Britten, Dr. Catherine Acholonu-Olumba, Zuni Elder Clifford Mahooty, Kimberley Ruff, Hopi Elder Martin Gashweseoma, Ronald Regehr, Ralph and Marsha Ring, Richard Fisher, Howard Middleton-Jones, Ray Urbaniak, Heyoka Ken Thornton, Dr. Stephen C. Jett, Linda Krumrie, Ros George, Gisela Ermel, César Reyes, Graham Hancock, Erich von Däniken, Gene D. Matlock, the late John Jay Harper, Jennifer Bolm, and my publisher David Hatcher Childress.

As always, special thanks and love go to my wife Anita Descault, who proof-read the manuscript and offered invaluable advice, and to my daughter Zia Ann David, of whom I am very proud.

Satellite photos courtesy of Google Earth.

Contents

"the inside real
and the out sidereal"

–Edward Dorn

(96) The Kachina dance to the rain-god, Hopi Indian Village, Shongho-pavi, Arizona.　　Copyright 1904 by Underwood & Underwood.

Right half of stereopticon photo, kachina dance,
Shungopovi village, Second Mesa, Arizona, 1903.

Chapter 1
Star Correlations
and Earth Chakras

"Follow wise Orion
Till you lose your eye,
Dazzlingly decamping
He is just as high."

–Emily Dickinson

Archaeoastronomical Quest

In July of 1997 I was driving the vast, desolate spaces of the high desert in northeastern Arizona en route to see one of the kachina dances held annually on the Hopi Reservation. The Hopi tribe currently numbers about 7,000 souls spread out across a dozen different villages. Dating back to the beginning of the 12th century AD, the original villages consisted of stone and adobe "apartment complexes" called pueblos, each of which contained an interior plaza. The sacred kachina ceremonies are performed in the plazas from about April until July, a few weeks after the summer solstice. The kachinas are spirits to which the Hopi people pray for rain and fertility in this harsh but stunningly beautiful land. Donning multi-colored costumes and masks, the dancers circle all day long in the plaza under the brutal desert sun. The droning beat of a single cottonwood drum accompanies their slow, stately dance while gourd and turtle shell rattles accent the persistent beat.

The kachinas are basically intermediaries between the realm of humans and the realm of the gods. Thus, their role is similar to that of angels in the Christian religion. Literally hundreds of different types of kachinas exist, each with its distinctive mask and ritual paraphernalia. Painted in primary colors with a multitude of various arcane symbols, these stitched rawhide or cloth masks come in all forms: circular, square, dome-shaped, cylindrical. Some are seen with horns, others with feathers or straggly hair. Many masks have either tube-like mouths or painted triangular mouths. They might instead have fangs or diamond-shaped teeth. Kachinas can appear with bug eyes, goggle eyes, slit-shaped eyes, or no eyes at all. A few masks even resemble space helmets worn by astronauts or perhaps even ETs!

In the process of impersonating the kachinas, the Hopi men –only males may perform the dance– are actually transformed into these benevolent spirit-messengers. In addition, the Hopi carve dolls called *tihuta* from cottonwood root. These dolls were traditionally used to teach the children about the various kachinas but are now also sold to collectors and tourists.

On my way to watch this unique Hopi ceremony, I had recently finished reading *The Orion Mystery* by Robert Bauval and Adrian Gilbert. In this bestseller the co-authors proposed what was called the Orion Correlation Theory. They had essentially discovered an ancient "unified ground plan" in which the layout of the pyramids at Giza directly corresponds to the pattern of Orion's belt in the sky as it appeared 12,500 years ago. According to the entire configuration, the Great Pyramid (Khufu) represents Alnitak, the middle pyramid (Khafre) represents Alnilam, and the slightly offset smaller pyramid (Menkaure) represents Mintaka.[1]

The central point of Egyptian cosmology was known as *Rostau*, the gateway to the *Duat*, or underworld (conceptualized as the afterlife realm). In a subsequent book, Graham Hancock and Robert Bauval clearly describe the earth-sky duality. "We have seen that the essence of this sacred 'Kingdom of Osiris' was the peculiar dualism with which it was connected to an area of the sky known as the *Duat*, close to Orion and Sirius on the western side of the Milky Way. We have also seen how the centre of the *Duat* was called Rostau and how Rostau, too, existed in both cosmic and terrestrial realms: in the heavens it was characterized by the three stars of Orion's belt and on earth by the three great Pyramids of Giza."[2]

Osiris, the god of death and resurrection, was commonly associated with Orion in ancient Egypt. The word *Sahu* refers to the "star-gods in the constellation Orion."[3] On the other hand, the Hopi word *sohu* simply means "star," with the most ritually important star pattern being Orion.[4] The Hopi even have a Sohu Kachina with a horizontal triad of stars on his crest. In addition, the Hopi word *tu'at* (also spelled *tuu'awta*) means "hallucination," "vision," or "mystical experience of seeing something extrasensory in nature or of déjà vu."[5] This word sounds very close to the Egyptian *Duat*—that seemingly illusory realm of the afterlife. (The renowned Egyptologist E. A. Wallis Budge indeed spelled it *Tuat*.) The Hopi term refers to just the sort of phantasmagoria one would encounter in the afterlife. Are these linguistic similarities merely coincidental or do they point to cultural interaction and mutual influence some time in the distant past?

With this Star Correlation theory of Egypt fresh in mind, I gazed idly in the distance as I slowly made my way toward the three equally spaced mesas upon which the Hopi had settled and constructed stone villages in a period following 1100 AD. Then it hit me: Could these also represent Orion's belt, I wondered? Perhaps here was yet another ground-sky relationship on the dry, expansive Colorado Plateau.

After witnessing the kachina dance, I returned home and got out my maps and sky charts in order to compare them. What I found astonished me. Either a currently inhabited Hopi pueblo or the ruins of an ancient Hopi village directly corresponded to every major star in the constellation! The earth reflected the sky with uncanny perfection. The migrating Hopi clans over a span of centuries had built a holistic pattern of pueblos on the ground that mysteriously yet undeniably mirrored Orion in the sky, with each village representing a specific star. I had to find out why. In other words, I had to "follow wise Orion." This propelled me on an archaeoastronomical quest that has lasted to this day.

The term for this relatively new science refers basically to the study of the way ancient people conceptualized the heavens, and the cultural effect that celestial phenomena had on their lives. It was, of course, "naked-eye astronomy" but was not any less complex than our contemporary endeavors. Or perhaps it was equally complex but in a radically different way. This sophistication did not involve technology and empirical science; instead archaeoastronomy interpolated mythology, spirituality, and ceremonial practices in the process of keen and persistent astronomical observation. It was essentially a gestalt: whole earth, whole sky, whole soul.

Arizona Star Patterns

In the depths of winter, Orion rises from the eastern horizon and gains its highest position in the sky. This in itself is amazing to see, but it is even more startling to watch this constellation rise out of the red dust of the Arizona desert. The stellar configuration of ancestral Hopi villages began to take shape in the mid-11th century and was finished by end of the 13th century AD. The construction of these "star shrines" basically achieved the unification of terrestrial and celestial.

I have borrowed the phrase "star shrines" from the Japanese culture. Frequently located in peaceful, rural areas, they usually enshrine a meteorite or round stone thought to have fallen from heaven—a sort of *omphalos*, or world navel. The meteorite is, of course, the physical embodiment of the cosmic link between earth and sky. These shrines are sometimes dedicated to three gods who were born from nothing and from which everything arose. One of the associations of this divine triad is Orion's belt.[6]

Extending from the giant hand of Arizona's Black Mesa that juts down from the northeast, three great fingers of rock beckon. They are the three Hopi Mesas, isolated upon this stark but majestic landscape to which the Ancient Ones were led very long ago. Directing our attention to this "Center of the World," we clearly see the close correlation to Orion's belt.

Mintaka, a double star and the first of the trinity to peek over the eastern horizon as the constellation rises, corresponds to Oraibi (Orayvi) and Hotevilla (Hotvela) on Third (or West) Mesa. The former village is the oldest continuously inhabited community on the continent, founded in the early 12th century.

Approximately seven miles to the east, located at the base of Second (or Middle) Mesa, the village of Shungopovi (Songòopavi) was reputedly the first to be established after the Bear Clan migrated into the region around the year 1100. Its celestial correlative is Alnilam, the middle star of the belt.

About seven miles farther east on First (or East) Mesa, the adjacent villages of Walpi, Sichomovi (Sitsom'ovi), and Hano (Hanoki) –the first of which was established prior to 1300– correspond to the triple star Alnitak, rising last of the three stars of the belt.

Nearly due north of Third Mesa's Oraibi at a distance of just over fifty-six miles is Betatakin Ruin in Tsegi Canyon, while about eight miles beyond is Keet Seel Ruin. (Betatakin is a Diné, or Navajo, word; Kawestima is the Hopi word for the site.) Located in Navajo National Monument, both of these spectacular cliff dwellings were built during the mid-13th century. Their sidereal counterpart is the double star Rigel, the left foot of Orion. (We are conceptualizing Orion as viewed from the front.)

Due south of Oraibi at an equal distance of fifty-six miles is Homolovi Ruins State Park, a group of four ancient Hopi pueblos. Homol'ovi was constructed between the mid-13th and early 14th centuries and represents the variable star Betelgeuse, the right shoulder of Orion.

Forty-seven miles southwest of Oraibi is the primary Sinagua ruin at Wupatki National Monument, surrounded by a few smaller ruins. (Sinagua is the term for a group culturally similar and contemporaneous to the Anasazi. Most archaeologists now refer to both groups as Ancestral Puebloans. The Hopi call their ancestors the *Hisatsinom*, or "Ancient Ones.") Built in the early 12th century, the celestial counterpart of Wupatki is Bellatrix, a variable star forming the left shoulder of Orion.

About fifty miles northeast of First Mesa's village of Walpi is the mouth of Canyon de Chelly and its eponymous national monument. In this and its side canyon, Canyon del Muerto, a number of ruins dating from the mid-11th century are found. Saiph, the triple star forming the right foot of Orion, corresponds to these ruins—primarily White House, Antelope House, and Mummy Cave. The Hopi term for the canyon is Söyaptup'ovi, which refers to its sandy ("spongy") bottom.

Extending northwest from Wupatki/Bellatrix, Orion's left arm holds a shield over numerous smaller ruins in Grand Canyon National Park, including Tusayan near Desert View on the south rim. Reaching southward from Homol'ovi/Betelgeuse, Orion's right arm holds a club above his head. This club stretches across Mogollon Rim, an escarpment that cuts east to west across northern Arizona. The club reaches southward to the Hohokam ruins near the modern-day metropolis of Phoenix. (The Hohokam were an earlier group than the two previously mentioned. They used irrigated rather than dry farming methods and constructed an extensive canal system. See Chapter 6.)

The head of Orion is a small stellar triangle formed by Meissa at its apex and by phi 1 and phi 2 Orionis at its base. It correlates to the 12th century Sinagua ruins at Walnut Canyon National Monument together with a few smaller ruins in the immediate region. The Hopi name is Wupatupqa, or "Long Canyon."

Solstice Interrelationships of Hopi Villages

Whereas the Giza terrestrial Orion from head to foot is oriented southeast to northwest, the Arizona Orion is oriented southwest to northeast. Of course, the pyramids are located west of the Nile River, while the Hopi Mesas are located east of the "Nile of Arizona," namely, the Colorado River.[7]

Another factor that eliminates mere chance in this mirroring of sky and earth is the angular positioning of the terrestrial

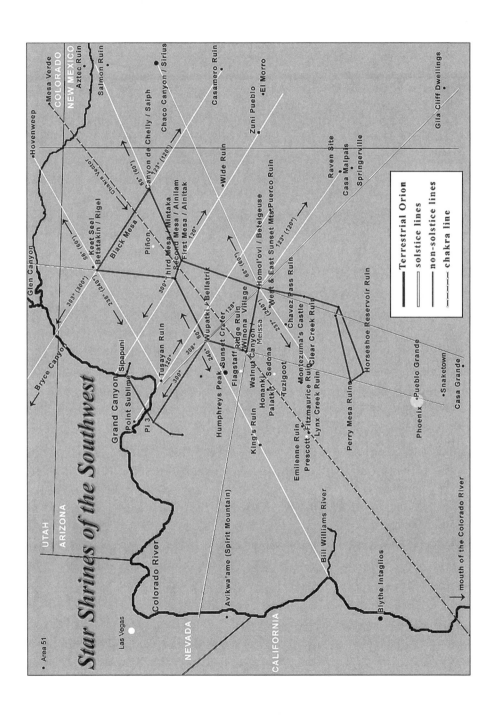

Star Shrines of the Southwest

Orion in relation to longitude. According to their cosmology, the Hopi place importance on inter-cardinal directions –that is, northwest, southwest, southeast, and northeast– rather than cardinal directions. They could not, of course, make use of the compass but relied instead upon solstice sunrise and sunset points on the horizon for orientation.

The sun-chief (in Hopi, *taawa-mongwi*) still performs his observations of the eastern horizon at sunrise from the winter solstice on December 21 (azimuth 120°) through the summer solstice on June 21 (azimuth 60°), when the sun god Taawa is making his northward journey. On the other hand, he studies the western horizon at sunset from June 21 (azimuth 300°) through December 21 (azimuth 240°), when Taawa travels south from the vicinity of the Sipàapuni in Grand Canyon to the San Francisco Peaks southwest of the Hopi Mesas.[8]

A few days before and after each solstice, Taawa seems to stop and rest in his winter or summer *Taawaki*, or "house." (The term solstice literally means "the sun to stand still.") In fact, the winter solstice ceremony called *Soyal* is performed in part to encourage the sun to reverse his direction and return to Hopi-land instead of continuing southward and eventually disappearing altogether.

The key solstice points on the horizon that we designate by the azimuthal readings of 60°, 120°, 240°, and 300° were incorporated in the relative positioning of the "star shrines." (However, these numbers for summer and winter sunrises and sunsets hold true only for this specific latitude.) If we stand on the edge of Third Mesa in the village of Oraibi on the winter solstice, for instance, we watch the sun set at exactly 240° on the horizon, directly in line with the ruins of Wupatki almost fifty miles away. The sun disappears over Humphreys Peak, the highest mountain in Arizona where a major shrine of the kachinas is located.[9]

Conversely, if we stand at Wupatki during the summer solstice, we see the sun rise directly over Oraibi on Third Mesa at 60° azimuth on the horizon. On that same day the sun sets at 300° azimuth, to which the left arm of the terrestrial Orion points. (There are a number of other solstice interrelationships that you can see on the map on p. 15. Also see azimuth diagram, p. 19.)

In this schema each village is connected to at least one other by a solstice sunrise or sunset point on the horizon. The interrelationships provided a psychological link between one's own village and the people in one's "sister" village miles away. Moreover, they reinforced the divinely ordered coordinates of the various sky cities brought down to earth. Orion and his Hopi manifestation named Masau'u (see next chapter) had spoken in a geodetic language that connected the Above with the Below (the Arizona Orion Correlation). In addition, Taawa/Sun had verified this configuration by his solar measurements along the curving rim of the *tutskwa*, or sacred earth.

Arizona Earth Chakras

Another alignment of ancient pueblo sites forms the Arizona Orion's grand chakra system, which indicates the direction that his spiritual energy flows. Derived from various ancient Hindu texts such as the *Upanishads*, the chakras system consists of a number of whirling wheels or vortexes contained in the subtle energy-body, which are aligned along the physical backbone. They receive and store life force called *prana*, each controlling a different area of the corporeal body.

Although this concept originated in India, some people may be surprised to learn that the Hopi also acknowledge chakras. However, the Hopi describe five psychophysical centers rather than the traditional seven. Southwestern author Frank Waters observes:

"The living body of man and the living body of the earth were constructed in the same way. Through each ran an axis, man's axis being the backbone, the vertebral column, which controlled the equilibrium of his movements and his functions. Along this axis were several vibratory centers which echoed the primordial sound of life throughout the universe or sounded a warning if anything went wrong. The first of these in man lay at the top of the head. Here, when he was born, was the soft spot, *kópavi*, the 'open door' through which he received his life and communicated with his Creator."[10]

Starting in the northeast at Mesa Verde National Park (Base or Root Chakra) in southwestern Colorado, a line runs southwest through Burnt Corn Ruins near the village of Pinon on Black Mesa (Sacral Chakra). This line continues southwest through Shungopovi/Alnilam on Second Mesa (Solar Plexus Chakra). Then the line intersects a mesa called Kachina Points (Heart Chakra) and passes near Grand Falls on the Little Colorado River (Throat Chakra). The line enters the foothills of the San Francisco Peaks and goes into the forehead of Orion at Walnut Canyon (Third Eye Chakra).

The line is extended farther into the red rock country of Sedona with its electromagnetic vortexes, passing Palatki ("Red House"), a small but gorgeously located ruin and pictograph (rock painting) site. In Verde Valley the newly energized vector ends at Tuzigoot National Monument, a major 13th century Sinagua ruin of over 100 rooms perched on a hilltop for the probable purpose of stellar observation (Crown Chakra). This line could, however, be extended even father southwest, ultimately reaching a point just north of the Colorado River's mouth. This is perhaps the place where the ancient Hopis migrating on reed rafts from the previous Third World (Era) to the current Fourth World entered the territory.

In this series of major chakra points, we see nearly a dozen Anasazi or Sinagua ruins and one still-inhabited Hopi pueblo perfectly aligned over a distance of over 275 miles within the framework of the tellurian Orion. The probability that these were randomly distributed is highly unlikely and increases the possibility that the Masau'u, Hopi god of the earth and the underworld, had directed their positioning.

This ley line forms Arizona Orion's grand chakra system that provides a conduit of *pranic* earth energy flowing southwest: from Mesa Verde, through the Hopi Mesas, into the evergreen forests of the San Francisco Peaks, and down to the Verde Valley. Walnut Canyon, by the way, symbolizes the terrestrial Orion's Third Eye, or pineal gland, which is etymologically derived from the Latin word *pinus*, or "pine cone."

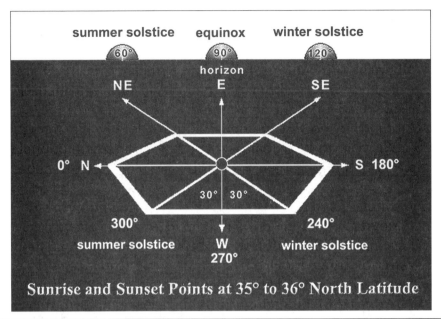

summer solstice   equinox   winter solstice

60°   90°   120°

horizon

NE   E   SE

0° N   S 180°

30° 30°

300°   240°

summer solstice   W   winter solstice
270°

Sunrise and Sunset Points at 35° to 36° North Latitude

1. Base Chakra = Mesa Verde, the Sun (Orion) Temple in southwestern Colorado.
2. Sacral Chakra = Burnt Corn Ruins near the village of Pinon, Arizona (corresponding to the Orion Nebula). 3. Solar Plexus (Navel) Chakra = Second Mesa and the Hopi village of Shungopovi. 4. The Heart Chakra = Kachina Points, a mesa southwest of Oraibi (also called Monument Point). 5. Throat Chakra = Grand Falls on the Little Colorado River. 6. Third Eye (Pineal) Chakra = Walnut Canyon Ruins in the foothills of the San Francisco Peaks. 7. Crown Chakra = Tuzigoot Ruins and the red rock country near Sedona in Verde Valley.

The Purpose of the Arizona Orion Correlation

Orion is sometimes depicted as holding a shield, lion's skin, or bow in his left hand. Projected onto the Earth, a curving line of six stars with Pi 1 at the top (south) and Pi 6 at the bottom (north) arcs across the eastern end of Grand Canyon. (See satellite overviews of The Orion Zone on p. 22 and p. 35.) This magnificent canyon functions as both the primordial "Place of Emergence" of the Hopi people and the destination for souls in the afterlife. Its chthonic energy flows through the constellation's shield and left arm to his shoulder (Wupatki/Bellatrix), revitalizing the rest of his torso and the ancient pueblos located there. His arm fundamentally serves as a spirit road between worlds. It might even fulfill a more astonishing purpose: namely, that of an interstellar stepping stone.

Many of Orion's stars are very distant. For instance, Meissa (lambda Orionis), the head of Orion, is the farthest major star at 1060 light-years away, while Bellatrix (gamma Orionis), Orion's left shoulder, is one of his closest at 240 light-years away. Betelgeuse (alpha Orionis), the constellation's right shoulder, is a variable star at 643 ± 146 light-years away. Rigel (beta Orionis), Orion's left leg, is 773 light-years away, while Saiph (kappa Orionis), his right leg, has a distance of 722 light-years. The three stars of the belt –Alnitak (zeta Orionis), Alnilam (epsilon Orionis), and Mintaka (delta Orionis)– are respectively 817, 1300, and 916 light-years from us.

However, pi 3 Orionis at the center of the shield is only 26 light-years away.[11] In addition, pi 3 is only slighter larger and hotter than our Sun. It is classified as an F6 V yellow-white dwarf star with a surface temperature of 6,000°-7,500° K. Our Sun is a G2 V yellow dwarf star with a temperature of about 5,700° K.[12] Stars with similar temperatures are generally the same size and age. Hotter stars are larger and younger, while cooler stars are smaller and older. In essence, pi 3 Orionis is quite a bit like the Sun, which is exactly what SETI (Search for Extra-Terrestrial Intelligence) researchers are looking for when they aim their giant radio telescopes toward the heavens to scan for signals of sentience.

Although life forms are probably ubiquitous throughout the universe, some scientists restrict their search to stellar objects closer to the Earth. According to Todd Henry, who oversees Project Phoenix, a "Best and Brightest Sample" includes only those stars within twenty parsecs (65 light-years) as well as those that are similar to the Sun in color, size, age, and temperature.[13] pi 3 fits all those requirements.

In fact, pi 3 Orionis is star number 2185 in the SETI Star Catalogue. According to Dr. Peter R. Backus of the Phoenix Project, this star is both too far north for its radio telescope in Australia and too far south for the one at Arecibo in Puerto Rico, given the limited amount of time allotted at the latter telescope. Thus, at the time of this writing pi 3 Orionis has not yet been surveyed.[14] In addition, pi 3 was # 7 on NASA's Top 10 target stars for the Terrestrial Planet Finder observatory, whose planned launch has unfortunately been cancelled due to lack of funding.[15] Still, this star is one of the most promising candidates for the existence of exoplanets and ET life.

210,000 years ago pi 3 was only 15 instead of 26 light-years away from us—and shining twice as brightly. Anatomically modern humans appeared in Africa at about this time. If one believes in direct astro-theological influences, then the closer proximity of the star may have jump-started our species with a volley of the intense Orion energy. An unconfirmed pi 3 Orionis B may also exist in the form highly variable dwarf cepheid star.[16]

Looking at the satellite photo on the bottom of p. 22, we see that the Arizona Orion Correlation's upper part is oriented southwest. The left arm extends from Bellatrix/Wupatki Ruin toward Grand Canyon. It passes Hopi Point on the South Rim, and terminates within the canyon near a butte named Osiris Temple, which celestially corresponds to pi 3 Orionis. The Egyptian underworld god Osiris was traditionally associated with Orion and is also analogous to the Hopi god Masau'u, nocturnal god of the underworld, death, and fire, but also of the earth plane. (See Chapter 2 for more on Masau'u.)

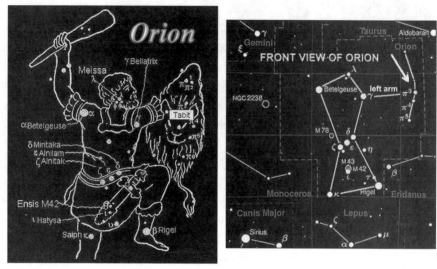

Pi 3 Orionis, also called Tabit, Arabic for "the Endurer," is in the middle of the left arm that holds a lion's skin or sometimes a shield or bow.

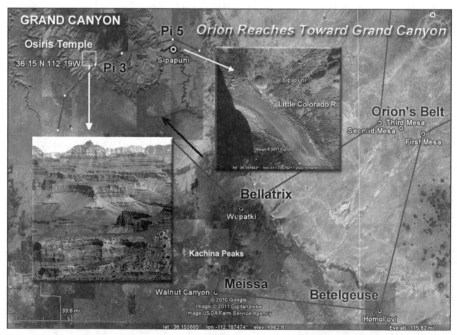

The black arrow follows the Orion energy extending northwest from Wupatki/Bellatrix, Orion's left shoulder, to a butte within Grand Canyon named Osiris Temple (pi 3 Orionis). The Hopi "Place of Emergence" called the Sipàapuni, literally "navel," corresponds to pi 5 Orionis.

Top: Osiris Temple at upper section. Bottom: Overview of a travertine dome called the Sipàapuni on the north bank of the Little Colorado River.

Looking toward the southeast, we see the location of the ancestral Hopi ruin site of Wupatki National Monument (corresponding to Bellatrix, left shoulder of the Arizona Orion Correlation). The San Francisco Peaks, home of the Hopi kachinas from July until December, are a few miles to the southwest. The Hopi Mesas are almost 50 miles northeast of Wupatki. The Sipàapuni is located on the Little Colorado River 3.5 miles upstream from its confluence with the Colorado River. Osiris Temple (corresponding to pi 3 Orionis) is downstream on the Colorado River.

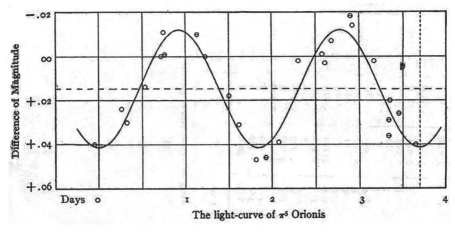

The light-curve generated by the binary star pi 5 Orionis
is a perfect sine wave.

Another astrophysically interesting star in Orion's bow or shield is pi 5 Orionis. (See left arm of Orion on star chart, p. 22.) According to Jim Kaler, Professor Emeritus of Astronomy at the University of Illinois, this is a stellar oddball. "Though observed for more than a century, Pi-5 remains an enigma."[17] At 1340 light-years away (roughly the same distance as the middle belt star Alnilam), it is a blue giant at least twice as hot as our Sun. This star is technically called an ellipsoidal variable binary. The pair rotates each other in an orbital period of 3.7 days, and the combined visual magnitude is, coincidentally, also 3.7.

Unlike an eclipsing binary, where the magnitude varies due to the occultation of the pair (in other words, one eclipsing the other), the variation in magnitude of an ellipsoidal binary is the result of the two stars each being gravitationally distorted from a sphere to an ellipse. That is, the stars are so close together that mutual tidal forces warp their shapes. Edward Gleason, manager of the Southworth Planetarium and astrophysicist at the University of Southern Maine, explains the celestial mechanics of ellipsoidal binaries. "The star's energy output is not constant along its surface due to the distortions, so as the stars within an ellipsoidal system rotate they show these different regions, which causes the system's apparent brightness (a combination of both) to vary in accordance to the sinusoidal curve."[18]

Light-curves generally plot on a graph the star's varying light intensity through time. Most binary stars have irregular and asymmetrical light-curves. One striking anomaly of pi 5 Orionis is the fact that this binary produces an absolutely perfect sine wave. In essence, its symmetry appears almost artificial. Could this possibly be a sign (no pun intended) of a higher intelligence manipulating the light sources to manufacture a regular pulse or precisely timed signal, almost like an interstellar lighthouse?[19]

This notion of artificial stellar manipulation is not unheard of, especially in light of a hypothetical Type II Civilization with the capability to harness and manipulate the energy of a whole solar system. In my book *The Kivas of Heaven*, I discuss the work of American astrophysicist Paul A. LaViolette, who claims that ETI (Extraterrestrial Intelligence) modulated the amplitude of the Crab Nebula pulsar by collimating a beam of synchroton radiation in order to construct a warning beacon. (Synchroton radiation is produced when charged particles are radially accelerated through rapidly spinning magnetic fields, such as those found in supernova remnants.) He believes that the galactic core periodically emits a volley of electromagnetic radiation, blasting the cocoon of Earth's atmosphere and causing solar disruptions, such as coronal mass ejections. LaViolette speculates that the most recent "galactic superwave" resulted in the mass extinction of Late Pleistocene megafauna. He believes that some benevolent, advanced civilization may be trying to send a signal of another impending discharge.[20]

In the case of pi 5 Orionis, the regularity of its pulsations may be an attempt by some ETI to direct our attention to this particular region of the sky, much like a yellow flashing light on the highway forces us to heed its location. In terms of the Arizona Orion Correlation, however, the terrestrial correspondence of this specific star is perhaps the most important locus in Hopi cosmology.

The previously mentioned Sipàapuni (also spelled Sipapuni or Sipapu) is a naturally formed travertine dome located in Grand Canyon on the north bank of the Little Colorado River a few miles upstream from its juncture with the Colorado River. It is about 60 miles west of the Hopi Mesas, from which periodic pilgrimages were made. In fact, the Hopi refer to Grand Canyon as Öngtupqa, literally "Salt Canyon," because ceremonial salt was gathered there.

Analogous to the Egyptian "Primeval Mound" that rose from the waters of the abyss during the creation of the world, Sipàapuni is the source of all life. Hopi legends state that the ancestral Hopi, known as the *Hisatsinom*, climbed through a hole at the center of this geologic formation from the subterranean Third World (or Era) to the current Fourth World. The Ancient Ones escaped the social chaos and spiritual decline of the previous epoch by ascending through a giant reed that poked through a hole in the Third World's sky. In one of my previous books I noted that the Hopi word *songwuka*, which literally means "big reed," is a reference to the Milky Way. The prefix *soo-* means "star" and the root *ngwuvi* means "climb," thus forming the etymons of *songwuka*—the "star-climb" through the galactic tunnel to a terrestrial existence on the sun-drenched Colorado Plateau.[21]

The Sipàapuni is not only a genesis,or birth, but also, paradoxically, a thanatos, or death. According to the Hopi belief system, after the body's demise, the soul returns to this chthonic region in Grand Canyon to reside in a parallel universe that mirrors our mundane life. Here we find *Maski*, or the house of the dead, "the gate of Masau's house," which is symbolized by either a whirlpool or a spiral petroglyph.[22] (The important deity Masau'u will be discussed in the following chapter). This final habitation is, of course, a gorgeous chasm where hordes of departed spirits or revenants roam.

A microcosmic analogue of the Sipàapuni is manifested as a simple round hole in every village plaza and in the floor of every kiva [kee-vah], the latter referring to a subterranean, communal prayer-chamber. These tunneling connections to the underworld collectively function as a sort of a shamanic subway system in which the seeking soul may journey to distant locations in the spirit world.

One description of a Hopi salt expedition in 1912 describes the Sipàapuni in detail.

"It was not long before the expedition found itself approaching *the* Kiva, the original sipapu through which mankind emerged from the underworld. Its outlines are indicated by soft, damp earth and an outer circle of bushes called pilakho (plur., pilakhotcoki). (Stems of this tough bush serve as the male sticks, i.e. the firedrills, when the new fire is kindled in the kivas during the Wuwutcim ceremony in November."[23]

The fertility aspect is also emphasized when participants earlier in the expedition would ritually copulate with a vulva-shaped black stone embedded in a smooth white stone. The black stone was about two inches in diameter and about eight inches deep, into which a lump of salt (symbolic semen?) collected at the bottom of the canyon was deposited on the way back home. Legends say that at this specific spot Kòokyangwso'wùuhti, or Old Spider Woman (who also created salt), turned herself into this stone to guide spiritual questers to the canyon.

In his autobiography Don C. Talayesva, youngest of the three participants on this same salt expedition, adds to the description of the sacrosanct Sipàapuni, including the fact that not only the Hopi but all humans originally emerged from this tellurian matrix.

> "At the very center was the original *sipapu*, the opening leading to the underworld. There was some yellowish water about two feet down which served as a lid to the sipapu so that no ordinary human could see the marvels of the underworld. This may be the fountain of youth which white men have sought in vain. Some ignorant, foolhardy Whites had plunged two poles into the sacred sipapu and left them standing against the west wall. Those profane fellows had desecrated the sacred spot where our ancestors—and theirs—emerged from the underworld. It was a great disgrace. The War Chief stood erect and shouted, 'At last we are here.' And sure enough, the spirits answered for the yellowish water bubbled up as if it were boiling."[24]

The late Harvey Butchart, professor of mathematics at Northern Arizona University, hiked this area over four decades later, and adds another anecdote of the continued desecration.

> "Up a side ravine I saw a salt spring, and my scramble to reach it was rewarded by a fine view down the river. Around the next bend I came upon the original Sipapu. It is a chocolate colored cone about twenty five yards wide at the base and ten yards across the flat top. A pool ten feet across occupies the center, and the bilious yellow

water hides the bottom. By the cupful the water is clear, and the taste is no worse than that of the mineralized river water. More gas than water is coming from the stem of this morning glory pool where, according to the Hopi, the ancestors of the human race emerged. Mr. McCormick of Flagstaff, who was here in his teens when his father and uncle were working the mines, tells how they would jump into the center of the pool. The gas would pop them to the surface for an unintended reenactment of the Hopi myth."[25]

As previously stated, this geologic formation is travertine, which is a type of limestone formed by mineral springs, much like the geothermal formations at Mammoth Hot Springs in Yellowstone National Park or the beehive dome at Hot Springs State Park in Thermopolis, Wyoming. The precipitation of calcium carbonate ($CaCO_3$) has also created the odd, dome-like structure at the bottom of Grand Canyon. We are reminded that the Great Pyramid was constructed of 2.3 million tons of limestone blocks, including highly polished casing stones of Tura limestone. Edward Leedskalnin built Coral Castle in Florida of mostly megalithic limestone blocks formed from coral. The construction materials for each of these human-made wonders might have provided a resonant frequency that aided in interdimensional travel.

Why did the Hopi traditionally make such arduous and even dangerous journeys to perform various ceremonies along the route, with mythological echoes reverberating every step of the way? Remember that the realm linked by the subterranean passageway is a former era called the Third World, destroyed by a deluge. (Most Hopi elders believe we are living at the very end of the Fourth World.) The souls of the dead also continue to journey to this watery underworld. In the Arizona Orion Correlation the celestial correspondence to the Sipàapuni is pi 5 Orionis, a binary with symmetrical sine wave photonic intensity.

In my book *The Kivas of Heaven*, I noted that this formation when seen from above appeared as a perfect circumpunct—a circle with a dot at its center. (See photo, bottom of p. 23.) This also served as the quintessential icon in Dan Brown's novel *The Lost Symbol*.

> "In the idiom of symbology, there was one symbol that reigned supreme above all others. The oldest and most universal, this symbol fused all the ancient traditions in a single solitary image that represented the illumination of the Egyptian sun god, the triumph of alchemical gold, the wisdom of the Philosopher's Stone, the purity of the Rosicrucian Rose, the moment of Creation, the All, the dominance of the astrological sun, and even the omniscient all-seeing eye that hovered atop the unfinished pyramid. *The circumpunct. The symbol of the Source. The origin of all things.*"[26]

Regardless of what one thinks of Brown's fiction, it must be admitted that he chose a simple yet potent leitmotif. In the case of the Sipàapuni, this ultimate source of all the Hopi may serve as a singularity point, a wormhole or Einstein-Rosen bridge to the spirit world. The "giant reed" that the Hopi ancestors ascended to reach the current world and that departed souls descend to attain the afterlife may be simultaneously a hyperdimensional energy conduit leading to the tellurian dimension and a vorticular tendril reaching deep into the archetype-archive of the subconscious of the living Earth (i.e. Gaia).

Perhaps we are dealing with a terrestrial portal or stargate accessed via what former NASA consultant and CBS science advisor Richard C. Hoagland has termed hyperdimensional physics.

> "Modified Einstein-Cartan Torsion Theory predicts that rotating mass uniquely distorts space-time ('the aether') — sending measurable torsion waves of energy spiraling outward from the center of the rotation: the Hoagland-Torun Hyperdimensional modifications propose that the ultimate source of this 'spin-field energy' is a rotating *hyperspatial 'gate'* [italics added]—allowing the energy to enter 3-space from higher dimensions."[27]

Upper: Sipàapuni with
Schwartzschild wormhole
superimposed. A stargate?
Middle: Sipàapuni seen at
river-level.
Lower: Torsion field twisting
spacetime.

31

Is this, then, the prime purpose of the Orion Correlation in Arizona? To point to the particular star system whence the Ancient Ones once traveled? It would be far easier for a Hopi elder to point to that star and say, "That's where we came from," or, "That's where our star ancestors came from." However, memories fade and people die. By constructing a configuration of stone villages during centuries of migration upon the high desert in order to reflect the Orion home-world, an everlasting monument was created in the form of star shrines. Perhaps the people of our current era, the precarious end of the Hopi Fourth World, are specifically the ones for whom this mirrored message of sky and earth was written.

Considering the vast number of stars in the sky, I must admit that it is a very long shot. A number of questions remains: Could this be the code that the Arizona Orion is trying to convey? Were the ancestral Hopi actually the children of star elders who originated in the heavens? An answer of "yes" to these questions would unequivocally alter the paradigms of our planetary evolution and prehistory. This leads to one last question: Are we prepared for the seismic shift in consciousness that such a far-reaching concept requires?

Hopi women climbing on pueblo, photo by Edward Curtis, 1906.

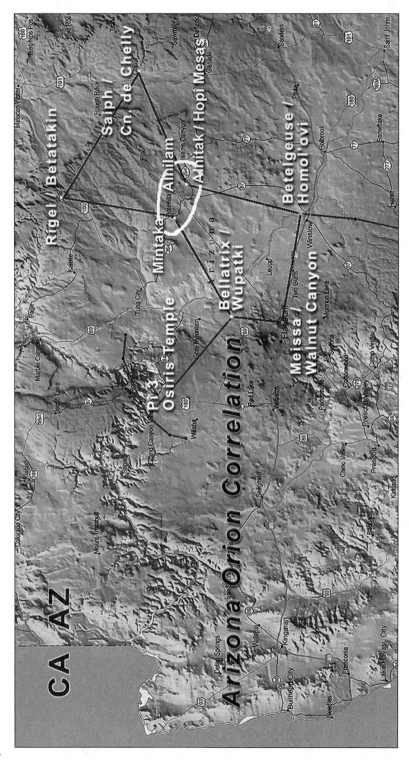

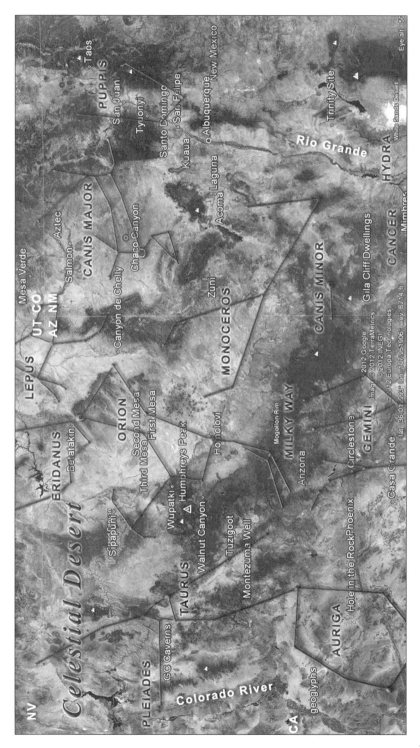

35

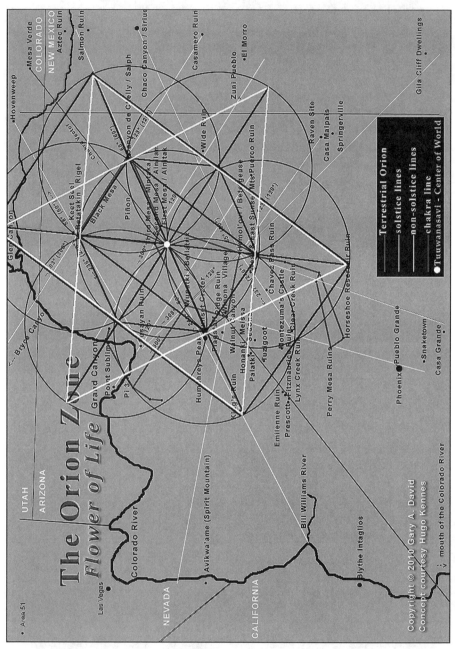

The Flower of Life with its sacred geometry blooms on the high desert of The Orion Zone. The inner rectangle's width is formed by the two feet of Orion (Betatakin and Canyon de Chelly) together with Humphreys Peak and East & West Sunset Mountains south of Homol'ovi.

Chapter 2
OZ (Orion Zone) Rising

"Nothing beside remains. Round the decay
Of that colossal wreck, boundless and bare
The lone and level sands stretch far away."

"Ozymandias," Percy Bysshe Shelley

Who Put the Ari- In Arizona?

My friend, the diffusionist scholar Gene D. Matlock, recently wrote: "Lately, the Turks, who still call themselves Ari (Aryan, Turanian, and Kurustan) are coming out of the closet and claiming to be the parents of all civilizations—even of Egypt." Given the fact that the deserts of both Egypt and Arizona host Orion Correlations, it is especially significant that an Aryan culture may have given birth to all the other cultures of the world—Arian, related to the name "Orion." The abhorrent repercussions of Nazism aside, this is not a mere folk etymology.

The late 19th-early 20th century Vedic scholar Bal Gangadhar Tilak claims that the Greek name for Orion is derived from the Sanskrit word *Agrayana*, which literally means "commencing the year." Tilak believed that the Aryan civilization flowered during the Age of Orion, about 4000 BC to 2500 BC—what Western astrologers call the Age of Taurus. In other words, the vernal equinox point, which slowly shifts backward due to the precession of the equinoxes (see discussion below), was located between Orion's right shoulder Betelgeuse and the Pleiades in the constellation Taurus.

The Sanskrit *agra* has the following denotations: "beginning, summit, apex, projecting, prominent." This corresponds to the Greek *oros*, or "mountain top," from which the English word "ore" is derived. The Sanskrit *ayana* means "going" but also refers to the equinoctial point or precession. This term corresponds to the Greek *ion*, present participle of *ienai*, "to go." When the guttural "g" and the final "a" of the Sanskrit term are dropped, we have "Arayan," or Aryan. In the Greek version, the initial "a" becomes an "o"—Or-ion.[1] In this context I am particularly interested in the term *Ari*, and how it got in the name Arizona.

The most obvious meaning is "arid zone"—simply, a dry place. Or considering the prefix *Ari-*, we may think of Ariel, the potent spirit of air and earth in Shakespeare's play *The Tempest*. In the Old Testament Book of Isaiah, Ari-el is an appellation for the city of Jerusalem and literally means "Lion of God." In Ezekiel the word refers to the "Hearth of God," or the altar upon which burnt offerings were made.

According to the *Oxford English Dictionary*, a 1599 reference for the word "zone" has the following meaning: "The constellation named Zone or the gyrdle of Orion."[2] In other words, within the larger constellation is the smaller star pattern known as his belt. Following Aristotle's usage, the Latin poet Ovid specifically refers to "Zona" as the three central stars of Orion. Thus, in the name Arizona (Ari-zona) is hidden the fiery belt of Orion emblazoned upon the sacred navel of the world, in this case the three Hopi Mesas located on the high desert of the southwestern United States.

About 1754 Padre Ortega first used the word "Arizona" when he penned it on a map, referring to the "Real of Arizona."[3] The Spanish word *real* means "military encampment," but the adjective form meaning "royal" is also implied. In addition, the Spanish term *arisco* can mean "surly," "churlish," or even "vicious." The word *ariete* means "battering ram" (suggesting the constellation Aries near Orion), and *arimez* means "projection"—all traditionally active, masculine, and violent attributes in keeping with the archetypal Orion, the Hunter. Furthermore, the Spanish term *zona* also refers to "belt" or "girdle" as well as to "zone," a distinctive area of land. Alternate spellings for

Orion include "Arion," "Oarion," and "Aorion," so the prefixes Ari- and Ori- might have been interchangeable.[4] The Greek *aristos*, as in "aristocracy" means "best" or "noblest," while the related Sanskrit word *arya*, as in "Aryan," means "of high rank"or "noble." The Italian word *aria* also means either "air," as in wind (of the "arid zone"?) or "melody." In light of all these etymologies, perhaps the padre was merely recording what was already established in the region we now know as Arizona.

The Hopi suffix *-sona* refers to a "craver" or "enthusiast," while *tsoona* means "forward, not shy, or having fun exuberantly"—all of which suggest characteristics of Orion. In addition, the term *orai* (like the first two syllables in "Orion") means "Rock on High" or "Round Rock,"[5] after which Oraibi was named, one of the initial Hopi Mesa villages. Furthermore, the Hopi word *soona* means "germ, kernel, edible part of any seed, or heart of a tree." Like the center of the constellation Orion, this could be a reference to the heart of Hopi-land, whence sprouts the sustenance of the sacred corn or other agricultural mainstays.

Once we acknowledge the possibility of cultural diffusionism rather than the more academically accepted isolationism, it is plausible that Indo-European speaking Aryans such as the Hindu Nagas (perhaps with the help of the Phoenicians) once sailed to the American Southwest and ascended the Colorado River to Arizona, where they shared linguistic concepts phonetically with the Hopi. Because of all these linguistic "coincidences," the semantic nexus I've described may have been trans-oceanically transported from the Middle East and northern India here to the high desert of Arizona.

This is not the place, however, to digress into this seemingly intractable debate. In my three previous books, I discuss various themes regarding "cultural diffusionism," such as the connections between the serpent cult of the Nagas and the Snake Clan of the Hopis. (See Endnote 85 on p. 379.) Suffice to say that the Egyptian reference in Shelley's poem quoted above resonates with certain cultural, cosmological, and mythical aspects found in the American Southwest.

Center of the World

In the first chapter of this book I discussed the Arizona Orion Correlation and the rather stunning implications of the particular orientation of this constellation as a template overlaid upon the Desert Southwest. This, however, was not the first time I had encountered a cosmo-geo correspondence. In the late 1980s while living in South Dakota's Black Hills and teaching on the Pine Ridge Reservation, I happened to meet the Oglala Lakota (Sioux) activist Charlotte Black Elk, the great-granddaughter of Nicolas Black Elk. This visionary medicine man, assisted by Nebraska poet John G. Neihardt, had written the classic Native American memoir *Black Elk Speaks*. At the time I met her, Black Elk was speaking and writing about her tribe's claim to Paha Sapa, or the sacred Black Hills, which she called the "Heart of Everything That Is" (*Wamaka Ognaka y Cante*). In satellite photos, this evergreen island in a sea of prairie grass indeed resembles a human heart.

The 1868 Fort Laramie Treaty had guaranteed the Lakota their homeland in perpetuity. But alas, a mere six years later, an onslaught of mining activities triggered its de facto abrogation. The raucous town of Deadwood rose overnight at the center of Lakota holy land to become the seething core of the last American gold rush. The gargantuan carving of four white presidents into Mount Rushmore during the mid-20th century was the final affront.

Ms. Black Elk was trying to reestablish the Lakota claim to the Hills over a century after they had been stolen by yet another broken treaty. Most academic historians consider the Sioux tribe's arrival in the area to be only about 1700 AD. On the contrary, she determined that the Lakota had lived in the Black Hills much earlier. To prove this point, she used the astronomical phenomenon called precession of the equinoxes, or the slow shifting through the ages of zodiac constellations along the ecliptic—one degree every 72 years. The Lakota constellations thus served as "non-material artifacts," fixing the astronomical period that the first annual sacred ceremonies of spring had been performed.

According to her calculations, this occurred when the vernal equinox was in the Dried Willow constellation (Aries and Triangulum), or as early as 3,000 years ago.

Black Elk gave me her photocopied essay describing a basic archaeo-astronomical concept that many other ancient cultures had also embraced: "Each principle star in the Black Hills Sacred Ceremonies of Spring is associated with actual land sites. The Black Hills are the mirror image of the star pattern."[6] The annual ceremonial cycle began after the vernal equinox and consisted of a series of rituals, each performed in and around the Black Hills at a specific location and time.

To simplify the following description, merely the main components of a more complex earth-sky template will be noted. The Pleiades, some of the stars in Orion, and Sirius comprise a celestial Buffalo that directly reflects various points in the Black Hills.[7] The Pleiades are the head of the bison, which correlates to Harney Peak, highest point in the range. This spot is where Charlotte's great-grandfather as a boy journeyed to the spirit world and received his Great Vision.[8] The bison's tail is Sirius, which relates to the lower southern Black Hills near the Cheyenne River. Two of the Buffalo's ribs are Rigel and Betelgeuse, which correlate to a central limestone plateau, whereas its backbone is the belt stars, which correlate to three small, prairie-like areas inside the thickly forested Hills. (Very recently, the Rosebud Sioux tribe offered to purchase one of these prairies known as the *Pe' Sla*, which the Lakota consider as the center of the universe.)

In addition, the iron-rich, geologic formation called the Racetrack surrounds the Black Hills like a red Sacred Hoop. It roughly matches up with the sidereal Winter Hexagon: Aldebaran in Taurus, Rigel in Orion, Sirius in Canis Major, Procyon in Canis Minor, Pollux/Castor in Gemini, and Capella in Auriga. Some of the stars in Gemini also correspond to the Bear Lodge, which is known today as Devils Tower, an impressive laccolith rising out of the plains of northeastern Wyoming. This is, of course, the location where the sci-fi classic *Close Encounters of the Third Kind* was also filmed.

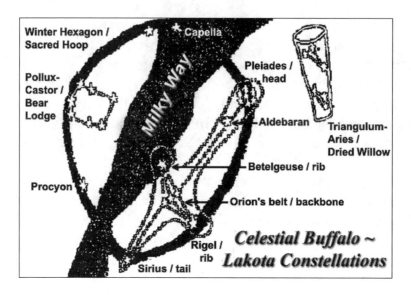

Winter Hexagon /
Sacred Hoop

Capella

Pollux-
Castor /
Bear
Lodge

Milky Way

Pleiades /
head

Aldebaran

Triangulum-
Aries /
Dried Willow

Betelgeuse / rib

Procyon

Orion's belt / backbone

Celestial Buffalo ~

Rigel /
rib

Lakota Constellations

Sirius / tail

Some believe that L. Frank Baum, author of *The Wonderful Wizard of Oz* (1900), got inspiration for the Emerald City while working as a journalist in Aberdeen, South Dakota. Off in the west lay the evergreen Black Hills at the heart of the Sioux Nation, to which settlers were currently flocking. The fictional name of "the great and powerful Oz" may have been influenced by Shelley's sonnet "Ozymandias," which is the Greek name for Ramesses II (also spelled Ramses, 1303 – 1279 BC), the puissant pharaoh of the 19th dynasty. In the lines that prefaced this chapter, the "colossal wreck" refers to his statue lying shattered in the deadly desert. The word *ozy* (derived from *ozium*) means "air" or "breath," while *mandias* means "to mandate" or "to rule" — thus, ruler of air, something invisible, insubstantial. Unfortunately, Shelley's cautionary poem against excessive human ambition went unheeded in the age of Manifest Destiny.

The creator of the delightful fantasy tales of Oz had his darker side too. As a response to the Wounded Knee Massacre that occurred on December 29th, 1890, Baum aired his racist beliefs five days later in an editorial: "The Pioneer has before declared that our only safety depends upon the total extirmination [sic] of the Indians. Having wronged them for centuries we had better, in order to protect our civilization, follow it up by one more wrong and wipe these untamed and untamable creatures from the face of the earth."[9] I guess he figured that Indian children wouldn't have the money to buy his books anyway, much less be able to read them.

Most ancient cultures acknowledged the essential concept of a center-place, the sacred heart or navel beyond whose boundaries lay chaos and a profane existence. The Romanian historian of religion Mircea Eliade comments on this archetype of the Center of the World in relation to the celestial realm, even when the notion is no longer an overt presence in the culture's myths or religion.

"Driven from the cult and replaced in mythologies by other themes, in the religious life the sky remains ever present by virtue of its symbolism. And this celestial symbolism in turn infuses and supports a number of rites (of ascent, climbing, initiation, royalty, and so on), of myths (the cosmic tree, the cosmic mountain, the chain of arrows connecting earth and heaven, and so on), of legends (e.g., magical flight). The symbolism of the Center of the World –whose immense disseminations we have seen– likewise illustrates the importance of celestial symbolism; for it is at a center that communication with the sky is effected, and the sky constitutes the paradigmatic image of transcendence."[10]

In an earlier book Eliade describes an "architectonic symbolism of the Center" that includes a sacred mountain, sacred temple, or sacred city forming a vertical axis in order to link the tripartite structure of the cosmos: underworld plane, earth plane, and celestial plane. "Hell, the center of the earth, and the 'gate' of the sky, are, then, situated on the same axis, and it is along this axis that passage from one cosmic region to another was effected."[11]

Charlotte Black Elk refers to Harney Peak in the heart of the Black Hills as "Mountain at the Center Where He Comes."[12] It is the place from which one may transcend to the celestial realm. Wind Cave in the southern Black Hills is the subterranean Place of Emergence, the initial wellspring of life and the origin of both the immense herds of buffalo and, subsequently, all the Sioux tribes. The Egyptian variation of the holy peak is, of course, the pyramid (and perhaps the flat-roofed tomb called a *mastaba*). The Hopi variation of the same archetype is the mesa, the flat-topped mountain ubiquitous in the American Southwest. (The term is actually a Spanish word literally meaning "table.")

Like the Egyptian *Rostau* (mentioned in the previous chapter) and the central Lakota mountain named Harney Peak, the corresponding region in Hopi cosmology is called *Tuuwanasavi*, a term that literally means "sand-middle."[13] The *Tuuwanasavi* is located very near the three main Hopi Mesas where the tribe had constructed their pueblos, which are basically ancient stone-and-adobe apartment complexes. Similar to the terrestrial-celestial dualism of the three primary structures at Giza, these natural "pyramids" directly correspond to the belt stars of Orion.

The *Tuuwanasavi* is the Hopi *axis mundi*, or central pillar of the world, and suggests the sandy "Primeval Mound" rising from the waters of the abyss during the Egyptian cosmogony.[14] In other words, the world was created by an island that rose from the primordial seas, just as water-saturated land would appear after the annual flooding of the Nile. Atop this island perched the *Benu* bird, otherwise known as the phoenix, which initiated cyclic time, rising from its own ashes at the end of every age.

Later, its more naturalistic form, a purple heron, would be depicted as sitting atop an obelisk located at Heliopolis ("sun-city"), the center of the Egyptian cosmos (now found in a suburb of Cairo). The island was sometimes conceptualized as an "Isle of Fire," and indeed the word "pyramid" may be related to the term "pyre." From the throat of the *Benu* bird issued the *Hikê*, or Divine Word (Logos), the "breath of life." During the Middle Kingdom the *Benu* was seen as the "soul of Osiris" (Orion).[15] In this context it is interesting to note that the Hopi word *hikwsi* literally means "breath, breath of life, vital force, vitality," but it also means "soul, living spirit."[16]

Wallis Budge defines the avian entity as "...a bird-god sacred to Ra and Osiris, and the incarnation of the soul of Ra and the heart of Osiris." The *ba* ("soul") of Ra (the sun god) and the *ab* ("heart") of Osiris are linked by a simple anadrome, or word reversal. The *Benu* was also apparently associated with Venus as the morning star that rises shortly before Ra, just as Osiris (Orion) had his heliacal rising in ancient Egypt on the summer solstice after an absence in the sky of a few months.[17]

Unlike the ancient Egyptians or the Maya of Mesoamerica, however, the Hopi were never pyramid builders. They instead sanctified this triad of geologic uplifts by constructing villages either on their summits or at their bases, according to the specific needs at the time they were built. The basic function, however, was still the same: to bring the astronomer-priests closer to the numinous architecture of the celestial realm. About a dozen of these villages remain inhabited today. The village of Oraibi on Third Mesa is the oldest continuously inhabited community on the North American continent. The Hopi have lived there for over 900 years.

As we saw in the previous chapter, the entry to the subterranean plane is known in Hopi as the Sipàapuni. Located at the bottom of Grand Canyon, this is perhaps the most sacred spot in the Hopi cosmos. I will further discuss the significance of Grand Canyon in terms of the Hopi *tutskwa*, or "territory," in Chapter 4.

The Hopi generally consider Orion as the most important constellation. The term *Hotòmqam*, or "beads on a string," refers either to his belt or to the constellation's three stars: Betelgeuse, Alnilam (middle belt star), and Rigel.[18] In fact, Orion's appearance shortly after midnight in the overhead hatchway of the kiva signals the start of *Soyal*, the winter solstice ceremony, which is the first and most important ritual of the annual ceremonial cycle. This stellar pattern thus synchronizes a solar ceremony.

Ironically, it is here on the high desert of Arizona that we also realize the truth of the hermetic maxim attributed to the Egyptian god Thoth: "As above, so below." I have called this region the "Orion Zone," and indeed its various anomalies at times seem as strange as Oz.

Stargate Vortex

Project Ozma, named after Princess Ozma in Baum's Oz novels, was the first systematic search for extraterrestrial intelligence. It was conducted in 1960 by radio astronomer Frank Drake at the Green Bank, West Virginia observatory. He targeted two particularly Sun-like stars, epsilon Eridani and tau Ceti, at 1420 MHz, the radio frequency at which hydrogen resonates. Unfortunately Drake found nothing but dead air. The alien D. J. had apparently fallen asleep.[19]

Epsilon Eridani, at 10.8 light-years away, is the third closest star to Earth, after alpha Centauri and Sirius. This orange solar youngster is less than a billion years old and only a third as luminous as our Sun. However, about a dozen years ago astronomers detected a Jupiter-like planet orbiting it. Epsilon Eridani b is the closest exoplanet yet found. They also discovered two asteroid belts plus a debris disk around the star that may also be hiding additional planets.[20]

This star is not unlike our sun in size and temperature, which suggests that the ancient cultures somehow obtained knowledge that this part of the sky may harbor life. Perhaps intelligent entities migrated to this hospitable planet from elsewhere in the cosmos. Then, using SOL (speed-of-light) technology, they traveled through what the Ancients called the *zalos*, a "whirlpool in the sky" (discussed shortly) to our Earth. In many cultures the subterranean realm of the underworld –for instance, the Greek Hades or the Egyptian *Duat*– also included the celestial realm of stars and planets. Chthonic rivers were conceptualized as streams of stars, like either Eridanus, which starts at Orion's sinister (left) foot, or the Milky Way, which forms a bridge across the night sky.

In 2006 other scientists working again at the Green Bank Telescope discovered "a giant, magnetic Slinky wrapped around a long, finger-like interstellar cloud" known as the Orion Molecular Cloud, which extends from Orion's belt to his sword. At a distance of 1,750 light-years, the radiation emitted from the cloud's interstellar hydrogen transmitted a signal—also at 1420 MHz on your radio dial![21] This helix or corkscrew pattern is located in the loins of Orion, a stellar nursery constantly producing new "star seed."

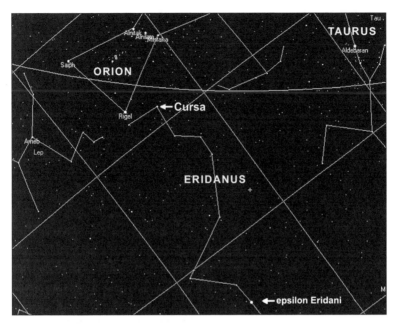

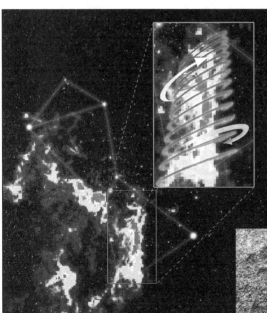

Upper: Star chart showing Eridanus flowing from Rigel, Orion's left foot. Middle: Magnetic helix wrapped around the Orion Nebula. Lower: Spiral petroglyph near Prescott, Arizona. A small, eroded spiral was carved at the two o'clock position.

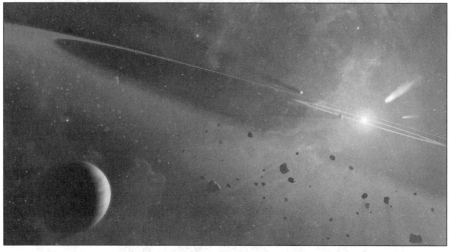

Artist's conception of epsilon Eridani, Jupiter-like planet, and dust debris from asteroid belt, NASA-JPL-Caltech.

Drake's Equation

N = N* • fp • ne • fl • fi • fc • L

N* = The number of stars in the Milky Way Galaxy. (100 billion)
   (Instead of N*, R* is sometimes used—the rate of formation of stars.)
fp = The fraction of those stars with planetary systems. (20% to 50%)
ne = The number of planets, per solar system, with an environment
   suitable for life. (1 to 5)
fl = The fraction of suitable planets on which life actually appears.
   (0% to 100%)
fi = The fraction of life-bearing planets on which intelligent life emerges.
   (0% to 100%)
fc = The fraction of civilizations with a technology that releases
   signs of their existence into space
   (i.e. communication). (10% to 20%)
L = The length of time such civilizations release detectable signals
   into space. (1/1,000,000th—survival of 10,000 yrs.)

When all these variables are multiplied, N = the number
   of civilizations in the Milky Way Galaxy whose electromagnetic
   emissions are detectable (via some form of communication).

Frank Drake's own solution to his equation, formulated in 1961,
   = 10,000 extraterrestrial civilizations in our galaxy alone.

Co-authors Giorgio de Santillana and Hertha von Dechend in their classic book *Hamlet's Mill* describe the ancient concept of a "whirlpool in the sky" near Eridanus. Also called the River, this constellation starts at the left foot of Orion and flows southward. (In the Star Correlation of the American Southwest, Eridanus corresponds to the upper Colorado River.)

"That there is a whirlpool in the sky is well known; it is most probably the essential one, and it is precisely placed. It is a group of stars so named (*zalos*) at the foot of Orion, close to Rigel (beta Orionis, Rigel being the Arabic word for 'foot'), the degree of which was called 'death,' according to Hermes Trismegistos [i.e., the Egyptian god Thoth], whereas the Maori claim outright that Rigel marked the way to Hades (Castor indicating the primordial homeland). Antiochus the astrologer enumerates the whirl among the stars as Taurus. Franz Boll takes sharp exception to the adequacy of his description, but he concludes that the *zalos* must, indeed, be Eridanus 'which flows from the foot of Orion.'"[22]

The whirlpool or vortex is an icon used in cultures around the world to signify an interdimensional portal, the transition between worlds, or a gateway between one reality and another. It is the doorway through which the shaman begins his or her ecstatic quest along the World Tree (*axis mundi*) from the physical to the spiritual plane. In essence, it is a stargate—but not like the portal on terra firma in the movie and TV series. It is instead a divine tunnel located in the sky through which the soul's transcendence is achieved.

But the morphology of the spiral is also manifested in the "vortex" areas located in many spots all around the Earth. For instance, many vortices are found in the Sedona, Arizona region. In her book *Terravision*, Page Byrant defines the term: "A vortex is a mass of energy that moves in a rotary or whirling motion, causing a depression or vacuum at the center.... These powerful eddies of pure Earth power manifest as spiral-like coagulations of energy that are either electric, magnetic, or electromagnetic qualities of life force."[23]

Vortices (or vortexes) can be likened to various acupuncture points upon the etheric body of the Earth. An electric (yang) vortex –Bell Rock and Airport Mesa, for instance– energizes and enlivens the body and the mind, creating or rejuvenating a sense of optimism or faith. On the other hand, a magnetic (yin) vortex –such as Red Rock Crossing– calms and heals the psyche. It also encourages the flow of creative or artistic energy and may even stimulate the brain's temporal lobe to variably induce vivid memories, visions, lucid dreams, and past-life or out-of-body experiences. An electromagnetic vortex –Boynton Canyon, for example– readjusts any physical, mental, emotional, or spiritual imbalances one may be experiencing. The native peoples have used these earth spirals for millennia, and they still remain a natural source of invigoration and regeneration.

According to J. E. Cirlot's *Dictionary of Symbols*, "The double spiral represents the completion of the sigmoid line, and the ability of the sigmoid line to express the intercommunication between two opposing principles is clearly shown in the Chinese Yang-Yin symbol."[24]

Comparative mythologist Joseph Campbell has written about a Navajo medicine man named Jeff King, who was born in New Mexico in the mid-nineteenth century and died at about age 110. From boyhood this traditionalist healer frequently visited a stone carving near a cave of a particular mountain near his home. This carving represented two entwined spiral snakes positioned with their heads pointing east and west. Unfortunately the sculpture was lost when a rock overhang collapsed and it was washed away.[25]

In this context it is interesting to note that over the shaved head of the boy-pharaoh Tutankhamun was found a linen skull-cap woven with minute gold and faience beads in the form of a pair of uraei—two sinuous cobras rearing up on its apex or crown chakra.[26] The double spiral in the form of serpents must have held significance in ancient Egypt as well.

In the previous chapter I discussed the Orion Chakra system in Arizona and mentioned the fact that the Hopi also acknowledge chakras. Most of us have at least heard about the Tibetan Tantric yoga system of kundalini, with a number of chakras, or energy wheels, aligned along the spinal column (*Susumna*). The word kundalini comes from *Kundala*, which means "coiled," and refers to the serpent energy asleep at the base of the spine.

The chakra system was certainly not restricted to Asia. Sir John Woodroffe (a.k.a. Arthur Avalon) remarks on other systems in the Western Hemisphere: "I am told that correspondences are discoverable between the Indian (Asiatic) Sastra and the American-Indian Maya Scripture of the Zunis [sic] called the Popul Vuh. My informant tells me that their 'air-tube' is the Susumna; their 'twofold air-tube' the Nadis Ida and Pingala. 'Hurakan,' or lightning, is Kundalini, and the centres are depicted by animal glyphs."[27]

Mirroring the structure of DNA, the "Pingala" and the "Ida" refer to subtle nerves that take the form of a double spiral. They wind around the physical backbone, channeling solar (masculine) and lunar (feminine) energy respectively up and down the spine.

An epithet for Huracan (or Hurricane), the lightning deity of the Maya, is "Heart of the Sky,"[28] the exact phrase used to describe the correlative Hopi sky god Sotuknang (or Sootukwanangw). The Hopi glyph and accompanying hand gesture for lightning is formed by a "...sinuous, undulating motion..."—namely, a sigmoid or spiral. Another Hopi design for lightning is a series of lozenges, while yet another is shaped like a modern expandable coat rack—both of which are two-dimensional representations of the 3-D double spiral.[29]

Many examples of the painted spiral exist in ancestral Puebloan pottery from the American Southwest, and the carved spiral is also found in the rock art of the region. As previously mentioned, the whirlpool or double spiral motif represents the "gate of Masau's house."[30]

Hopi God of Death and the Alien Greys

Masau'u (also spelled Masau or Maasaw) is the Hopi god of the underworld, death, fire, and the earth, but he is also god of transformation. He was present when the *Hisatsinom* emerged upon the surface of the earth and began to make their migrations; he was there again when they finished them after many centuries.[31] The Hopi consider the building of villages as a way of marking the boundaries of their territory—"leaving footprints," so to speak. It is thought that Masau'u directed the people on their exodus, telling them when to go and where to stop along their route. In essence, this Hopi god established the star pattern of villages on the Arizona desert (discussed in Chapter 1).

Masau'u is sometimes also conceptualized as either the Great Spirit or the Creator. On August 4th, 1970, a Hopi spiritual elder from Hotevilla named Dan Kachongva sent a letter to President Nixon on behalf of a number of others.

> "We, the True and Traditional religious leaders, recognized as such by the Hopi People, maintain full authority over all land and life contained within the Western Hemisphere. We are granted our stewardship by virtue of our instruction as to the meaning of Nature, Peace, and Harmony, as spoken to our People by Him, known to us as Masau'u, the Great Spirit, who long ago provided for us the sacred stone tablets which we preserve to this day. For many generations before the coming of the white man, for many generations before the coming of the Navajo, the Hopi People have lived in that sacred place known to you as the Southwest, and known to us to be the *spiritual center of our continent.* [italics added]."[32]

The words "land and life," or in Hopi, *tutskwa i'qatsi* (also spelled *techqua ikachi*)[33], are frequently found together in order to express the enduring Hopi principle of environmentalism long before the birth of the contemporary ecological movement. Similar to the stone tablets that Yahweh presented to Moses, Masau'u gave four stone tablets to the Hopi at the beginning of the Fourth World, just before they began their migrations that lasted centuries and eventually brought them back along a spiral path to the center-place, the three Hopi Mesas. These tablets collectively represent the Hopi deed to their land, a map, a life-plan, and a covenant with the Great Spirit.

Masau'u kachina doll,
Katsinam Collection,
Prescott Public Library,
Prescott, Arizona.

Artistic conception of the Hopi god Masau'u by Jack Andrews, 2012.

One of the gateways of Masau'u is located near the Sipàapuni at the bottom of Grand Canyon, the portal through which the *Hisatsinom* emerged from the past Third World to the present Fourth World. As described in the first chapter, the Hopi periodically journey to this sacred area to gather ritualistic salt. Therefore, one of their names for Grand Canyon is *Öngtupqa*, literally "Salt Canyon."[34]

Masau'u is the only nocturnal deity in the Hopi pantheon. As my book *The Orion Zone* argues, Masau'u is the terrestrial equivalent of Orion, ritually the most important constellation in Hopi cosmology. The Hopi believe that Masau'u can travel across the entire earth before morning arrives, so distances mean nothing to him. What better way to express Orion's movement from the eastern to the western horizon during the course of the night? The warfare and hunter qualities of Orion can be equally attributed to Masau'u.

This primordial god wears a mask with large open round eyeholes and a large round mouth. His head is huge and bald, resembling in shape and texture a summer squash, and his forehead bulges out in a ridge. His feet are as long as a human forearm, and his body is gray. In fact, the root word of his name is the Hopi word *mas*, which actually means "gray," but it also means "corpse." The related word *mas'at* means "wing," perhaps referring to the soul's flight through the *Maski*, or the "underworld."[35]

In any case, the description of Masau'u from Hopi legends is very close to contemporary images of the classic extraterrestrial Grey. In particular, he seems to fit the typology of the "tall Grey," usually 7 to 8 feet tall with a large nose but possessing the other physical characteristics of the smaller version. In the mind-boggling literature of exopolitics, the tall Grey is usually described as a biological hybrid of small grey aliens and humans. He frequently appears as either an overseer of the small Greys or a leader of diplomatic envoys between his race and the shadow governments of the U.S. and other countries.

Former Navy Intelligence Advisor William Cooper describes one meeting with the Eisenhower administration at Holloman Air Force Base in New Mexico. "Later in 1954 the race of large nosed Gray Aliens which had been orbiting the Earth landed at Holloman Air Force Base. A basic agreement was reached. This race identified themselves as originating from a Planet around a red star in the Constellation of Orion which we called Betelgeuse. They stated that their planet was dying and that at some unknown future time they would no longer be able to survive there."[36]

The tall Grey sometimes performs the role of head surgeon in the medical procedures and genetic manipulations performed on UFO abductees. On the other hand, this type is often times considered less hostile than the robotic and emotionless manner of the smaller Grey. The tall Grey's character is consistent with that of Masau'u, who as a benefactor assists the Hopi in their agricultural pursuits.[37]

My personal experience of talking to various Hopis regarding Masau'u is that some see this as a taboo subject altogether and will simply not discuss him. Others are more open, possibly because of clan affiliations, e.g. the Fire Clan, or *Kookopngyam*, which views Masau'u as a tutelary deity.

Spiraling back to the theme of the astro-eddy, I previously stated that the ancients perceived a "whirlpool in the sky" or stargate located around the region of the constellation Eridanus. At the head of the River is the star Cursa, which is called "the Footstool" of Rigel, located 3° to the northwest of Orion's left foot. (See star map, top of p. 47.)

The double star Rigel (corresponding to the Betatakin and Keet Seel ruins in the Arizona Orion Correlation) is thought by some investigators of ETI (extraterrestrial intelligence) to be the home-star orbited by a planet from which the small grey aliens traveled to our Earth.

"The first type is the short gray humanoids with the large heads, which resemble embryos and average about four and half feet in height. They are from a solar system that revolves around Rigel. Rigel is a double bluish-white star on the left foot of Orion, about 800 light years from Earth. They have problems with their glands, particularly with their sebaceous glands, which make it difficult for them to digest food. These glandular problems were caused mainly by exposure to radioactivity during a nuclear war their race fought in the distant past, many thousands of years ago."[38]

Let's put aside the moot possibility of previous nuclear holocausts on distant exoplanets and pose a more immediate question: Did the small Greys possibly pass through this stargate or wormhole that the Ancients recognized as a celestial whirlpool? Cursa itself is an anomaly among stars. Located 89 light-years away and having a size and mass about three times that of our Sun, it is one of about two dozen stars that suddenly and inexplicably produce huge flashes, perhaps related to a magnetic shift. In 1985, for instance, it increased by an amazing three magnitudes (or a factor of 15) and stayed that bright for over two hours until it faded back to normal brilliance.[39] Perhaps this relatively quick burst of light was the result of some interdimensional travelers passing through a whirlpool portal in the star Cursa.

Millennial Mill

Co-authors De Santillana and von Dechend describe the eddy, or *zalos*, as a celestial mill whose millstone has fallen to the bottom of the ocean. During the Golden Age of peace and abundance, it ground out only auriferous material. During successive ages (Silver, Bronze, and Iron), it ground salt, rock, and finally sand. This cosmic quern grinding temporal kernels, so to speak, is a metatphor for the astronomical mechanism called precession of the equinoxes, mentioned above in connection with the Lakota constellations.

The central shaft of this celestial machine is the previously noted *axis mundi*, or North Pole extended into the heavens toward the pole star. During the 26,000-year precessional cycle, the spindle makes a giant wobble, much like a spinning top or gyroscope. This wobble is clockwise, whereas the rotation of the Earth is counterclockwise. Precession is basically due to the fact that the Earth is not a perfect sphere but bulges at the equator, which consequently affects the gravitational pull of the Sun and the Moon on our planet. The wobble causes the Earth's axis to point to various points along a great arc, and over the course of the cycle the axis points to one star or another, which is then identified as the pole star. For example, in about 3000 BC the pole star was not Polaris but Thuban, or alpha Draconis. About the time Plato was suggesting that Greek myths referred not to human and divine figures but to astronomical bodies (see quote below), the pole star was Kochab, or beta Ursa Minoris. In 12,000 years the North Pole will point to Vega, or alpha Lyrae.[40]

As a result, the constellations or signs of the zodiac very slowly slide –one degree every 72 years– in a relative motion backward (that is, they "precess") along the inclined loop of the ecliptic, which is the apparent pathway of the Sun and the planets. The vernal equinox point, or the locus where the ecliptic crosses the celestial equator, thus shifts almost imperceptibly throughout the ages. (Both the ecliptic and the celestial equator are great circles. The point where the two cross is called the "frame," or *skambha*, literally "world pillar" in Sanskrit.[41] The ecliptic is the plane of the Earth's orbit projected onto the celestial sphere, whereas the celestial equator is the plane of the Earth's equator extended into outer space.) Currently on the first day of spring, the sun rises in the constellation Pisces, the Age of the Fish, which symbolizes Christ, but will soon rise in Aquarius, the Age of the Water Bearers—heralding the new age of enlightenment. (Some claim this has already happened.

However, the transition is by no means a rosy scenario. De Santillana and von Dechend believe that with each age's passing, the mill becomes unhinged, the fiery axle is dislodged from its hole, and a great cataclysm descends upon the Earth. The world tree is uprooted, the celestial pillar chopped down, and humans must pick up the pieces and begin again. Myths from all over the world encode these serial global catastrophes.

For instance, one Greek myth describes this cosmic catastrophe. The god Phoebus Apollo, also known as the sun god Helios, had failed to dissuade his impetuous son Phaethon from taking the reins of his chariot and driving it across the heavens. The Roman poet Ovid provides a narrative in astronomical terms, with father admonishing son.

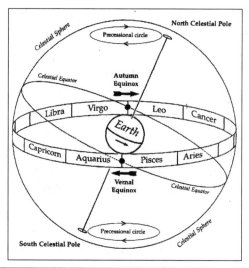

The *Carta Marina* of Olaus Magnus (16:h century) shows the "horrenda caribdis," i.e., the Maelstrom, on the lower right, with ships, destructive sea-animals, and icebergs on the left.

"… the firmament circles round forever / And carries with it distant stars and planets / At whirling, blinding speed which mazes all / But me, who with a wary hand drive clean / Through the swift courses of the sky. But you? / Can you ride counter to the whirling axis / Of space, of sky, and yet ride clear? Perhaps / You dream unearthly forests on your path: / Cities of gods, and temples pouring gifts, / Yet all the way is filled with hidden terror, / And if you hold the road, the hornèd Bull [Taurus], / The enchanted Archer [Sagittarius], the open mouth / Of the wild Lion [Leo], Scorpian [Scorpius] and Crab [Cancer] / With hairy, knife-like tails, claws reaching / Each against each, to face the other, / Are in your way."[42]

The son's hubris became his downfall, literally, after he lost control of the horses. Enraged Zeus saw the debacle and struck down the youth with a thunderbolt. Phaethon plunged in a fiery mass to earth, drowning in the River Eridanus. Perhaps the spinning chariot wheels analogically replace the archetypal revolving mill. Three-and-a-half centuries before Ovid, the Greek philosopher Plato in his work *Timaeus* had recognized in the myth its hidden celestial code:

"There have been, and will be again, many destructions of mankind arising out of many causes; the greatest have been brought about by the agencies of fire and water, and other lesser ones by innumerable other causes. There is a story, which even you have preserved, that once upon a time Phaethon, the son of Helios, having yoked the steeds in his father's chariot, because he was not able to drive them in the path of his father, burnt up all that was upon the earth, and was himself destroyed by a thunderbolt. Now this has the form of a myth, but really signifies a declination of the bodies moving in the heavens around the earth, and a great conflagration of things upon the earth, which recurs after long intervals…"[43]

During the Golden Age (about 6600 – 4500 BC), the vernal equinox sun rose in Gemini, while the autumnal equinox sun rose in Sagittarius. In this period the galactic axis, or Milky Way, served as a broad arch linking two opposite regions of the sky: the galactic center (between Scorpius and Sagittarius) and the galactic anticenter (between Gemini and Taurus). Scientists now assert that the region around Sagittarius harbors a black hole at the heart of our galaxy.

De Santillana and von Dechend comment first on the cosmic structure of the initial epoch and then on what happened after the mill became dislodged, ending the Golden Age. "The three great axes were united, the galactic avenue embracing the 'three worlds' of the gods, the living, and the dead. This 'golden' situation [subsequently] was gone, and to Eridanus was bequeathed the galactical function of linking up the 'inhabited worlds' with the abode of the dead in the (partly) invisible South. Auriga had to take over the northern obligations of the Galaxy, connecting the inhabited world with the region of the gods as well as possible."[44] In other words, the River that linked the upper land of the gods, the middle land of the humans, and the lower land of the departed no longer was the Milky Way but was instead the constellation Eridanus. The chariot that has crashed and burned becomes the constellation Auriga. Bernadette Brady summarizes this cosmic process in terms of the Greek myth.

"Eridanus touches the feet of Orion as it wanders southward and in this location, close to Rigel, it is believed to be the river into which the great millstone fell, at the time of the tilting of the table, when the mill was dislodged from the North Pole. This falling, whether of a millstone or of Phaethon, caused the whirlpool (called *zalos*), whose effect on the world we know as precession. Santillana and von Dechend talk of this myth as a mythological history. They consider the story of Phaethon as one of the great stories of the fall of one world age and the beginning of another, the historical recording of the shift of the equinoctial colure from the Milky Way, the river of life, to Eridanus—the Sun breaking out of its orbital path to finally come to rest on the ecliptic.

"Thus Eridanus took over the great mythological and theological role of the Milky Way. The next time you look at Eridanus, recognize you are looking at a living myth, as is the case with all constellations. This is the river of life, the source of all water, the river that came to be considered the band around the center of the world once the Milky Way was abandoned by the Sun. This was the river to the otherworld, the way to a different place, the Yellow Brick Road."[45]

So we come back to OZ, which is the Orion Zone. Some might say that I have already lingered too long in the ozone. But let's stay here a bit longer.

Orion, Lord of the Mill

Why did ancient cultures chose the rotary mill as a metaphor for precession? *Hamlet's Mill* presents the master of the mill in his variable guises, the most accessible to modern readers being, of course, Hamlet. However, no grinding contraption appears in Shakespeare's play at all. The bard's source was the 12th century Danish historian Saxo Grammaticus, whose relevant character was named Amleth. This version apparently lacks any mention of the cosmic mill as well. A contemporary of Saxo, the Icelandic historian Snorri Sturluson penned another Norse version, which calls the mill-master Amlodhi. Here we finally see the trope, which is referred to as Grotte, literally "axle-block." Located on a skerry (i.e. a small, rocky island), "Amlodhi's Mill" or "Amlodhi's Churn" is a kenning for the sea, but more specifically, "navel of the sea," or *Umbilicus Maris*.[46] (See bottom of p. 58.)

This bizarre "naval navel" was formed when the boat transporting the mill sank. Sturluson also narrates yet another version of the tale, in which appears a character named Frodi—alias Freyr, the Nordic form of Titan and also the great-grandson of Odin. Whereas the Amlodhi story contains nine maidens, the

Frodi story also involves the feminine—two giantesses, Fenja and Menja, who worked as slaves at the mill. Frodi told them to grind out "gold and peace and prosperity" but he worked them so hard that finally a Viking named Mysing came along and killed the overlord. With Frodi's age of peace ended, Mysing then told the pair to grind salt. "They had ground on for a short time only when the ship sank, and where the sea poured into the eye of the hand-mill was a whirlpool there afterwards in the ocean. It was then that the sea became salt."[47]

Another word for our pelagic belly button is maelstrom. This curious word is derived from *mala*, "to grind," and *stroom*, "stream." Related words include "meal," which is ground up grain, and even the term "mill" itself. Norse skalds traditionally called gold "Frodi's meal." Half a world away in the Desert Southwest, the Hopi word *tumala* means "work." The chief women's work in Hopi culture consists of grinding corn. A *mata* is a stone grinding-bin, also known as a metate.[48]

The theme of slavery is also found in the biblical story of blind Samson grinding in the Gaza prison house (Judges 16). Incidentally, the Finnish name of the cosmic mill is Sampo. Samson had previously slain a thousand Philistines with the jawbone of an ass, after which he drank the water that God had caused to flow from it (Judges 15). De Santillana and von Dechend suggest that this is actually a celestial jawbone, specifically the "watery Hyades" in the constellation Taurus.[49] It it interesting to note in this context that the man who gave King Frodi his mill was oddly named "Hangjaw."[50] Samson's pulling down the two middle pillars of the house in which three thousand Philistines were carousing, and which ultimately led to both his and their deaths, may be an echo of the toppling of the *skambha*, or world pillar. Of course, the only constellation that depicts a figure known to have at least temporarily gone blind is Orion, the Giant located in the heavens adjacent to Taurus, the Bull.

The archetypal master of the mill wears many masks, each according to his particular culture and era, but de Santillana and von Dechend finally settle on one. "The Lord of the Mill is declared to be Saturn/Kronos, he whom his son Zeus dethroned by throwing him off his chariot, and banished in 'chains' to a blissful island, where he dwells in sleep, for being immortal he cannot die, but is thought to live a life-in-death, wrapped in funerary linen, until his time, some say, shall come to awaken again, and he will be reborn to us as a child."[51] Again, the chariot wreck; again, the chains; again, the island.

Anthropologist Francis Huxley comments on the nexus of themes upon which we have been ruminating.

> "*Cronos* [or Kronos] is traditionally assimilated to *Chronos*, Time, although the words come from different etymological roots—*Cronos* perhaps from *Coronis*, 'the crow,' and Chronos from a root meaning 'to grind,' 'to wear out,' or 'to erode.' As Cronos is often figured as a miller, this conflation of meaning makes sense. Moreover it is plain that if Time is a Great Reaper, the corn he cuts has to be threshed and ground. Then, too, Cronos had a Latin counterpart, Saturn, whose name probably comes from that of an Etruscan god but is traditionally supposed to come from the verb *serere*, 'to sow.' This folk-etymology is worth taking seriously, simply because those who took over the worship of Saturn did so. It then becomes clear that we inherit the notion of time as both reaper and sower, which makes Cronos the god of the harvest."[52]

At this point we should remember that Saturnalia was the Roman festival of fertility and purification at the winter solstice, honoring the ruler of the Golden Age. Perhaps the debauchery, licentiousness, and overall *Carnival* atmosphere at year's end reflected the chaos that occurred at the change from one world-age to the next. In addition, the master-slave role reversal suggests the ascension of a new epochal ruler and the deposing of the old, such as the banishment of Kronos to the cryogenic sleep of his golden cave in Tartaros. Yet in the mythological landscape where geography is frequently confused with uranography, de Santillana and von Dechend still are compelled to remind us: "And the immense storm-swept abyss of Tartaros is not a cavern under the ground, it belongs somewhere in 'outer' space." — i.e. the celestial realm.[53]

The Roman god Saturnus was said to use a falx, a sickle-like tool that predated the scythe, which, of course, connotes the Grim Reaper[54] (associated with the Hopi god of death, Masau'u). The astrological and alchemical symbol for the planet Saturn also resembled this curved weapon. Huxley additionally claims that Orion wields not a straight sword but a falx, falchion, or billhook — the "bill" specifically being a crow's bill. So the god Saturnus, the planet Saturn, and the constellation Orion are all related, as my book *The Kivas of Heaven* has pointed out.

Maybe it is more than a coincidence, then, that a Saturn 5-class rocket will send the Orion Multi-Purpose Crew Vehicle (OMPCV) into space. Scheduled launch date is late 2017. It will take a crew of four astronauts to the Moon, near-Earth asteroids, and eventually Mars.[55]

As we all know, these are mere fledgling trials in our space-faring adventure. Like the "lone and level sands" of Shelley's poem, the stars in our galaxy "stretch far away" — 100 billion of them. Farther still are those sidereal mysteries burning and expiring in incomprehensibly distant galaxies. These spinning pinwheels or glistening disks number 100 billion or more, each with countless stars of their own. As Drake's Equation (p. 48) attests, the possibility of sentient life is vast.

Surely there are civilizations somewhere in the depths of the cold abyss whose technologies are thousands or perhaps millions of years more advanced than ours. They may even have mastered "whirlpools in the sky" (wormhole travel). But how many of them eventually self-destruct, becoming "colossal wrecks"? Or perhaps the shift in world-ages, the unhinging of the Cosmic Mill with resulting global cataclysms, have naturally wiped out untold civilizations through no fault of their own.

In our interstellar loneliness, we long to hear a response to our feeble SETI-signals — even though the entities may, like the Hopi underworld god Masau'u, be fundamentally different from us in form and function. Resting on the Orion Arm of the Milky Way, our solar system awaits a sign from the Lord of Time that life in the universe is not anomalous but ubiquitous.

Chapter 3
Egyptian Orion—
Psychedelic Barley God

The Divine Beer of Eternity

In the previous chapter I quoted de Santillana's and von Dechend's description of the Lord of the Mill as being "wrapped in funerary linen." This clearly resonates beyond the European stage. It is, in fact, a perfect evocation of an Egyptian mummy swathed in linen, an embodiment of Osiris, deity of death and resurrection, whose soul resides in the stars of Orion. Richard Hinckley Allen informs us that the ancient Egyptians also knew Orion as "Smati-Osiris, the Barley God."[1] However, Wallis Budge defines Smati as "a bull-god"[2]—perhaps a reference to Orion's position adjacent to Taurus in the sky. On the other hand, the word *smet* refers to "a kind of grain or seed used in medicine," and *smet-t* refers to "slave, servant, serf."[3] Thus, domesticated cattle, which played a key role in agriculture (especially the growth of grain), were incorporated into an astro-theological system that, as we shall see, included a psychotropic dimension.

In their book *Black Genesis*, Robert Bauval and Thomas Brophy theorize that a black-skinned race of pastoralists lived originally in east Africa and subsequently in the highlands of northern Chad when the Sahara was still lush and green. In this region and later in southwestern Egypt, they constructed a number of megalithic stellar observatories. After the desert began to dry out circa 3500 BC, these "cattle people"-turned-"star people" migrated to the Nile Valley where they established the roots of the early dynastic culture of Egypt.

> "Orion was known as Sah, and this constellation was associated with Osiris and the pharaoh who, in turn, was also symbolized as a celestial bull and the celebrated Apis Bull of Memphis. Further, all of these clues involving cattle and megalithic astronomy specifically involving Sirius, Orion, and the Big Dipper strongly suggest a link across the centuries of religious ideologies between the prehistoric society of the Sahara and that of pharaonic Egypt."[4]

Returning briefly to the rogue's gallery of "miller-narians" encountered in Chapter 2, we find that De Santillana and von Dechend have even managed to induct Dionysus into the ranks, comparing him with the Finnish figure of Kullervo. "A crow [Cronos?] then advises Kullervo to drive the cattle into the marshes and to assemble all the wolves and bears and change them into cattle."[5] Thus, wild beasts are transformed into domestic animals, useful for agriculture. This parallels Dionysus' taming lions or tigers to use them to draw his chariot. (See facing page.)

> "Although not all dying gods were associated with vegetation, the death and rebirth of Dionysus was based on fertility rites, marking the seasonal changes of the year. In fact, Dionysus' association with the grapevine, and the wetness of juice, stimulated much dryer aspects of the harvesting process, namely grain and agriculture. Additionally, given that the bull was a symbol of generative power, and a desired animal to plow the fields when castrated, Dionysus could very well have been related to Taurus, the Bull."[6]

The Dionysian role of vintner may have even been preceded by his role as brewer. Mythologist Robert Graves comments: "...Dionysus the Wine-god is a late superimposition on Dionysus the Beer-god also called Sabazius, [which] suggests that *tragedy* may be derived not from *tragos*, 'a goat', as Virgil suggests, but from *tragos*, 'spelt' — a grain used in Athens for beer-brewer."[7]

Dionysus procession, Roman Empire mosaic, El Jem Museum, Tunisia, photo by Damian Enwhistle, 2010.

Statuettes of Egyptian beer-making, Rosicrucian Museum, San Jose, CA.

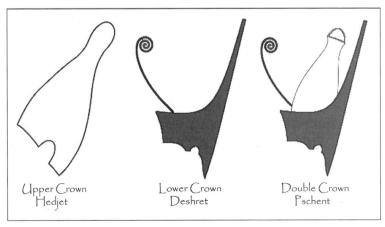

We also may recall that Dionysus was the culprit that got Orion inebriated, just prior to the latter being blinded by King Oenopion. In addition, the Greek historian Herodotus identifies the Egyptian Osiris as Dionysus and Isis as Demeter.

The ancient Egyptians apparently could brew what they called "the divine beer of everlastingness." The phrase *heq-t-enth-Maat* means "'beer of truth'—a kind of divine beer drunk by the 12 gods who guarded the shrine of Osiris."[8] The twelve gods may actually refer to the zodiac constellations. In addition, the term *neter* is generally used to refer to a "god," whereas the identical word not only means "wine, strong beer" but also "stream, canal."[9] An alternate spelling of the "god" reference is *nether*, which is orthographically the same as the English word for "under" or "below," as in netherworld or underworld. The Egyptian *nether* also means "natron," a salt used in the mummification process.[10] One Egyptian word for "barley" was *ta*, and *Neter ta* refers to "heaven," supposedly the afterlife and not simply the sky.[11]

In the afterlife "field of reeds," grain was grown, just as it was in life on earth—except larger and more bountiful. Wallis Budge comments: "…it is said that Osiris makes Pepi [Pepi II, a Sixth dynasty pharaoh] 'to plough corn and to reap barley.' From this passage we are probably right in assuming that Osiris was, even at this early period, identified with the Grain-god Nepra. This view is, moreover, supported by the statement that the deceased drinks the emissions of Osiris and eats what comes forth from him, *i.e.*, he lived on the moisture and meal which formed the Grain-god."[12]

Osiris-Neper was the personification of barley, wheat, or sorghum, whose identity was later entirely absorbed by Osiris. "The identification of Osiris as a corn-god is proved by the relief at Philae, in which corn is seen growing out of his mummified body, and by the custom of making a figure of the god in grain on a mat which was placed in the tomb. The germination of the grain typified the germination of the spirit-body of the deceased."[13] Thus, drinking the "moisture" of Osiris, namely, the divine beer, and eating his "meal," or sacred ground barley, assured that the spirit-body (*sahu* or *Sah*) would sprout in the afterlife.

My colleague and friend Jeff Nisbet writes that the Old

English word *bere* denotes "barley," which is probably also the derivation of the word "beer" itself. The name town of North Berwick, Scotland, on the Firth of Forth also comes from this root. "Lamb Island, a.k.a. The Lamb, sits about a mile from the seaside town of North Berwick, and was the central island of three that I claimed mirrored the layout of the belt stars of the constellation Orion, which, according to the hotly debated Orion Correlation Theory, were also mirrored in the layout of the 'Gizamids.'"[14]

We recall the poem by Robert Burns about John Barleycorn, whom mythologist Donald A. MacKenzie has called the "Scottish Osiris." "There were three kings into the east / Three kings both great and high / And they hae sworn a solemn oath / John Barleycorn should die." Of course, the three kings, or the Magi, connote Orion's belt. The miller crushed his bone marrow between a pair of stones, and the consumption of his blood (namely, beer or whisky) produced intoxicating joy.[15] It is interesting to note that the Egyptian word *ber* means "gateway"(stargate?), whereas the Egyptian term *berber* refers to "a loaf of bread of a pyramidal shape."[16]

Having been identified with the same word as this Egyptian one, the Berber tribe, who call themselves the Amazigh ("free people"), resides in the Maghreb — the area in northern Africa west of Egypt. In my book *The Kivas of Heaven*, I describe various Berber symbols and architecture to corresponding ones in the Hopi culture of the American Southwest. (See next page.) For instance, the Berber checkerboard is a symbol for barley, whereas the same ancestral Hopi petroglyph refers to the night sky or the Milky Way, (Remember that Orion is the Egyptian god of barley.) Constructed of five squares, the Berber equilateral cross, which represents "bird," corresponds to the Hopi equal-armed cross symbol, which signifies "star" — in this case, on the shield of the sky god Sotuknang. The Berber icon for seeds and fertility corresponds to the Hopi symbol for woman and fertility. The Berber crow's beak corresponds to the Hopi glyph for war — both of which resemble the head, feet, and hourglass shape of Orion. A Berber amulet-shape is the same as the previously mentioned Hopi coatrack symbol for lightning. And finally, the lozenge-shaped Berber eye resembles the Hopi pottery design that signifies a celestial gateway.[17]

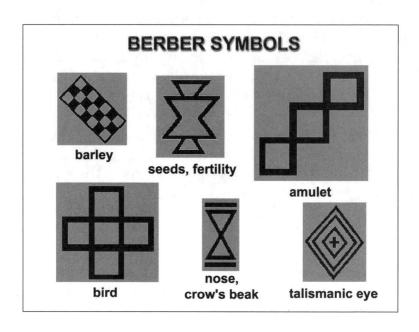

In ancient Egypt, barley was apparently considered masculine, whereas wheat was considered feminine. "The Berlin Papyrus (c. 1800 B.C.) contains directions for the oldest known pregnancy test. The test involved wetting cereals with urine. If barley grew, it meant the woman was pregnant with a male child; if the wheat grew, she was pregnant with a girl. If neither grew, the woman would not give birth."[18] (If both grew, would male-female twins be born? Or would the result be a hermaphrodite?)

We also recall that Greek legends identify Demeter (the Roman Ceres, from which the word "cereal" is derived) as the Corn Mother, and not the Corn Father, e.g. Osiris. (Corn, of course, refers to wheat and barley, not to maize.) Although Demeter was primarily associated with wheat, she also ruled over barley production. Barley may have even appeared first in civilization's agricultural development. "...of the two species of corn associated with her in Greek religion, namely barley and wheat, the barley has perhaps the better claim to be her original element; for not only would it seem to have been the staple food of the Greeks in the Homeric age, but there are grounds for believing that it is one of the oldest, if not the very oldest, cereal cultivated by the Aryan race."[19] (Recall the discussion of Aryans, which began Chapter 2.)

Unas was the last pharaoh of the Fifth Dynasty, and his pyramid at Saqqara, whose ceiling is carved with five-pointed stars, contained some of the Pyramid Texts inscribed on its inner chambers. These verses describe his journey through the *Duat*. Like Orion, Unas was a hunter, not of animals but of gods. In a rather grisly fashion, the various deities were butchered, boiled in cauldrons, and eaten—flesh, heart, liver, entrails. It is said that he consumed both the Red Crown of Lower Egypt and the White Crown of Upper Egypt.[20] (See drawing, bottom of p. 67.) The ancient Egyptians made beer out of the red grain (barley), whereas bread was made with the white grain (wheat).[21] These two-color-coded crowns perhaps symbolically refer to barley (*šma*) and emmer wheat respectively. "In his hunting expedition Unas journeyed over every part of the day sky and the night sky. The strength he derived from eating the gods enabled him to become the chief of the oldest gods of heaven, and the equal of the giant Orion." He thus possessed the gods' will, absolute power, wisdom, and everlasting life—never mind the contradiction of slain gods.[22] We recall that cannibalism was paradoxically a main motif of the Golden Age. For instance, Cronos devoured all of his children except Zeus, whom the infant's mother Rhea switched with a swaddled stone.

The myths of Unas may have even eventually led to human sacrifice in Egypt. The optimum victim, oddly enough, was supposed to have red hair, which represented either ripe cereal grains or a particular fungus that invades them.

> "Osiris, the corn-spirit, was annually represented at harvest by a stranger, whose red hair made him a suitable representative of the ripe corn. This man, in his representative character, was slain on the harvest-field, and mourned by the reapers, who prayed at the same time that the corn-spirit might revive and return (*mââ-ne-rha*, Maneros) with renewed vigour in the following year. Finally, the victim, or some part of him, was burned, and the ashes scattered by winnowing-fans over the fields to fertilize them."[23]

Orion, Celestial Entheogenesis

The ultimate question remains: Why do all these religious connotations regarding bread and brew exist? Surely a simple beer-buzz is not the path to enlightenment or immortality, to which a plethora of binging college fraternity parties attest.

The answer, I believe, lies in the connection between the Egyptian barley god, Smati-Osiris, and the word "smut"—not pornography but a type of parasitic fungus that infests various cereal crops. Barley is particularly susceptible to ergot (*Claviceps purpurea*), a rust that invades both cultivated grains and wild grasses. This sclerotium, however, contains psychoactive properties that, when ingested, elicit hallucinations.

In Greece the crimson-colored fungal corruption was called

erysibe, and, indeed, one of the epithets of Demeter was Erysibe. Some suggest it played a major role in the Eleusinian Mysteries, the ceremonies that occurred every five years in late September or October at Eleusis, a town located on a fertile plain a dozen or so miles northwest of Athens. Sworn to secrecy under penalty of death, initiates drank a barley potion called *kykeon,* laced with the psychedelic ergot and herbs. Although today not much is known about these rituals, they probably involved chanting, music, ecstatic dance, and dramatic invocations. It is interesting to note that toward the end of the ceremony, a bull (most likely symbolizing the constellation Taurus) was sacrificed.[24] Chemist Albert Hofmann, who first synthesized LSD in 1938 and experimented with its effects, writes about the Greek entheogen ("generating the divine within").

> "We have no way to tell what the chemistry was of the ergot of barley or wheat raised on the Rarian plain in the 2nd millennium B.C. But is is certainly not pulling a long bow to assume that the barley grown there was host to an ergot containing, perhaps among others, the soluble hallucinogenic alkaloids. The famous Rarian plain was adjacent to Eleusis. Indeed, this may well have led to the choice of Eleusis for Demeter's temple, and from the growth of the cluster of powerful myths surrounding them and Triptolemus that still exert their spell on us today."[25]

The symbolism of the Mysteries certainly included the myth of Demeter's daughter Persephone, who was abducted and raped by Hades, lord of the underworld. The former, which represented cultivated grain and by extension the amenities of civilization, was seized by the latter, which represented the dark, moribund fungus and the primal forces of wild nature. Persephone is doomed to spend the colder part of the year with Hades in the underworld, and this pact keeps the chaos of the chthonic energies at bay. The demigod Triptolemus ("threefold warrior"—perchance, something to do with Orion's belt?), whose name seems particularly appropriate (Trip-tolemus), was an apostle of Demeter, who traveled the world in a wingèd chariot drawn by serpents, spreading the knowledge of agriculture and, presumably, the mind-expanding virtues of barley-beer.

The Eleusinain Mysteries, specifically the Lesser Mysteries, additionally included ingestion of *Psilocybe*, a variety of magic mushrooms, or perhaps *Amanita muscaria*. Author John Major Jenkins suggests that the latter species is an *imago mundi*, or model of the tripartite world of sky, earth, and underworld. He specifically says that the mushroom stipe (or stalk) is the cosmic pivot of the previously mentioned Finnish Sampo, with the white-flecked, red cap corresponding to the star-strewn dome of the sky, referred to as its "many ciphered cover." Circular or spiral rings are also distributed along the stipe.[26]

Herodotus claims that the Greek Mysteries were imported from the Lower Egyptian town of Sais, where he also says the grave of Osiris lies. (Plutarch says that both the birthplace and tomb of Osiris is Busiris.) Herodotus furthermore states that he knows more than he can say about the Mysteries, which took place around a circular pond with tall stone obelisks in the vicinity, so apparently the secretive aspect of the rites was imported to Greece as well.[27]

I talked earlier about two royal headdresses in connection with the pharaoh Unas: 1. Red Crown, or *deshret*, and 2. White Crown, or *hedjet*. An alternate spelling of *deshret* is *tesher-t*, while the same word refers to a red pot or vase used in funerary ceremonies. The related word *tesher* refers to red grain. An alternate spelling of *hedjet* is *hetch-t*, while *Hetch-a* is the name of a singing god or grain-god.[28] The Red Crown comes from Lower Egypt and the Delta region, which is why its hieroglyph –one of the oldest, by the way– was in some cases used to designate "water-ripple." This perhaps brings us back to the whirlpool symbol.

Ethnopharmacologist Stephen R. Berlant theorizes that the distinctive morphology of the White Crown was influenced by that of the pin-stage primordium of *Psilocybe cubensis*, one of the magic mushroom species indigenous to Egypt.[29] Remember that the pre-dynastic climate when the Mysteries probably began was much moister, allowing fungi to thrive. In addition, mushrooms tend to grow prolifically on cattle manure, so the ceremonial bovine aspect found in Greece was obviously present in Egypt as well. From The Pyramid Texts we read: "Neferirkare' (Pepi II) is the bull of heaven, who once suffered want and decided –literally gave in his heart– to live on the being of every god, who ate their entrails when it came to pass that their belly was full of magic from the Isle of Flame [the Primordial Mound]."[30]

In an ancient Egyptian tale from the Westcar Papyrus called "King Cheops and the Magicians," Queen Reddedet (Khentkaus) gave birth to triplets: Wosref (Userkaf), Sahure (Sahu-re), and Keku (Neferirkare', or Pepi II)—the first three pharaohs of the 5th Dynasty. They were all born with headdresses of lapis lazuli and limbs covered with gold. The bluish-purple hue of the former may represent the fruiting bodies of the ergot (species *purpurea*) in symbiotic embrace of the latter, namely, the golden grain. The color may also reflect the purple-blue of Hades' hair as well as the royal color of Demeter's robes. ("In antiquity 'purple' meant crimson."[31])

In the narrative the four goddesses of childbirth (Isis, Nephthys, Heket, and Meskhenet) made three crowns as gifts to the three kings: 1. *hedjet*–White Crown, 2. *deshret*–Red Crown, and 3. either *pshent*–Double Crown, or *atef*–Osiris' *hedjet* with ostrich plumes. These were placed in bins of barley, exposed to a rainstorm, and then put in a storeroom for 14 days. "So they fashioned three royal crowns, and they placed them in the corn. Then they caused the heavens to turn into a storm and rain, and they turned back to the house and said: Would you please put the corn here in a locked room until we can come back on our northward journey? So they placed the corn in a locked room."[32] Reddedet then purified herself for 14 days in preparation for the beer-making. Two weeks is the period between infection of the grain by fungal spores and the appearance of sclerotia, which resemble tiny mushrooms.[33]

Regarding the Egyptian story, it is surprising that Berlant mentions psilocybin mushrooms sprouting from the moist barley but does not consider the possibility of infestation by ergot, which seems to have been the primary hallucinogen of the Greater Mysteries of Eleusis. The Red Crown of Lower Egypt, where the Mysteries took place, may even be symbolic of the ergot rust. Ergo, the fungus ergot may be summed up metonymically as the Red Crown, which, when ingested, causes extreme vertigo and phantasmagoria—in other words, a psychedelic trip.

The spiral on the crown also signifies both the proboscis of a honeybee, the insect that aids in the pollination of barley, and, as previously mentioned, swirling or rippling water. In addition, the Greek "mother of the gods" named Rhea and by association Demeter were both considered Queen of the Bees. Freemason Robert Hewitt Brown remarks: "[The beehive] was one of the emblems of the Eleusinian Mysteries. The goddess Rhea… was represented with a beehive beside her, out of the top of which arose corn (wheat) and flowers, denoting the renewal of the seasons and the return of the sun to the vernal equinox." Her name literally means "flow"—either of water or, because of her marriage to Chronos, of time.[34]

One version of Orion's birth deals with a poor beekeeper named Hyrieus, who was impotent but wanted a son. Zeus, Hermes, and Poseidon urinated on a bull hide, buried it, and nine months later the infant Orion emerged. In this case, Orion was son of an apiculturist.

Another ancient Egyptian artifact that incorporates the spiral is the *Wadjet* (*Udjat*), or Eye of Horus, sometimes also known as the Eye of Ra. Generally recognized as a protective and healing amulet, the *Wadjet* was once torn from the falcon-god Horus by his vicious brother Set but was restored by the shaman and divine magician Thoth. One possible avian variation of the deity is the Gyrfalcon, or "gyre-falcon" (*Falco rusticolus*), a species that hunts for its prey in a circling pattern. We might think of Y. B. Yeats' poem called "The Second Coming," which describes the shifting of the World Age. "Turning and turning in the widening gyre / The falcon cannot hear the falconer; / Things fall apart; the centre cannot hold; / Mere anarchy is loosed upon the world, / The blood-dimmed tide is loosed, and everywhere / The ceremony of innocence is drowned…"

The "centre" is, of course, the *axis mundi*, or mill-axle, which was known in ancient Egypt as the *djed* pillar, or the "backbone of Osiris," a.k.a. Orion. The ancient Egyptians, of course, did not use the rotary mill. They instead milled grain with abrasive stones on flat slabs, somewhat like the Hopi of the American Southwest. Prior to the women's arduous work of grinding, however, the grain had to be pounded in limestone mortars with wooden pestles so the chaff could be separated from the kernels. Thus, the pestle serves this symbolic vertical function of the mill, along with the *djed*.

Horus in turn gave the *Wadjet* to his dead father, Osiris, who ate it, causing his resurrection. This icon was traditionally made into cakes, which probably contained the powerful alkaloid ergot. The Pyramid Texts state: "To say four times: A royal offering to the *ka* [etheric double] of Neferirkare' [Pepi II]. Osiris Neferirkare', take to thyself the eye of Horus. It is thy cake; eat thou. A cake of offering, a *wdet*-cake [*Wadjet*-cake]."[35] Wallis Budge comments on the importance of the custom. "The gods nourished themselves with celestial food which was supplied by the Eye of Horus, that is to say, they supported their existence on the rays of light which fell from the sun which lit up heaven, and they became beings whose bodies were wholly of light."[36]

Here we see Smati-Osiris as undisputed Lord of the Cosmic Mill, who dines on celestial grain, and whose soul resides in Orion. He strides across the sky with his sidereal bull Taurus. His body is formed not from corruptible flesh but from pure light. Inexorably swirling at his feet is the whirlpool (wormhole?) of the ages the Ancients called the *zalos*. (See Chapter 2.)

Orion, the Shining One

The possibility of interstellar travel may not be the result of simply a physical, nuts-and-bolts craft. Instead the celestial wanderers may have employed interdimensional "archaic techniques of ecstasy," to use Eliade's phrase that refers to shamanism in general. Perhaps eons ago adepts learned the secrets of the Mysteries and began to inhabit "light-bodies" or "rainbow-bodies," which are sort of like etheric containers for their souls. Investigative mythologist William Henry talks about the Bon tradition of Tibetan Buddhism, whereby various meditation practices refine and rarify the five traditional elements of matter in order to create a vehicle free from the limits of space and time. "A teacher of yogi who has acquired the highest forms of accomplishment can manifest what is called 'the rainbow body' or 'body of light.' Usually this happens after death, but it has been known to happen at other times and in front of witnesses. It is not so much a 'body' but rather a *vortex of energy* [italics added] into which these adepts can transform themselves on dying. In Tibetan terms they 'dissolve into space like a rainbow.'"[37] Again, energy vortexes are the underlying structures whereby transcendence of the physical realm is achieved.

Musicologist and scholar of Western mystery traditions, Joscelyn Godwin says that this particular concept was part of the universal Perennial Philosophy that recurs in various guises throughout the ages.

"As in shamanic, Masonic, and other later initiations, the candidate was placed in a trance, his consciousness taken out of his body, and in this state he experienced higher states of being and met some of the denizens of the invisible worlds. Some were demonic, others beneficent; Proclus describes certain of them as forms of light that take on human shape. Through direct experience the candidate would learn that he could live freely without his physical body, and that the gods he worshipped were perfectly real. Then he would return to earth fully convinced of his immortality and prepared to meet death fearlessly, knowing it as the gate to freedom and his soul's true home."[38]

This "gate to freedom" may be the same type of stargate that many Native Americans have described as an entryway to Earth, a sort of "immortal portal" through which star elders or celestial ancestors descend from hyperspace to our three-dimensional realm. Adrian Gilbert, co-author of *The Orion Mystery*, reminds us that the five-pointed hieroglyphic for "star" is transliterated as *s'ba*, a word that also means "door."[39] Like Hamlet's Mill, it is revolving, with both ingress and egress possible. Da Vinci's pentagonal Vitruvian Man is the supreme human manifestation of the sidereal vortex. To use an anagram, the *ba's s'ba* is the skylight through which flies that human-headed bird (soul).

Shifting the letters of another anagram, the *akh* flees the *kha*—the eternal light separates from the ignorance and shadowy corruption of the flesh. Lucie Lamy, daughter of the renowned Egyptologist R. A. Schwaller de Lubicz, defines the former term: "Another of the subtle parts of Being, *akh* plays a considerable role in the sacred language. *Akh* is a state, a quality, and an activity, signifying the spirit; radiant, transcendent light; and the transfiguration by this light. *Akh* is at the origin and at the end of all vital experience of becoming conscious."[40] The Coffin Texts describe Orion sailing his boat over the sky's *akhakh*, which Budge translates as "flowers (of heaven), *i.e.*, stars."[41] Spell 227 says: "I indeed am Osiris [Orion], I indeed am the Lord of All, I am the Radiant One..."[42] It is interesting to note that the Egyptian word *akhakhu* means "blossoms, flowers," whereas the Hopi word *àaqawu* means "wild sunflower."[43]

We recall from Chapter 1 that the *Duat/Tuat*, which refers to the afterlife realm, is a homophone of the Hopi word *tu'at*, which signifies a mystical vision. Co-authors Philip Gardiner and Gary Osborn very kindly cite my work in regard to a Celtic connection that they made. "The word 'tuat' also forms part of the name of the mythical Celtic gods, the Tuatha dé Danaan, a race of 'Shining Ones' who are said to have arrived in Ireland before the present inhabitants. The pronunciation of 'Tuat-ha' is strikingly similar to the Hopi *tuu'awta* and provides further evidence for the early worldwide distribution of knowledge from a single source."[44]

The Egyptian *akhu*, then, were "light-beings" or "divine spirits," and the *Åakhu* were the "spirit-souls of the gods of the Tuat."[45] Hancock and Bauval claim that the *Akhu* may have been the Predynastic cadre of demigods known as the Shemsu Hor, or the "Followers of Horus," whose reign lasted over 13,000 years, or half the precessional cycle.

> "The plural word '*Akhu*', is normally translated as 'Venerables'. Yet... a close examination of the full range of meanings that the ancient Egyptians attached to it suggest that another and far more intriguing possibility exists—one that is concealed by so generalized an epithet. To be specific, the hieroglyphs for *Akhu* can also mean 'Transfigured Beings', 'Shining Ones', 'Shining Beings', or 'Astral Spirits'—understandably identified by some linguists with the stars."[46]

Based on Budge's definition of these entities as "wise, instructed folk," Hancock and Bauval suggest, however, that they were actually an enlightened and learned class of humans, or "...an élite of highly initiated astronomer-philosophers."[47]

In the previous chapter I spent quite a bit of time discussing Orion's left foot Rigel and the celestial whirlpool in the adjacent constellation Eridanus. If we focus in the other direction on Orion's head, we find that the main star Meissa (lamba Orionis), or its Arabic name *Al Maisan*, literally means "the shining one." This third magnitude star is the apex of a small triangle, with its base formed by a pair of 4th magnitude stars, phi 1 and phi 2 Orionis. These "little twins" are known as Heka and Hike—in Arabic, *Al Ha'qa*, or "white spot." We recall that the Egyptian *Benu* bird (phoenix) perched atop the pyramidion issues the *Hikê*, the "breath of life" or "divine word." It is ironic that the Sumerian (Allen calls it "Euphratean") name for the faint pair is

Mas-tab-ba-tur-tur.[48] A mastaba is, of course, a flat-topped pyramid tomb. In this context we hear the echo of the Hopi god of death, Masau'u, who, as I have argued, is the deified manifestation of Orion. In addition, we recall one Greek version of Orion's death that involves Artemis shooting an arrow at his head while he is swimming in the sea, perhaps the Milky Way itself.

This stellar trio (phi 1 Orionis, phi 2 Orionis, and Meissa) may be conceptualized as the two physical eyes resting below the Third Eye chakra of Orion's head. As we saw in Chapter 1, this upper sidereal point corresponds in the Arizona Orion Correlation to Walnut Canyon located in the evergreen foothills of the San Francisco Peaks, the sacred home of the Hopi kachinas. The Third Eye, of course, is related to the pineal gland, which literally means "pine cone" due to its shape.

The Arabic name for Meissa is *Ras al Jauzah*, the "head of Orion." However, *al Jauzah* literally means either "walnut" or a "black sheep with a white spot on the middle of its body." Considering his truculent and bellicose character, Orion was clearly a black sheep.[49]

Using WISE, or the Wide-field Infrared Survey Explorer telescope, NASA scientists have recently found a circular nebula that completely surrounds Meissa. Approximately 130 light-years in diameter, this molecular ring appears as a huge green dust cloud encompassing the giant Orion's head. This great, star-forming region of the sky might be seen as big-headed Orion with his boastful and belligerent nature. On the other hand, this celestial circle might be construed as the divine nimbus or halo of the Shining One in all his cosmic glory.[50]

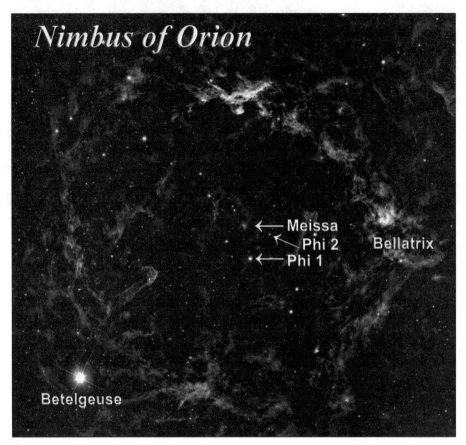

Nimbus of Orion

Meissa
Phi 2
Phi 1
Bellatrix
Betelgeuse

Upper: At the center of the circular nebula (a giant green halo 130 light-years in diameter) is Meissa, Orion's head, with ph 1 and phi 2 forming the base of a small triangle. Meissa might also be considered as the Third Eye, while the smaller pair of stars as the corporeal eyes. At lower left of the photo is the variable red supergiant Betelgeuse, Orion's right shoulder. To the right of Meissa is Bellatrix, the constellation's left shoulder.

Facing page, lower-left: Petroglyph at Nephthys Hill, Dakhla Oasis, about 225 miles west of Karnak on the Nile. At the top is a right footprint and at the bottom is probably a left handprint, perhaps of the person who carved this slab. The human figure is possibly one of the earliest depictions of Orion. In his left hand is a staff, or perhaps a stalk of barley; in his right is a club. To the figure's right is a bow and some arrows, as well as a backpack. The large triangular shape above them has been interpreted as a wristguard. However, it may instead represent a yardang, which is a natural, pyramid-shaped hill. Alternative historians may deem it an actual pyramid, and the truly fanciful may see a delta-shaped, extraterrestrial craft hovering in the air.

Facing page, lower-right: Sahu, the god Orion with a five-pointed star above.

A Few Cognates From the Hopi and Ancient Egyptian Languages

• The Hopi word *saaqa* means "stepladder."
• The Egyptian name Saqqara was the place where the first step pyramid was built.
• The Hopi word *hikwsi* means "breath, breath of life, vital force, vitality."
• The Egyptian word *hikê* meant "life-breath" issued from the *Bennu* bird (phoenix) during the cosmogony.
• The Hopi word *tu'at* means "mystical vision, illusion."
• The Egyptian word *Tuat* (or *Duat*) meant "the afterlife," where mystical insight is achieved.
• The Hopi syllable *ka-* (as in kachina, *katsina*—an angel-like spirit messenger) was borrowed from outside the Pueblo Southwest.
• The Egyptian word *Ka* meant "vital essence, etheric double, guardian angel."
• The Hopi word *sohu* means "star." (For the Hopi, the most important constellation in a ritual sense is Orion.)
• The Egyptian word *sahu* meant "stars of Orion."

These linguistic correspondences indicate a common knowledge-base globally distributed in ancient times by a unified source—either terrestrial or ET.

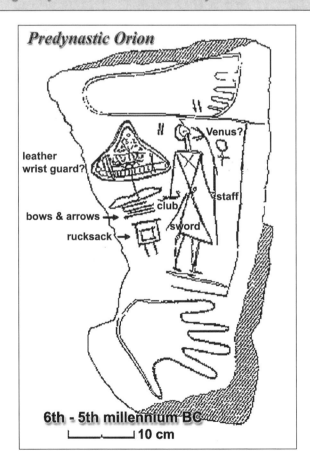

Predynastic Orion

leather wrist guard?

bows & arrows →

rucksack ←

‖ ‖

Venus?

staff

club

sword

6th - 5th millennium BC

⊢————⊣ **10 cm**

SAHÛ-ORION.

83

Hopi man and youth impersonating ancestral spirits during bean-planting ceremony,Arizona,1893, from INDIANS by Joanna Cohan Scherer, Crown Pub., Inc. Photo by James Mooney, Bureau of American Ethnology.

Chapter 4
Grand Canyon
and the Hopi Underworld

Romantic Grandeur and Archaic Culture

Grand Canyon is a magnificent geological manifestation of the Hopi underworld. Over 275 miles long, 18 miles wide at its greatest extent, and over one mile and two billion years deep, this breathtaking rift in time is essentially beyond words. It continues to elude us. Descriptives fall flat. Many have tried, most have failed to convey the power it has to seize our imagination and galvanize our higher selves. Naturalist writer John Muir sometimes comes close, despite his occasional antiquated rhetoric.

"Yonder stands a spiry cathedral nearly five thousand feet in height, nobly symmetrical, with sheer buttressed walls and arched doors and windows, as richly finished and decorated with sculptures as the rock temples of India or Egypt. Beside it rises a huge castle with arched gateways, turrets, watch-towers, ramparts, etc., and to right and left palaces, obelisks, and pyramids fairly fill the gulf, all colossal and all lavishly painted and carved. Here and there a flat-topped structure may be seen, or one imperfectly domed; but the prevailing style is ornate Gothic, with many hints of Egyptian and Indian."[1]

As we shall see, perhaps he intuitively knew more than he realized.

In the late 19th century geologist Clarence Dutton and others tried to capture the chasm's Romantic immensity by naming some of its buttes as exotic places of worship: Osiris Temple (mentioned in Chapter 1), Isis Temple, Horus Temple, Temple of Set, Brahma Temple, Shiva Temple, Vishnu Temple, Deva Temple, Buddha Temple, Solomon Temple, Zoroaster Temple, Apollo Temple, Jupiter Temple, Juno Temple, Venus Temple, Diana Temple, Thor Temple, Confucius Temple, Mencius Temple, Holy Grail Temple, Masonic Temple. Other names of its natural features evoke the misty mythological past: Merlin Abyss, Excalibur Tower, Lancelot Point, Guinevere Castle, Galahad Point, Gawain Abyss, Wotans Throne, Walhalla Plateau, Freya Castle, Vulcans Throne, Tower of Babel, Cheops Pyramid, Ariel Point, Ottoman Amphitheater, Krishna Shrine, Hindu Amphitheater. Still others simply suggest the canyon's overwhelming majesty: Point Imperial, Cape Royal, Point Sublime, Cape Solitude, Angels Window, Sky Island, Bright Angel Trail.[2]

Even the park's brochure waxes poetic: "Perhaps no landscape on earth is as startling to the observer as the vast yet intricate face of the Grand Canyon.... The world seems larger here with sunrises, sunsets, and storms taking on an added dimension to match the landscape. It is a land to humble the soul." Yet language simply cannot match the sheer experiential ecstasy of Grand Canyon.

Years ago my wife Anita and I stopped at Lipan Point after a day spent lingering on the South Rim. She was tired and stayed back at the car, while I walked out to a precipitous peninsula of rock. As I sat cross-legged, gazing dreamily into the distance, I could feel tranquil waves of healing energy, negative ions, or some ineffable force blissfully flowing out of the canyon in slow, rhythmic breaths. Slipping into a meditative state, with my brainwaves drifting downward from Beta to Alpha, I slightly shifted my eyes out of focus and squinted against the setting sun. After a few moments I began to see swirling, Van Gogh-like forms take shape on the 3-D canvas of the canyon. Luminous orbs surged from one pinnacle or butte to another—dancing spheres of electric lime-green and fuchsia balancing briefly on the top of one spire, then streaming off to another in a rush that gave me the distinct impression that they were conscious, living beings of light. Eventually these sensations began to fade, although I couldn't tell how long the experience had lasted.

Totally relaxed and floating on clouds of euphoria, I sauntered back to the car. My wife noticed immediately that something had changed within me, some shift of my inner axis, though she didn't mention it until later. We drove home, mutually agreeing not to speak for a long time.

In the holistic world of Grand Canyon, I'm sure this sort of altered perception, or something akin to it, is not uncommon. The unique phenomena many people encounter here are probably why various tribes had visited and even inhabited the canyon for thousands of years, despite the challenges of its harsh topography and climate.

More than 250 archaeological sites have been excavated below the rim.[3] There could easily be 10 times that number or more, but because of the inhospitable and inaccessible nature of the terrain, we just haven't found them all yet.

Archaeologists believe that a Desert Culture known as the Pima Complex migrated southward from the Mojave Desert starting about 4,000 years ago and began to thrive in Grand Canyon, perhaps as much for aesthetic and spiritual reasons as for pragmatic ones. Early evidence of this habitation includes animal effigies called split-twig figurines. Many of these small willow twigs twisted into the shape of a generic game animal had been cached beneath rock cairns inside of ceremonial caverns of Redwall limestone. (See p. 90.) Hunters supposedly used the figurines in sympathetic magic to lure various animals, such as bighorn sheep and mule deer. Sometimes they were pierced with small sticks to represent spears. These are some of the oldest artifacts yet discovered beneath the rim. For instance, scientists from the University of California tested one figurine found in a huge cave in Marble Canyon and came up with a date of 2145 BC ± 100 years.[4]

Archaeologists say that the Ancestral Puebloans started to inhabit the canyon about 700 AD, with the greatest influx being about 1150. Except for periodic Hopi salt expeditions, the area was abandoned by 1300, partly because of the Great Drought that occurred in the last quarter of the 13th century.

One of the largest sites is located on the Unkar Delta and its vicinity, downstream from Tanner Trail. This aggregate of nearly 100 structures was positioned on broad, sandy terraces that provided ample arable land. The construction included pueblos with large rooms and well-made, round kivas. This may have been a winter home, with the farmers moving up to the cooler North Rim in summer to become again like the hunter-gatherers of old. The delta is surrounded by brilliant vermillion cliffs, hence its name—the Paiute word *unkar* meaning "red stone."[5]

Author and world explorer David Hatcher Childress speculates that the word *Unkar* might actually be a linguistic borrowing from ancient Egypt. *Ankh-Ka* or *Ankh-Ra* merges the key of life with either "guardian spirit" or "sun god."[6] In addition to the Egyptian names of various buttes in Grand Canyon noted above, we see that the Egyptian theme constantly seems to recur. During his monumental boat-trip down the Colorado River in 1869, John Wesley Powell himself borrowed an Egyptian term.

"I walk down the gorge to the left at the foot of the cliff, climb to a bench, and discover a trail, deeply worn in the rock. Where it crosses the side gulches in some places steps have been cut. I can see no evidence of its having been traveled for a long time. It was doubtless a path used by the people who inhabited this country anterior to the present Indian races—the people who built the communal houses of which mention has been made. I return to camp about three o'clock and find that some of the men have discovered ruins and many fragments of pottery ; also etchings and hieroglyphics on the rocks."[7]

By "etchings and hieroglyphics," Powell undoubtedly meant petroglyphs, or rock carvings. He made this observation where the aquamarine waters of the Little Colorado River slip into the green jade waters of the main Colorado. In 1890 a prospector named Ben Beamer settled in this area and built a stone cabin. It is likely that instead erecting a new structure, he simply renovated the ancient one.

NOONDAY REST IN MARBLE CANYON.

J. W. Powell made the first reconnaissance of the Colorado River in 1869.

Split-twig figurine found in Grand Canyon.

Looking down the Colorado River from near the Confluence.

Celestial Shrine of the Ages

As implied above, an encounter with Grand Canyon is primarily a spiritual experience. Regardless of one's religious or cultural background, the scale of the natural architectonic spans of stone and time is so immense that one's spirit is simultaneously humbled and exalted. When I took my adopted brother, friend and colleague Shree Subash Chandira Bose, who lives in Tamil Nadu, India, to the South Rim for the first time, he was simply overwhelmed by the "divine spiritual energy rising from the bottom of the Grand Canyon."[8]

George Wharton James, an early 20th century popular writer, photographer, and lecturer, aptly describes the transformative power of the place: "To me this Canyon is the Holy of Holies, the Inner Temple, where each man may be his own High Priest, open the sacred veil, and stand face to face with the Divine. And he who can thus 'talk with God' may not show it to his fellows, but he knows within himself the new power, calmness, and equanimity which he has gained, and he returns to life's struggles thankful for his glimpses of the Divine."[9]

Archaeologist Douglas W. Swartz, who excavated Unkar Delta in the 1960s, describes a visit to the Hopi Sipàapuni, discussed in Chapter 1:

"The hike seemed endless in the heat. The sun beat down on us from a cloudless sky, and the reflection from the cliff walls made it even hotter. But when we finally reached our destination, it was well worth the effort. For suddenly, there in front of us, was the origin of a people — as sacred to the Hopis as Bethehem to the Christians, Mecca to the Moslems, and Benares to the Hindus. We circled the dome, trying to understand its geological structure: a travertine or similar formation produced by the mineral content of an artesian spring that for ages had poured onto the dome, slowly increasing its height. Climbing to the top over its slightly loose, grainy surface, we found in the center of the dome the pool of bubbling yellowish water through which the ancestors had emerged into this world. The sanctity of the spot affected us all, and for much of the time we were there we spoke very little."[10]

One account after another taps into this universal reservoir of meaning, both aesthetic and sacred, that Grand Canyon with its gigantic geologic expanse contains. On the other hand, cultures separated by millennia would certainly have different perceptions of the potency of this place. Colin Fletcher, who in 1963 became the first person to walk the length of Grand Canyon below the rim, ruminates on the divergent worldviews of the ancient *Hisatsinom* and us, the moderns. "Because this man lived in a different age, the surface of his answers would clearly be different from mine. He could not ponder on the marvel and mystery of a Redwall that had been built by the remains of countless tiny organisms that are in a tenuous sense our ancestors. He would undoubtedly think in terms of some kind of god. And his god, I felt sure, was the Spirit of the Rocks."[11]

This "Spirit" finds its particular manifestation in the Hopi deity Masau'u, discussed in Chapter 2. In fact, the cave of Nukpana, or "Evil One" (another name for the ambiguously baffling Masau'u) is located very near the Sipàapuni. Only a warrior (*kaletaka*) or a member of the Masau'u-Coyote-Kokop (Fire) phratry of clans may enter this "House of the Dead," but visitation by at least one participant in the salt expedition is required.[12]

Masau'u himself is said to have a dual nature. Beneath his death-gray, blood-encrusted mask is a handsome youth, who wears beautiful, long turquoise ear pendants.

"The Hopi say he is really a very handsome great man of a dark color with fine long black hair and that he is indeed a great giant. When the Hopi came up from the Underworld and looked about them in fear, the first sign they saw of any being of human form, was the great footprints of Masauwu. Now Masauwu only walks at night and he carries a flaming torch. Fire is his and he owns the fiery pits [of the underworld]. Every night Masauwu takes his torch and he starts out on his rounds, for he walks clear around the edge of the world every night."[13]

In the same vicinity of the canyon is also located the House of the Koyemsi, or Mudhead. He wears a sack-like mask with gourd-knobs for ears and one knob on the top of the head. His eyes and mouth are tube-like, and his head and body are daubed with red-brown clay. He is a sacred clown originally from Zuni Pueblo, although he frequently appears at Hopi kachina dances. Zuni elder Clifford Mahooty says that these beings are the mentally disabled or deranged spawn of incest or other sexual aberrations. The late 19th century archaeologist and ethnographer Jesse Walter Fewkes saw that a number of Mudheads appeared at the Powamu, or Hopi Bean Planting Ceremony held in February. He remarked that they "...danced and sang, performing certain obscene acts which need not be described."[14] (See drawing on the bottom of p. 96.)

Grand Canyon undeniably includes the full range of sensibilities, from sacred to profane, divine to evil, embodying in its length, breadth, and depth the famous quip by American poet Walt Whitman (1819–1892): "Do I contradict myself? / Very well then I contradict myself, / (I am large, I contain multitudes.)"[15] Leigh Kuwanwisiwma, director of the the Hopi Cultural Preservation Office, comments on the overall significance of the wondrous abyss: "All this canyon land is covered with our footprints. It's where we had our genesis; where some of our clans farmed and lived until we were called to the mesas. It is where our spirits go when we die. It is where we learned the Hopi way of life, and the lessons that guide us. And the key lesson is the lesson of humility."[16]

If New Mexico is called the Land of Enchantment, surely Arizona with its Grand Canyon could be called the Land of Enshrinement. In Chapter 1, I discussed the celestial shrines formed by the terrestrial template of Orion projected on the high desert—his left arm reaching out to Grand Canyon. The late anthropologist of the Southwestern pueblos Fred Eggan summarizes Hopi cosmology vis-à-vis the Grand Canyon.

"The most important shrines or sacred areas are in the Grand Canyon where the Little Colorado River flows into the Colorado. Here the *sipapu*, or place of emergence, is physically present in a large raised pond. Here is their 'source,' the place of emergence from, and entrance to the underworld. Here the deceased Hopi live and respond to the prayers of their descendants. In this area are salt deposits that are periodically visited to gather salt, essential to their diet, with shrines to Spider Woman, who created the salt, and the Twin War Gods, who are her grandchildren and the protectors of the Hopi and their domain. Here, too, are many of their early villages in which their world-view was shaped, and which are still shrines to their descendants. Only Hopis initiated into Wuwutsim, the Tribal Initiation [or New Fire Ceremony], could journey to this area, since the trip was physically difficult and involved danger since the spirits of the dead lived in this region and Masau [Masau'u], the God of Death, had his major home in the cliffs. The Salt journey from Oraibi took several days, and involved stopping at Moenkopi for final preparations and the making of offerings and rituals at a number of shrines along the 'salt trail.'"[17]

A Hopi legend says that before departing on their migrations the Hopi met Masau'u, who said he would return at the end of the Fourth World, the conclusion of the current temporal cycle. This theme is akin to the return of the Mayan Kukulkan or the Aztecan Quetzalcoatl at the end of the world-age. Echoing the final chapter of the Book of Revelation, Masau'u also stated: "I'm the first but I'm also going to be the last." ("*Pay pi as nu' mootiy'angw pay nu' piw naat nuutungktato.*")[18]

Welsh author Jon Manchip White places the God-centered

yet evolutionary philosophy of French paleontologist and Jesuit priest Pierre Teilhard de Chardin in the context of Grand Canyon.

"Stepping away from those falls of stone, you can only trust in Teilhard's belief that that blunt and twisted chaos down there is our Alpha point, that God in His own good time (which is not *our* time) will raise us to the Omega point where everything will meet again in Him. There are moments at the Grand Canyon when I am gripped by the thought that the instant of death might be like this. The Canyon might be as close as we can come while living to the sensation of sinking into eternity, being carried to heaven by an Archangel, or being hauled into Paradise by our hair, like a Muhamadan . . ."[19]

Ogre kachinas at *Powamu* ceremony, Walpi, Arizona, 1893,
James Mooney, Bureau of American Ethnology.
(See other kachinas at same Bean Planting ritual on p. 84.)

Right: Hopi drawing of Masau'u, 1903, Bureau of American Ethnology.
Round helmet with multi-colored spots. On top are twigs with prayer feathers. Body painted red and black. Neck kilt and rabbit-skin rug, shirt, and kilt around the body. Two circles on the breast made from human bones. Yucca whip in each hand. Cloud symbol upper-right.

Maya scholar Augustus Le Plongeon notes that spots of the leopard skin were frequently associated with Osiris.

Below: Drawing of Zuni Koyemsis, or Mudheads. Two figures wear fawn-skin bandoliers. Painted spots on middle figure.

Hopi Cosmology

The architectural structure of the Hopi underworld is basically a mirror image of the terrestrial plane. It is also a perfect embodiment of the hermetic maxim "As above, so below." This concept is illustrated in the description of a spirit-journey to the nether realm made by the Hopi "Sun Chief" Don Talayesva during a serious illness at the Sherman School for Indians in Riverside, California. After a series of disturbing visions and bizarre encounters, he arrived at Grand Canyon.

> "Soon I came to a great canyon where my journey seemed to end; and I stood there on the rim wondering what to do. Peering deep into the canyon, I saw something shiny winding its way like a silver thread on the bottom; and I thought that it must be the Little Colorado River. On the walls across the canyon were the houses of our ancestors with smoke rising from the chimneys and people sitting out on the roofs."[20]

Not only is the Grand Canyon the ancestral Place of Emergence whence the Hopi as a people transitioned from the previous Third World (or Era) to the current Fourth World via the Sipàapuni located on the Little Colorado River, but the canyon is also the destination of individual spirits of those recently deceased. The previously mentioned *hikwsi*, the "life-breath," "breath-body," or shade travels the harrowing roads to the chthonic plane in order to exist in much the same way the body did while living on the surface of the earth, enjoying similar pursuits. Life and afterlife are not distinct states of being but rather two phases of the same continuum or recurrent cycle. The Hopi consider an individual's death not as a loss to the family or clan but merely as a change in status. It is as if the departed person were being initiated into a new order.

When one dies in the upper world, one is born in the lower world and begins existence there as a baby. However, this new stage eventually bestows certain responsibilities and supernatural powers. On a daily basis the spirit rises through the

Sipàapuni and looks east toward the three Hopi Mesas, mirroring the belt stars of Orion. The spirit then ascends to the heavens to become a cloud-kachina, bringing rainfall, fertility, and health to virtuous villages or individuals (One Hearts), whereas wicked Hopis or sorcerers (Two Hearts) receive only drought or windstorms. Thus the spirit continues to play an active role in the life of the village it once inhabited. Anthropologist Mischa Titiev sums up this overall schema.

"The notion that life and death are merely two stages in a continuous cycle of events has far-reaching consequences on the structure of Hopi society. For the individual it offers a kind of immortality that helps to soften the shock of death; for social units such as the clan it provides a sense of stability based on the feeling that death cannot lessen its total membership in the two worlds; and for the pueblo or tribe as a whole it serves as a guarantee of permanence. Thanks to the operation of such a set of beliefs, the Hopi regard their dead not as outsiders who are lost to the living community, but as powerful members of society, whose sphere of activity has been changed for a time from the upper realm to the lower."[21]

In addition, when one dies in the lower world, one is reborn in the upper world—thus completing the continuous cycle. However, the Hopi do not consider this as a personal or individual reincarnation but think of it in tribal or general terms as a conscious force returning to the terrestrial plane. "By the concept of *hikwsi* human beings are linked to the immanent force of the world. The human *hikwsi* is a 'portion' of the life-giving force that enfolds the entire world and invests all elements, manifesting in them differently. In the Hopi perception of things, even the sun, the moon, the wind, the stars, and the clouds, are alive and related."[22]

John D. Loftin, Professor of Religious Studies, adds to the discussion of the numinous *hikwsi*, which, as I mentioned in Chapter 2, is related to the Egyptian concept of *Hikê*.

"*Hikwsi* is thus the 'spark' of deity which each Hopi embodies and which returns to the sacred ('giver of the breath of life') after death. Breath, moisture, cloud, fog have all been referred to by the Hopi in describing the spiritual essence of the universe. Moisture, or rather a certain aspect of moisture, is perceived by the Hopi as the 'spiritual substance' of the cosmos and receives a name kept secret from the uninitiated. In fact, a primary purpose of the initiation of all Hopi youths into the Kachina cult is to inform them that the 'spiritual substance' is their origin, nature, and destiny. That the cosmos was created and is sustained by the 'spiritual substance' is common knowledge among adult Hopis, a position perhaps best revealed by their emergence mythology."[23]

The spirit's ability to modulate between the world below as a wraith and the world above as a cloud-kachina indicates what may be called a three-tiered, shamanistic cosmos found in many cultures around the globe. This cosmic structure consists of an underground spirit realm that usually involves water in the form of oceans or rivers and a celestial spirit world that involves perceptions of clouds or flight, with a mundane middle plane located between these two vertical polarities. Cognitive archaeologist and South African rock art specialist David Lewis-Williams sees this as a basic function of the human nervous system.

"Taken together the neurologically generated experiences of traveling underground and flying are, I argue, the origin of notions of a tiered cosmos. This is, I believe, the best explanation for so universally held beliefs that have no relation to the material experience of daily life. Such beliefs were not inferred from observations of the natural environment. Nor did they easily and swiftly diffuse from a single geographically located origin because they made excellent sense of the world in which people lived. Rather, they are part of the in-built experiences of the full spectrum of human consciousness."[24]

Returning to Hopi cosmology, we see not only a duality between the houses of the living (i.e. the Hopi Mesas) and the houses of the dead (i.e. the *Maski* in Grand Canyon) but also a temporal duality. Specifically, when it is day in the upper world, it is night in the lower world; when is is summer in the upper world, it is winter in the lower world. During the time that the winter solstice ceremony is being held on the earthly plane, the spirits on the subterranean plane are making *pahos*, or prayer feathers during their summer solstice. (See diagram on p. 104.) Again, Titiev explains the synergistic dichotomy:

"By far the most profound effect of the duality concept is exerted on the structure of the ritual calendar. This is due to the fact that life in the other world is supposed to reflect life on earth so exactly that corresponding cere- monies are performed simultaneously (with the seasons reversed in the two spheres....) Thus we find that the con- cept of the year's duality is another feature which under- lies the entire structure of Hopi ceremonialism. On the one hand, it throws into sharp relief the reversal of con- ditions between the living and the dead, but on the other hand, it emphasizes the bonds between them and pro- vides a basis for synchronous, co-operative activities between the inhabitants of the two realms."[25]

In addition, the Hopi cosmos includes two solar houses—one in the southeast and one in the northwest. Also conceptualized as kivas, these two resting points on the horizon are owned by the primal deity named Hur'ingwùuti, or Hard Objects Woman. She is associated with solid things of the earth, such as shells, corral, turquoise, beads, silver, copper, and sometimes the moon and stars. The two kivas, which are both located in oceans (presum- ably the Atlantic and Pacific), correspond respectively to the win- ter solstice sunrise and the summer solstice sunset. The sun god Taawa, who is the Creator and father of humankind, rises from the eastern kiva and puts on first a gray fox skin (dawn) and then a yellow fox skin (morning), which are both hanging on the ladder. He travels over the earth and at dusk descends the ladder of the northwestern kiva, shaking the turtle shell rattle also hanging on the ladder as he enters to the kiva to sleep with Hur'ingwùuti. She is a crone during the day and is transformed into a beautiful young woman when the sun arrives in the evening.[26]

The Cosmic Turtle and the Dual Lion-Gates

In *The Kivas of Heaven*, I demonstrated that in many cultures the turtle is associated with Orion's belt. For instance, a sand mosaic from Acoma Pueblo in New Mexico shows three dots on the shell, with the one on the right slightly higher like the star Mintaka. The native name for this pueblo is *Ako*, and the Hopi call it *Aakookavi*. This latter term is a cognate of the Hopi word *aaku*, or "ladle, spoon," which, like the turtle's carapace, has a concave/convex shape. The Hopi also wear turtle shell rattles on their right calves during kachina dances. Furthermore, at New Mexico's San Juan Pueblo the Turtle Dance is performed during the winter solstice, whose ceremony is synchornized by the appearance of Orion in the overhead hatchway of the kiva. The Tewa word *'Oku* means "turtle" but it also means "hill." The native name for the San Juan Pueblo is *O'ke*.

Incidentally, the Maya associate the turtle with Orion's belt, as exemplified in an 8th century AD mural at Bonampak in Chiapas, Mexico. The Cosmic Turtle of the Maya was cracked by the Maize God named One Hunahpu at the end of the previous Mayan age or cycle. (This is analogous to the dislodging of the Cosmic Mill, discussed in Chapter 2.) The Mayan word for "turtle" is *ak*, and their word for "star" is *ek*. In addition, Mayan glyphs carved in 669 AD on the stele of Monument 6, which was found in the town of Tortuguero in southern Tabasco, Mexico, contain the only December 21st, 2012 date known to exist in all of Mesoamerica. The stele was sculpted to commemorate the construction in 510 AD of a kiva-like sweat bath called a *pibnaah*.

The name *Tortuguero* means "turtle" or "land of the turtles." The divine ruler of this place was named Ahku'ul K'uk', or "Turtle-Quetzal" —a reptilian-avian hybrid.[27]

Given Orion's multicultural association with the turtle, it is significant that the Hopi solar deity Taawa shakes a turtle shell rattle to announce his crepuscular presence at the northwestern kiva of Hur'ingwùuti, as mentioned in the preceding section.

I have written elsewhere[28] that Orion disappears from the heavens in late April and is not seen seen again until mid-July when it rises in the east before dawn, the latter technically known as its heliacal rising. The setting sun of late spring eventually blots out the constellation's presence in the western sky, so the last time it can be seen is called its heliacal setting. During this time the Hopi plant sweet corn called *tawaktsi*, which fully ripens by July and is distributed for the final kachina dance of the season called *Niman*. This type of corn is associated with the nadir, or underworld to which Orion seems to be departing.[29] The rest of the corn, which is planted after the constellation has gone below, is harvested in the fall. Thus, the constellation descends to his subterranean house and remains there for the duration of the sowing period in an apparent attempt to stimulate germination and growth during the agricultural season.

The upper diagram on the facing page shows terrestrial Orion in relationship to Grand Canyon. 270° azimuth is where the sun (Taawa) sets on the vernal (and autumnal) equinoxes, while 240° is where it sets on the winter solstice—the latter directly in line with both the ruins at Wupatki (terrestrial Bellatrix) and Humphreys Peak. The sun sets on summer solstice over Tatahatso Point, a prominent overlook above Marble Canyon.

The lower diagram shows Orion's left arm pointed downward into Grand Canyon, possibly directing his energy at Osiris Temple. (See Chapter 1.) The setting constellation slides northwest and appears to enter into that great nether realm. In 1100 AD (approximate time that the first pueblos were being constructed on the Hopi Mesas), Orion was last seen on April 18th, shortly after eight o'clock in the evening. While these stars are hidden in the Maski during the lengthening spring days, the sun sets over the Sipàapuni at 290° azimuth on April 26th. Taawa reached his summer house in the northwest (300° azimuth) on June 21st, and lingered there for a few days. (Solstice literally means "sun stands still.")

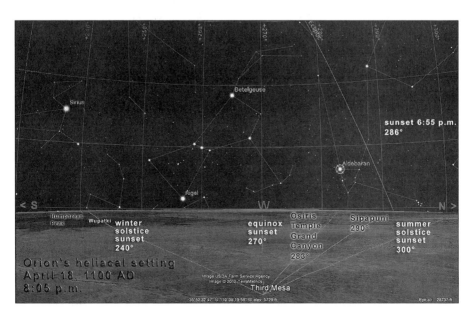

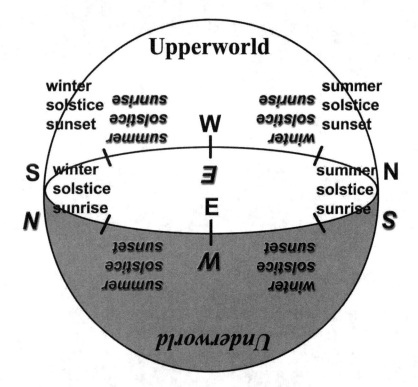

Hopi Cosmology

Imagine you are facing west....

Upperworld directions in regular font.

Turn the book upside down:
Underworld directions in italics.

The horizontal plane of the earth's surface bisects the sphere. The underworld is a mirror image of the upperworld. North and south in the two hemispheres are opposite of each other. The summer solstice sunset in the upper world becomes the winter solstice sunrise in the lower world, etc.

Orion ascends from the underworld after an absence of about 2½ months to arrive during the start of the monsoon season. This is approximately the same period as the Egyptian mummification process.

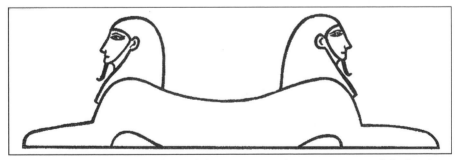

Aker is the Egyptian guardian of the eastern and western gates of the horizon through which the sun ascends and descends on its daily journey. Instead of sphinxes, the pair is sometimes represented with lion heads and the sun resting on its back.

The structure of the Hopi calender also seems to reflect Orion's annual sojourn in the underworld. Oddly enough, the Hopi pair certain months at different times of the year by giving them the same names. For instance, the following months have identical names: December and July (that is, the beginning and end of the kachina season), January and August, February and September, March and October, June and November. The remaining two months, April and May, have different names. No major ceremonies may be held during that time, although kachina dances are performed in the plazas.[30] Of course, April and May are the primary sowing months when Orion in the underworld assists the sprouting corn plants with his grounded celestial energy, urging them upward to the sunlight.

According to the Hopi cosmological system, when the sun sets in the west, it is thought to travel eastward through the underworld in order to arrive at its sunrise point. Martin Gashweseoma, Hopi Fire Clan elder from the village of Hotevilla, recently stated that the Creator lives under ground.[31] The Creator is conceptualized as either Taawa or Masau'u. (I have previously contended that the Hopi equate the latter with Orion.) The sun's subterranean journey produces daytime in the lower world, while it is nighttime in the upper world. This is precisely the case in Egyptian cosmology. In fact, the two respective nether realms are quite similar, each additionally incorporating judgement, purgatory, or punishment.

In my series of books about Hopi star knowledge and legends, I have provided substantial evidence linking the two cultures that are separated by both space and time. Loftin also emphasizes that commonality: "The Hopi are viewed by and large—and not without cause—as a very conservative, slow-to-change people who have clung tenaciously to their law, their way of life, their land, and their religion for centuries, demonstrating at times an almost incredible degree of stability, comparable perhaps to the Old Kingdom in Egypt."[32]

To continue with a previous theme, the Hopi Turtle Kachina (*Káhayla*) is also known as the Hunter Kachina (*Maak*), considered a guardian or warrior figure—all attributes of the archetypal Orion.[33]

We have found a number of words that sound alike and that also connote turtle, turtle-shape, or star: *Ako, aaku,'Oku, O'ke, ak, ek, Maak,* etc. We should not be surprised, then, that another word for the Egyptian *Duat* (or *Tuat*, discussed in Chapter 1) is *Akert.*[34] In this context it is interesting to note that the Hopi word *atkya(q)* means "down, down there, down below" and refers to the underworld. An alternate denotation is "area to the southwest of the Hopi villages," which contain ruins such as Wupatki.[35]

The lion god Aker was guardian of the chthonic portals. "There are two gates to the Underworld, in the east and the west, each guarded by the foreparts and head of a monstrous sphinx known as Aker."[36] The name literally means "one who curves," i.e. the horizon.

Author Murry Hope draws the distinction between the Old Kingdom's conception of the deity and the later version.

"The oldest known lion god was Aker, who was seen as guarding the gate of the dawn through which the sun-god passed each morning. From the Pyramid Texts it is clear that this deity's role and attributes were clearly defined in the Early Empire. In later dynasties it was believed that during the night the sun passed through a kind of tunnel (wormhole?) which existed in some nether region, each end of which was guarded by a lion-god, the two deities being called Akeru (or Akerui)."[37]

Hence, we see the later leonine god with a head at each end of the body, signifying the sunrise and sunset domains. (See drawing on p. 105.) The Hopi cultural hero named Tiyo once journeyed to the kiva of Hur'ingwùuti ensconced on an island in the western ocean. Before descending the ladder, he was confronted by two pumas (mountains lions), which he subdued by blowing on them a medicine called *nahu* (literally, "plateau whip-tail lizard") that he had obtained from Kòokyangwso'wùuti, Old Spider Woman.[38] Located on a plateau about 10 miles from the Bandelier National Monument in New Mexico is a pair of life-size, sculpted stone mountain lions surrounded by a circle of upright, huge stone slabs.

Re-enforcing the *ak* phoneme in connection with the turtle, the Egyptian word *paqit* means "tortoise or turtle shell," and one turtle god is named *Qeq-ha*.[39] We are reminded of the celestial carvings on the ceiling of the tomb of Senemut, chief architect of the 18th Dynasty pharaoh Hatshepsut (circa 1500 BC). The inscriptions include Orion/Osiris, Sirius/Isis, Saturn/Horus, Mars/Set (all on barges), Geb/earth in the form of a goose, Aries, the Pleiades, and a pair of turtles—the latter perhaps representing the rising and setting of Orion.

The name of the Akeru, lion-guardians of the dual portals to the underworld, are possibly related to the Hopi word *koro*, which is a cave or small cavity in a cliff wall. This may tantalizingly lead us to the nether realm, as we shall see in the next chapter.[40]

Stone Lions Shrine, near Frijoles Canyon, New Mexico. This highly eroded, sculpted pair of crouching pumas within a tufa limestone circle about 30 ft. in diameter was obviously a site of great ceremonial significance for the Ancestral Puebloans. Charles F. Lummis called it "a strange aboriginal Stonehenge."[41] Several miles to the south is a second pair of effigy stone lions. Photo courtesy of Alexey Sergeev, 2008.

Chapter 5
Grand Canyon Cave Enigma

Kinkaid's Cave (What and When)

Perhaps no other Grand Canyon story evokes more mystery than that of Kinkaid's Cave. I probably get asked more questions about this topic than any other regarding the Southwest. Either history or hoax—it has been the focus of sustained controversy. The bare bones (no pun intended) of the scenario are as follows.

On April 5, 1909 the *Arizona Gazette,* Phoenix's main evening newspaper that later merged with the current *Arizona Republic,* ran a front-page article of about 2,200 words in length, which, if true, completely demolishes the isolationist archaeological paradigm that dominated the 20th century. ("Isolationism" posits that the ancestors of all Native Americans crossed the Bering Straits tens of thousands years ago and migrated southward down an ice-free corridor to populate both North and South America. The opposing theory, called "cultural diffusionism," sees pre-Columbian mariners arriving on both coasts from different geographical and cultural regions around the world to settle the continent. Most academic archaeologists, of course, have tried to discredit the latter theory.)

The headline of the article reads "EXPLORATIONS IN GRAND CANYON." The sub-headlines were: "Mysteries of Immense High Cavern Being Brought to Light," "JORDAN IS ENTHUSED," and "Remarkable Finds Indicate Ancient People Migrated From Orient."[1] I will discuss Professor S. A. Jordan below.

The main character of this story is one G. E. Kinkaid, "...the explorer who found the great underground citadel of the Grand

Canyon during a trip from Green River, Wyoming, down the Colorado, in a wooden boat, to Yuma, several months ago." In fact, the *Gazette* published a short article on March 12th of the same year, which describes "Kincaid" (his name spelled differently in the earlier piece) traveling in October, 1908 down the Colorado River and arriving in Yuma in the spring. He carried a "fine camera" with which he took over 700 photographs, now apparently all lost or deliberately hidden. The last sentence of the earlier article is inexplicably understated but reveals Kinkaid's plans for a second expedition. "Some interesting archaeological discoveries were unearthed and altogether the trip was of such interest that he will repeat it next winter in the company of friends."

The cavern was located down a sheer cliff 1,486 feet from the rim of the canyon. On its eastern wall Kinkaid noticed "...stains in the sedimentary formation about 2,000 feet above the river bed." The mouth of the cave was, he said, "...nearly inaccessible... but I finally reached it with great difficulty." (Is this yet another understatement?) At the entrance were steps thirty yards long carved into solid rock, which led down to the former level of the river. (He must have assumed that the level of the Colorado River was much higher during the time the cavern was inhabited.) As quoted on p. 88, Major Powell also noticed carved stone steps in the vicinity of native ruins.

The main passageway was hewn and chiseled into the rock at right angles, "...straight as could be laid out by an engineer." It was 12 feet wide at the opening and led horizontally into the side of the cliff for hundreds of feet. At about 57 feet, two side-passages branched off to the right and left. Located off of these smaller passageways were a number rooms with oval-shaped doors and round ventilation shafts in the walls, which were about three-and-a-half feet thick. These rooms varied in size from those of "...ordinary living rooms of today..." to spaces "...30 by 40 feet square." Tunneling past the two perpendicular passages, the main passageway eventually led to a "...mammoth chamber from which radiates scores of passageways, like spokes of a wheel."

The article estimates that the complex contained a total of "Several hundred rooms..." that could easily hold 50,000 people, although this may be a journalistic exaggeration. However, one room, thought to be the main dining hall because it contained cooking utensils, measured about 40 by 700 feet. Other structures included round granaries "...such as are found in the oriental temples." They were made of what looked like "...a very hard cement" and contained various types of seeds. In addition, there was a "...very large storehouse..." 12 feet high and accessible only from its roof. This room had two copper hooks extending from the edge at the top, which may have supported a ladder. Two side passageways respectively measured 854 feet and 634 feet long.

The article speculates that the front of the complex may have served as "...warriors' barracks," while the subterranean interior portion is perhaps where "...far into the under-world will be found the main communal dwellings of the families."

The article states that the cavern is perfectly ventilated, with a steady draft of air blowing through it, indicating another outlet somewhere on the surface. More on this shortly.

The relics Kinkaid discovered are what we now call OOParts ("out-of-place artifacts"). These included artistically crafted vases, urns, copper and gold cups as well as copper weapons "...sharp-edged and hard as steel." The article also lists various copper tools, a gray metal resembling platinum, as well as slag, matte, and charcoal, indicating the smelting of ores. He also found glazed and enameled pottery, water vessels, stone tablets inscribed with some sort of hieroglyphics, and "cats eyes" scattered on the floor, each yellow stone "...engraved with the head of the Malay [Malaysian] type." He stated that the initial purpose of his journey was simply "looking for mineral," probably gold or silver, so these finds must have, to use contemporary patois, blown him away.

Other artifacts were even more unusual. For instance, the article identifies one as "The Shrine":

"Over a hundred feet from the entrance is the cross-hall, several hundred feet long, in which are found the idol, or image, of the people's god, sitting cross-legged, with a lotus flower or lily in each hand. The cast of the face is oriental, and the carving shows a skillful hand, and the entire is remarkably well preserved, as is everything in this cavern. The idol almost resembles Buddha, though the scientists are not certain as to what religious worship it represents. Taking into consideration everything found thus far, it is possible that this worship most resembles the ancient people of Tibet. Surrounding this idol are smaller images, some very beautiful in form—others crooked-necked and distorted shapes, symbolical, probably, of good and evil. There are two large cactus [sic] with protruding arms, one on each side of the dais on which the god squats. All this is carved out of hard rock resembling marble."

Although the statue is described as Buddha-like, sitting in a yogic lotus posture, "oriental" in the early 20th century sometimes referred to Egypt. Author Frank Joseph comments: "Although it suggested a Buddha figure to them, their description of the artwork seems more reminiscent of the Nile Valley deity Bes. Portrayed in Egyptian temple-art as an asiatic dwarf similarly holding a lotus in each hand, Bes was the divine patron of war, appropriately enough, given the weapons found in profusion at the Colorado River site."[2]

Perhaps the most intriguing discovery occurred in an area the article calls "The Crypt." The walls of this chamber, one of the largest rooms in the complex, slanted back at an angle of approximately 35°. Lying supine on shelves hewn into these rock walls were a number of adult male mummies covered with bark-fabric and clay. The bodies were arranged, one per shelf, in tiers going up to the ceiling. Urns, cups, and broken swords had been placed next to the bodies. The article states that the artifacts on the lower levels seemed cruder than the ones above, the latter indicating a "higher stage of civilization." Kinkaid mentioned that he place one of these mummies upright and photographed it, lit by his flashlight.

In one unventilated part of the cavern, Kinkaid noticed a "...deadly, snaky smell..." which, he says, may have actually been "...deadly gas or chemicals used by the ancients." He continues in this vein: "The whole underground installation gives one of shaky nerves the creeps. The gloom is like a weight on one's shoulders, and our flashlights and candles only make the darkness blacker. Imagination can revel in conjectures and ungodly daydreams back through the ages that have elapsed till the mind reels dizzily in space." Whew! The morbid sentiment evoked in this bit of prose certainly does resonate with feelings about Masau'u, the Hopi death god, and his lugubrious "house," which is located in Grand Canyon.

My publisher David Childress has written that this cave was possibly a necropolis comparable to the rock tombs in the Valley of the Kings in Egypt, where, of course, numerous mummies have also been found.[3] My friend Jack Andrews, who has studied this story for over 30 years and is perhaps the world authority on the subject of Kinkaid's Cave, has given the complex the appellation of "Lost City of the Dead in the Grand Canyon." I strongly urge readers who are interested in further details of the story to consult his meticulously documented, thoroughly researched website. His book and video on the subject are forthcoming.[4]

The article speculates that the installation "... was of oriental origin, possibly from Egypt, tracing back to Ramses." Then it comments on the archaeologists of the Smithsonian, which was apparently funding the expeditions (plural). "If their theories are borne out by the translation of the tablets engraved with hieroglyphics, the mystery of the prehistoric peoples of North America, their ancient arts, who they were and whence they came, will be solved. Egypt and the Nile, and Arizona and the Colorado will be linked by a historical chain running back to ages which staggers the wildest fancy of the fictionalist."

The newspaper also reinforced some of its readers' racist views. "One theory is that the present Indian tribes found in Arizona are descendants of serfs or slaves of the people which inhabited the cave. Undoubtedly a good many thousands of years before the Christian era, a people lived here which reached a high stage of civilization." So here we find a high culture, originating during the time of the Gizamids (as some have called them) or at least during the period of the New Kingdom, constructing very far from home a massive installation in what is possibly one of the Seven Natural Wonders of the World.

However, the article, as originally published, contains a few contradictions. (Some printed and Internet versions have minor deletions and variations. I am using the one Jack Andrews copied from microfilm at the Phoenix Public Library.) In regard to the "hieroglyphics," one sentence reads: "These writings resemble those on the rocks about this valley." Deleted altogether in some versions, this statement refers to the native petroglyphs found in the area surrounding Phoenix, not to ancient Egyptian ideograms.

Also, some republications of the article contain this sentence: "Similar hieroglyphs have been found in southern Arizona." The authentic version instead contains the following: "Similar hieroglyphics have been found in the peninsula of Yucatan, but these are not the same as those found in the Orient. Some believe these cave dwellers built the old canals in the Salt River Valley." The first sentence refers to Mayan glyphs and the second to the Hohokam. The latter people constructed major agricultural canals built between the 7th and 14th centuries AD where the Phoenix metropolis now sits. (See Chapter 6.) The anonymous newspaper writer or writers seem/s to be implying that the glyphs found in the caves were more like those of the Maya than those of the ancient Egyptians. In addition, he or they wanted to include the theory that the cave may have been constructed by ancient Arizonans, not ancient Egyptians. Were they just trying to cover all the bases? This story has as many twists and turns as the passageways in the cave itself.

Dramatis Personae (Who)

Who are the characters that are either directly or indirectly involved in this scenario, and did they ever really exist? Two names mentioned briefly at the end of the article were indeed real persons. W. E. (Warren Eliphalet) Rollins (1861 – 1962) was a Taos, New Mexico visual artist, and Arnold Hermann Ludwig Heeren (1760 – 1842) was an early Egyptologist who believed that that culture was initially influenced by the Indus River Valley region. The other people who play a part in this story are not so easy to identify.

In regards to the previously mentioned Professor S. A. Jordan, for instance, we draw a blank. The article states that the Smithsonian Institution was then conducting an investigation of the cavern system, which was supervised by Jordan. "Under the direction of Prof. S. A. Jordan, the Smithsonian Institute [sic] is now prosecuting the most thorough explorations, which will be continued until the last link in the chain is forged." However, inquiries to the Smithsonian, including a telephone call by David Childress prior to 1992 and a 1999 letter from Jack Andrews, elicited merely curt responses that sum up the article as basically a "myth."[5] But as Andrews points out, the story never explicitly states that Jordan was an employee of the institution; he may have merely been free-lancing, and thus not technically on employee records.

Newspapers in the early 20th century were not as assiduously proof-read like they are today, and of course there were no clever devices such as spell-check. A discrepancy exists, for example, between the "Kincaid" spelling in the initial brief article in March and the "Kinkaid" spelling of the April news article. In regard to the spelling of S. A. Jordan's name, if we move on the keyboard one key to the right, we have D. S. Jordan—and a door is thrown wide open.

David Starr Jordan, M.S., M.D., Ph.D., LL.D. (1851 – 1931) was a major scientific figure of his day, as well as an educator and a philosopher. After graduating from Cornell in 1872, he was a Professor of Biology at Butler University in Indiana. He also served as both the nation's youngest university president at Indiana University and the first president of Stanford University. His manuel on ichthyology was the standard text for a half century, and he had an interest in zoology and botany as well. Furthermore, he was the director of the Sierra Club from 1892 to 1903.[6]

In 1902 he published a book titled *The Blood of the Nation: A Study in the Decay of Races by the Survival of the Unfit*, which promoted a radical theory of eugenics. (The title was later changed to *The Human Harvest*.) He believed that wars essentially eliminated the most fit, allowing the genes of the unfit to be passed on to future generations. Thus, he became heavily involved in peace activism, serving as the chief director of the World Peace Foundation from 1910 until 1914. He also was a member of the board of trustees of the Human Betterment Foundation, which promoted the compulsory sterilization of "insane and feeble-minded patients." This organization was thought to have proved to the later Nazi regime the feasibility of large-scale sterilization programs.[7] This tall, broad-shouldered intellectual was a walking contradiction. "An apostle of Puritanism and of Nordic superiority, he was also an ardent defender of freedom and a champion of progressive reforms."[8]

Jordan was also listed on the 1925 membership rolls of the Bohemian Club based in San Francisco.[9] Founded in 1872 as a private gentlemen's social club for literati and artists, it gradually devolved into a haven for successful businessmen, wealthy entrepreneurs, CEOs, defense contractors, and power brokers.

To this day in the redwood forests of Sonoma County an annual summer retreat called Bohemian Grove hosts numerous elites from the world of politics, Fortune-500 corporations, the banking industry, and the military. Sequestered from public view, they perform dramatic skits and pseudo-pagan rituals, complete with musical productions, pyrotechnics, and a 40-foot-tall owl statue made of concrete. Members engage in collective catharsis, smoking cigars (or perhaps something more potent), binge-drinking and peeing in the woods like college fraternity boys. Rumors abound of libertine behavior or even homosexual acts. Bohemian Grove has basically become a playground for the rich and renowned: executives, legislators, judges, attorneys, dignitaries, diplomats, and high muckety-mucks of sundry stripes. Presidents in attendance have included Eisenhower, Nixon, Reagan, and the Bushes. Most recently it is even thought by some to be a bastion of the New World Order and the global cabal.[10]

Already one of the country's foremost ichthyologists, Jordan was appointed president of Stanford University in 1891. In 1906 he was offered but declined the post of Secretary of the Smithsonian, due to the San Francisco earthquake.[11] The main question is: Did he put off his duties at Stanford University long enough to visit Grand Canyon? Indeed he did.

Left: David Starr Jordan, 1909,
The Popular Science Monthly.

Below: Charles D. Walcott,
1908.

On Grand View Point.   Copyright, 1899, by H. G. Peabody.

Left:
Grand View Point,
1899, the area from
which D. S. Jordan,
C. F. Lummis,
and others made
their descent into
Grand Canyon
the year before.

Below:
from *Titan of Chasms,
the Grand Canyon of
Arizona,* travel essays
published by
the Santa Fe Railway
Company.

In the summer of 1898, Jordan and his wife traveled to Grand Canyon with one of his closest friends, explorer and author Charles F. Lummis, whom he describes as follows: "He is a journalist by profession, a human geyser of the first water, bubbling with enthusiasm."[12] Lummis even named his son Jordan to show their friendship. For many years Lummis (who was also a personal friend of Teddy Roosevelt) edited a magazine named *Out West*, which lists Jordan on the staff, as well as author Mary Austin (*The Land of Little Rain*, 1903) and Sharlot M. Hall, who was appointed as official historian for Arizona in 1909. Lummis sums up this "Wonderland": "I have spoken of the Grand Cañon of the Colorado as the gorge in which all *famous* gorges could be lost."[13]

The party descended to the river down Grandview Trail. "The remarkable old winding trail down which we made our way to the turbulent river (a stiff trip, especially on the return) was the work of the noted guide, John Hance, a native of east Tennessee." They also made side trips to Walnut Canyon, Sunset Crater, and Acoma Pueblo in New Mexico.[14] Grand Canyon apparently made the deepest impression (no pun intended) on Jordan.

But did it affect him enough so that he returned to Grand Canyon in 1908 – 1909? His autobiography states that in June 1908 he was called by the federal government to investigate the protection of fisheries along the U.S.-Canada border for the Joint International Fisheries Commission. His research would have entailed an extensive area from Passamaquoddy Bay west through the Great Lakes all the way to Puget Sound. At that time he was recovering from a "...very trying episode..." that had occurred the previous academic season, which involved his strong opposition to a recalcitrant bout of student "...beery conviviality." He probably just longed to get out of Dodge and escape the inebriated college kids.

In the summer of 1908, he traveled to Eastport, Maine, in order to begin working his way toward the Pacific along the boundary of the two countries. However, a setback occurred "...toward the very end of the year [1908]..." when a key Canadian figure suddenly resigned, leaving the survey unfinished until a more complete survey could be started again in the summer of 1909.[15]

Upon hearing the news of the survey's unexpected suspension, he probably began to return to Palo Alto some time in late fall, although his autobiography is vague (perhaps intentionally so) on this point. From his writing it is impossible to tell how much progress he had made along the border when he was told to call off the fisheries study until the following year. Perhaps he was still traveling westward during the time when Kinkaid was starting down the Colorado River from Green River, Wyoming. If he happened to meet up with Kinkaid, he might have been persuaded to join the expedition purely in the interest of his primary field, ichthyology. The fortuitous opportunity to increase his scientific knowledge and engage in a great adventure to boot might have been too hard to pass up. After all, he had already experienced the magical lure of Grand Canyon a decade before, and the trip from Yuma back home would have been, as they say, a piece of cake.

The archaeological discoveries described in the *Arizona Gazette* article would, of course, have precluded any disclosure to the world at large of their cultural diffusionist nature. According to the isolationist theories that began to dominate academia at the turn of the century, it is simply impossible for ancient Egyptian or Asian relics to be found anywhere in the New World. In addition, with the Smithsonian involved at the highest level, a few greedy and/or shady collectors of rare or exotic artifacts possibly got wind of the find, used their great wealth to covet the even greater treasures that were shipped back east, and then covered up the whole story. Except for that pesky newspaper in Phoenix!

We have evidence that D. S. Jordan corresponded with another character in our story—the person who would have received the artifacts from Arizona, one Charles D. Walcott.[16] In the article Kinkaid states: "I gathered a number of relics, which I carried down the Colorado to Yuma, from whence I shipped them to Washington with details of the discovery." Presumably he sent them to the Smithsonian, because, as the article also says, Kinkaid "...has been an explorer and hunter all his life, thirty years having been in the service of the Smithsonian Institute [sic]."

Charles Doolittle Walcott (1850 – 1927) served as the fourth Secretary of the Smithsonian Institution from 1907 until his death. (See his photo on the bottom of p. 117.) During his time in

Washington he became a very adept administrator, making many influential connections. Stephen Jay Gould, paleontologist and historian of science, writes that Walcott was one of the Smithsonian's finest secretaries.

> "...he also had his finger—or rather his fist—in every important scientific pot in Washington. He knew every president from Theodore Roosevelt to Calvin Coolidge, some intimately. He played a key role in persuading Andrew Carnegie to found the Carnegie Institution in Washington, and worked with Woodrow Wilson to establish the National Research Council. He served as president for the National Academy of Sciences and the American Association for the Advancement of Science."[17]

Although he was an autodidact with little formal higher education, Walcott made major contributions to the field of paleontology. His discovery of the diversity of Cambrian fossils in the Burgess Shale of British Columbia was probably his greatest achievement. In fact, it was during years 1908–1909, the period of the Kinkaid expedition, that his first work in this area was made. Despite his summer research and field work, he still managed to to keep a busy schedule as secretary of the Smithsonian, overseeing the institution with a hands-on approach.[18]

One story about his tenure at the Smithsonian hints at his early connection to Grand Canyon. "After Walcott became secretary of the Smithsonian Institution, he read all the manuscripts prepared by staff members, including a report by a young anthropologist working for the Bureau of American Ethnology. Evidence of a hitherto unknown tribe of Indians had been found in Grand Canyon; the evidence consisted of stone fireplace rings. Walcott commented that these were from his campsites and the manuscript disappeared."[19]

As a 29-year-old, athletically built assistant for the newly formed United States Geological Survey, Walcott had indeed camped in Grand Canyon, earning $50 per month for his work. Under Captain Clarence E. Dutton, he had studied the geological formations along Kanab Creek, which starts in southern Utah and flows south into Grand Canyon. In early fall of 1879, he reached the mouth of Kanab Creek, a few miles upstream from Havasu Canyon, where he gathered trilobites and other fossils.

J. W. Powell, the great-granddaddy of Grand Canyon exploration, remarks on Walcott's continued work.

"In 1882 Mr. C. D. Walcott, as my assistant in the United States Geological Survey, went with me into the depths of the Grand Canyon. We descended from the summit of the Kaibab Plateau on the north by a trail which we built down a side canyon in a direction toward the mouth of the Little Colorado River. The descent was made in the fall, and a small party of men was left with Mr. Walcott in this region of stupendous depths to make a study of the geology of an important region of labyrinthian gorges. Here, with his party, he was shut up for the winter, for it was known when we left him that snows on the summit of the plateau would prevent his return to the upper region before the sun should melt them the next spring. Mr. Walcott is now the Director of the United States Geological Survey."[20]

Walcott spent the entire winter of 1882-3 studying in detail the geology and paleontology of the eastern part of Grand Canyon. His maps specifically show Nankoweap Valley, Kwagunt Valley, Chuar Valley, and Unkar Valley. As we have seen in the previous chapter, the latter site was the location of large Anasazi pueblos. Walcott was, of course, also interested in archaeology, and he was even president of the Washington Branch of the Archaeological Institute of American from 1915 – 1917.

That winter Walcott was more solitary than Thoreau had ever been. Walcott's biographer Leon L. Yochelson writes about this brief period of his life isolated at the bottom of Grand Canyon: "His assistant was unable to endure the depression caused by living in these depths and finally left him, so that for a while Walcott conducted many lonely climbs in an exceedingly dangerous region."[21]

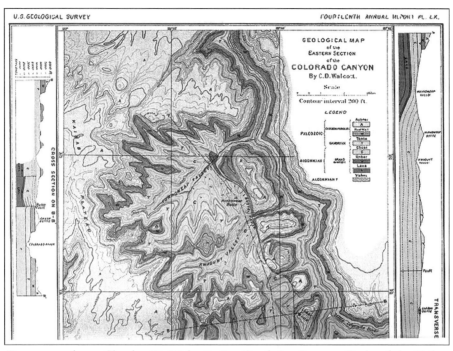

Topo map from Charles D. Walcott, *Pre-Cambrian Igneous Rocks of the Unkar Terrane, Grand Canyon of the Colorado, Arizona*, USGS survey report, 1895. At lower-right is Little Colorado River. To the northwest are Kwagunt Creek and Nunkoweap (now usually spelled Nankoweap) Creek.

Left: Walcott at Grand Canyon, 1915. Photo courtesy of Smithsonian Archives. Midway between Shiva Temple and Hopi Point is Walcott Butte, named by G. Wharton James.

123

During that period spent studying geological strata and fossils, Walcott might have accidentally stumbled across Kinkaid's cave. He may have even climbed up, entered it, and actually discovered the artifacts—deciding ultimately to remain reticent because of the firestorm it would undoubtedly have caused. Or he might have merely glimpsed a rectangular opening high on the the cliff wall and made a mental note of this oddity. Either way, the anomalous experience would have gnawed at him for over a quarter century until he had the opportunity to commission a clandestine expedition the year after he was appointed Smithsonian secretary.

On the other hand, he might have been stunned by the unexpected arrival of a few out-of-place relics and the report of an ancient subterranean citadel lost in the very labyrinth of canyons he long ago had wandered though. Another possibility could have involved his colleague and Stanford University president David Starr Jordan, who probably would have written to him about the incredible nature of the complex that he and Kinkaid had found on their trip down the Colorado River. (Letters that rock the scientific boat are easily disposed of, however.) Speculations like this are endless and will go on as long as the cave's location remains an enigma.

The main character of our story, G. E. Kinkaid, is perhaps the one most shrouded in mystery. The first article states that he hailed from Lewiston, Idaho, and the second says that "Mr. Kinkaid was the first white child born in Idaho..." The first white child born in what later became the State of Idaho was Eliza Spalding at Lapwai in 1837. But if the article's references not the State but Idaho Territory, signed into law by President Lincoln in March of 1863, then Kinkaid would have to have been very young to put in 30 years of service at the Smithsonian by 1909—specifically, about 16 years old. Perhap math was not the reporter's best subject in high school. (In that respect, he and I are alike.)

A few inconclusive genealogical clues about the Kinkaid (or Kincaid) clan in Idaho can be discussed. Records show an Alvis A. Kincaid in 1906 as vice-president and superintendent of the substantial Evergreen Mine (gold and copper) located eight miles from Grangeville, Idaho, which is near Lewiston. He was born in 1858, which makes the time-frame about right. However, his birthplace is listed as Kentucky. Alvis Kincaid had five brothers and sisters, including a G. D. Kincaid. Did he or one of his brothers possibly look for other minerals in Grand Canyon a few years after establishing the Idaho mine? "Mr. Kincaid has gone into mining to follow it the rest of his life and is putting that fund of wisdom, skill, and enterprise into it which has brought him success in other lines."[22]

Many in the Kinkaid/Kincaid clan moved to northern Idaho in the late 19th century, including George A. Kinkaid, born in Kansas in 1865. From a genealogical website, we find the following bit of information: "George was not listed in the household in Kansas in 1885. It is believed he had come to Idaho prior to this date. What brought him to Idaho?"[23] Good question. In addition, a Kinkaid Lake is located in the Idaho Panhandle.

I have one more scrap of information (again, courtesy of Jack Andrews) about Kincaid, before turning to Location-Location-Location! Diffusionist researcher Barry Fell in his book *Saga America* presents a photo of an alabaster egg with the engraved cartouche of the pharaoh Tutankhamen. It was found in Idaho around 1900 by the great-grandfather of Kathy Kincaid, who had its authenticity confirmed by Frank A. Norick, University of California curator.[24] This artifact may have been found not in Idaho but inside the cave complex in Arizona and carried back home to Idaho by Kincaid, where it still is in the possession of his great-granddaughter.

Coordinating the Coordinates (Where and How)

The second *Arizona Gazette* article has a very strong indication of where the cave might be located. However, Kinkaid in his own words strongly discourages any curious treasure-seekers from trying gain access to the installation. "It is located on government land and no visitor will be allowed there under penalty of trespass. The scientists wish to work unmolested, without fear of archaeological discoveries being disturbed by curio or relic hunters. A trip there would be fruitless, and the visitor would be sent on his way." In other words: Keep out!

Unlike today, quite a lot of mining activity occurred in Grand Canyon during the years around the turn of the century. Claims were staked in Nankoweap Canyon, for instance, whose eponymous trail had originally been used by Indians but further developed in 1882 by Powell and Walcott.[25] Robert Stanton, who conducted a railroad survey 1889 – 1890 along the Colorado River for a proposed rail line that thankfully never was built, is quoted as saying at that time: "In the Grand Canyon are some of the richest gold mines ever discovered, I noticed a good many prospectors on the trip, and while at Yuma, on my way here, I was told that three new mining towns have been started near the mouth of the Little Colorado River."[26]

John D. Lee, who was executed in 1877 for the massacre two decades before of 140 non-Mormon pioneers at Mountain Meadows, Utah, was rumored to have carried out sacks and sacks of silver and gold from a source somewhere in the canyon. The legend of his lost mine endures to this day. Characters like Seth B. Tanner (discussed at length in David Hatcher Childress' book *Lost Cities & Ancient Mysteries of the Southwest*), William Wallace Bass, and George McCormick all had mining operations in the "Little Colorado Mining District."[27]

Thus, Kinkaid was wise to issue his warning against trespassers. On the other hand, one wonders if it was merely part of a cover-up against illegal or unethical excavations of ancient Egyptian or Asian artifacts. Childress envisions the scenario of the artistic and cultural anomalies being stored (in other words, permanently concealed) in wooden crates inside some huge Smithsonian warehouse, like in the final scene of the movie *Raiders of the Lost Ark*. Apocryphal accounts also speculate that they were transported to San Diego and dumped from a ship into the Pacific. (Again, we wouldn't want to rock the boat!) Others believe that the cave might have been cleared out of all its precious relics soon after their discovery and distributed among wealthy collectors—then its entrance dynamited shut.

Kincaid was quite precise in describing the location of the cavern, which some cave-seekers have apparently chosen to ignore. (One account, for instance, places the cave inside Isis Temple.) Kinkaid writes: "Some forty-two miles up the river from the El Tovar Crystal canyon, I saw on the east wall, stains in the sedimentary formation about 2,000 feet above the river bed." Hence he provides both the approximate coordinates and the elevation above the the the river, as well as the type of rock strata in which he found the cave had been carved. El Tovar was the name of the hotel built by Fred Harvey at the northern terminus of the Santa Fe Railway line. It opened in 1905, and Grand Canyon was proclaimed a national monument three years later. The mouth of Crystal Creek is downstream and about eight miles northwest of the hotel, as the raven flies.

If we go upriver from the mouth of Crystal Creek 42 miles, we arrive at a spot just south of where Kwagunt Creek enters the Colorado from the southwest. Less than a half mile farther north is Kwagunt Rapids, designated as Mile 56 (measured from Lee's Ferry to the north). William H. Calvin remarks on the mammoth landscape of this area in a journal of his journey downstream on a raft : "The east Kaibab Monocline has pushed the North Rim up as high as 2,700 meters in places, while the South Rim is more like 2,100 meters high. If we look carefully back up Kwagunt Creek's canyon, we can see one of the highest points on the North Rim towering in the distance. It is more than a mile high from where we are, about the height of a 500-story building."[28] A little south of Mile 61 is the Confluence—the place where the Little Colorado River merges with the Colorado.

North of the Little Colorado and east of Marble Canyon is the broad expanse of Marble Plateau, also poetically marked Blue Moon Bench on some maps. (The canyon north of the riparian juncture is technically called Marble Canyon, although it is equally grand.) Located on the Navajo Reservation, this is a sparsely populated region of sagebrush, yucca, and galleta grass, with juniper dotting the occasional bluff. Dominating the western vista is the North Rim, but the lower South Rim sees most of the tourist action. Wind, sunlight, and solitude on this empty plain are your constant companions.

The rim of Marble Plateau above Kwagunt Rapids has an elevation of about 6,000 ft. and is composed of Conconino Sandstone. Kinkaid claimed that the cave is located 1,486 feet below the rim, at a level of 4,514 feet. It lies in a stratum called the Supai Group, which is a formation of sedimentary rocks consisting of red sandstone, siltstone, and shale laid down in the Pennsylvanian Period between 290 and 330 million years ago. The cavern system may even extend downward to the underlying Redwall Limestone formation (the "marble" of Marble Canyon). "The top of the Redwall Limestone is marked by karst erosion, typical of many limestone areas today, particularly those in warm, humid regions such as Kentucky and Puerto Rico. Sinks, caves, and underground channels were dissolved in the limestone, and deep ravines and stream valleys developed as caverns collapsed."[29] Karst topography is created when water erosion causes the dissolution of carbonate rocks, such as limestone or dolomite.

A blowhole system also exists in northern Arizona at a higher rock stratum called Kaibab limestone. A blowhole is an earthfissure that is connected by sinuous, subterranean passageways to other blowholes miles away. The air emitted depends on variations in atmospheric pressure. During summer months, cooler late-night air usually enters the earth when the air pressure above ground is higher than that below. This cool air, filled with soothing negative ions and nontoxic levels of radiation, is then expelled in the afternoon when reverse conditions prevail. The chilly breezes of nature's "air conditioner" sometimes blow out at over 30 miles per hour. The blowhole adjacent to the famous Wupatki ruin ball court must have been a blessing to the players.

A total of nine blowholes have been found in northern Arizona, although others may exist. Locations include: west of Wupatki, west of Sunset Crater, southwest of the San Francisco Peaks, near Meteor Crater, and near Sedona almost 50 miles away. The whole blowhole system contains contains a volume of over seven billion cubic feet.[30]

SECTION	FORMATION	THICKNESSS IN FEET	LITHOLOGIC CHARACTER
FEET 5000-	Kaibab limestone	300	Dense yellowish-gray to grayish-yellow dolomitc limestone containing much chert near top, and yellowish-gray to pale-orange calcareous sandstone
	Toroweap formation	280	Massive buff limestone between two red-bed sequences
4000-	Coconino sandstone	600	Very fine-grained to medium-grained crossbedded pale-orange to white sandstone
Spring 1	Hermit shale	270-320	Red sandy shale and fine-grained friable sandstone
Spring 3	Supai formation	950	Alternating light-brown sandstone and moderately red siltsone; near base alternating red shale and blue-gray crystalline limestone
3000-			
	Redwall limestone	500	Light-gray and grayish-blue crystalline limestone containing chert
2000- Spring 4	Muav limestone	415	Bluish-gray limestone and dolomite having a mottled appearance, and numerous thin beds of buff or greenish material
Spring 8	Bright Angel shale	0-325	Greenish micaceous, sandy shale containing beds of purplish-brown sandstone
	Tapeats sandstone	0-300	Brown slabby crossbedded sandstone
Spring 7	Unkar group		Conglomerate, limestone, shale, quartzite, and sandstone
1000- Spring 9	Vishnu schist		Gneiss and schist, intruded by siliceous and mafic rocks and pegmatitic dikes
0-			

Marble Canyon, looking upstream toward Kwagunt Rapids.

129

Fissures, or "earth cracks," that occur in the Kaibab limestone layer may have openings with smooth, vertical walls three to six feet wide and up to 100 feet long. Spelunkers have explored one fissure near Wupatki to a depth of 275 feet and another near Lomaki ruin (in Wupatki National Monument) to a depth of over 500 feet. These areas also show a small but measurable decrease in gravity. The length of the whole blowhole system is estimated to be about 700 miles![31]

The cavern system in and around Grand Canyon is certainly extensive.

> "In northern and central Arizona, the Kaibab Limestone (Lower Permian) and its equivalents are karstic. North of the Grand Canyon, subterranean openings are primarily widely spaced fissures up to 1,000 ft (300 m) long and 250 ft (75 m) or more deep. South of the Grand Canyon, the fissures are more closely spaced and a few shallow caves are present. East of Flagstaff, there is an area of open fissures. These fissures are over 300 ft (90 m) deep, up to 1,000 ft (300 m) long, and up to 3 ft (1 m) wide. They cut the Coconino Sandstone, as well as the Kaibab Limestone."[32]

The entire cavern system may indeed be the physical manifestation of the legendary Hopi underworld. It is even possible that the travertine Sipàapuni is connected to Kincaid's catacombs. This cave-complex could furthermore have been the very refuge that the Ant People offered the Hopi to survive two separate world-cataclysms.

Ant Antecedents

One of the most intriguing Hopi legends involves the Ant People, who were crucial to the survival of the Hopi people—not just once but twice. The First World was apparently destroyed by fire (possibly volcanism, asteroid strikes, solar coronal mass ejections, or earthquakes), and the Second World was destroyed by ice (Ice Age glaciers or a pole shift). During these two periods, the virtuous members of the Hopi tribe were guided by a certain cloud by day and a certain star by night that led them to the sky god Sotuknang, who in turn took them to the Ant People (*Anu Sinom*). As a sort of "chosen people," the Hopi were taken by them into subterranean caves and given refuge and sustenance. In this legend the ants are portrayed as generous and industrious, giving the Hopi food when supplies ran short and teaching them the merits of food storage.[33] In fact, the reason why the ants have such thin waists today is because they once deprived themselves of provisions in order to feed the Hopi. By chance, the constellation Orion also has a thin waist.

When Orion dominates winter skies, the ants are deep in their "kivas" (ant hills). Although this seems contradictory, the zenith and the nadir are actually one shamanic axis comprising the under-world. Two separate realms exist in the Hopi cosmology: the surface of the earth as the site of human activity and a combined sky/underground region as the home of the spirits, in particular the kachinas. Both the ant mound with its dark tunnels and the kiva with its *sipapu* (a hole in the floor symbolically linking it to the underworld) embody the nether plane. This paradoxically arches upward across the skies to serve as home to the star spirits. By the way, the Sanskrit *ki* means "ant hill" and *va* means "dwelling."[34]

Each February inside their kivas the Hopi perform the Bean Sprouting Ceremony, or Bean Dance, called *Powamu*. During this time the fires are continuously kept ablaze, turning these under-ground structures into superb hot houses. This ritual may com-memorate a time when the *Anu Sinom* taught the Hopi how to sprout beans inside caverns in order to survive. (See historic photos of *Powamu* on p. 84 and p. 95.) The related Hopi word *a'ni himu* means "sacred being, one who is venerated."[35]

The *Arizona Gazette* article states: "On all the urns, on walls over doorways, and tablets of stone which were found are the mysterious hieroglyphics, the key to which the Smithsonian Institute [sic] hopes yet to discover.... The engraving on the tables [tablets?] probably has something to do with the religion of the people." If these incisements were indeed Egyptian in ori-gin and not native petroglyphs or Mayan glyphs, then the link that the article talks about had indeed been forged between the Nile and "the Nile of Arizona," i.e. the Colorado.[36]

Another possible connection comes in the figure of an archaeologist named J. O. Kinnaman (1877 – 1961). Born near Bryan, Ohio, he studied at the University of Chicago under Professor Frederick Starr and received a Ph.D. from the University of Rome in 1907. Incidentally, both Frederick Starr and the previously discussed David Starr Jordan were stock-holders in the magazine *Out West*, published by Jordan's friend Charles Lummis.[37] Perhaps Starr and Jordan were even related.

In 1894 as an undergraduate, Kinnaman traveled with his physician-father to Egypt and met the great British archaeologist Sir William Flinders Petrie—right at the Great Pyramid, no less! In a taped lecture given in northern California about 1955 at a private home of an anonymous Freemason, Kinnaman (also a Mason) discussed his Giza research over a period of 11 years with Petrie (a Mason as well). He matter-of-factly stated that they by chance had jointly discovered a secret entrance on the south side of the Great Pyramid, which led to inner chambers that held records from Atlantis and an anti-gravitation machine allowing for the construction of the pyramid. He claimed that the structure was built over 35,000 years ago.

As Director of Research for the Kinnaman Foundation, Stephen Mehler says in an article on the subject that the two men swore a non-disclosure oath to "...the highest government officials in Great Britain and Egypt..." However, Kinnaman's semi-private talk to a few individuals apparently broke that oath. Mehler writes that Dr. Albert J. McDonald, President and Executive Director of the Foundation, knew Kinnaman personally.

"He informed me that Dr. Kinnaman had stated that one of the functions of the Great Pyramid had been as a giant radio system. By virtue of the huge crystal stored in a chamber 1,100 feet below the bedrock of the Giza Plateau, Egyptian priests could send telepathic messages around the world! According to McDonald, one of the places Dr. Kinnaman said these messages were sent was the Grand

 quote continued on p. 134

Petroglyphs of Ant People, northern Arizona. Note to the right: "crowsfeet," a warrior symbol. The figure on the left may be receiving celestial energy.

Wordplay: Ant-tics

- In the Bible the Nephilim are the "giants in the earth."
- Ancient Hebrews, Arabians, and Syrians all referred to Orion as "the Giant."
- The Sumerian term NFL (not football but Nefilim, Nephilim) means "those who came from Heaven to Earth."
- But… the Aramaic word *nephîliâ* is the name for Orion.
- And… the Hebrew word *nemalim* means "ants."
- The name Orion originally comes from the Indo-European word *morui*, which means "ant."
- The Hopi word *anu* means "ant."
- The Hopi word *naki* means "friend."
- On Sumerian seals the Anunnaki are seen as wingéd sky gods.
- Mature ant colonies produce winged ants.

Canyon! Dr. Kinnaman may have known about the find in the Grand Canyon in 1909 and even known Professor S.A. Jordan, but we have no documentation of this as of yet."[38]

Incredible as it may seem, ancient Egyptians may have been telepathically communicating with the cave-complex in Grand Canyon. Did the Ant People somehow transmit their vast trove of ancient knowledge from Egypt in order to assist the ancestral Hopi in their time of need? Could the Ant People have actually transported themselves via an interdimensional wormhole or time-tunnel to their ant colony in Arizona? If that's going too far, how about this?

Did they instead sail down the Red Sea in ships, cross the Indian Ocean, ply the vast distances of the Pacific on the eastward-moving conveyor belt of the equatorial countercurrent until they came to the Gulf of California, then sail up the Colordo River against the flow, perhaps using ropes or poles, in order to reach their destination at the Confluence? (For more on this possibility, see Chapter 12.) Diffusionist researcher Jim Bailey comments on the state of Egyptian and Phoenician ship building.

"Around 1500 B.C. an Egyptian barge took two obelisks of Queen Hatshepsut down the Nile. It was two hundred feet long and eighty feet wide and weighed, with its load, 1,500 tons. This was admittedly a river boat, but there is evidence that the Egyptians had seagoing ships that could carry two hundred men and others that had accommodation both for horses and for chariots. At about the time of Queen Hatshepsut's barge, ships of five hundred tons were being built in the Phoenician city state of Ugarit. Egyptian shipbuilding was ahead of that of Rome."[39]

So perhaps it was a joint Egyptian-Phoenician venture. Columbus's flagship, the *Santa Maria*, was puny by comparison—a mere 80 to 100 tons. The adage back in the Bronze Age must have been: the land divided, the water united.[40] "The role that tradition especially assigns to the Phoenicians as the merchants of the Levant was first developed on a considerable scale at the time of the Egyptian 18th dynasty. The position of Phoenicia, at a junction of both land and sea routes, under the protection of Egypt, favoured this development, and the discovery of the alphabet and its use and adaptation for commercial purposes assisted the rise of a mercantile society."[41]

The 5th century AD Egyptian scholar Horapollo comments on the significance of the ant to Egyptian culture. "To represent *knowledge*, they delineate an ANT, for whatever a man may carefully conceal, this creature obtains a knowledge of: and not for this reason only, but also because beyond all other animals when it is providing for itself its winter's food, it never deviates from its home, but arrives at it unerringly."[42] This insect, then, is the creature of secret or hermetic knowledge.

The verse-preface of Gerald Massey's massive (no pun intended) epic poem "Ancient Egypt: The Light of the World" is as follows:

"The revelation of the Old Dark Race;
Theirs was the wisdom of the Bee and Bird,
Ant, Tortoise, Beaver, *working human-wise*; [italics added]
The ancient darkness spake with Egypt's Word;
Hers was the primal message of the skies:
The Heavens are telling nightly of her glory,
And for all time Earth echoes her great story."[43]

So ant wisdom is not only arcane but also celestial.

Okay, let's get back to Arizona. Kinkaid stated that 42 miles upstream from the mouth of Crystal Canyon is Kwagunt Rapids, near where the cave is located. The name *Kwagunt* or *Qua-gun-ti* is a Paiute word meaning "quiet man," referring to a Paiute Indian born in the 1850s who lived in that region. During the spring he and his family would descend into Grand Canyon to collect *yant*, an edible species of agave cactus. During the fall they would ascend to the Kaibab Plateau to gather pinyon nuts and hunt deer.[45]

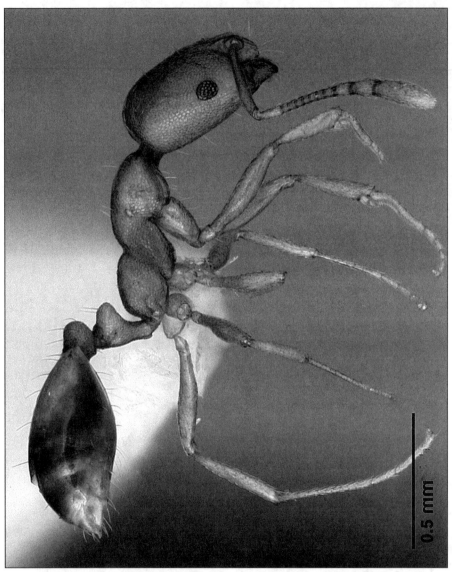

Pharaoh Ant (*Momomorium pharaonis*), originating possibly in West Africa. Elongated head, yellow to reddish brown body, darker abdomen with stinger.

David Hatcher Childress in *The Enigma of Cranial Deformation* observes: "An aspect of genetics, that appears not to have been given the attention it deserves, can help resolve this mystery. It is the elongated skull or the 'dolicho-cephalic' head that many members of the eighteenth Egyptian dynasty possessed, including Nefertiti's famous husband Akhenaten, and her even more famous relative Tutankhamen.... However, we are talking of a skull shape that goes well beyond the normal human shape, to the point that biologists have attributed it to a rare disease, some even to extraterrestrial sources."[44]

Akhenaten, 18th Dynasty, 1351–1334 BC, with his child, shown with elongated skull, which he is also thought to have had. The serpent or vulture on his uraeus resembles the ant's mandibles. His almond-shaped eyes and neck are like the ant's, and he has spindly arms and legs like the ant. His upper body resembles the ant's thorax and his lower body mirrors the ant's abdomen.

However, the similar Hopi word *Kwaakwant* means "membership of the Kwan or One-Horn Society," but it literally means "agave-fruit."[46] On a mundane level these warriors protect the villages and their various rituals from physical or spiritual trespass. This society meets in the Lance Kiva, named for the long agave stalks its members carry. This spike of the agave, or century plant, can grow over over 10 feet tall.

On a spiritual level the Kwan Society is associated with the underworld and death. During the harrowing *Wuwtsim*, or New Fire Ceremony held in November to initiate young men, they are responsible for kindling the fire. "The One Horn Society is the most powerful of all Hopi sacred societies or fraternities and is regarded with great awe by the Hopi, for it is the duty of these priests to look after the dead. They are in charge of the spirit upon its journey from this world into Muski [*Maski*], the under world or spirit world of the Hopi."[47] *Wuwtsim* is said to belong to Masau'u, Hopi deity of death, and counterpart to the Egyptian god Osiris (Orion). (See graphic of Masau'u on p. 53.) During this ritual the Kwan members address their purification to the kachinas of the Grand Canyon's Salt Cave (mentioned in the previous chapter) "...where there are stalactites (*lepena*) believed to be connected in some occult way with the horns on their helmets."[48]

The phratry (group of clans) called the Horn-Millet is comprised of certain totems such as mountain sheep, elk, deer, antelope, and various kinds of ants. These include red ant (*pala'anu*), flesh ant (*toko'anu*), which is "a large dark red ant with a painful sting,"[49] big ant (*woko'anu*), and black ant (*sisiw'anu*), otherwise known as "pissant" because it gives off a urine scent. The black ant in particular is associated with sorcery, and the Millet people are especially suspected of being witches.[50] Indian millet (Hopi name *leehu*, scientific name *Orzopsis hymenoides*) and galleta grass (Hopi name *söhö*, scientific name *Hilaria jamesii*) grow particularly well where anthills prevail. Galleta grass (*söhö)* is attached to prayer-sticks during the winter solstice ceremony, and the related Hopi word *sohu* means "star." Incidentally, Anu was the Egyptian name for the ceremonial city of Heliopolis, across the Nile from the Great Pyramid. It once housed the *ben-*

ben stone atop an obelisk in the Temple of the Phoenix.

I am basically saying that Kwagunt Rapids may be associated with the Hopi Kwan society, whose domain is the underworld. The whole area of eastern Grand Canyon, which includes the Little Colorado River, is considered in Hopi cosmology –or what British scholar Richard Maitland Bradfield has called "Hopi Cosmognosis"[51]– to be the nether realm of the dead and perhaps even the subterranean complex of the Ant People.

Postscript: Grand Canyon Expedition 2012

Some researchers have made various claims to have actually explored Kinkaid's Cave, although these remain unsubstantiated. In the cyberspace world where memes are created and transmitted in a nanosecond, the story just gets "curiouser and curiouser." For instance: "John Rhodes after 3 years of field research reportedly discovered the Grand Canyon city, which is now being used as a museum for elitist groups and has lower levels that are being used by 'super secret black book operatives', which can only be entered via a stainless steel door at the bottom of a stairwell deep within the 'city' that is guarded by a very lonely soldier staring into the darkness... dressed in a white jumpsuit and armed only with an M16 assault rifle to ward off his imagination."[52] To quote a 1994 report by this self-proclaimed "CryptoHunter":

> "Most importantly, after three years of intense research and field explorations into the Grand Canyon area, I believe that I have finally located the Hopi Sipapuni underworld that G.E. Kincaid initially discovered in 1909. I have acquired physical evidence indicating anomalous activity occurring during that time period, new interpretations of an ancient Hopi prophecy supports the 'story' of Kincaids [sic] discovery and I, and a close colleague of mine, have stood upon the same ground where Kincaid once stood in awe. Evidence of this recent discovery has been relayed to several key people across the United

States for security purposes. A more detailed report of this discovery is forthcoming and will be made available to the public in the very near future."[53]

So far, nothing further of this claim has come to light. Surprised?

In May of 2012, I joined a team of eight other investigators to reconnoiter various anomalies I had first noticed on Google Earth in the region north of the Little Colorado River and east of Marble Canyon near the Salt Trail Canyon, where for centuries Hopis have descended on their pilgrimages. In particular I saw on the rim near the Confluence a perfect rectangle exactly one mile long and three-quarters of a mile wide. On the ground these turned out to be dirt roads made by tire tracks. But one has to ask: Who would make such a geometrically straight roadway, and for what reason? In addition, extending from both the length and the width of the rectangle on two sides are parallel lines that can be seen in the satellite photo. (See bottom of p. 144.) However, no lines could be seen on the ground. Further research on this is needed, but this could possibly be the remnants of some agricultural system used to support inhabitants of the cave-complex.

Near the rim about three-quarters of a mile in a straight line northeast of the Sipàapuni is what appears to be a low, pentagon-shaped mesa with artificial structures and even a couple kivas on top. It also has tire tracks leading up to it. But because of the rough terrain threaded with precipitous ravines, we were unable to get close enough during this trip to investigate.

Another anomaly we stumbled upon appears to be a quasi-megalithic ceremonial amphitheater of some sort. It is located on the broad plateau about three miles northeast of the Marble Canyon rim and about four-and-a-half miles north of Salt Trail Canyon on the Little Colorado River rim. This (again) pentagon-shaped structure measures about 70 feet long and 50 feet wide. The limestone blocks, some weighing more than a ton, are approximately two to three feet long and one to two feet wide. The blocks are stacked without masonry three to four feet high, forming walls a foot or so thick. An entrance to the structure was on the north, where horizontal slabs of rock formed a partial flooring.

One of our team members, David Childress, presented the hypothesis that it was constructed as a sheepfold. However, that would require heavy equipment, such as a backhoe, to drive or be hauled down dirt roads from at least the nearest Navajo village of Cedar Ridge, which is almost 17 miles away. That would not be much of a problem. But since there is no visible quarry near the structure, the equipment would have had to break the upper limestone strata into slabs, then place them one on top of the other. However, no scratch marks or sharp breaks on the blocks are visible. Why go to all that trouble to corral sheep? Wouldn't a pickup load of cedar posts and a bale of barbwire be much easier? The purpose of a sheepfold is twofold: keep the sheep in, and the coyotes out. This structure might do the former but certainly not the latter. This remains one enigma of many in the area.

About 500 feet west of this structure is a smaller stone circle approximately 10 feet in diameter. However, some of the blocks are as large as those in the other structure. This is surely not a sheep corral, but what could be its function? It is perhaps something akin to the horseshoe-shaped Hopi shrine known as a *herradura*, or even an astronomical observatory.

This is a very remote area. During the four days spent camping in the area, we saw only three other people—a sheepherding Navajo grandma and grandpa living in a travel trailer with their granddaughter. However, their solitude could soon possibly be disturbed.

In cooperation with the Navajo Nation, a company from Scottsdale is planning to build a massive complex covering 420 acres near the Confluence. "The project plans include multiple motels, shops and restaurants, a tramway to the bottom of the canyon, a 1,400-foot elevated river walk and Navajo cultural center, amphitheater and museum."[54] The complex would be dangerously close to culturally sensitive areas, including Hopi and Zuni religious sites such as the Sipàapuni and the Salt Cave. To go forward with such a Disneyland-type complex would be, to quote one of the team members Chris O'Brien, "sacrilegious and possibly illegal." Another member, Ron Regehr, who is a Cherokee-Chocktaw-

Chickasaw and retired aerospace engineer from Moab, Utah, states: "This is sacred ground; as sacred to the Puebloans as The Wailing Wall is to Jews, Mecca is to Muslims, and The Church of the Nativity is to Christians. It is the Holy Land of the Americas."

On the last day of our expedition, we witnessed at least two helicopters repeatedly diving into the Little Colorado River gorge below the rim. Suspended from a cable beneath one was what appeared to be a water pipe. Each time the helicopter emerged from the canyon, it flew out sans the pipe (or whatever it was). When the chopper saw we were observing and filming, it began to fly undetected below the rim. A ranger from Grand Canyon National Park later gave the explanation that the Bureau of Land Management was reintroducing native fish, such as humpback chub, to the river. Sounds fishy to me...

The complex is to be called Grand Canyon Escalade.

- escalade – a scaling or mounting by means of ladders, esp. in an assault upon a fortified place; also, a high-priced Cadillac SUV
- escapade – a reckless adventure or wild prank, esp. one contrary to usual or proper behavior

Perhaps we should heed the words of President Theodore Roosevelt, when he proclaimed at the edge of Grand Canyon in 1903: "Leave it as it is. You cannot improve on it. The ages have been at work on it, and man can only mar it. What you can do is to keep it for your children, and for all who come after you, as the one great sight which every American... should see."[55]

Quasi-megalithic circle on the East Rim near the Confluence.

Author and videographer Chris O'Brien filming the quasi-megaliths.

Zuni elder Clifford Mahooty surveying the smaller stone circle.

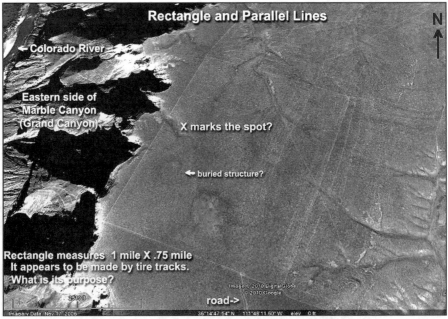

Rectangular form made by tire tracks near the Confluence,
with parallel lines at the right.

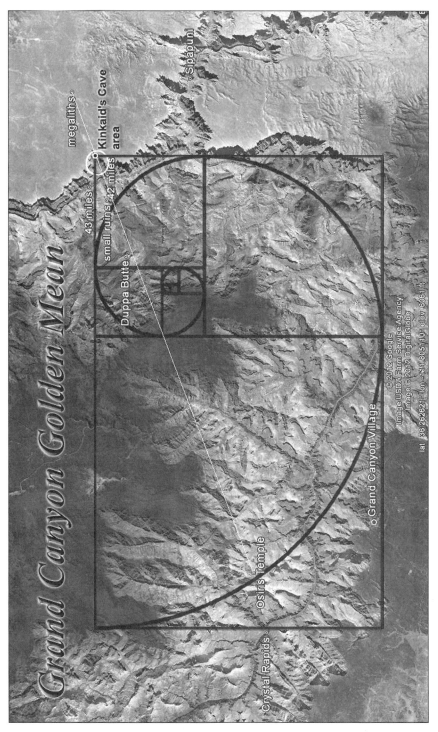

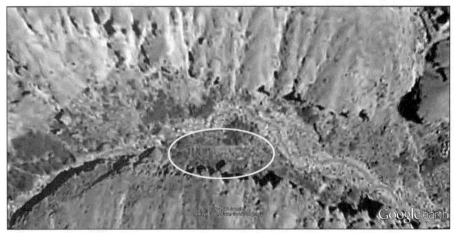

Satellite overview photo of ruins from 4,250 ft. altitude, located about 1.25 miles from the mouth of Kwagunt Creek. Grand Canyon expert Harvey Butchart: "The ranger scouting party of 1928 reported seeing a lost city of at least twenty-five rooms near here. Later, the man who claimed to have seen it, disclaimed his find. The city has never been rediscovered but a terrace on the south side of the stream and just west of the river narrows is said to have a number of room outlines on it."[56]

On the facing page the *New York Times* article from March 8th, 1896 describes a mummy found in a cave not far from the mouth of East Verde River in Arizona. The article speculates that the unfortunate person was walled up in a cave and left to starve or suffocate. Propped up against the wall in a sitting position, the mummy was the result of a natural mummification process due to the arid climate. Finely crafted artifacts were found next to the mummy. Although the article does not provide the exact height of the individual, it states that he was unusually tall and had a skull that resembled an Aztec rather than a Toltec. His teeth were like those of "the canine tribe," perhaps indicating a Chichimec. (See Chapter 7.)

Although a number of naturally dessicated mummies have been found in the American Southwest, a Peruvian physician-anthropologist named Guido Lombardi claims that the Anasazi may have also practiced intentional mummification for ceremonial reasons. In the 1890s, for instance, amateur archaeologist Richard Wetherill found a mummy in a cave in a gulch near Blanding, Utah. It came to be known as Cut-in-Two-Man due to an incision in his hips and abdomen that had been sewn together with braided human hair in a crude attempt to save him. Lombardi believes he was deliberately eviscerated because he was better preserved than most other mummies. In addition, dismembered arms and legs of others were found next to the mummy, perhaps as ritual offerings. Also, a "trophy head" with an elaborate hairdo and face painting was discovered in a cave in northeastern Arizona. It appears to have had the skull removed and the face and scalp sewn back on, Lombardi said.[57]

THE MUMMY OF A CLIFF DWELLER FOUND.

Reported Discovery by a Hunter in Arizona.

From The St. Louis Globe-Democrat.

PRESCOTT, Arizona, March 2.—The mummy of one of the ancient cliff dwellers of Arizona, the first of undoubted authenticity ever discovered, has been found by a hunter well known in Northern Arizona, John McCarty. In a cliff dwelling on the Verde River, a dozen miles north of the mouth of the East Verde, he noticed that when one of the walls was hit with metal a hollow sound emanated. This led to the discovery of a sort of crypt. In this crypt the mummy was discovered. It had evidently been propped up in a sitting position against the wall, though there were indications that the cliff dweller of long ago had been walled up alive, and there left to die of starvation or suffocation. By the side of the mummy were found several broken pottery bowls and a stone axe, and in the vault were picked up a dozen obsidian and flint arrowheads, several of them exceptionally large sized and of rare workmanship.

The mummy, which weighs twenty-one pounds, was taken away by the finder on an Indian litter, dragged behind a burro, till a wagon road was reached. It is now in this city. The body is that of a male, and is of unusually great stature. The skin, which is broken in several places, revealing the bones, is of the color of dried beef. The trunk is perfect, the skin covering it being unbroken. In the skull, however, lies the element of greatest interest. The formation is entirely different from that typical of the ancient dwellers in the valleys of Arizona. The valley dwellers were Toltecs of almost Caucasian cranial features. The skull of the mummy, with forehead retreating from the nose and large rear development, is of the Aztec type. The teeth are entire and well preserved, and protrude as in the canine tribe. As the mummy showed signs of disintegration, McCarty has given it a coat of varnish, preparatory to placing in an air-tight glass-covered box.

Chapter 6
Canals and Pyramids —
Earthworks of the Hohokam

The Grand Canals of Arizona

When we hear the word "earthworks," we generally think of stone-and-earthen structures such as the massive, flat-topped pyramid in the metropolis of Cahokia, located across the Mississippi from modern-day St. Louis. (Cahokia is contemporary with Chaco Canyon. See Chapter 7.) We may also recall the enigmatic Serpent Mound in the Ohio Valley, of which Ross Hamilton has so eloquently written, along with the other Pre-Columbian mounds in that region.[1] Or we might remember various mounds in the American Southeast: the bird-effigy mound at Poverty Point, Louisiana; the flat-topped pyramids at Winterville Mounds in Mississippi; others at Moundville in Alabama; and one more at Etowah Mound in Georgia—all located along the 33rd parallel.[2] The numerous henges and barrows of England might even come to mind. But rarely do we consider the Desert Southwest as a place replete with earthworks.

An indigenous group called the Hohokam, however, were the master earth-movers of Arizona. They inhabited the Phoenix Basin (also at about 33° north latitude) between 450 AD and 1450 AD—the so-called "Hohokam Millennium." Some authorities conversely claim that the Hohokam had migrated to the region as early as 300 BC—about the time of Alexander the Great and the Ptolemaic Dynasties in Egypt. Their name is a Tohono O'odham (Papago) word meaning "those who have vanished," or more literally, "all used up."[3] Of course, no draft animals or wheelbarrows were ever used in their construction projects. Relying instead on mere woven carrying baskets, digging sticks, and stone implements, the Hohokam created one of the world's most extensive irrigation systems. In fact, both north and south of the Salt River now sucked dry by the modern metropolis, they built the largest canal network in Pre-Columbian America north of Peru.[4]

The "Hohokam heartland" receives only about 7 to 10 inches of rainfall annually and temperatures exceed 90° F –and sometimes as much as 25 degrees higher– for three months out of the year. Nonetheless, these hearty farmers created an estimated total of 500 miles of canals to irrigate nearly 30,000 acres in the Valley of the Sun—an area the size of South Carolina. Separate canal networks measured up to 22 miles in length, and about one million person-days were needed to construct the trunklines of this massive dendritic system.[5] As the early Southwest archaeologist H. M. Wormington comments, "The scope of the canal project suggests comparisons with the erection of the huge pyramids of Egypt or the great temples of the Maya."[6]

The main canals leading from Salt River and Gila River measured nearly 75 feet across at the top and 50 feet wide at the bottom.[7] South canal no. 3 at Park of the Four Waters appears to have been about 12 feet deep, though most of the distribution canals were between two and four feet deep.[8] From the Salt River near Pueblo Grande (a major Hohokam site discussed below), North and South canals each extended almost eight miles long and sent water to villages nearly 10 miles away from the riparian flow.[9] So well constructed were these canals that 19th century Mormon settlers successfully employed and improved the pre-existing system. Some waterways were lined with a concrete-like substance known as caliche, so that even today they could be incorporated into the modern water system for the Phoenix metro area.[10] These main canals branched into smaller lateral canals with headgates to divert the water into the network of fields.

Overall, the construction of the canal system was, quite simply, a colossal undertaking. Archaeologist Stephen H. Lekson remarks on the hydraulic wonderworks. "By the end of the Colonial Period (900/950), Hohokam canals had reached levels of technological and organizational complexity unprecedented in the Southwest, and indeed most of North America—well beyond the control of village-level authority."[11]

At the risk of failing to give credit where credit is due, I have to question whether or not the Hohokam had "outside" assistance in the construction of this monumental irrigation project. Author Ernest Snyder seems to have similar doubts: "The organization and coordination for the planning, construction, maintenance and operation of the system must have required social and civic efforts far beyond what might be expected of a primitive people one step removed from a hunting and gathering existence."[12] Coincidentally, this scenario almost exactly mirrors that of the transition between pre-Dynastic and Dynastic Egypt.

But if we disregard the "who" and focus on the "what," one must admit that this technological savvy allowed a florescence of culture virtually unprecedented in North America. Archaeologist Stephen Plog remarks on this success story in terms of the number of people who were fed. "The Phoenix Basin achieved a total population of between 30,000 and 60,000, one of the highest densities of people –living along the largest system of irrigation canals– anywhere in prehistoric North America." This was larger than the population of London during the same period.[13]

Adobe Abode and the Home Field Advantage

Unlike the Ancestral Puebloan stone structures to the north, most of the Hohokam adobe dwellings have melted into the desert in the last five hundred years. During the Pioneer Period (450 – 700 AD) the low desert people lived in semi-subterranean pit house structures with jacal walls made of slim vertical poles and mud. Typically two to five houses were clustered around a central plaza with their doorways facing inward. This architectural arrangement known as the *rancheria* suggests a kinship system, with related households forming a clan that contained 16 to 20 individuals.[14] Each compound had its own communal cooking area, trash mound, and cremation cemetery.

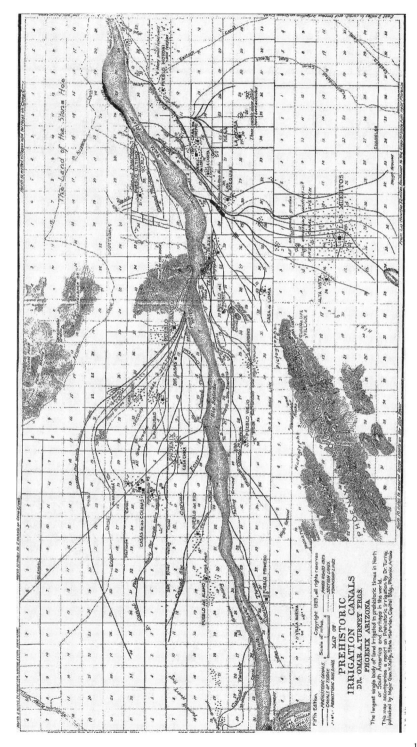

Emil W. Haury, who in 1964–5 excavated the Hohokam site of Snaketown. He is standing in an irrigation canal.

Drawing by Michael Hampshire. Hohokam pit house village during Pioneer Period (450 – 700 AD). Woman lower-left using paddle-and-anvil method of pottery making, as opposed to coil-and-smooth method of the Anasazi/Sinagua.

In contrast to the inhumation custom of the Anasazi and Sinagua, the Hohokam had elaborate cremation rituals with ceramics and lithics burned along with the deceased. Associated with the mortuary ceremony were buried caches of deliberately destroyed stone effigies and clay figurines of both humans and animals.[15] Two classes of humanoid figurines have been found at Hohokam sites: torsos and heads. Mid-20th century archaeologist John C. McGregor explains: "The torsos are strongly suggestive of similar human figurines found in the Basket Maker culture of the [Colorado] plateau, and this latter group may well have taken the idea of modeling them from the Hohokam. The heads find no close parallel in the Southwest, but are strongly suggestive of those typical of the Archaic horizon in the Valley of Mexico."[16]

Also found among the cremated remains were rectangular schist palettes with raised borders, frequently incised or sculpted with birds, snakes, lizards, or various animals. Additional offerings to the dead included fine pottery vessels, copper bells, quartz crystals, and *Glycymeris* shells from the Gulf of California or the Pacific that were etched with the acidic juice of the saguaro cactus to form designs. At any rate, we might conclude that the emphasis on cremation is symbolic of the phoenix himself rising from his ashes on the Phoenix Basin. In addition, vanity for the Hohokam was no different than it is for us; they admired themselves in pyrite mirrors similar to ones found in Mayan ruins.

During the Colonial Period (700 – 900 AD) ball courts began to be extensively used. Lekson remarks, "Ball courts are the sine qua non of the Hohokam."[17] More than 225 of the former structures have been found at over 160 different sites in Arizona, from Wupatki in the north to below Tucson in the south. However, over 40% of them are located in the Phoenix Basin.[18] The court itself was probably an *imago mundi* of earthen construction in the form of an oval depression with raised embankments and sometimes a smoothed or plastered floor. The players used a ball made from *guayule*, a rubber-like substance from a plant native to Chihuahua, in order to decide their cosmic fate. Only three balls have been found in the Southwest.[19] Unlike the Maya, no evidence of human sacrifice has been found.

Horned toad on *Glycymeris* shell
etched with fermented cactus juice.

Five-pointed star (Venus?)
on red-on-buff shallow bowl.

Red-on-buff bowl with swastika.
The Hopi use also this icon on dance
rattles—*aya,* or "moisture rattle."

Schist earplug, Snaketown.
This is the "earmark" of the
Ancient Mariners. (See Chapter 12.)

Schist palette with coiled rattlesnakes.
Used either for grinding pigments
or for crematory rituals. Courtesy of
American Heritage Administration.

The oldest and largest court was found at a site the Akimel O'odham call "place of the rattlesnakes," or Snaketown, about 19 miles due south of Pueblo Grande. This oval playing area was 197 feet in length and 16 feet in height, with its embankments allowing for over 500 spectators.[20] In addition to the sacred connotation of the game, David R. Wilcox, chief archaeologist for the Museum of Northern Arizona, believes that it served the economic function of linking dispersed settlements in an exchange system, thereby fostering trade between different native groups: Hohokam, Sinagua, Salado, and Mogollon.[21] Much like modern sporting events, the competitive aspect between various "hometowns" was mixed with the commercial aspect. (In my own youth, I rooted for the Indians.)

Hohokam Pyramids, a.k.a. Platform Mounds

The primary architectural development of the Sedentary Period (900–1150 AD) was the use of the platform mound, which served as a ceremonial civic center or specialized sacred precinct. Over 40 of them were located in the Phoenix Basin alone.[22] Whereas the ball court represented a communitarian or egalitarian phase of Hohokam development, the platform mound signaled a shift toward a more hierarchical social structure.[23] The earliest mounds began as circular accumulations of earth, rubble, and trash capped with caliche, though sometimes they were accompanied by retaining walls. The earlier round mounds apparently served a ritual function, whereas the later rectangular mounds suggest a residential area for the elite, although the two were not mutually exclusive. Mounds may have functioned as dance platforms or stages for performances. Arizona archaeologist Jefferson Reid comments: "In appearance like a *truncated pyramid with a flat top* [italics added], platform mounds apparently served as a stage-like area for performing ceremonies. That this custom was borrowed from Mexican peoples seems certain."[24]

Rectangular platform mounds were constructed with rounded corners, oriented to a north-south axis. In addition, wooden palisades or adobe compound walls signify a restricted visual and spatial access to ceremonial activities. The further segregation of an elitist class of priesthood from the "commoners" is demonstrated by the construction of domicile and storage rooms on top of the platform mounds of the later period. Again, McGregor observes: "There were also massive adobe-walled enclosures which were filled in and formed raised platforms on top of which structures were built. It has been pointed out that similar pyramidal bases were found in Mexico."[25] Unlike the ball court phenomenon which spread across both low desert and upland regions, this type of North American flat-topped pyramid was restricted to the major tributaries of Arizona.

Platform mounds averaged 2 to 12 feet high, and the amount of dirt and rubble needed to fill in the outer adobe-walled enclosure ranged from 2,800 to over 700,000 cubic feet. Imagine hauling all that in a woven basket on your back! The two largest Hohokam platform mounds, Pueblo Grande and Mesa Grande (see pp. 160-1), required no fewer than 50,000 person-days each to construct them. Within the larger Hohokam sphere of influence, archaeologists have found a total of 120 platform mounds at different 95 sites.[26]

How were those monumental earthworks pragmatically accomplished? Clearly, a combination of complex bureaucracies and centralized management, which supervised architectural planning, engineering, construction, and labor coordination, had produced the branching canal systems as well as the plethora of pyramid projects. Archaeologist Mark D. Elson describes the type of hierarchical society necessary to get the job done.

"Of course, the Hohokam did not build these structures quickly. The large mounds undoubtedly took many people many years to build. Such sustained commitment strongly suggests that by the time the Hohokam began to build platform mounds, their society featured highly ranked persons who inherited territories, could command the labor of commoners, and had the foresight required for long-term planning. Indeed, the labor needed to build the large Hohokam mounds rivals that needed to construct some of the large temple mounds in

Hawai'i, where nobles had the divinely sanctioned power of life and death over the lower classes. Perhaps Phoenix Basin leaders had similar powers, allowing them to conscript laborers to build their mounds."[27]

The Pueblo Grande (PG) platform mound measured 300 feet long, 150 feet wide –the size of the proverbial American football field– and 25 to 30 feet high Over 720,000 cubic yards of fill –granite, sandstone, river cobbles, and dirt– were used to construct this truncated pyramid.

On the southeast corner of the platform mound was a room with an unusual corner door to let in the rays of the summer solstice sunrise, which fell against another door in the south wall. The former door also lines up with one more solstice observatory called Hole-in-the-Rock on Papago Buttes about 2.5 miles to the northeast. The last rays of the winter solstice sunset would have also entered the southern doorway, so the room was undoubtedly used to calibrate the Hohokam agricultural calendar.

On the southwest corner of the mound was found a number of debris-filled cells, which included a human burial and the skeleton of a large bird. (Some inhumation was practiced in the later stages of Hohokam development.) In this area were also discovered four giant adobe columns four feet in diameter and six feet in height, evenly spaced in the center of the room. This odd type of architectural feature has only been located on platform mounds and probably served a ceremonial purpose.

Surrounding the platform mound was an adobe wall three feet thick and up to eight feet high. The rooms, compound walls, and courtyards later built atop this artificial mesa were apparently designed in a labyrinthine fashion to emphasize their hierarchical function. In addition, Hopi pottery, shells, stone beads, obsidian nodules, and piles of stone axes were unearthed in an area to the north. Because of Pueblo Grande's commanding view of the surrounding landscape, a few 19th century settlers were known to have sat atop this monumental example of Hohokam architecture to enjoy their picnics. One such individual was the Freemason Darell Duppa, who actually named the city of Phoenix. (See p. 160.)

The Great Houses of the Fin de Siècle

During the latest stage of Hohokam development, namely, the Classic Period (1150 – 1450 AD), the development of the Hohokam pyramid burgeoned, becoming larger and higher through time. Lekson succinctly underscores this essential architecture. "Platform mounds became the most conspicuous and (presumably) important monumental form of the Classic Period."[28] Of course, weeds had begun to overtake the ball courts starting at the end of the 11th century. According to archaeologist David Gregory, however, the mound-canal link was still strong. "Classic period mounds are consistently associated with major sites situated on canals that drew water directly from the Salt and Gila rivers, and these sites are regularly spaced along the canals."[29]

Also during the Classic Period, at least three and probably more adobe "great houses" three to four stories high were built, the most famous of which is the astronomical observatory and administrative center at Casa Grande Ruins National Monument located about 40 miles southeast of Pueblo Grande. In the construction 1,440 cubic yards of dirt and 600 roof beams were used. The ponderosa pine and white fir beams, each 13 feet in length, had to be hauled and/or floated down the Gila River from 60 miles away.[30] The entrenched walls measured four feet thick at ground level and two feet thick at the top.[31]

These "great house" structures were also frequently surrounded by adobe compound walls. "In the last century [viz., the 19th], when the rich agricultural potential of the Phoenix Basin was rediscovered by European-American settlers, the Pueblo Grande site was put under cultivation to produce cotton. Even the three-story big house was demolished and its fill was used to help level fields."[32] This major archaeological ruin once rested where Van Buren St. is today—about one-quarter mile to the north of the platform mound.

The 14th century was not kind to the Hohokam (or for that matter, to the Europeans, if we recall the Black Plague). What had been competitive rivalry during the ball court period escalated into violence and warfare between communities, manifested by increased defensive hilltop sites. But the final Hohokam coffin nail, so to speak, proved to be deluge followed by drought. In the mid-1300s these riverside communities were hit particularly hard. Floods occurred in 1357, 1358, and 1359, followed by a two-year extreme dry spell in 1360 and 1361. Then in 1381, 1382, and 1384, floods plagued the Phoenix Basin again—with 1382 the most devastating one in 480 years, overwhelming their irrigation network. A decade of drought followed, ultimately finishing off the stalwart and resourceful society.[33] Perhaps by that time the river-farmers had had enough and simply headed for the hills.

But clearly the architectural Big Four —canals, ball courts, pyramids, and great houses— were the key factors that allowed these desert dwelling people to inhabit and even thrive in their extremely harsh region for well over a thousand years.

Left: Clay effigy head, 900–1100 AD, Grewe site east of Casa Grande.
Upper-right: Hohokam "wrestler," clay, elongated skull, 700–900 AD, Van Liere Ranch Site.
Lower-right: Olmec "wrestler," basalt, possibly 400 BC, Veracruz, Museo Nacional de Antropología.

Top: Author by PG platform mound. Bottom: Drawing Michael Hampshire.

Author's wife Anita Descault atop northeast corner of Pueblo Grande truncated pyramid, measuring 300 ft. by 150 ft. and up to 30 ft. in height. 720,000 cubic ft. of fill were used in construction. Rocks were carried from 1 to 2 miles away. Caliche, a cement-like soil, was mined nearby. Adobe rooms on the rectangular mound stressed the separated, elite status of their inhabitants.

Located 8 miles east of Pueblo Grande, Mesa Grande (c. 1100 – 1400 AD) was 27 feet high, larger than a football field, and home to 2,000 Hohokam.[34]

"Great House" with protective roof at Casa Grande National Monument. Photo by NPS, 2003. It also served as an astronomical observatory. Round or rectangular holes in the walls apparently provided observation points for summer solstices, equinoxes, and lunar standstills. In addition, the platform mound there may have also been connected with the celestial realm. "[David R.] Wilcox suggested that the manipulation of astronomical information used to schedule ceremonial events was part of elite activities at the Casa Grande platform mound. The sun, moon, certain planets, stars, and constellations were thought to be supernatural powers that shamans, priests, or chiefs sought to control for human benefit. Such control was possible through the possession of esoteric knowledge manipulated and guarded by society's leaders."[35]

Historic Model of Casa Grande Ruin with Great House and platform mound

Chapter 7
All Roads Lead to... Chaco

The Sun Stands Still

A lone sentinel named Fajada (Spanish for "banded") Butte rises 380 feet above the floor of Chaco Canyon in northern New Mexico. It is located four miles southeast of Pueblo Bonito, the largest ruin in the canyon and the center of this massive pre-Hispanic urban complex. Near the top of the eastern side of this butte, the now-famous Sun Dagger petroglyphs (rock carvings) were rediscovered in 1977 by artist-turned-archaeoastronomer Anna Sofaer. Three upright slabs perpendicular to the cliff face had been positioned about four inches apart by the Ancients in order to direct sunlight onto a pair of spirals –one large and one small– carved into the vertical surface of the butte, thereby creating a golden solar sliver that slices through the petroglyphs. This happens at approximately 11:15 in the morning of each summer solstice. Three other daggers of sunlight on different positions of the spirals also indicate the winter solstice as well as the vernal and autumnal equinoxes.

The sandstone slabs that collimate the sunlight are five times heavier than the largest foundation stones in the great kivas of Chaco Canyon, weighing approximately 4.5 tons each. They measure 6 to 10 feet high, 2 to 3 feet wide, and 8 to 20 inches thick. If indeed positioned by humans, these megaliths must have been extremely ponderous to manipulate.

In addition, an artificial ramp had been constructed on the southwestern side of the butte in order to facilitate access to the obviously ceremonial site. It was 700 feet long and rose 280 feet above the valley floor. Despite the difficulty in climbing the geological structure as well as its lack of water, 35 small dwellings and a round kiva have been found on the higher bands of Fajada Butte. The presence of manos, cooking pots, hearths, and burned corn cobs suggests long-term residence at the site.[1]

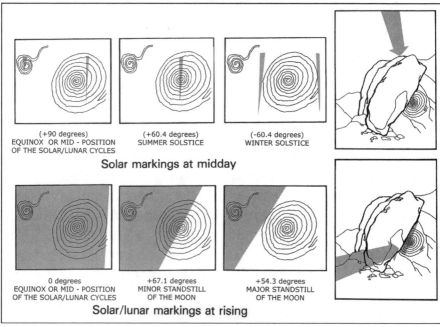

"Sun Dagger" spiral petroglyphs and rock slabs directing the sunlight. Slivers of light designate the solstices and equinoxes; shadows designate the major and minor lunar standstills (which occur every 18.6 years.)

Fajada Butte during a summer thunderstorm.

Pueblo Bonito against south-facing cliffside.

Road Warriors and Shaman Runways

The incredible archaeo-metroplex of Chaco Canyon was the Big Apple of its day. In fact, the "Great House" of Pueblo Bonito, which contained as many as 700 rooms, was the largest apartment complex in the world until a bigger one was built in New York City in the 1880s. A dozen or so other large pueblos were constructed in the canyon between about 850 AD and 1130 AD. Chaco Culture National Historical Park today is another UNESCO World Heritage Site. Because I have already discussed Chaco Canyon in my previous three books (*The Orion Zone, Eye of the Phoenix,* and *The Kivas of Heaven*), I will take up only a few relevant points.

An extensive road system radiated outward from Chaco Canyon. For the most part it was aligned strictly north and south. These roads were conceptualized not only as the transportation network for import and export of "goods and services" but more importantly as sacred pilgrimage-avenues that mirrored the pathways of spirits.

The Chacoans constructed over 400 miles of roads, most of which converge upon Chaco Canyon. They were an average of 30 feet in width, although some were nearly 10 feet wider. The longest segments of the roads were 40 to 60 miles in length, connecting half a dozen outlying sites with the Middle Place. The major construction period was between 1075 and 1130 AD—the last phase of the Chaco run. One authoritative source sums up the magnitude of the project: "This road system is undoubtedly the great single achievement of prehistoric man in the Southwest."[2]

The roadway surface consisted of packed earth or bedrock and was bordered by berms of dirt, sand, or rubble. Ramps and stairways of masonry were built to cross canyons and buttes. At times, stairs were even cut into bedrock in order to traverse steep ravines. "The generally straight, undeviating bearings of the roads suggest that they were laid out or 'engineered' prior to their actual construction, although what specific techniques were used is not certain."[3] In other words, this road system was built according to an archaic blueprint or pre-conceived plan and was not merely a construction accomplished a posteriori.

Why undertake such a massive project, when beasts of burden or wheeled carts were unknown? (Architects of the great houses did, however, use giant sandstone disks to support the roofs of the great kivas. These disks were probably rolled into place, so the idea of the wheel did occur to these people.) Many believe these roads have a raison d'être that is more than simply pragmatic. Author Kathryn Gabriel has devoted an entire book to the Chacoan road system.

"Some archaeologists refer to the roads as ceremonial ways, while others say their nonutilitarian purpose, supplemented with other evidence, suggest that they are 'monuments to social organization,' projects *much like the pyramids or standing stone formations* [italics added]. Much as they do in Mesoamerican societies contemporary with the Anasazi, the road fragments may reflect an insatiable appetite for order, by underscoring cardinal direction or an astronomical alignment."[4]

Comparable to monumental structures such as the Great Pyramid or Stonehenge, this massive road network made a grand statement: Don't mess with the Masters of the Universe! The concrete expression of these concepts of social hierarchy, Gabriel says, were mostly likely imported from the pyramid-building cultures to the south, which also built straight roads connecting ceremonial cities.

Along certain segments of the roads, double or even quadruple parallel pathways were constructed to ritualistically revivify an ancient cosmological map and invoke the Myth of the Eternal Return. "...the parallel avenues are possibly the symbolic representation of the multiple paths down which the people traveled in the ancestral journey from the place of emergence to the Middle Place. Pilgrimage down these divergent corridors into parallel paths may have then reactualized and validated the origin myths and opened cosmological channels over which spiritual energy was conducted."[5] In this context it is significant that the word for road in Tewa, a Pueblo language, literally means "channel for the life's breath."[6]

The people of Chaco also built a series of signal towers for communication via mirrors of pyrite or mica during the day and torches at night. In addition, horseshoe-shaped masonry shrines called *herraduras*, usually open to the east, have been found along the route. These have been compared to the lights along an airport runway. (We are talking here about beacons of spiritual offerings, not runways for ET spacecraft, though proponents of the Ancient Aliens theory will probably draw the latter conclusion.)

So what's the big deal about a north-south line? For an agrarian culture such as the Pueblo people, the concept of this straight alignment must have been an abstraction with awe-inspiring spiritual implications. North is the direction of immutable circumpolar stars sweeping around the celestial axis, the Milky Way's ghost road extending beyond this life. South, on the other hand, is the way the sun god journeys in winter.

The summer and winter solstice points on the eastern and western horizons –the four spots forming an X– were related to the mundane agricultural calendar of life arising from the earth plane. The north-south highway would conversely lead to the timeless realm that spirits inhabit after death.

In the cosmology of the ancient Pueblo people, north is the direction of both the afterlife and the underworld. This subterranean, fourfold womb of the Earth Mother and the Corn Mother called the *Shipap* (similar to the Hopi Sipàapuni at the bottom of Grand Canyon) was also the place of emergence where the ancestors ascended from the previous world or era to the current one.

Chaco Canyon was the sacred Middle Place, to which newborns migrated and from which souls returned after their bodies' death via ceremonial roadways to the spirit world. The "heart" of the cosmos was an *axis mundi*, a convergence-point of the four cardinal directions. This vertical axis was located at the midpoint between the nadir and the zenith. The former was, in fact, represented on Earth by the direction of north, whereas the latter by the south.

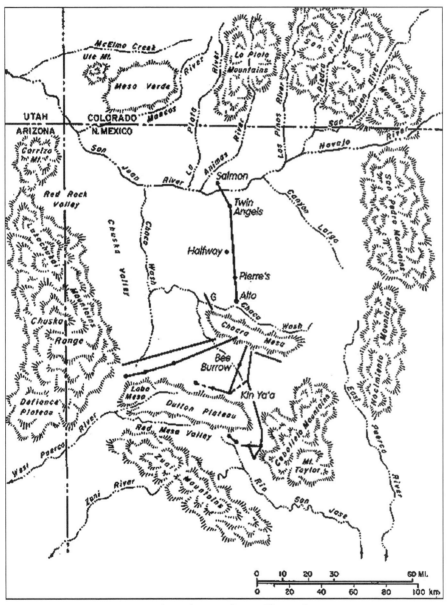

Major roads radiating from Chaco Canyon.

Stars revolving around the Pole Star above a great kiva in Pueblo Bonito.

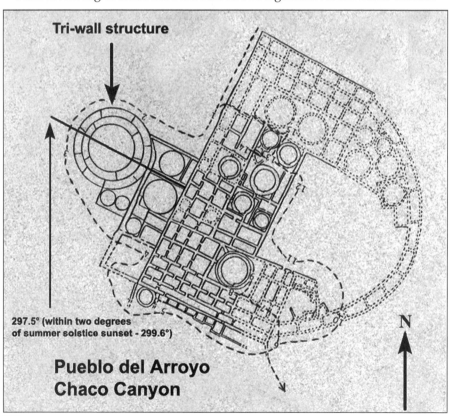

Tri-wall structure

297.5° (within two degrees
of summer solstice sunset - 299.6°)

**Pueblo del Arroyo
Chaco Canyon**

N

In this cosmology the actual physical location of the nadir is Kutz Canyon, a few miles southeast of Salmon Ruins. In the opposite direction the zenith finds its location at Hosta Butte, 12.5 miles northwest of the Chacoan outlier of Casamero Ruin.

Anna Sofaer comments on the "cosmographic expression" of Chaco Canyon as it relates to the surrounding area:

"In the ceremonial architecture and astronomy of the Chaco culture the north-south axis is primary. Most of the great kivas have approximate north-south axes and the kivas generally have niches primarily located to the north. The axes of two major ceremonial structures of Chaco Canyon, Pueblo Bonito and the great kiva, Casa Rinconada, are within 1/4 degree of north. A bearing within 1/2 degree of north-south has been noted between two high ceremonial structures which are intervisible –Pueblo Alto and Tsin Kletzin– the former of which is itself aligned to the cardinals."[7]

This mysterious meridian combined with the effect of colossal Chacoan architecture and exotic trade goods were the means by which an exclusive group of despots could project sociopolitical power over their subjects, who, like the serfs in the medieval feudal system, provided the royalty with tributes of food and craft items. Come to think of it, the period when all this was taking place generally coincides with the European Middle Ages.

How, specifically, did these ancient people achieve an exact north-south line? One method, a nocturnal one, might have gone something like this: Light a signal fire on a clear night while a second person maintains it. Then walk backward with eyes fixed on Polaris, constantly aligning the fire with the North Star as you proceed southward. Drive stakes or poles into the ground at regular intervals to mark your path. Walk until you can barely see the fire. Then start a second bonfire at your spot, which signals the first fire tender to join you.

More competent than I in such matters, William H. Calvin suggests a diurnal method that he calls "leapfrogging gnomons."

Balance a long pole (the gnomon, probably a spruce tree) vertically, stabilizing it with guy-ropes. Follow the tip of the shadow throughout the day to find its shortest length that occurs at local noon, and then stake that point. Secondary method: find the two longest shadow-points of the pole in both the morning and afternoon, stake these points and stretch a rope between the pair of pegs, thereby determining an east-west line. Then bisect the rope and align this center-point with both the gnomon and the noon marker.

Send a second team carrying another gnomon southward as far as line-of sight can be maintained. This team temporarily erects the pole. Back at the first site, stand north of the noon-point and look past both the bisected rope and the gnomon toward the second gnomon in the southern distance. A blanket tied to the top of the first pole together with a halyard-like rope that pulls the "flag" either east or west could signal the second team where to position and affix their pole.

Once the second gnomon is stabilized, the first team bypasses the second one and walks generally southward with another pole—again, to the limits of inter-visibility. Then the process is repeated. The two teams thus leapfrog each other on down the line, which ultimately runs north to south.[8]

One might think that this labor-intensive method would use up too many heavy logs to be practical. It is well documented, however, that over 215,000 huge trees were cut and hauled from between 20 and 50 miles away in order to build the massive structures in Chaco Canyon. The Ancients were apparently accustomed to such arduous tasks. Once the poles were used to determine the meridian, they were perhaps incorporated into the architecture.

Bow-and-Arrow Buildings

I have suggested that the arrow-straight roads leading into Chaco Canyon might have symbolized the shaman's inter-dimensional flight across the landscape of the spirit world. It is probably more than a coincidence, then, that half the large pueblos constructed in the canyon took the architectural form of the bow.

For instance, Pueblo Bonito is the largest of over a dozen masonry structures in Chaco Canyon. Its semicircular "bow" faces northward, while its "string" runs precisely east-west along the southern side. Its south-north axis is, in fact, just .2° east of true north—an accuracy comparable to the geodetic measurements of the Great Pyramid in Egypt. Thus, this edifice is metaphorically shooting its spiritual energy northward along the so-called Chaco Meridian (107° 57' 26.5" W) toward the entrance to the underworld, physically located in Kutz Canyon—the cosmological nadir. (See discussion of the Chaco Meridian below.)

Another example of the bow motif is Pueblo Alto, constructed on the plateau overlooking the north rim of Chaco Canyon. As its Spanish name implies, this 90-room building was specifically located to mark the termination of the Great North Road, which extends nearly 40 miles to the north. The axis of this bow-shaped structure is 1.1° west of true north. The curved portion of the building faces south, so it is symbolically shooting its arrow southward along the Chaco Meridian toward the cosmological zenith point at Hosta Butte about 35 miles away.

Exactly 2.3 miles due south of Pueblo Alto on a mesa top south of the canyon is Tsin Kletsin. The axis of this pueblo, which also had about 90 rooms and three kivas, was only 1° west of true north. So, it too is shooting an arrow southward toward this same butte and the nearby Kin Ya'a Ruin with its four-story tower kiva. The Navajo name Kin Ya'a, by the way, means "House in the Sky."

The north-south axis between Pueblo Alto and Tsin Kletsin bisects the line running west to east between the two largest pueblos in Chaco Canyon: Bonito and Chetro Ketl. The latter is possibly a bow-shaped structure, although it is not oriented along the cardinal directions.

Another bow-shaped structure whose curve faces roughly south is Hungo Pavi. The name of this Great House is the only one that could be considered Uto-Aztecan—the others are either Spanish or Navajo. The phrase Hungo Pavi may be related to the Hopi word *hongap*, meaning "arrow material."[9] This 150-room pueblo lies nearly two miles southeast of Bonito. Its north-south axis was oriented 4.8° east of true north.

Pueblo del Arroyo, located about 400 yards west of Bonito, contained about 285 rooms. It is also bow-shaped, although its curve is facing southeast toward, according to Anna Sofaer, what is called a minor lunar standstill. Major and minor lunar standstills are part of an 18.6-year cycle in which the moon rises and sets a certain number of degrees north or south of both the summer and winter solstice sunrise and sunset points on the horizon. The specific number of degrees depends on the latitude of a given place. (See floor plan on p. 170. This diagram, however, shows a near-summer solstice sunset line.)

Sofaer has determined that most of the structures in Chaco Canyon are, in fact, astronomically aligned.

"Twelve of the fourteen major Chacoan buildings are oriented to midpoints and extremes of the solar and lunar cycles. The eleven rectangular buildings have internal geometry that corresponds with the relationship of the solar and lunar cycles. Most of the major buildings also appear to be organized in a solar-and-lunar regional pattern that is symmetrically ordered about Chaco Canyon's central complex of large ceremonial buildings. These findings suggest a cosmological purpose motivating and directing the construction and the orientation, internal geometry, and interrelationships of the primary Chacoan architecture."[10]

A cadre of astronomer-priests most certainly collaborated with the architects of the Great Houses in order to accomplish such celestial and geometrical precision.

Why did the urban planners of Chaco choose the bow or the D-shape for many of their buildings? The structures, especially those with a north and south axis, may have symbolized the shaman's arrow-straight flight either to the underworld or the sky world. The extensive road system that ran parallel to or even directly coincided with some segments of the Chaco Meridian may have served as a terrestrial map for these cosmic aviators.

The bellicose Hopi Bow Clan once lived at Aztec Ruins in

northern New Mexico. The Hopi call this ancestral site *Hoo'ovi,* or literally "arrow-up place."[11] The *Hisatsinom* of Chaco Canyon called on this particular clan to journey southward in order to institute the great Salako (Shalako) ceremony in the canyon, now also performed at Zuni Pueblo in western New Mexico. Their specific ritual expertise was apparently needed toward the beginning of the 12th century. This was shortly before Chaco was abandoned, partly due to the 50-year drought between 1130 AD and 1180 AD. Perhaps these shamanic elites were summoned to walk southward down the main road to Chaco in a desperate attempt to stave off the inevitable.

But even the common person with no psychic flight training could appreciate this longitudinal excess. Standing rooted upon the earth-axis (the Chaco Meridian) and looking either north (toward the nadir) or south (toward the zenith), one could certainly feel the cosmographic power of the sun at noon as it achieved its own meridian passage from east to west. And for the Ancients, the sun was so much more than a burning ball of gas. It was in fact a primary deity that assisted in the cosmogony. The Hopi, for instance, believe that Taawa (the Sun) is himself the Creator. Other Pueblo groups have similar mythical traditions. Again, Ms. Sofaer comments:

"The arrow, and the bow-and-arrow, are associated with the sun in the cosmology of the historic Pueblo peoples, who are descendants of the Chacoan people. In certain Pueblo traditions the arrow is seen as a vertical axis and as relating the nadir and the zenith... or the world below and above. In a version of the Zuni creation story, the Sun-Father gives his sons bows and arrows and directs them to lift, with an arrow, the Sky-Father to the zenith. In other versions, the sun directs his sons to use their bows and arrows to open the way to the world below for the Pueblo people to emerge to the earth's surface and to the sun's light. At the solstices, the Pueblo people give offerings of miniature bows and arrows to the sun. The sun is depicted by Pueblo groups as carrying a bow and arrow."[12]

About 33 feet west of the Sun Dagger on Fajada Butte (mentioned at the beginning of this chapter) is a bow-and-arrow-shaped petroglyph carved on a vertical wall. Above it is a spiral petroglyph; the two together measure about 9.5 inches by 14 inches. The bow exactly mirrors the groundplan of Pueblo Bonito, with the arrow corresponding to the north-south wall. However, the nock is not affixed to the bowstring (the southern east-to-west wall), so the arrowhead is consequently pointed toward the south.[13] (See p. 178.)

The petroglyph-pueblo relationship remains a mystery. Does the spiral symbolize the sun, a whirlpool, or a portal? What lies in the ground beneath its center? The park's asphalt road has paved over the answers, probably forever.

Big Shots In the Great House

The first three Great Houses constructed in Chaco Canyon were Peñasco Blanco at the western end, the initial sections of Pueblo Bonito in the middle, and Una Vida at the eastern end. According to a 1996 dendrochronology (tree-ring dating) study called the Chaco Wood Project, these were begun between about 850 and 865 AD.[14] Pithouse villages had been located earlier in the vicinity; for instance, Shabik'eschee, circa 550 – 700 AD, contained 70 pit houses and a Great Kiva.[15] However, this pueblo-triad was the first major construction projects in the canyon.

Many archaeologists consider Pueblo Bonito to have been the sociopolitical and ceremonial center of Chaco Canyon. Room 33 in the northern section of the pueblo may have been the mortuary crypt where the rulers or even the founders of the complex were interred. (Was the man who assigned the numbering system for Pueblo Bonito perhaps a Freemason, or was this merely a coincidence?) The largess of artifacts recovered from this single, tiny room is staggering. Archaeologists Stephen Plog and Carrie Heiten generally describe the finds:

"Room 33 held the remains of at least 14 individuals and the richest assemblage of artifacts ever uncovered in the Pueblo Southwest, although it is one of the smallest rooms in the pueblo with dimension of ~2 × 2 m. More than 30,000 objects were recorded and cataloged from this small room. Most (>95%) of these objects were beads, pendants, or other items made from minerals such as turquoise and jet or shell. More turquoise, at least 25,000 pieces, was recovered from this one small room than from all other prehistoric sites in the entire Southwest combined."[16]

(A specifiic description of the artifacts found in Room 33, including the hoard of turquoise, is given in the next section.) The room may have been among the first built at Pueblo Bonito. It was located at the center of the initial arc of rooms that opened to the southeast. Additional rooms were later added onto this curve in order to develop the true bow shape that opened due south. A lintel between Room 32 and 33 was tree-ring dated to 852 AD, but the outer growth rings are missing, so the construction date might have been even earlier. In fact, AMS (accelerator mass spectrometer) median dates for two burials are 821 AD and 817 AD.[17]

The restricted access of Room 33 may indicate that it was used as a sacred precinct where the elites practiced an ancestor cult. This hierarchy was apparently established very early in Chaco Canyon history and was sustained for over two-and-a-half centuries. Once again, Plog and Heitien:

"In most hierarchically organized groups, elites constitute only a small proportion of the population. In Chaco, nonelites, even if they resided in the larger great houses, may have been interred in the abundant cemeteries associated with the small-house settlements. Only those with the highest social ranking may have been interred in great houses, where powerful and unusual objects and materials such as turquoise, cacao, cylinder vessels, and macaws were much more abundant and some of the most significant burial crypts served as microcosms of the Chacoan world."[18]

Left: Petroglyph
of spiral and
bow-and-arrow
atop Fajada Butte.

Below: The spiral
begins where the
park's asphalt
road now is, so
we probably will
never know what,
if anything, lies
beneath.

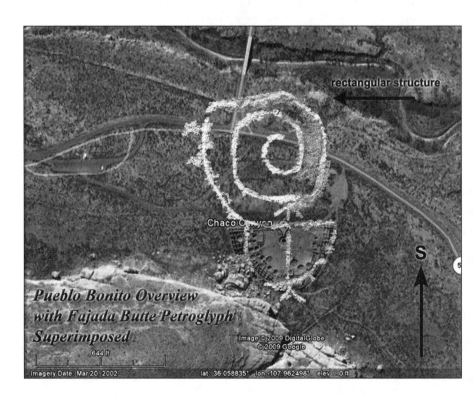

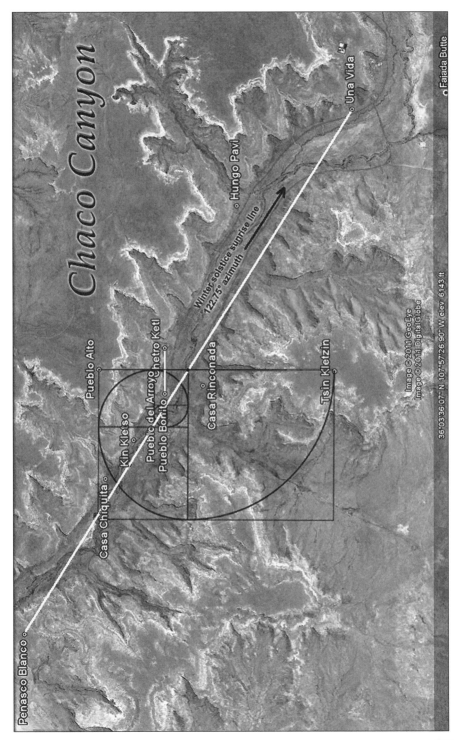

The 4-inch hole that had been cut in the wooden floor of the eastern portion of Room 33 may have functioned in a manner similar to a *sipapu*, or the symbolic tunnel to the underworld found in every kiva. Significant caches of artifacts were found at each of the four corner posts, which suggest that the small room may have functioned as an *imago mundi*, where the powers of the cosmos were concentrated in the four ordinal directions (northwest, southwest, southeast, and northeast). This quaternary pattern may have focused the ancestors' spirits at the quincunx of the room's center, thus designating the absolute heart of Chaco Canyon.

Begun at about the same time as Pueblo Bonito (circa mid-9th century AD), Peñasco Blanco to the northwest may have functioned as the astronomical observatory for the canyon. The well-known pictograph (rock painting) reputed to represent the 1054 AD supernova is located on the cliffside north of the oval-shaped Great House, which contained 215 rooms. The impressive view southeast down the canyon is unobstructed, providing a perfect observation post for ancient sky watchers. The elevations of both this pueblo and Una Vida, another Great House of 160 rooms located six miles to the southeast, are over 6,200 feet (6,280 feet and 6,250 feet respectively), so intervisibility would have been possible. (The elevation of Room 33 of Pueblo Bonito is somewhat lower at only 6138 feet.)

The axis of the canyon that runs between these two great houses is basically a winter solstice sunrise line. The Hopi, whose ancestors most likely resided in Chaco at some point, consider this period of the agricultural calendar to be the most ritually significant. The actual line between the two pueblos is 122.75° azimuth, whereas the winter solstice sun rises at 119.6° azimuth. This three-degree discrepancy may be the result of the actual position of the sun-watching station, which may have been slightly different than the location of Peñasco Blanco.

Particularly striking in this Chaco Canyon schema is the fact that a north-south line between Pueblo Alto and Tzin Kletzin exactly bisects this winter solstice line. As previously mentioned, the former line extends for 2.3 miles, and is less than a half-degree from a true north heading. The point at which it intersects the winter solstice line is precisely three miles from both Peñasco Blanco to the northwest and Una Vida to the southeast. Not only that, the ratio of the distance between Pueblo Alto-Tsin Kletzin (2.3 miles) and the distance between Tsin Kletzin and the point at which it intersects the northwest/southeast winter solstice line (1.42 miles) happens to be the Fibonacci number of 1.618. (See Golden Mean Spiral overlaid on satellite image on p. 179.)

Even more astounding is the fact that Pueblo Alto, a Great House located at the terminus of the north-south road, was constructed in the mid-11th century, whereas Tsin Kletsin, a Great House located on South Mesa, was constructed at the beginning of the 12th century. If all these relationships between locations are the result of something other than a series of mere coincidences, this means that the specific loci for the schema must have been determined long before these two pueblos were built, since the winter solstice line was established in the mid-9th century.

In addition, the north-south line almost exactly bisects the west-to-east line between Pueblo Bonito and Chetro Ketl, a 580-room Great House constructed in the mid-10th century. Also, Pueblo del Arroyo, which lies a quarter-mile west of Pueblo Bonito, is bisected by the winter solstice line.

The Big Shots surely had a big plan, a comprehensive pattern that encompassed the whole canyon. Even before they were constructed, the pueblos' geodetic relationships were predetermined. Not only was the architecture of the individual structures considered, but also the architectonics of the gestalt formed the theocratic oligarchy's monumental expression of its power.

Turquoise Town

Considering Chaco Canyon's solar emphasis as well as its multiple architectural alignments with solstice and equinox points on the horizon, one would think that gold would be king. But as far as I know, no golden artifacts, gold nuggets, or even gold flecks have ever been found at Chaco, despite the substantial deposits of the mineral in New Mexico, Arizona, and south-western Colorado.

On the contrary, Chaco-plex was a big-time turquoise town. The primary reason for this was not native lore but this miner-al's foreign lure down the line—that is, to the south. Archaeologist David R. Wilcox comments on the stone trade.

"Let there be no doubt about the value of turquoise in Mesoamerica; it was valued in both West and Central México as in no other world area. The symbolic penetra-tion of this commodity was almost universal; it stood for the words of priests and kings, as a special-purpose cur-rency available in the great markets and *tianguis* [Nahuatl term for open-air market]; for rain; for fertility in both nature and humanity; and for maize. It was used in elite exchanges as *prestige* [italics added] gifts, in elegant cos-tumes, and in general decoration. It permeated the iconography of the Mesoamerican world as no other min-eral compound or natural substance did, outdoing even jade. Once a flow of it was established as part of the Mesoamerican trade structure, we may suppose that great efforts would have been made to maintain that flow, and even to increase it."[19]

The great amuletic, curative, and religious properties of turquoise rest on its dual symbolism: both blue sky-stone and green earth-stone. As above, so below. Because of its varying shades from blue to green, turquoise was sometimes confused with the jade mined extensively in Guatemala.

The Aztec term for turquoise is *xiuitl* or *chalchihuitl*. The pre-historic Cerrillos mine, located in fact at "Mount Chalchihuitl," had been a huge operation for at least 1,200 years. It was over 130 feet deep, 200 feet wide at the top, and 100 feet wide at the bottom. Tens of thousands of tons of the mineral were extracted with nothing but hornblende and andesite hammerstones that weighed an average of 20 pounds.

Chalchiuhtlicue was the Aztec goddess of sweet (as opposed

to salt) water, whose name literally means "She of the Jade (or Green) Skirt." As mentioned, green jade and blue-green turquoise were often conflated. She especially controlled ground water, such as lakes, rivers, streams, cenotes, and lagoons. In this aspect, she was associated with serpents. Chalchiuhtlicue was sister or sometimes wife of the rain god Tlaloc and served as patroness of childbirth. She is sometimes depicted as wearing a turquoise nose plug.

The Hopi correlative goddess was named Huru'ing wùuhti, or "Hard Objects Woman," which refers to blue turquoise (southwest), red coral (southeast) and white shells (northeast.) Her house was in the northwest (yellow), the place where she welcomes the sun god Taawa while he rests at the summer solstice sunset for four successive days.[20]

Chaco Canyon was a vast repository of turquoise mined all over the Southwest, but especially in New Mexico. The Center Place became, in fact, the central clearinghouse for the coveted mineral. Witness this inventory of the turquoise cache interred at Pueblo Bonito that was found during the Hyde Expedition of 1897–99. Geologist Stuart Northrop summarizes the contents of Room 33.

"...[G. H.] Pepper described the contents of a small burial room about 6 ft. square, which, among many other items, included the amazing total of 24,932 turquoise beads and more than 700 turquoise pendants. One skeleton, for example, had associated with it a total of 5,891 beads and several pendants of turquoise, the largest pendant being 45 mm. long. A still more gorgeously arrayed skeleton had 8,385 beads and more than 500 pendants; these had originally been worn as wristlets, anklets, and ornaments over the breast and abdomen; on the left wrist alone were found 2,388 beads and 194 small pendants. Near the skeleton was a remarkable cylindrical basket 6 in. high and 3 in. in diameter, onto which had been cemented a mosaic of 1,214 pieces of turquoise. Inside the basket were found 2,150 beads, 152 small pendants, and 22 large pendants, the largest of which measured 36 by 27 by 3 mm. Pepper concluded that Cerrillos was the chief source of this turquoise, that the burials represented persons of considerable rank, and that at this time the Chaco people were at the height of their esthetic arts."[21]

In modern times the Navajo (Diné) are famous around the world for their turquoise and silver jewelry. This exquisite craft-work more or less epitomizes the Southwest. Archaeologists believe –and it is just an educated guess– that the Navajo migrated from the north into the Four Corners region about 1500 AD. However, it is curious that this tribe possesses legends regarding Chaco Canyon, which was abandoned almost four centuries before this tribe supposedly came into the area.

Navajo stories talk about settling near a pueblo called Kinteel (Kîntyél), or Broad House, which, they say, was in the process of being built but not yet finished. One source identifies this as Chetro Ketl, completed in 1054 AD, which was, coincidentally, the same year as the massive supernova explosion depicted in previously mentioned pictographs at the western end of Chaco Canyon. "Some time before, there had descended among the Pueblos, from the heavens, a divine gambler, or gambling-god, named Nohoílpi, or he Who Wins Men (at play); his talisman was a great piece of turquoise."[22]

This Gambler challenged the men at Chaco Canyon to various games and contests, in which they wagered their property, their wives, their children, and even themselves as slaves. Then the Gambler said that he would give them back everything if they would build him a palace, so the people of Chaco began to do his bidding in hopes of regaining their former lives. That's when the Navajo tribe showed up.

One young Navajo man was selected and prepared by the gods to confront the Gambler and beat him at his own game. With supernatural assistance the Navajo eventually triumphed. Finally, with a "Bow of Darkness" he shot the Gambler (i.e. the Big Shot) into the sky like an arrow. Some accounts have him being aerially projected due south into Mexico.[23]

Other versions even claim that the Gambler was himself Hispanic, who, while sojourning in the sky world, received a new kind of wealth: horses, sheep, pigs, goats, and chickens. He later would return to earth with these, thereby dominating the American Southwest.[24]

Although translating myth into history has its problems, we nevertheless see a possible Mexican connection to Chaco Canyon as well as the dual motifs of: bow-and-arrow (the Gambler's quick exit from Chaco south into the heavens) and turquoise (his talisman). The Gambler's legacy can be seen today in the Fire Rock Casino recently built near Church Rock, a few miles east of Gallup, New Mexico.[25]

The Navajo conceptualize turquoise as a piece of the sky fallen to earth, similar to the Gambler with his chunk of magical turquoise falling into Chaco Canyon. If a blue stone is thrown into the river, they believe it will produce rainfall. New Age advocates claim that the protective qualities of turquoise foster spiritual cleansing, prosperity, success, and good fortune.[26]

A Longing for Longitude

Arizona professor James Q. Jacobs discovered what he called the Chaco Meridian in 1990. He noticed that a number of significant archaeological sites were aligned to roughly the 107th degree of west longitude. The Big Horn Medicine Wheel in north-central Wyoming on the western slope of the Bighorn Mountains, for instance, just happens to be located on the same meridian as two large stone pueblos built from the 12th to the 13th centuries AD by the Hitsatsinom (formerly called the "Anasazi"). The sites are known as Aztec Ruins and Salmon Ruins in northern New Mexico. These are in line with the massive ceremonial metro-center in Chaco Canyon that began construction in the mid-9th century. Jacobs later extended the line southward to include the adobe pueblo of Paquimé (also called Casas Grandes, see Chapter 9) in Chihuahua, Mexico, built from the 13th through the 15th centuries.[27]

Stephen Lekson, apparently unaware of Jacobs' geodetic findings, published a book in 1999 titled *The Chaco Meridian: Centers of Political Power in the Ancient Southwest*. His hypothesis envisions an oligarchy of high status elites centered in Chaco Canyon who exerted theocratic authority over an extensive territory up and down the longitude line. He believed this "political-prestige economy" eclipsed or even subsumed the local subsistence economy by facilitating imports from the south.

These trade items included macaw feathers or even whole birds. In a field where the descriptive language tends to be bone-dry, the maverick Lekson observes: "When macaws reached the northern Southwest, they were hotter than Hula Hoops. Pueblo histories... suggest that the political structure of the Great Southwest was a case of macaws and effects."[28] (Archaeology doesn't need to be dull. Any archaeologist who uses such word-play and quotes Ezra Pound's *Cantos* to boot, as Lekson does, is okay in my book. And it is my book, to steal another of Lekson's quips.) Other "exotic goodies" included parrots, copper bells, and abalone or olivella shells.

The major commodity heading south would have been turquoise, mined mostly either in the vicinity of the present town of Cerrillos south of Santa Fe or from the equally rich mines at Old Hatchita and Azure in southwestern New Mexico, a few miles west of the Chaco Meridian.

Most evidence points to an influx of goods into Chaco Canyon rather than a redistribution to the outlying areas—except for the exports south along the Meridian to Mexico. This reinforces the totalitarian model of political control over the local population. For reasons unknown, the *hoi polloi* who lived in smaller communities outside "downtown Chaco," as Lekson puts it, periodically journeyed to the Center Place. Like Emerald City, the monumental architecture of this "Turquoise City" was meant to awe the rubes from Kansas or similar backwaters. Unlike the modesty of previous *Hisatsinom* buildings, the style was rigid, geometric, formal, and even severe—a grand statement in stone.

The commoners may have brought craft items such as pottery, woven textiles, and other sundry wares as well as surplus food into the urban center in order to trade for the overwhelming spiritual powers that the elites possessed. This possibly allowed the former to take part in sacred healing rituals or seasonal religious rites. If so, the Meridian Mystique was partly responsible for this relationship. Lekson remarks on the path to power.

> "The people supported the Lords of the Great House through levies and taxes; the Lords did not work. A proto-bureaucracy of administrators and officials took care of business. Leaders were buried in elaborate crypts in the oldest part of the oldest building, with rich offerings and, possibly, their retainers. Buildings and built environments were the principal expression of power: Great Houses, ritual landscape, regional sight-lines, earth-monuments (now called roads) and astronomical alignments that were rapidly evolving toward regional geomancy."[29]

As the influence of Chaco (circa 850 – 1125 AD) gradually waned in the 12th century, the "Chaco hegemony," as Lekson calls it, eventually shifted to other sites—first to Aztec (1110 – 1275 AD) in the north and then to Paquimé (circa 1250 – 1450 AD) in the south. (See Chapter 9.) He tentatively includes another site along the meridian called Culiacán, located nearly 400 miles south of Paquimé. (See Chapter 10.) This gradual development along the Meridian, however, was not an unconscious evolution; it was instead a deliberate, politically calculated shift of power across distance and through time. As the decades passed, the memory of Chaco became increasingly talismanic—the sacred place due north where the ancestors once lived.

Dog Town

> "For all the toll the desert takes of a man it gives compensation, deep breaths, deep sleep, and the communion of the stars. It comes upon one with new force in the

pauses of the night that the Chaldeans were a desert-bred people. It is hard to escape the sense of mastery as the stars move in the wide clear heaven to risings and settings unobscured. They look large and near and palpitant; as if they moved on some stately service not needful to declare. Wheeling to their stations in the sky, they make the poor world-fret of no account. Of no account you who lie out there watching, nor the lean coyote that stands off in the scrub from you and howls and howls."[30]

My previous books put forth the notion that *Mositsinom*, or the First People, constructed a pattern of villages in the American Southwest that mirrors the heavens. In particular, the three Hopi Mesas correspond to the belt stars of Orion, and Sirius, what we call the Dog Star, corresponds to Chaco Canyon. (See the map on p. 15.) Thus, the largest ruin-complex in the region reflects the brightest star in the sky.

I furthermore posited that a group called the Chichimecs, or "Sons of the Dog," inhabited Chaco and was the driving force behind the construction of the monumental architecture. The symbol of this group was the bow, and they were indeed a tribe of semi-nomadic hunter-gatherers. However, they finally settled into these pueblos, which they coerced the ancestral Hopi, Zuni, Laguna, Acoma, etc. to build for them. As a pre-Aztec people, the barbaric Chichimecs eventually migrated into the valley of Mexico, where they became a major power.

The word *Chichiman* means not only "Place of the Dog" but also "Place of Milk."[31] Some say this refers to the milky substance of the maguey cactus. However, it is interesting to note that the Hopi word for Sirius, the Dog Star, is *Ponotsona*, which literally means "belly sucker," or "one who sucks milk from the stomach," i.e. a mammal. Frank Waters states: "This is the star that controls the life of all beings in the animal kingdom."[32]

In ancestral Puebloan cultures, canines, which include coyotes, wolves, wild dogs, and foxes are associated with witchcraft and even cannibalism. The Hopi word *powaqa* means "sorcerer, wizard; member of a society believed to operate from Panlangw or Hopqöyvi."[33] Palangw refers to "a place near Chinle [a village in eastern Arizona, near the mouth of Canyon de Chelly][34], and Hopqöyvi is "a mythical place in the northeast where marvelous building was accomplished by *powaqam*, 'sorcerers'."[35] That place is, of course, Chaco Canyon. Homophonically related to the term *powaqa* is the prefix *pok-* or *poko-*, which means both "dog/possessed animal" and "shoot-arrow."[36]

In her powerful novel titled *Ceremony*, Leslie Marmon Silko from Laguna Pueblo describes in free verse a "witches' conference":

"Way up in the lava rock hills / north of Cañoncito / they got together / to fool around in caves / with their animal skins. / Fox, badger, bobcat, and wolf / they circled the fire / and on the fourth time / they jumped into that animal skin.... / Then some of them lifted the lids / on their big cooking pots / calling the rest of them over / to take a look: / dead babies simmering in blood / circles of skull cut away / all the brains sucked out. / Witch medicine / to dry and grind into powder / for new victims."

Silko even claims that the coming of the White Man was the result of sorcery:

"The wind will blow them across the ocean / thousands of them in giant boats / swarming like larva / out of a crushed ant hill. // They will carry objects / which can shoot death / faster than the eye can see. // They will kill the things they fear / all the animals / the people will starve. // They will poison the water / they will spin the water away / and there will be drought / the people will starve."[37]

In the late 1990s a controversial theory of "Anasazi" cannibalism was introduced by Arizona State University professor Christy G. Turner II and his late wife Jacqueline A. Turner in their book *Man Corn*, the title of which is derived from the meaning of the Aztec word *tlacatlaolli*. The term means "sacred meal of sacrificed human meat, cooked with corn."[38] The authors present extensive forensic and archaeological evidence that human bones found in Chaco and elsewhere in the region showed signs consistent with food preparation. (This material is covered in my previous book *The Kivas of Heaven*.) However, archaeologist George H. Pepper back in 1920 had provided preliminary evidence of cannibalism at Chaco Canyon.

> "During the period of our work in Pueblo Bonito some of our Navajo workmen cleaned out a number of rooms in Penasco Blanco and in one of these a great many human bones were found. Some of these, including portions of the skull, were charred, and the majority of long bones had been cracked open and presented the same appearance as do the animal bones that have been treated in a similar way for extraction of the marrow. It would therefore seem that these Pueblo Indians, either through stress of hunger or religious reasons, had occasionally resorted to the eating of human flesh."

Also, he suggests that other evidence in Pueblo Bonito points to the same practice. "The finding of cracked and calcined human bones in some of the rooms brings up the question of the eating of human flesh by the people of this pueblo."[39] Lekson additionally remarks that the Navajo were looking for turquoise and found a sizable cache among the more grisly objects at Peñasco Blanco. He also states that in 1890 F. T. Bickford noticed the presence of human skull fragments in this pueblo as well.[40]

At the other end of the canyon, Una Vida was known by the Navajo names of "witchcraft woman's home" or "house of a woman who makes you thin by starving you." This latter name "...relates to a common local legend of a witch renowned for her practice of holding human hostages atop nearby Fajada Butte."[41] Thus, we see evidence of both witchcraft and cannibalism at the the early pueblos: Peñasco Blanco at the northwest, Pueblo Bonito in the middle, and Una Vida to the southeast.

About 1,575 yards south of Una Vida and just over 75 yards northeast of Fajada Butte is a site known as Chaco 1360. It had 18 masonry surface rooms, a number of pit houses, five kivas, and a trash mound. In one pit house constructed in the early 800s, the skeletal remains of six humans and two dogs were found.

Oval-shaped Peñasco Blanco, constructed in the mid-9th century AD, with kivas and possible ancient road (seen above).

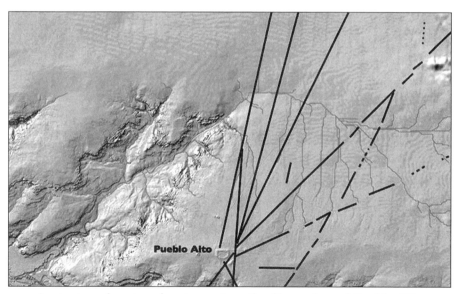

Ancient road system fanning out north of bow-shaped Pueblo Alto, located on the plateau .6 miles from the northern rim of the canyon.

Turner speculates that one was an adult male, 35 to 40 years old, with a slight frame, suggesting he was not used to hard physical labor—someone like either a shaman-priest or one who was chronically ill. An adult female was also found lying on a twilled mat with a long beaded necklace and two arrow points in her torso, as well as a wound in her elbow caused by a wooden spear or dagger. Skeletons of a two-year-old and an infant were also found. In addition, the skulls of a one-year-old, probably with anemia, and an infant were found in a ventilator shaft. Because of the fact that the bodies were not ritually buried and showed signs of carnivore damage, Turner believes the deaths were the result of violence sometime between 920 and 1040 AD.[42]

One of the most interesting aspects of Site 1360 is that it had, in the words of archaeologist Peter J. McKenna, who conducted the initial dig, "...a thriving dog population." It was, in fact, a kennel. The remains of a total of 67 canines were found, both puppies and adults. In its day, this site might have been called Dog House.[43]

An observer at the other end of the canyon, stationed at Peñasco Blanco at about its initial construction date of 860 AD would have gazed toward the eastern horizon in the pre-dawn hours about a month after the solstice to see the heliacal rising of Sirius. Specifically, the Dog Star rose on July 23rd, 860 AD at 4:25 a.m. With the sky gradually brightening, the sun was still 12 degrees below the horizon as the brilliant star rose at azimuth 108°. Less than two centuries later and to the north of Pueblo Bonito, Pueblo Alto would be constructed at 108° azimuth in relation to Peñasco Blanco. Thus, from that latter astronomical watching place the star would appear to rise over Alto, which in Spanish means "tall" or "high." Was this point a little over two-and-a half miles away already fixed at an early date in the mid-9th century? Was Alto constructed at this precise location because it was a rising point of Sirius from the vantage of Blanco? Ancient sky watchers would have certainly hailed the annual summer return of the "belly sucker" to Chaco after its disappearance in the spring.

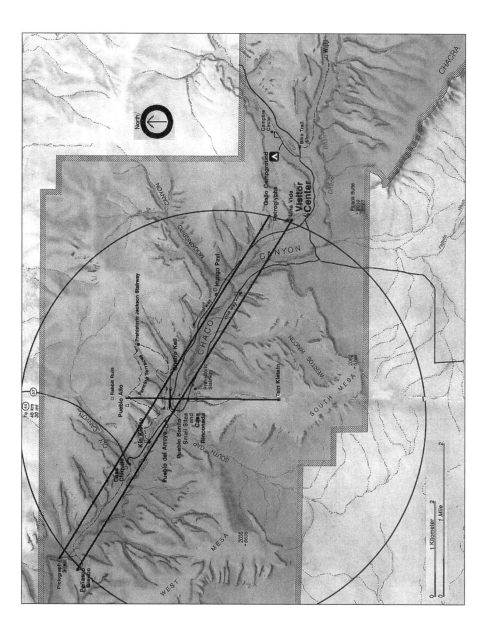

Chapter 8
Mimbres—A Pre-Columbian
Counterculture In New Mexico

Spaced Out In New Mexico

In the late 1960s and early 1970s, New Mexico became a magnet for those seeking an alternative lifestyle. All over this semidesert landscape, exotic varieties of communes sprang up like magic mushrooms after a rainstorm. One typical example of this phenomenon was portrayed in the 1969 classic film *Easy Rider*. It was not, however, the first time an alternative lifestyle occurred among the pinyon and sandstone mesas. One may have already developed a thousand years earlier.

Centuries before the fierce Chiricahua Apache battled or evaded American troops and Pancho Villa fought with the U.S. Cavalry along the Mexican border, an indigenous culture peacefully inhabited southwestern New Mexico. Its members took the art form of painted pottery to a new level. Today we call these people Mimbres, a Spanish word meaning "willows," though we have no idea what they called themselves. They may well have been fleeing the urban decadence of both Chaco Canyon in the northwestern part of the state and, a bit later, Paquimé in Chihuahua, Mexico. (See the next chapter for more on the latter.) These rustic individualists could have caused one of the first back-to-the-land movements in North America.

Their territory started near the 33rd parallel on the headwaters of the Mimbres River, which originates at the Continental Divide. The river flows southward toward the arid Deming

Plain, where it plunges underground and ultimately empties into the Rio Grande drainage system. Rainfall here is precious. For the upper river valley it is a little over 17 inches annually, while for the lower valley it is just about 9 inches. Approximately 15 major villages were located along this basically north-south line.

During the early 11th century AD, these growing villages consisted of aboveground "pueblos"—apartment-like architectural structures characteristic of the American Southwest. The Mattocks Ruin, for instance, consisted of 192 stone-and-adobe rooms distributed among four room blocks arranged around a central plaza. It rested on a terrace above the west bank of the Mimbres River a mile south of the current post office in the eponymous Mimbres community.[1] (See map on the next page.)

Like most Mimbres pueblos, this village was built right on top of what archaeologists call "pit houses"—single-family, isolated dwellings customarily constructed before the 11th century. These earlier semi-subterranean structures were usually rectangular or square. Four large posts set into an adobe floor near the corners supported a gable roof made of smaller branches. This sort of domicile was the norm before the communal craze took hold.

From a historical standpoint, Mimbres culture is divided into three phases: the Early Pithouse period from 200 to 550 AD, the Late Pithouse period from 550 to 1000 AD, and the Classic Mimbres (or Surface Pueblo) period from 1000 to 1130 AD.[2]

Old Town Ruin is located downstream toward the south upon a grassland of mesquite and creosote bush. Although it was extensively excavated, this major pueblo has not yielded much archaeological data because it had also been extensively pot-hunted. The painted pottery –more on this shortly– was so coveted that the looters pillaged most of the primary Mimbres sites, beginning in the late 1800s through the 1970s. Sometimes they even used bulldozers or backhoes, leaving the dwellings pockmarked with unsightly holes as evidence of their greed. The late Southwestern novelist Tony Hillerman called these perpetrators "thieves of time." This wanton destruction has made archaeological research of Mimbres culture difficult or in some cases impossible. Not much is left at many of the ancient villages.

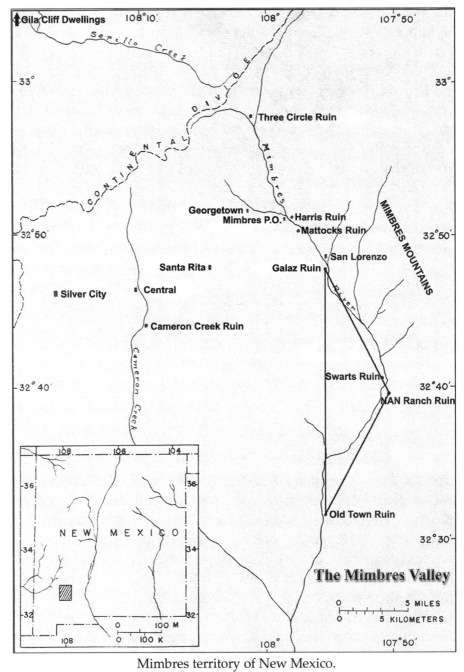

Mimbres territory of New Mexico.
The area within the triangle was the heart of Mimbres culture.

Brothers and Sisters of the Back-to-Nature Guild

Material wealth among various families who lived in the Mimbres pueblos was pretty much the same. Some individuals may have played defined roles in their community, such as astronomer-priests or ceremonial leaders (similar to the social situation at contemporary pueblos), but the general standard of living was basically equal for everyone. Unlike Chaco Canyon, a lack of variation in skeletal remains proves that the diet was similar for all members of the community. The idea of "the haves versus the have-nots" was simply not a factor.

Archaeologist Stephen Lekson describes the general cultural emergence.

"Famous for its pottery, Mimbres was more than just a pretty vase. Sprawling one-story masonry Mimbres settlements were, perhaps, the first real pueblos in the Southwest. Fueled and tethered by large-scale canal irrigation systems, Mimbres villages were truly permanent-sedentary over many generations—and grew to remarkable size. The largest Mimbres village sites had up to 500 rooms and –unlike Pueblo Bonito and other Great Houses [in Chaco Canyon]– most of those rooms were habitations. To cope with high densities and deep sedentism, Mimbres developed the earliest forms of kachina ceremonialism. These were remarkable achievements, but the florescence did not extend to architecture. Masonry and layouts were irregular and informal, compared with Four Corners ruins and, regrettably, compared with Chaco. Rough river cobble walls were the norm, and we search in vain for a right angle at Mimbres buildings."[3]

Like nature, the Mimbres seem to have abhorred straight lines. Their architecture was nonetheless a first step in the grandiose style of the pueblos that began to rise all over the Southwest, beginning in the early 900s. This was an initial development but certainly not a paramount example. For the Mimbres people, buildings were designed for comfort and convenience, not style and statement. Unlike Chaco, nothing about them was monumental.

As Lekson suggests (with one of his characteristic bad puns), the Mimbres' painting of pottery rather than the making of it was their cultural signature. The technical skill in actually forming the mostly hemispherical bowls was not anything special. On the other hand, the exquisite iconography painted in black on the ceramics was a cultural epitome. The Mimbres are known today as the prehistoric "painters" of the Southwest; their canvas was clay.

Jesse Walter Fewkes, renowned early 20th century archaeologist and ethnologist of the Southwest, comments on their high artistic merit. "In the author's judgment no Southwestern pottery, ancient or modern, surpasses that of the Mimbres, and its naturalistic figures are unexcelled in any pottery from prehistoric North America. This superiority lies in figures of men and animals, but it is also facile princeps in geometric design. Since the author's discovery of the main features of this pottery, the Mimbres Valley has come to be recognized as a special ceramic area."[4]

J. J. Brody, a contemporary expert on Mimbres pottery, sums up the achievement: "The hallmarks of Mimbres Black-on-white [pottery] are complex nonfigurative, representational, or narrative paintings, often made with an elegant line and powerful and dynamic masses and always placed within framed picture spaces. The contrast between indifferent pottery and fine painting argues that a distinction should be made between the two, for only the latter is at all remarkable."[5]

The artwork consists of some abstract or geometric forms painted in black or brown with yucca brushes on a white or cream-colored slip. Usually the exterior was left undecorated, while fine rim lines on the bowl defined the interior visual space. The composition was extremely diverse and aesthetically complex: fine parallel lines, parallel wavy lines, spirals, interlocking scrolls or frets, cross-hatching, diamonds, rhomboids, checkerboards (usually inside bird, animal, or human figures).

Naturalistic designs include a veritable menagerie. Mammals

such as deer, rabbits, antelope, bighorn sheep, bears, mountain lions, wolves, dogs, coatis, and bats were painted. Avian examples range from macaws or parrots to cranes, turkeys, eagles, and quails. Among representations of reptiles and amphibians are turtles, frogs, horned toads, lizards, snakes, and tadpoles. A variety of insects were also depicted, including grasshoppers, locusts, spiders, dragonflies, and moths or butterflies.

Fish make up a surprisingly high percentage of the total pottery imagery—about 10 to 15%. Many of these painted fish are very large when compared with human images depicted on the same bowl. This may have been just a visual representation of a "big fish" story, or it could be evidence that the Mimbres traveled regularly to the Gulf of California, where larger ocean fish abound. Given the great quantities of marine shells found at Mimbres villages, the latter is probably the case. In addition, ichthyological portrayals include both fresh-water and salt-water species.[6] The shortest distance between Mimbres, New Mexico, and the Gulf is about 325 miles, near the modern town of Puerto Peñasco, Sonora. Whatever the actual route was, however, it was certainly not straight and thus considerably longer.

Mimbres artists frequently displayed human figures in profile by painting solid black bodies, plain arms and legs, simple noses and mouths, and diamond-shaped eyes with a dot for the pupil. These delineations sometimes depicted events from daily life (what Brody calls "narrative"), including hunting scenes, dancing scenes, ceremonial scenes, childbirth scenes, and even a few pornographic scenes. In essence, Mimbres pottery design was both utterly unique and universally expressive, speaking directly to our humanity across nearly nine centuries.

Although naturalistic themes were superbly rendered, supernatural elements were also present. Mythical creatures such as the plumed or horned serpent are seen. In addition, therianthropes (part-human and part-animal) suggest a deep shamanic tradition. Fewkes deems these "problematical animals." In some cases the chimeras depicted are so bizarre that they rival anything Hieronymus Bosch or Salvador Dali ever painted. We have to wonder what these pot makers were smoking.

Right: Mimbres black-on-white pottery bowl, two bighorn sheep, therianthrope, and human head.

Left: two crosses may represent stars. Geometric designs may represent the entoptic imagery experienced in the initial stages of a psychedelic event. (See discussion of mind-altering substances below.) Both bowls: Dallas Museum of Art.

Men with fishing lines in mouth of human-fish hybrid.
(This somewhat resembles Peter Benchley's *Creature*.)

Two human figures, Dallas Museum of Art.

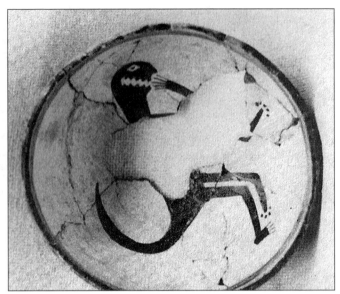

Above: Dinosaur-like creature with feline left foot and right hand.
(The bowl is damaged.)
Below: "Bird-man" holding fish.

Above: Figure with an enormous phallus supported by three smaller men.
He holds two curved sticks (boomerangs?) and has spiked hair or a punk headdress.

Below: Ritual copulation scene. The figures carry staves or curved sticks.

As stated above, the Classic Mimbres Phase ranged from 1000 AD through about 1130 AD. The culture's demise almost exactly coincides with the abandonment of Chaco Canyon. Author Rose Houck describes the dynamics of the Mimbres' strategic location before the culture began to wane in the first part of the 12th century.

> "The changes among the Mimbres coincided with major changes at Chaco Canyon, an important Anasazi center 225 miles north of the Mimbres core. Chacoans were involved in a vast trade network, part of it with Mexico. Turquoise was heading south, and copper bells and macaw feathers were being carried north. The Mimbres Valley was a likely stop along this well-worn route, and the Mimbres may have acted as middlemen in the Chaco-Mexican connection, perhaps housing and feeding the bearers in return for some of the goods being transported."[7]

One Mimbres pueblo named Galaz contained the burials of 11 macaws or parrots. These non-indigenous birds, of course, inhabit the jungles of southern Mexico over 1,000 miles away. This points to an extensive trade network with the south. At the same pueblo archaeologists found greenstone, or jadeite, which also originates from Mesoamerica. Galaz along with Old Town even kept live macaws imported from Mexico.

Old Town may have been the first major stopping point on a Paquimé-to-Mimbres-to-Chaco Canyon trade route. In addition, Galaz and Old Town are located on an exact north-south line with a longitude of 107°55'15" —2.3 miles east of what Lekson has called the "Chaco Meridian." This, he believes, is a series of villages intentionally positioned along a longitude line that stretches north to south from Aztec Ruins and Salmon Ruins in northwestern New Mexico, past the Mimbres territory, through Chaco Canyon, and down to Paquimé (also called Casas Grandes) in Old Mexico.

One would think that Mimbres pottery would have been widely traded because of its extraordinary artistic quality. On the contrary, the quantity of commodity-ceramics was very low. A few ceramic exports have been discovered in outlying areas, especially to the south, but that number is negligible. In addition, archaeologists have found virtually no ceramic imports in the Mimbres Valley.[8] The people were simply not interested in designs or techniques from outsiders.

A huge amount of Mimbres pottery was produced, but not for commerce. Self-expression or ritual visualization must have been more important than merchandise exchange. In the Mimbres region as a whole, an estimated 125,000 bowls were manufactured over a period of 125 years (the Classic period). From Mattocks Ruin alone, 4,000 bowls were unearthed.[9] If the top priority was not the bottom line, so to speak, then what prompted such prolific pot making and painting?

Mimbres Book of the Dead

The Mimbres followed the custom of depositing bones of deceased family members beneath the floor of the living room. Even infants and children who succumbed to disease or malnutrition were buried there. Like some archaic cultures and a few modern ones, the Mimbres maintained living shrines to the dead in their homes. The only difference is that today the dearly departed are not generally stored domestically—that is, onsite.

In one room of the NAN Ranch Ruin, for instance, 50 individuals were interred—the largest number of single-room burials in the Mimbres Valley.[10] This room also contained a wealth of funerary goods. In particular, adult female graves contained a large number of mortuary vessels. This along with the favored eastward orientation of their bodies suggests a matrilineal society.[11] (More on this below.)

The cosmology of the ancient Puebloans totally integrated the world of the living and the world of the dead. The ancestors were thus kept close at hand –or I should say, close at foot– in a symbolic underworld, while the entry/exit ladder through the roof of the dwelling represented the link to the celestial world.

The Hopi of Arizona believe that the spirits of the ancestors return to the villages in the form of clouds to bring life-giving moisture to the high desert. The immediate ancestral presence may have even served an oracular function, providing secret formulas for scheduling and coordinating rituals to increase rainfall.[12] More than the focus of mere ancestor worship, the deceased kin continued to play an essential and integral role in pueblo society.

The hemispherical bowl may itself have been an icon of the sky dome. A small "kill hole" was customarily made in the bottom of the bowl in order to release the spirit of the clay vessel, which was considered a living being. If the bowl was "killed," then the spirits could use it in the afterlife. The spirit could also fly up through the hole, which is analogous to the hole in the floor of every kiva (which, we recall, is a subterranean prayer-chamber). This small hole, in Hopi called a *sipapu*, leads to a passageway that connects the physical and spiritual worlds.

Painted pottery bowls were the dominant burial offerings. In the Mimbres region as a whole, over 25,000 of them had been used as funerary vessels.[13] Black-on-white bowls were present in 68% of Mimbres graves, although most burials contained only one vessel—thus reinforcing the egalitarian nature of the ancient society.[14]

The bowl was placed either over face of the deceased as a mask, with the kill hole aligned to the Third Eye Chakra, or over the top of the cranium as a sort of skullcap, with the hole aligned to the Crown Chakra. (See Fewkes' burial drawing, facing page.)

According to the Hopi, the latter is the "door to the Creator," through which consciousness arrives and departs. An open "door" means that an individual is receptive to the inner visions of the spiritual realm. These sacred messages traditionally included the directions for ancient migrations. The sky god Sotuknang thus addressed the first people: "Your kópavi [vibratory center on top of the head] will lead you. This inner wisdom will give you the sight to see a certain cloud, which you will follow by day, and a certain star, which you will follow by night. Take nothing with you. Your journey will not end until the cloud stops and the star stops."[15]

Left: Bowl with decapitation scene. Figure wears a horned serpent headdress, suggesting worship of what the Aztecs later called Quetzalcoatl. The Mimbres may have practiced human sacrifice, or this may be a representation of Mesoamerican customs.

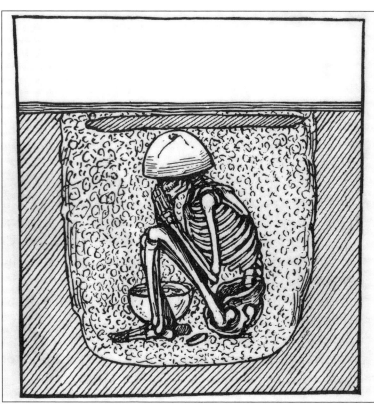

The *Phowa* (also spelled *Powa*), or "transferring consciousness at the time of death," is a Tibetan meditative practice that involves the Crown Chakra. W. Y. Evans-Wentz, compiler and editor of *The Tibetan Book of the Dead*, comments on the process. "The art of going out from the body, or transferring the consciousness from the earth-plane to the after-death plane, or any other plane, is still practiced, in Tibet, where it is known as *Pho-wa*."[16]

Rock art expert Ray Urbaniak of St. George, Utah, speculates that the *Phowa* is associated with the Hopi *Powamu* ceremony held in February. "The Powamu 'Bean Planting' ceremony, in my opinion, is analogous to the Tibetan Phowa ceremony, and reinforces my theory on the Mimbres burial practice. The beans crack open, the life force energy is released, and the bean husk or shell is discarded!"[17] In other words, the inverted bowl with its ritually punctured hole was placed on top of the deceased' head, thereby corresponding to the *kópavi* in the skull.

After surveying over 2,000 images painted on Mimbres bowls, scholar Marc Thompson presents the following conclusions regarding that culture's comprehensive "cult of the dead."

"(1) Representational Mimbres depictions are of supernatural figures, underworld characters, mythical creatures, and celestial bodies. (2) Analysis of action and identification of individuals permit chronological ordering of motifs from episodes recorded in Mesoamerican and Southwestern myth and folklore. This allows for visual reconstruction of oral traditions into a pictorial 'Book of the Dead' comparable to that from ancient Egypt. (3) These bowls were made for the dead and depict scenes from the journey to and through the underworld. The bowls may also have served as mnemonic devices in rituals (enactments of myths) at burials and probably reflect a highly structured and multifaceted cosmology found throughout Mesoamerica and the ancient Southwest. Additionally, painted Mimbres figurative motifs may have played a role analogous to that of the scenes from the *Iliad* and *Odyssey* found on Archaic Greek vessels."[18]

In this series of masterfully painted bowls, are we indeed seeing a Mimbres' *Book of the Dead* tantamount to the Egyptian *Book of the Dead*, the Tibetan *Bardo Thödol*, or the Mayan *Popol Vuh*? Fewkes comments that one of the bowls is reminiscent of what is called a "prayer stance," also found in Dynastic depictions. "The attitude of the arms suggests an ancient Egyptian at prayer."[19] Inside his body is double step-pyramid design, and on his back is a smaller figure, probably a male child or dwarf. Curiously, the person has a large fish attached to his nose. (See bowl below.)

This image is possibly a hallucination generated in the chaotic realm of what the ancient Egyptians called the *Duat,* or the Afterlife. It is worth remembering that the Hopi, some of whose ancestors undoubtedly inhabited the villages of the Mimbres Valley, had a word that sounded similar: *tu'at,* which actually means "hallucination" or "mystical vision." In fact, E. A. Wallis Budge, former director of antiquities at the British Museum, spelled the Egyptian term almost exactly the same: *"Tuat"*—a reference to that illusory realm of the after-death plane.[20] So, to echo my friend and diffusionist scholar Gene D. Matlock, both the name and the game are the same.

Mimbres For Peace, Drugs, and Women's Lib

I previously stated that the Mimbres society, unlike the massive city-state of Paquimé (see next chapter), was generally non-hierarchical and pacifist. Once again, the bones tell the story. Archaeology professor Ben A. Nelson: "Skeletal evidence for warfare in the Mogollon area is not strong prior to A.D. 1200, despite the removal of thousands of Classic Mimbres burials. Disarticulated burials and trophy skulls are found at Paquimé around A.D. 1200 – 1400, and [we can] infer a condition of chronic warfare from these osteological patterns."[21]

We also see a plethora of violence to the north at Chaco concurrent to a relative paucity of it at Mimbres. But not only was the period of Mimbres peace remarkable for the Southwest, it was also unusual for almost anywhere else in the world.

"This remarkable people created paintings on pottery for six hundred years (A.D. 550 – A.D. 1150) with almost no incidents of warfare. In contrast, Europe during the same period was a world wrenched by strife and dominated by severe religious imagery. The central symbol was the judging Christ, and the most vivid scenes were those that portrayed the agonies awaiting the damned in Hell. In the Southwest, meanwhile, the Mimbres were painting images reflecting a world viewed as something of an amicable cosmic circus."[22]

Although archaeologist Steven A. LeBlanc found evidence of early massacres, scalping, and trophy head taking in the wider Mogollon region, this violence did not extend into the Classic Mimbres period.[23]

So, if life on the idyllic Mimbres River was something of "an amicable cosmic circus" within a geographically anomalous pocket of peace, we might be witnessing the rare case of a prehistoric counterculture. Was some tyrannical proto-Nixon sitting in his palace up at Chaco along with a bunch of sycophantic reactionaries, complaining about the dopers down on the

Mimbres, who cohabited in sloppily built communes while they made weird paintings on pottery? Wouldn't this decadence ultimately lead to the downfall of Civilization?

11th century politics aside, the odd mixture of complex geometric designs and phantasmagorical imagery on ceramics does open the possibility that altered states of consciousness were involved in the creative process. Archaeologists have already established via ancient artifacts the widespread use of *Datura* and nicotine. (See my book *The Kivas of Heaven* for more on the former mind-altering plant.[24]) Some have also speculated on the use of so-called entheogens (literally, "creating god within") such as peyote cactus or psilocybin mushrooms. In the case of the latter, for instance, Mimbres bowls clearly depict either actual mushrooms or the tops of ceremonial wands shaped like a pileus, or mushroom cap. On one Internet site dedicated to the entheogenic tradition of the Mimbres, Bob Cox states: "Mimbres figurative pieces are often whimsical and include many bizarre creatures. The same inspiration at work in many of the geometrics was probably invoked for some of the figurative art. There are a few bowls painted with mushroom-like shapes, but the dominant clue to their inspiring presence is in the pahos [prayer sticks] and in paho ceramic depictions with mushroom-like tops and in the visionary geometrics."[25]

Experimentation with investigative psychedelics may have played a significant role in Mimbres culture, if it was anything like our version of the counterculture. This together with the watchwords of artistic innovation, sexual freedom, sensuality, gender equality, fraternity, and feminism must have made the Mimbres a unique folk for their time.

Psilocybin usage is hard to prove, given the perishable nature of the fungus. If mushrooms were indeed the head-trip of choice, then the particular fertility aspects of their phallic morphology cannot be overlooked. The only evidence we have is the spectacular imagery painted on the bowls by –most likely– women. They provide a visual record of their daily life, their dreams, their exploration of inter-dimensional realms, and their spiritual longings. Again, from the same website:

"They [the Mimbres] may well have been a matrilocal culture, as are many modern pueblo societies. The women had roles (as revealed by Mimbres burial practices and ceramic art) of probable equal value to those enjoyed by the men. They appear to have been the ones responsible for the expressive decoration on the pottery in which they were often included in ritual scenes. Men and women viewed both their own sexuality and that which they observed in nature to be both sacred and whimsical, if the pottery record can be trusted. Their casual and sacred use of entheogenic mushrooms would have been consistent with this view, as psilocybin fosters sensual feelings and an egalitarian approach to their expression."[26]

Architectural design was clearly not the forte of the Mimbres people. They crafted a huge amount of pottery, mainly shallow bowls—although the quality of the ceramics was merely average. The importance here was the visual space that these bowls provided for paintings. They excelled in both abstract, geometric designs and naturalistic representations. Some of the scenes even took on a hallucinatory aura, which suggests the possibility that alternate realities were being explored via the use of psychotropic plants.

Perhaps this experimentation with mental states other than the mundane, baseline reality was connected with a cult of the dead. The mythology that developed during repeated interdimensional journeys to the underworld may have been tantamount to that of ancient Egypt, or at least served a similar function. The copious images produced during the apex of the Mimbres culture (1000 – 1100 AD) may even be compositely viewed as a "Book of the Dead."

The lifestyle and priorities of these rural inhabitants of the Mimbres River Valley were radically different from those of the large urban areas in both Chaco Canyon and Paquimé. The Mimbres apparently lived in peace and aesthetic harmony. At the very same time the Chacoans not far away were engaged in violence, psychological intimidation, and even cannibalism. Were the former living as free spirits "doing their own thing" in opposition to the mainstream culture that valued hierarchical control and a monumental architecture designed to awe the lower classes into submission?

Archaeo-anthropology is extremely difficult when all we have are a few mute artifacts. As humanly expressive and emotionally evocative as this painted pottery is, we can only speculate on the character of the culture that produced it. We unavoidably project our own Zeitgeist, historical prejudices, and worldviews upon the Mimbres. The human need to explore the alternate realities of the subjective, non-physical realm is, however, universal. The psycho-nauts of the Mimbres Valley were apparently doing just that.

Bearded (non-Indian?) figure holding staff (or sword?)
with mushroom-shaped pommel.

Chapter 9
Paquimé—Mummies, a Meteorite, and the Macaw Constellation

Casas Cosmos

Paquimé was for the birds. Literally. This UNESCO World Heritage Site located about 100 miles south of the U.S.-Mexico border in the Rio Casas Grandes Valley of Chihuahua had the region's densest population for its time—both human and avian, but more on the latter below. 1250 AD is generally accepted as its founding as an urban entity, although this date is sometimes disputed. Archaeologists have also discovered evidence of a preceding period they call "Viejo," when pit houses or small adobe pueblos were inhabited. People may have settled shortly after the Mimbres culture's collapse in about 1130 or even as early as the mid-11th century. (1250 was a few decades before the onset of the 25-year Great Drought in the American Southwest, and 1130 was the beginning of a slightly lesser drought but lasting twice as long.)

Stephen Lekson briefly sums up the ultimate importance of the urban surge: "Paquime was the most wonderful city ever built in the Pueblo Southwest: Mexican ballcourts, effigy mounds, and 'pyramids' surrounded a huge poured-adobe Great House pueblo."[1] In his most recent book, he goes even further with hyperbole: "Paquimé was Chaco on steroids, or Chaco gone to finishing school. The southern city was everything Chaco tried but failed to be. And I think its region was at least as large as that earlier, simpler city."[2]

Paquimé's planned layout incorporated a massive U-shaped,

terraced pueblo that has been structurally compared to Taos in New Mexico only much larger. The main building measured about 800 feet from north to south and 250 feet from east to west. Surrounding large courtyards, walls made from adobe blocks three feet long and two feet thick rose 40 to 50 feet high—up to six stories tall. Charles C. Di Peso, who did the primary archaeological survey of Paquimé in the 1950s and 1960s, called it a "high-rise."[3] This enormous proto-apartment complex contained as many as 2,000 rooms.

Acequias (canals) ran throughout the pre-Hispanic metropolis, using water diverted from warm springs about two-and-a-quarter miles away. Three large reservoirs also supplied the inhabitants with water, and urban amenities included a drainage-and-sewer system. There was even a walk-in well, accessed via descending steps and a floor with, strangely enough, a human skull embedded in it. The plan also integrated 18 ceremonial platform mounds and a few effigy mounds representing a cross, a bird, and a horned serpent representing Quetzalcoatl or Kukulkan.

The city additionally contained the classic I-shaped ballcourts found much farther south in Mayan territory. Unlike the previous isolationist settlements of the Mimbres to the north, cosmopolitan Paquimé "…represents an intersection of southernmost Pueblo and northernmost Mesoamerica."[4]

Other Mesoamerican architectural motifs found at Chaco Canyon also occur at Paquimé. These include T-shaped doors, colonnades, "sleeping platforms" (or shelves the width of a room), and massive disks used as structural post supports. The T-shaped door or window is found north into Colorado and south as far as the Mayan city of Palenque in Chiapas, Mexico.[5]

Although no kivas per se are found at Paquimé, a ceremonial room in the "House of the Serpent" is considered a proxy kiva due to its large subterranean chamber with a ramp entry on the south side. This compares to those in square or rectangular kivas of the 12th century Mogollon culture of western New Mexico and eastern Arizona. The building gets its name, by the way, because of an image of a plumed or horned serpent carved on the wall of this "kiva."

Oriented north and south, a serpent mound effigy about 370 feet long was also constructed on the western side of the city. Into its caliche eye was carved a horned serpent with dorsal feathers and a backward-pointing horn, similar to a petroglyph of Awanyu found at Tshirege Ruins near Los Alamos in New Mexico. Its tail points to Arroyo de Los Monos, the largest spring in the region located a little over nine miles from the city. This water source also has horned serpent petroglyphs adjacent to it.[6]

Three Mummies and a Meteorite

A maze of tombs was found within the main pueblo. Inside one crypt, a number of seated mummies with their knees raised were discovered, wrapped in linen and surrounded by jewelry and pottery. The treatment of these mummies resembles those found in various cliff dwellings around Chihuahua.

A bricked adobe tomb in the middle of another room (Unit 11) contained a lenticular meteorite that measured 38" x 29" x 18" and weighed 3,407 lbs. (Another source estimates its weight at 5,000 lbs.) A yoke of 26 oxen was required to haul it out. However, the meteorite was clearly not in situ. Both its provenance and the method of its transport without the means of draft animals remain a mystery. Carefully swathed in the same type of cloth as the mummies, it was obviously an object of great reverence.[7]

"...the inhabitants of the small town of Casas Grandes [Paquimé] 240 km south of the Paso del Norte searched the neighboring ancient temple ruins of the 'Montezuma Casas Grandes' for treasure and found in the middle of a large room a sort of grave with an immense block estimated at 5,000 pounds weight carefully wrapped like an Egyptian mummy in a coarse linen cloth. The Casas Grandes was the dwelling place of the Montezuma Indians and accordingly the entombment of the meteorite took place before the conquest of Mexico by the Spaniards."[8]

Adobe walls of Paquimé Pueblo
(also called Casas Grandes), Chihuahua, Mexico.

Meteorite found inside Paquime Pueblo,
Museum of Natural History, Smithsonian Institution.
It appears to have been sawed in half, so it may have actually been larger.[9]

Other burials in this "city of palaces" (Lekson's characterization again) include a crypt inside a platform mound or truncated pyramid where defleshed bones in large ceramic jars were deposited. In addition, two apparently high-status adult males were buried in another crypt along with a huge amount of grave goods. Above this pair were interred scores of disarticulated individuals (archaeological lingo for torn apart). These may have been servants or kin sacrificed to the rulers. Like Chaco Canyon, this later municipality seemed to have spurned the egalitarian model once adopted by the Mimbres (the latter discussed in the previous chapter).[10]

The rulers at Paquimé may have in fact used their special relationship with their ancestors residing in the underworld to consolidate power on the material plane. Trophy skulls and necklaces of finger bones have been unearthed here, which, along with other mortuary practices, may have had ritual significance and have aided in the acquisition of esoteric knowledge from the spirit world. Unlike the emotional comfort we might feel today by keeping one's relatives ashes on the mantle, these talismanic bones of the dead aided in communication across the threshold of worlds. The messages received were probably not always easy to take, but they had the ancestors' weight of authority behind them and thus were more credible. In addition, a temporal continuity was maintained between generations, both living and dead. Anthropologist Gordon F. M. Rakita comments on this interaction of mundane and spirit worlds.

"The ancestor cult at Paquime, through its focus on exclusivity and power negotiations, helped maintain elite authority. This was achieved through securing and maintaining a special role for elites as priests in negotiations with ancestors in the afterworld, a process involving the manipulation of human remains. Membership in the cult would have been limited to elites with their exclusive rights to positions of authority. Ritual practices would have been conducted periodically and involved extension of the ancestors' liminal power into the world of the here and now."[11]

In the T-shaped ball court on the southwestern side of the House of the Pillars, a number of other ceremonial burials were found. Beneath the lid of a central marker, or "spirit hole," was placed a man's skull on top of another man's skeleton in a flexed position. This hole is analogous to the Hopi *sipapu* found in every kiva, which is the symbolic access to the underworld and the source of all water or fertility.

Renee Opperman describes the strange ball court internment.

"In the southern end of the field another burial cache was found underneath the floor. It was comprised of a woman whose severed right arm was placed over her shoulders, and covered by a pregnant woman lying on top of her. The northern end was marked by a wooden upright staff and a third burial cache. At the bottom of the cache was an articulated body of a woman with a man's skull on top of her, topped by the disjointed body of a woman, whose severed feet are articulated."[12]

Past the boneyard chaos of skulls and dust, weary souls long ago had flown into the sky's watery abyss.

Birds and Arrows

¿Que fueron de Paquimeños? Who were the Paquiméans, and whence their origin? Charles Di Peso claimed that the site was the "Fallen Trade Center of the Gran Chichimeca." He writes, "It is believed that sometime around the year 1060 AD a group of sophisticated Mesoamerican merchants came into the valley of the Casas Grandes and inspired indigenous Chichimecans to build the city of Paquime."[13]

Unfortunately, Di Peso miscalculated his dating of Paquimé due to faulty assumptions regarding tree-ring data. In fact, he got it wrong by about two centuries. Lekson, on the other hand, suggests a cultural thrust from the north rather than one from the south. In other words, the Chaco modality shifted—first to Salmon and Aztec Ruins to the north in the early 12th century, and then to Paquimé to the south in the mid-13th century. At the end of the temporal chain of ancient cities, Culiacán's demise was early postcolonial. By the mid-16th century this last site was a ghost town. (See Chapter 10.)

The pottery made at Paquimé, like that of the future site of Culiacán to the south, was polychrome: black-and-red geometric and naturalistic designs on a light-tan background. Many religiously important representations are found: regular snakes or horned serpents, macaws, or macaw-headed men. Artisans even painted macaw-headed serpents, turtle-headed macaws, and other therianthropes (animal-human hybrids). This suggests that, in addition to a priestly culture, a shamanic cult may have influenced the ecclesiastical polity. Real creatures (birds and snakes) were frequently depicted in ceramic effigies or appliqué, while mythical creatures were painted on pottery (horned serpents, macaw-headed serpents, shamans transforming into macaws, and double-headed macaws with diamond-shaped bodies).[14] The two different media may have been used to represent the material and spiritual worlds respectively.

The VanPools, a husband-and-wife archaeological team, comment:

"We have argued that images of males, especially those painted with pound signs [i.e. #], portrayed tobacco shamanism and the 'classical three-part shamanic journey' [i.e. zenith, middle place, nadir]. The shamans smoked tobacco (perhaps laced with datura or peyote alkoloids), danced, prayed, meditated, fasted, and practiced sleep deprivation and auto violence to induce an ecstasy trance. While in a trance they lacked a discernable pulse and appeared to be dead. Their spirits traveled to the 'other'-world in the form of macaw-headed anthropomorphs, where they communed with supernaturals before returning to the mundane world, having defied death."[15]

Above: Plumed serpent ceramic pot, red and black on tan background.
Below: Flying shamans with # signs. One at left has arrowhead headdress,
one at right has a macaw headdress and circumpuncts on legs and belly.

Above-left: Male effigy pot, red and black on brown.
Above-right: Male smoker with # signs and macaw heads on legs,
red and black on tan.
Below: The scarlet macaw may have seemed like a wise elder
to the Paquiméans. The species can live up to 60 years—
more than twice the average human lifespan for the period.

These shamanic flights into the astral realm may in fact explain at least one of the purposes of the arrow-straight roads built on a north and south axis across New Mexico, and perhaps provides the rationale for the entire Chaco Meridian that stretches from northern Wyoming to Sinaloa, Mexico. (See Chapter 7.) Author and ley line researcher Paul Devereaux claims these pathways served as topographic vectors for the shaman's out-of-body experiences.

"The shaman, of course, was the person who used trance-inducing methods in order to enter the spirit worlds on behalf of the tribe. This 'shaman's journey' was what we would call today an "out-of-body" experience, which was often envisaged as magical spirit flight. Could it be that the lines of shamanic spirit flight became translated onto the landscape as straight lines of various kinds in certain societies? Flight is, after all, the straight way over the land— 'as the crow flies', we say. Another phrase with a similar meaning is 'as straight as an arrow', and arrow symbolism was strongly associated with shamanic flight."[16]

Birdland

A more appropriate simile might be "as the macaw flies." Scarlet macaws (*Ara macao*) are associated in Pueblo cosmology with the sun. The sun god's home is in the south or southeast, the direction he travels in the winter. In Hopi directional symbolism, southeast corresponds to the color red and to the totemic birds of either the macaw or the parrot. The sun's annual journey northward brings fertility to the land during the spring and summer. Thus, macaws are also connected to the multicolored Indian corn. In addition, the macaw's brilliant hues of red, scarlet, crimson, chrome yellow, and purplish blue suggest a rainbow. Macaws are consequently associated with rainfall as well.[17]

In one Hopi legend, a beautiful maiden had once spurned six suitors in succession: Yellow Cloud (northwest), Blue Cloud (southwest), Red Cloud (southeast), White Cloud (northeast),

Black Cloud (above), and Gray Cloud (or all colors together, i.e. the underworld). A rain deity named Paváyoyk'ashi, who lived far to the south (perhaps at Paquimé), heard about this and decided to try and win her. He dressed up like a Flute player or certain handsome kachinas and took a bow with a quiver of arrows made of a panther skin and proceeded northward, where he met the girl in her father's field. (Whether "panther" refers to the Mexican jaguar –*Panthera onca hernandesii*– or to the North American cougar –*Puma concolor couguar*– is unclear, but probably the former.) She was so taken by the Paváyoyk'ashi that she acquiesced to be his bride.

Meanwhile Old Man Coyote heard this story and vowed to get the maiden for himself. He traveled to the southern land of warmth and captured a macaw as a present. After he got back to Hopi-land, the maiden was struck by the bird's beauty and accepted the gift. Later that night Coyote went to Paváyoyk'ashi's northern house and stole his colorful raiment and bow-and-arrows. Next morning in this guise he tricked the maiden into sleeping with him, whom she thought was the rain deity.

When she found out Coyote's true identity, the maiden was dejected; but Paváyoyk'ashi was furious. He returned to his home in the south and bided his time. Eventually he caused a great storm with thunderclouds, strong winds, and heavy rain to form over the Hopi Mesas. Finally the rain deity got revenge on Coyote by striking him dead with a bolt of lightning.[18]

This myth contains a number of primary elements: macaws, rain, rainbow clothing, bow-and-arrows, lightning, and canine (coyote). These are all connected in some way to Chaco Canyon located 392 miles due north. Macaw feathers and whole birds were an integral part of the sacred ceremonies at Chaco and other places in the Southwest. The highly coveted feathers were used on masks, fetishes, prayer-sticks, and were worn in the hair. This was an attempt to harness the macaw's symbolic power of warmth and moisture on the sometimes frigid but usually dry high desert.

Whatever their spiritual or psychological effects, scarlet macaws were big business, and Paquimé was quite possibly the macaw capital of the Southwest (or Northwest, if your frame of reference is Mexico rather than the United States). Over 400 of these beautiful birds whose native territory is in the jungles of southern Mexico were found among the ruins of this northern node of the ancient Pan-American Highway. In addition, nearly 100 military macaws native to Chihuahua were unearthed. Also found here were other avian species, including thick-billed parrots, ravens, owls, white pelicans, Canada geese, and more than 300 turkeys.[19] It must have been a bird-lover's paradise—a veritable Mexico Macao!

As I have witnessed in the village of Oraibi in the 1990s, the Parrot Clan still performs kachina dances on the Hopi Mesas of Arizona. It is somewhat jarring to see the spirit of the multicolored tropical bird invoked upon the arid, mauve-and-buff-colored landscape, but perhaps that is just what is needed to induce rainfall. The Parrot Clan's *wuya*, or specific ancestral and mythical being(s) with which it identifies, includes both the parrot (*Rhynchopsitta pachyrhyncha*) and the scarlet macaw (*Ara macao*).[20]

Macaws were taken from their nests in the humid lowlands at about seven weeks of age and carried in baskets to Paquimé. There they were hand-raised by aviculturalists and kept in rows of rectangular adobe pens—over 50 in all. Due to the birds' nasty disposition and razor-sharp beaks and talons, these pens were equipped with heavy cylindrical plugs in their doors to allow easy access.[21]

From Paquimé, the macaws were transported north along the Chaco Meridian—first to the Mimbres area of southern New Mexico, then to Chaco Canyon, on up the line to Salmon Ruins, and finally to Aztec Ruins. However, scarlet macaws have also been found to the northwest at a number of Arizona ruins, including Point of Pines, Grasshopper, Turkey Creek, and Wupatki.

In the generation before Google Earth, co-authors William Ferguson and Arthur Rohn published many aerial photos of ruin sites in the Southwest in their ironically groundbreaking book on the Anasazi. They comment on the feasibility of this course. "The authors flew over the terrain from Casas Grandes in Chihuahua, Mexico, to Chaco Canyon. An Indian could have followed this route without crossing any mountains and without ever being far from water."[22]

A total of 29 mature macaw skeletons were found at Pueblo Bonito in Chaco, with 14 in one room alone, and 36 in the entire canyon. Nine macaws were found at Salmon Ruins, some ritually buried. Red ocher was found on the body of one bird and the same substance on merely the bones of another.[23] Lekson adds: "Excavations at Salmon Ruins produced macaws in a wide range of contexts and a few from Aztec."[24] The low number of birds found at Aztec West (only two birds and one feather) might be the result of the low number of buildings actually excavated there.

Needless to say, the Paquiméans got around. Literally tons of shells from the Gulf of California were found at the site. In addition, 2.1 kilograms (4.6 lbs.) of turquoise and 14.6 kilograms (32.19 lbs.) of copper were discovered at Paquimé—the former imported from the north along the Meridian, probably from Chaco Canyon. Turquoise sources included the large prehistoric mine near Cerrillos, New Mexico, as well as Hachita and Burro in the southwestern part of the same state. The mineral was also mined in the Cerbat Mountains north of Kingman, Arizona, and the Globe-Miami area of the same state.[25]

Perhaps the copper came from Barranca del Cobre in the Sierra Madre to the south. From this raw material the craftspeople had made inlaid turquoise, shell jewelry, and copper bells for exports. The small amount of turquoise actually found at Paquimé is probably the result of a brisk trading business. The people additionally crafted shell trumpets, pottery hand drums, and stone carvings.

Each archaeologist seems to have his or her own theories regarding the possible cross-cultural influences on Paquimé. One website sums these up nicely.

"Since the 1990's, archaeologists have variously attributed the Paquime phenomenon primarily to stimulation by the Aztatlan Mercantile System, immigration from Mexico's west coast, inspiration by Anasazi refugees, newly established empire by Chaco Canyon Anasazi elites, a combination of mercantile system stimulation and Anasazi inspiration, emergence of indigenous leadership, local manipulation and control of prestige goods and social and ideological concepts, and combinations of possibilities."[26]

Take your pick. However, one compelling study of skeletal remains recovered from archaeological sites both in the American Southwest and the Mexican Northwest compares dental structures of various ancient tribal groups. Christy Turner, who did controversial research of cannibalism in and around Chaco Canyon, concludes from the evidence: "In sum, dental crown morphology suggests the populations of Casas Grandes [Paquimé] had close epigenetic connections with people living in Sinaloa and in the Mimbres area. These relationships are closer than between Casas Grandes and another sample of Chihuahuan dentition." He also states that Paquimeños teeth and the Hohokam teeth recovered from the Phoenix Basin to the northwest had the lowest number of similar characteristics.[27]

Sinaloa is the area to the south of Casas Grandes where, as we will see, Culiacán was located, and the Mimbres area is to the north of Casas Grandes in New Mexico. Turner's dental evidence thus reinforces Lekson's belief that the major migrations were centered along the north-south axis, i.e. the Chaco Meridian. Independent researcher Richard D. Fisher calls this the Monsoon Meridian, because of the persistent and frequently violent summer monsoons that sweep northward off the Gulf of California and to an extent the Gulf of Mexico and across the Mexico-U.S. border into the Southwest.[28]

Astro-Avian Correlations

The Paquiméans did not have a writing system, so it is impossible to determine the exact astro-spiritual dimensions of the scarlet macaw. We can only speculate what role the bird played in their religious life. We know from the plethora of images painted on pottery that this particular fowl was a crucial element in their worldview. The great amount of time and effort expended in transporting and raising these birds in captivity demonstrates the reverence they must have had for them. Perhaps they were even considered wise, old souls, given their lifespan, which in some cases may have been twice that of the average human lifespan at that time. They were not simply pets, but instead teachers and spiritual guides. Because of the basic characteristics of a shamanistic society, the relationship between animals and people was radically different from what we experience today. And because birds are creatures of two worlds, earth and sky, it makes sense that the people of Paquimé may have tried to find this avian archetype in the celestial realm.

Many sources state that the scarlet macaw was culturally associated with the sun. Its brilliant red and yellow plumage makes this solar connection seem quite obvious. However, there may have been a nocturnal association as well, when the sun was journeying through the underworld.

My previous books propose a star correlation system in which the patterns of a number of constellations have been projected on the Desert Southwest. Suffice to say here that this was an attempt shared by many cultures worldwide to make the earth mirror the sky. The unified cosmos demonstrated by the hermetic dictum "as above, so below" found its expression in a terrestrial template honoring the star gods that the shaman-priests monitored each night. The precision of their observations makes the astronomical knowledge of the average contemporary urban dweller seem paltry in comparison. (Growing up in suburban Cleveland, Ohio, for instance, I could only recognize two constellations—Orion and the Big Dipper. But that's another story.)

In my book *The Kivas of Heaven*, I describe a sidereal projection that incorporated all the constellations of the Winter Hexagon: Orion, Taurus, Auriga, Gemini, Canis Minor, and Canis Major. Additional research has shown me that the pattern can be extended further to include the zodiacal constellations of Cancer and Leo.

The region of the Mimbres in southwestern New Mexico has been overlaid with the constellation Cancer. The basic personality traits of the astrological water sign seem in keeping with the general character of the Mimbreños. This culture had a tendency to withdraw from the world at large and seek security and emotional happiness within the confines of its home-pueblos and its kinship relations. (See Chapter 8.)

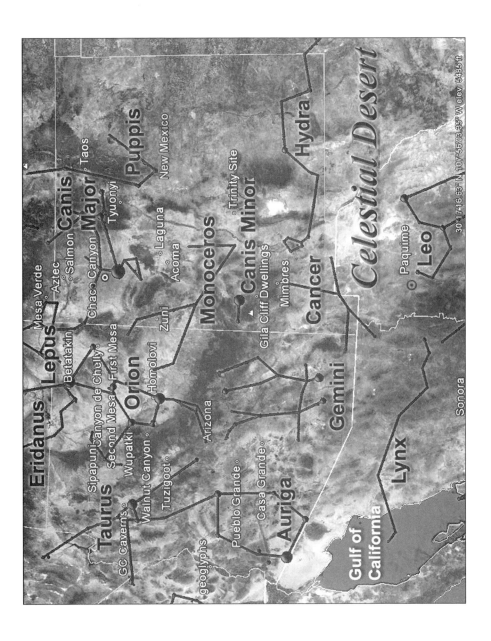

Leo ~ the Scarlet Macaw Constellation

The remains of over 400 scarlet macaws (*Ara macao*) have been found at Paquimé. The birds were transported from a region 300-600 miles to the south, or bred onsite.

The "lion's mane" of Leo (also known as the Sickle) corresponds to the bird's beak, while Regulus is the talons. Theta and Denebola are the long tail, and Delta is the blue tail-covert feathers (the sky). Like Leo, the scarlet macaw was associated with the sun (the red and yellow feathers).

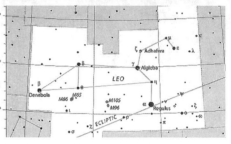

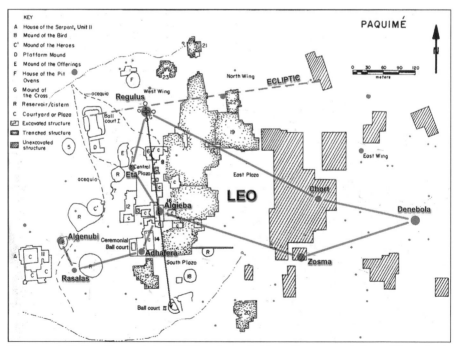

The constellation Leo rotated 180° and overlaid on the groundplan of Paquimé. The celestial bird's beak (Algenubi) correlates to the Mound of the Bird, and its talons (Regulus) correlates to the Mound of the Cross.

On the other hand, the Paquiméans, whose region was over-laid by the fire sign Leo, wanted to be the center of attention during the apex of its regal and magisterial culture. The extent of its influence was far and wide, and its fierce ambition to perpetuate its extravagantly urbane lifestyle knew no bounds. The pre-Columbian metroplex was a steady solar presence around which the smaller villages revolved.

Paquimé celestially corresponds to Regulus, the primary star of the constellation. In ancient Persia this was considered one of the Four Guardians of Heaven or Four Royal Stars: Aldebaran in Taurus, Regulus in Leo, Antares in Scorpius, and Fomalhaut in Piscis Austrinus.[29] The four most important zodiac signs traditionally were the three just mentioned and Aquarius rather than Piscis Austrinus.[30] Ptolemy considered Regulus to have the same character as either Mars or Jupiter. The star was linked to noble intelligence, courage, and candor but also to violence, destructiveness, and honor that is short-lived or eclipsed.[31] As we shall see, this proves to be an ill omen.

Equinox Sacrifice

Although they potentially live a long time, most of the scarlet macaws at Paquimé were raised for just under one year, when their first set of tail feathers was fully grown. The birds were then ritually sacrificed, their feathers plucked, and their bodies formally buried on or near the vernal equinox.[32] Richard Fisher comments on the symbolic nature of the ceremony.

> "The design of the structures previously interpreted as ceremonial macaw birthing chambers, with their anthropomorphic male "plugs" that fit into round female macaw stones, brings my analysis back to fertility. Though these enclosures have been called macaw nesting boxes, macaws are not likely to breed or nest under the conditions these boxes present. Our alternative suggestion is that the Scarlet Macaws were seen to exit Mother Earth during

major religious ceremonies, such as at the spring equinox,
and were then lifted by the priest to greet Father Sky."[33]

Thus, the birds emerged from the earth through an anthro-
pomorphic birth canal, were proffered to the sky gods, and then
their sacrificed remains were interred so that their spirits could
fly through the underworld, thereby enhancing agricultural
fecundity. Again, the VanPool couple: "Macaws at Paquimé may
have also been used in ceremonies related to maize maturation,
occurring during the vernal equinox with water rituals. The
macaw burials at Paquimé, with birds being laid out in spokes,
are further suggestive of the macaws' being intended to represent the rays of the sun. Perhaps the vernal equinox ceremonies
at Paquimé were to propagate the ever-important corn cycle."[34]
Macaw burials of eight macaws symmetrically arranged in
"spokes" with heads pointed outward may have also represented the four cardinal points (equinox sunrise/sunset points plus
the north-south meridian) and the four intercardinal points (solstice sunrise/sunset points).

Placement of the ritually killed birds in the earth was a
mimesis of the celestial journey of Leo through the western gate
to the underworld. On March 21st of 1250 AD (approximate
founding date of metropolitan Paquimé), Regulus perched on
the western horzizon about two hours before sunrise, while the
whole constellation set just before sunrise. (This is technically
called a cosmical setting, when a star sets as the sun rises.) The
celestial bird was in essence symbolically sacrificed to the rays of
the rising sun and then entered the netherworld.

Let's go back more than a centuy to the earlier Viejo period.
On March 21, 1128 AD, Regulus happened to be conjunct Mars.
Six days before the equinox in that same year a conjunction of
Regulus, Mars, and a nearly full moon occurred while three other
planets were in close alignment: Uranus, Saturn, and Jupiter.
This unusual show in the heavens may have initially caught the
attention of the sky watchers at the new settlement of Paquimé.

Nearly four months later Regulus achieved its true heliacal
setting on July 11th. The sun was about 12° below the western

horizon a little after eight o'clock in the evening. During the annual agricultural cycle, the maize that was planted shortly after the vernal equinox grew with the help of monsoon rains that arrived in July. This agrarian period was aided by the scarlet macaw constellation that descends to the underworld in order to engender chthonic life forces.

Around harvest time exactly two months later at about 5 a.m. on September 11th, an extremely rare occultation occurred during the heliacal rising of the constellation. That is, the planet Venus completely eclipsed the star Regulus, with the sun 12° below the eastern horizon. (See p. 240.) As mentioned at the beginning of this chapter, the year 1130 is generally given for the collapse of the Mimbres culture in southwestern New Mexico. This was also the beginning of a half-century drought. Was this anomalous celestial event in 1128 a signal for Mimbres exiles to move southward in order to inhabit the Casas Grandes Valley and begin the hatching of Paquimé? Was this a sort of prehistoric 9-11?

This might seem like an exaggeration, but the rarity of the Venus-Regulus occultation may have been extremely alarming to ancient astronomers. Between 1000 AD and 3000 AD, there are only four cases of this event: (a) Sept 11, 1128 AD, (b) July 7, 1959 AD, in our lifetime, (c) 2044 AD, in the lifetime of some of us, and (d) 2271 AD, in the lifetime of the crew members of the starship Enterprise (but this last one is dubious).[35] Hence, 1128 was the first time anyone in historic times had seen this sort of occultation.

How might the Paquiméans have interpreted this "high strangeness"? The planet Venus is associated in a number of Mesoamerican cultures with the plumed or horned serpent—Kukulkan to the Maya and Quetzalcoatl to the Aztecs. The occultation of Regulus by Venus might have appeared as a symbolic merging of avian and ophidian. Indeed, the Paquimé painters portrayed this motif in the polychrome pottery that depicts creatures with macaw heads and snake bodies. Some images interpreted as either beaked macaws or horned snakes may in fact be a conflation of the two. In the architecture of Paquimé, we also find the Mound of the Bird adjacent to the House of the Serpent and the serpent effigy mound.

Star-Crossed Macaw

As shown on p. 230, the Mound of the Cross corresponds to the star Regulus when the constellation is overlaid upon the city. This equal-armed platform is roughly aligned to the cardinal directions but, for some reason, is slightly offset 2°– 4° from the true directions. (One source claims the north arm is 4.5° west of north, the west arm is 4° south of west, whereas the east and south arms are strictly cardinal.[36]) The central observation locus may have been used to determine the agricultural calendar by using bumps or other geographic features on the horizon to mark the summer and winter sunrise and sunset points, much like the Hopi *tawamongwi*, or sun watcher, still does today in Arizona. An equal distance between these two sets of points on the eastern and western horizons would mark the equinoxes—the vernal quarter of the year being the time when scarlet macaws were ritually sacrificed.

It has also been suggested that the Mound of the Cross was the ritual center of Paquimé, and the ceremonial heart or hub of the whole region.[37] If so, it may have functioned as the shamanic *axis mundi* of the cosmos, the consecrated spot whence the shaman-priests took flight and transformed into scarlet macaws. Indeed, we find on some polychrome pottery the depiction of men growing wings at their elbows and feathers at their wrists. These figures are also wearing kilts with a black-and-white checkerboard design, which, as previously stated, may be symbolic of the sky or the Milky Way. It has further been suggested that the public (exoteric) space of the Mound of the Cross has its private (esoteric) correlative in the cross-shaped room on the eastern side of the pueblo.[38] (See satellite photo on p. 235.)

In rock art of the American Southwest, an equilateral cross is thought to represent the planet Venus, the celestial embodiment of Quetzalcoatl. The Tarahumara, who live in Sonora and Chihuahua, also identify this same sort of cross with the planet.[39] When the constellation Leo is projected upon the groundplan of Paquimé, Regulus rests on the Mound of the Cross. Hence, the coterminous planet and star were both manifested in the very rare 1128 AD occultation at the heliacal rising of this heart of the constellation.

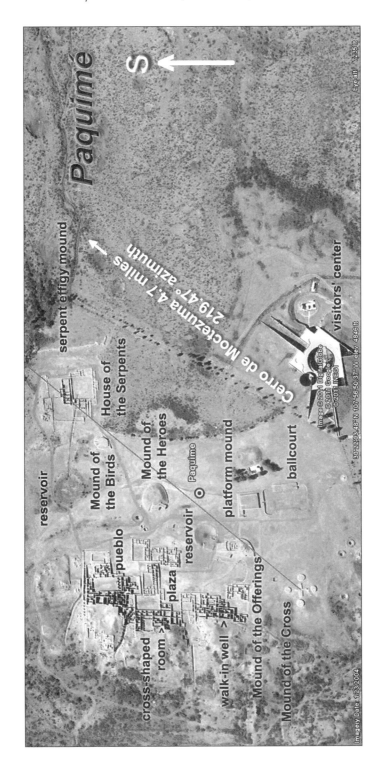

We should remember that Regulus was conceptualized in many Old World cultures as the heart of Leo, the Lion. In Egypt, for example, Leo corresponded to the leonine Sphinx on the Giza Plateau in the Zep Tepi, or First Time (Era) in 10,500 BC, the precessional Age of Leo. On this date at the vernal equinox, Leo, which achieves its heliacal rising with the sun 12° below the horizon, rests on the eastern horizon as the Sphinx stares directly at this celestial phenomenon.[40] Graham Hancock describes this initial world-cycle: "Here is what the Ancient Egyptians said about the First Time, Zep Tepi, when the gods ruled in their country: they said it was a golden age during which the waters of the abyss receded, the primordial darkness was banished, and humanity, emerging into the light, was offered the gifts of civilization."[41] Thus, the constellation Leo first gained primacy 12,500 years ago, or about halfway around the precessional cycle.

The Sphinx is located on 29° 58' 31.03" latitude. Perhaps it is merely a coincidence that Paquimé's Mound of the Cross is located at 30° 22' 03.35" latitude. The difference between the respective parallels is approximately 23.5 minutes, or about 27 miles. (At 30 ° latitude, 1 minute of latitude = 1.15 statute miles.[42]) The distance on a great circle between the two sites is 7489.32 miles. Is this tiny discrepancy between the respective latitudes of the Sphinx and the Mound of the Cross enough to rule out the possibility that Paquimé was consciously located on this geodetically significant parallel of the Earth?

In the New World case, we are seeing Regulus as the talons of the regal scarlet macaw perched upon the ecliptic rather than the heart of the lion. (Regulus is the closest bright star to the ecliptic.) This platform was probably a ritualized space, perhaps even before the major building occurred at Paquimé. This locus may have been the inception of the city that would gradually begin to fledge during the 13th century AD.

At a distance of 4.7 miles southwest of Paquimé lies Cerro de Moctezuma, a prominent mountain that can be seen for many surrounding miles. The Paquiméans built a round tower, or *atalaya*, on its crest with four symmetrical rooms inside. This "watch tower" was constructed for the probable purpose of communication via intervisibility. They may have used of pyrite mirrors by day and bonfires by night in order to relay signals from distant villages, which also could have been seen from the summit, thereby creating a signaling network across large tracts of the Sonoran desert. Also built on the mountain were a small adobe pueblo, a possible reservoir, and a number of anomalous structures consisting of stone walls, circles, and rectangles.[43]

Some have interpreted the masonry walls as forming a conch shape, while Di Peso called the stone structures a "temple" dedicated to the Aztec wind god Ehécatl, a human aspect of Quetzalcoatl.[44]

In the city proper, the line-of-sight starts at the Mound of the Cross, skirts the Mound of Offerings, and passes the Mound of the Heroes and the Mound of Birds to bisect the House of Serpents on its diagonal. In fact, the room in the southwestern corner of the building contains a narrow window that faces the mountain, which could be clearly seen from a well worn seat.[45]

Cerro de Moctezuma is 219.47° azimuth in relation to the Mound of the Cross. At about 10 o'clock on the evening of the vernal equinox in 1128 AD, the traditional day of the ritual sacrifice of macaws, Leo arrived at the meridian, or highest point in its arc across the sky. Regulus in conjunction with the red planet Mars was at 219° azimuth, so it would have been hovering over Cerro de Moctezuma in the distance. At this time the constellation was projected on the ground, with Regulus/Mound of the Cross as its talons and the Mound of the Birds as its beak.

One avian myth that perhaps refers to Paquimé is known to the Zuni, who call themselves the *Ashiwi*, a pueblo people who live in northwestern New Mexico. Their ancestors were wandering from their Place of Origin in Grand Canyon and trying to find the Middle Place, their final homeland. While staying at a spot on the Little Colorado River, they were given a choice of two gifts: either a plain white egg or an egg with beautiful blue spots. One group of Zunis chose the colorful egg, out of which hatched a raven, and this, of course, dismayed them. Another group chose the plain egg, which produced a parrot with resplendent feathers. The former group stayed in the north, while the latter group journeyed southward.

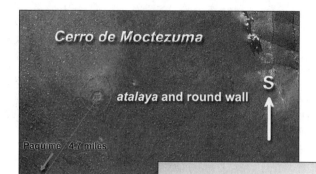

Satellite view of
Cerro de Moctezuma
from 7,910 ft.
El Pueblito
("little pueblo")
is about 1 mile north
of the "watchtower."

Cerro de Moctezuma
may have served as a
communication center
for the entire region.

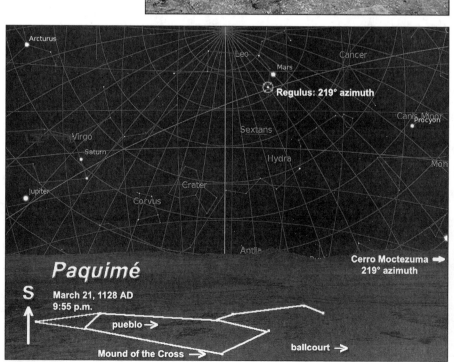

The group that had chosen the parrot finally arrived at the Land of Everlasting Sunshine.[46] There they founded a magnificent city in a warm climate with abundant sources of water. Archaeologist Linda Cordell states: "The Casas Grandes Valley itself is wide, fertile, and relatively well-watered, and the indigenous, Mogollon-like population experienced a general population growth."[47] The city had an irrigation system at least comparable to if not surpassing that of the Chaco Canyon complex. Frank Waters comments: "Inside the city was a large reservoir filled by a ditch run from the river a few miles to the north. From this reservoir rock-walled underground ducts led throughout the city. They possibly served as both a water system and a sewage system."[48]

At some point about three centuries later in the mid-15th century, the stars must have aligned in a cluster of negative aspects, because Paquimé experienced a precipitous collapse. As one theory goes, the city's demise was caused by a tremendous deluge, which also destroyed the whole Third World (Era). A Hopi myth describes the destruction of *Palatkwapi*, the legendary Red City of the South: "...now the Bálölöokongs [water serpents] were shooting forth from the ground with streams of water in all parts of the village, from the fireplaces in the kivas, in the houses from the water vessels, and in fact everywhere. Water began to fill the houses in the village. Soon the houses began to fall, burying many of the inhabitants under falling walls."[49] Being made of mud instead of stone, these walls were susceptible to the violent water erosion of an inundation. The Hopi version of the flood is echoed almost word for word by the Mayan *Popol Vuh*: "The desperate ones ran as quickly as they could; they wanted to climb to the tops of the houses, and the houses fell down and threw them to the ground..."[50]

Another theory posits extinction by fire. In this scenario, the city was apparently sacked and burned, with plaster scorched and vigas charred. More than 80 corpses lay unburied in the streets and inside rooms, while the macaws were left to starve in their pens.[51] A rather sad ending to this grandiose but bellicose Mexican metropolis.

Regardless of which element played a part in its ending, the sophisticated City of the Scarlet Macaws thrived for over three centuries. Its impressive astronomical knowledge was evident in the groundplan that mirrored the constellation Leo. Well versed in both the solar and stellar realms of the cosmos, this Pre-Columbian municipality was truly at the regal heart of the Land of Eternal Sunlight.

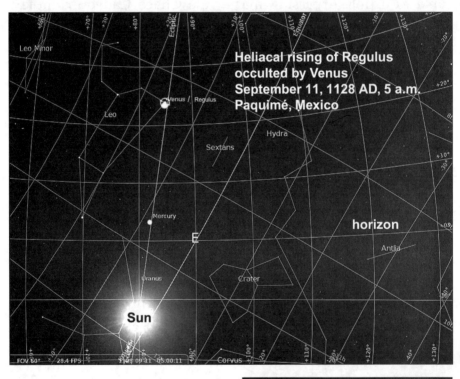

The fact that Regulus is egg-shaped may be just a coincidence. It bulges at the equator because of its rapid rate of spinning. Photographed by the CHARA array, Mt. Wilson, California.

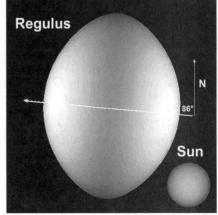

Chapter 10
The Lost Empire of Aztlán

"'Over the Mountains / Of the Moon,
Down the Valley of the Shadow,
Ride, boldly ride,' / The shade replied
'If you seek for Eldorado!'"

Edgar Allan Poe

The Conquest of Culiacán

In 1930, geographer Carl Sauer along with Donald Brand made an "archaeogeographic reconnaissance" of an area along the central Sinaloan coast of Mexico called Aztlán (or Aztatlán), which some people claim is the mythical homeland of the Nahua people and but also of the Uto-Aztecan speakers. (These include the Hopi, Pima-Papago, Ute, Shoshone, Comanche, Yaqui, Tarahumara, Huichol, and other tribes.) Exactly four centuries earlier, Nuño de Guzmán had reconnoitered the same region in search of the fabled Seven Cities of Cibola, or the Seven Cities of Gold. He called the territory that he surveyed "Tierra Caliente del Nuevo Galicia" (Hot Land of New Spain). It was in fact the elusive El Dorado that Guzmán sought.

The name Aztatlán is, in fact, found on a 1570 atlas drawn by the cartographer Ortelius. (See map on p. 243.) Although its climate was temperate, it was hardly a paradise. The basic landscape is bush savanna and scrub steppe. Today the coastal strip and the foothills west of the sierras are covered by dense patches of *monte*—leafless, gray, thorny shrubs virtually impassible except where foot paths are maintained. This tough vegetation is interspersed with occasional columnar cacti, such as pitaya and saguaro. However, the land is copiously watered with rivers

241

flowing larger than those in the more arid region to the north. It was enough to let a cultural nexus flourish.

Archaeologist Stephen H. Lekson remarks on the territory's major cultural center: "Culiacán Viejo was the last great city on the precolonial west coast, and it became the jumping-off point for early Spanish explorations into the trackless north. Prehistorically, it was the center of the Aztatlan tradition, an archaeological entity with Mesoamerican pottery but lacking, apparently, ball courts and pyramids."[1] Spanish accounts do, however, point to artificial elevations identified by a number of terms: *promontorio pequeño*, *arcabuco*, and *monton de tierra algo alto*—i.e. platform mounds.

No excavations were permitted, but Sauer and Brand also found numerous dwelling mounds –some 40 to 50 yards long– that were actually individual houses buried by erosional deposition and detritus. Some of the mounds were positioned in rows; others were arranged around a square, which suggests a central plaza.

From this evidence they concluded that the site of Culiacán, located along the Culiacán River, was an adobe town "of urban extensiveness."[2] This was an understatement. Later excavations revealed that most of the houses had thatched walls and roofs rather than adobe. Nevertheless, this was no podunk outpost.

The pueblos that the Spanish had found in 1530 were *"muchos muy grandes."* The whole of the Culiacán Valley was, in fact, studded with them. Most Spanish accounts stress the population density of the area. One account describes it as "...peopled in some very large plains; the population reaches to the sea; a very beautiful river flows through the midst of the population; it abounds in all kinds of food." Another says that "...the land was more densely peopled than has been seen in the Indies, nine leagues of it were lined with pueblos on one side and the other, spaced at a distance of three-quarters to half a league, each one with five or six hundred houses." A further account incidentally comments that the province was "...the most densely inhabited which was seen along the ocean and had the best looking women." (An ugly fringe benefit of the Guzmán expedition?) Yet another: "...the chieftains who came in to submit recorded more than two hundred pueblos that were subject to the lords of Culiacán."[3]

Right: Huitzilopochtli as human, perhaps a *pochtecatl* with a sack and quincunx-shield, Codex Telleriano-Remensis, 16th century.

Below: On this map "Aztatlan" is marked at about 30° north latitude. Rio Guaiaual (Rio Tamazula?) empties into the Gulf of California opposite the tip of the Baja.

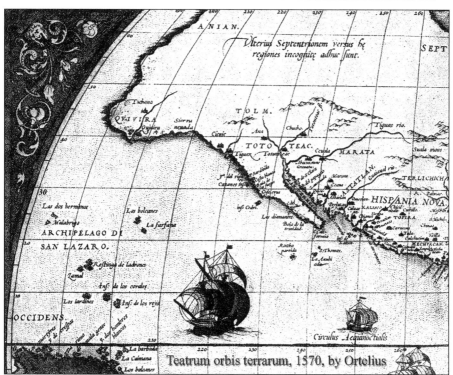

Teatrum orbis terrarum, 1570, by Ortelius

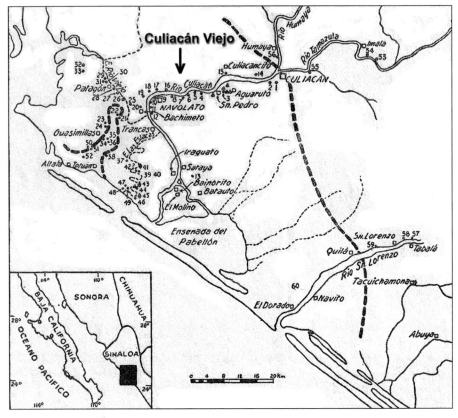

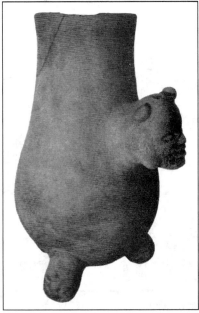

Above: map showing archaeological excavations at Culiacán, Sinaloa, Mexico, 1945.

Left: Tripod effigy vessel with horned human head.

One native source commented on the imperial nature of local governance. "…the province was inhabited by unnumbered pueblos to the sea and was most flourishing, the governing chief Ocelotl had subjected to his rule some of the mountain Indians and had in his house two hundred porters and a hundred servants to grind meal, and the town of Sentispac [at the southern end of the region] contained ten thousand Indians without the subject Indians who were ten thousand more." In other words, this was not simply an idyllic, non-hierarchical, hunter-gatherer society.[4]

"The people of Aztatlán were lowlanders, tillers of the soil on a large scale, fishermen, *salinero* ["salt producers"], and they lived in warfare with the dwellers of the barrancas, who were cannibals."[5] (Were the latter a reference to the Chichimecs of the Sierra Madre to the north?)

By one account, the Spanish met 80,000 warriors near the modern town of El Dorado, although this is probably an exaggeration.[6] Estimates from other encounters are far less, though still substantial: "…there was one body of more than ten thousands Indians bravely adorned with feathers."[7] The Spaniards also characterized the men as great archers, who additionally used round shields made of withes.[8] With the exception of one major battle, however, the natives pretty much surrendered sans struggle. Perhaps the Aztatlánians had a ruler similar to Moctezuma, whose omens of doom and disaster a decade earlier had sealed the fate of the Aztec at Tenochtitlán.

The nutritional triad of maize, frijoles, and squash had been traditionally grown, along with chili peppers, eggplants, and guava. The agricultural abundance is exemplified by the fact that Guzmán's troops were fed in one town alone for a month-and-a-half. Cotton was produced for cloth, and domesticated turkeys were kept perhaps both for food and feathers. Dogs were also a part of village life.

Ceramics equal in quality to anything found in Mexico were produced. "During conquest times, Culiacán… is known to have been the northern outpost of high culture on the West Coast. It is singular therefore that from this decidedly peripheral region should come pottery which ranks with the best wares of the continent."[9]

Some pottery bowls were polychrome, painted in red, yellow, white, black, and orange. They displayed a wide range of geometric designs, including spirals, scallops, circles, helixes, funnels, dots, dot-dashes, cross hatches, interlocking stepped frets, stripes, diamonds, triangles, serrated figures, bar panels, wavy panels, and checkerboard patterns. Naturalistic designs included birds, feathers, fish, and fantail monsters.

Culiacaños also crafted terra cotta animal effigies as well as human effigies with pancake heads, coffee-bean eyes, and prominent, hooked noses. In addition, some of the odd figurines had pointed or gargoyle-shaped heads. Some of these representations had undeniably non-Indian facial features.

Tripod bowls and vases were also found, along with clay cylinder seals similar to those used in Sumer. A variety of assorted artifacts were unearthed, including whistles, spindle whorls, and clay pipes shaped like lizards or even one that resembled a triceratops dinosaur. (See p 248.) Large ollas had been used as burial urns for bones stripped of their flesh. (I will spare my readers the details.)

Bird plumage was used in headdresses, most likely macaw or parrot feathers imported from the south. Ornaments were crafted from pearls, shells, gold, silver, and even turquoise—the latter imported from the north. The people also sailed the wide river and probably the seashore with rafts made of reeds lashed with calabashes.

All pueblos of the Culiacán Valley were located on a floodplain. Guzmán's first expedition was nearly wiped out at the town of Aztatlán by a summer inundation. This expedition, on the other hand, also wiped out almost all archaeological traces of the natives by employing a scorched earth policy. The *modus operandi*: pillage and incinerate.

Sauer and Brand somewhat bitterly comment on the difficulty of their archaeological field work: "Our area was almost completely destroyed because it was overrun in 1530 and 1531 by about as hard a gang of killers as Spain let loose anywhere in the New World and because in those days there was no stay upon the killing propensities of the conquerors."[10]

Culiacán polychrome pottery (orange, yellow, red, black, white).

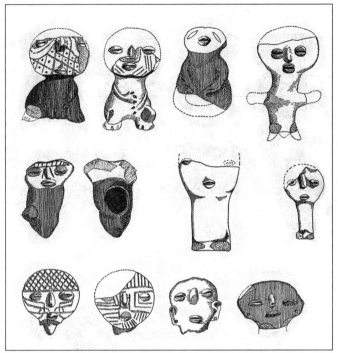

Terra cotta human effigy heads.

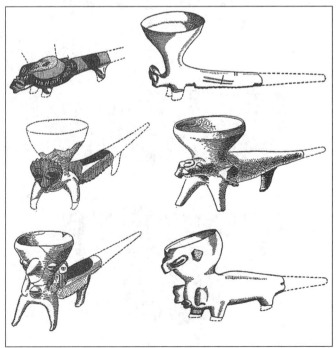

Culiacán clay pipes.

Just five years after the expedition, between 1535 and 1536, about 130,000 Indians died of measles and smallpox in the valley.[11] During this same period thousands more were enslaved and exported from the country. Sheer desolation was left in the wake of the Spanish *entrada*. It must indeed have seemed like a wake. The region had reached its cultural apex around 1450 AD and declined thereafter. Guzmán's terror campaign was just the coup de grâce to Culiacán. Archaeologist Isabel Kelly, who performed excavations in the area during the mid 20th century, comments on this cultural genocide. "It is evident that this is [or was] no weak, marginal culture. A heavy population, village organization, markets, intensive agriculture, and technological skill in a variety of materials all indicate a sophisticated and well-advanced culture. This is the picture at the time of the Conquest—a flourishing culture, which was wiped out within a very few years through brutal exploitation and heavy disease toll."[12]

Chicomoztoc, the Crooked Hill

Although Sauer and Brand believed that this relatively high civilization was a northern frontier settled by people from the south rather than by pre-Aztecans from the north, the indigenous population had a different take. "Local patriotism indoctrinates the youth of Sinaloa with the belief that Culiacán was the 'crooked hill' of Aztec migration."[13]

Skeletal evidence from the vicinity of Culiacán indeed supports this latter interpretation.

"On the whole the ancient inhabitants of Aguaranto [a main site at Culiacán], of medium stature and small heads, appear to be racially intermediate between the Mexicans and the larger Southwestern types. This is not in any way surprising when we consider the location of the site and the traditional story of the wanderings of the Nahua tribes [i.e. Aztec]. The broad noses and low head reveal, perhaps, remnants of an older population akin to the Basketmakers."[14]

The name Culiacán comes from the Nahuatl word *colhuacán*, which means either "Place of the Ancestors" or "Place of the Hill Bent Forward," namely, "crooked." Colhuacán can also have the sense of "Twisted Hill." This great hill was said to have been located in the midst of the waters of Aztlán (or Aztatlán), which means "Place of Whiteness" (*aztatl* = "whiteness").

This may be a reference to salt. As mentioned above, Sauer identifies the Aztatlánians as *salineros*, or "salt producers." In this case, sodium chloride is the result not of mining but of the interaction of sunlight drying up saline marshes to leave a film of encrusted salt. This is culturally akin to the salt gathering expeditions that the Hopi, the Zuni, and other Pueblo people undertake annually.

The name Colhuacán also denotes "Place of Those Who Adore Coltzin." This refers to the Aztec god who is twisted, bent, or curved.[15] Coltzin may correspond to the ithyphallic Humpbacked Flute Player known in the American Southwest as Kokopelli (in Hopi, *kokopilau*)—the first syllable of each figure being identical. One theory connects this figure with the Aztec *pochtecatl* (pl., *pochteca*) from Mesoamerica, who carried a sack of goods on his back and announced his arrival at a pueblo by playing his flute. This wealthy, highly respected long-distance merchant was a vital geographic link between north and south.

The delightful land of Aztatlán, at least in ancient times, was replete with herons, cormorants, cranes, ducks and other waterfowl. (The *atl* in the middle of the country's name in Aztec language also means "water.") Two additional denotations of Aztlán are "Place of the Heron" (an aquatic bird) and "Place of the Reeds" (an aquatic plant). As I stated in my book *Eye of the Phoenix*, the heron is the naturalistic version of the mythical phoenix, the Egyptian bird that rises from the ashes of its pyre at the end of each temporal cycle and is reborn. The reed, on the other hand, is a universal symbol of high culture and civilization recognized all over the world.

In *The History of the Indies of New Spain*, Fray Diego Duran writes that Moctezuma I (also called Motecuzoma the Old, 1441 – 1469) had dispatched 60 wizened sorcerers from Tenochtitlán in order to find the place where the ancestors had once lived without aging. This original location of Chicomoztoc, or the Seven Caves of Aztatlán, was also where lived Coatlicue, "the Mother Goddess of the Earth Who Gives Birth to all Celestial Things." It was additionally the place that her son, the war-and-sun god Huitzilopochtli, was born.

At the beginning of their journey, the shamanic elders gathered on the hill of Coatepec ("Mountain of the Serpent") in Tula (or Tollan, another "Place of the Reeds"). They traced magic symbols on the ground, invoked demons, and smeared themselves with a special ointment. These rituals allowed them to change into birds, ocelots, jaguars, jackals, and wild cats. This, incidentally, is reminiscent of the *nagual* phenomenon described in the books of anthropologist and mystic Carlos Castaneda. They then proceeded in various animal forms toward Chicomoztoc, located supposedly 300 leagues away. (If the journey was made by normal means, the distance on foot to the proto-Aztec center seems plausible. A league is the distance that can be walked in one hour. Of course, this varies due to terrain. Culiacán is a bit over 600 miles to the northwest. This would mean the average speed would be 2 m.p.h. Average walking speed for an adult on a straight pavement is about 3 m.p.h., so this does not seem unreasonable, given that part of the route traversed over the Sierra Madre.)

The Aztec envoys arrived in Aztatlán on the shores of a great lake in the middle of which rose Colhuacán. They assumed their human form again and saw people in canoes fishing and farmers peacefully tending their plots. The sorcerers soon discovered that Colhuacán was the "Hill of Eternal Youth," inside of which were numerous caves and grottoes. Coatlicue, "She of the Serpent Skirt," lived on top of this magical hill. (Yet another meaning of the name Colhuacán is "Place of the Snakes.")

An old servant who attended her became miraculously younger and younger with each step up the hill. The sorcerers were unable to follow him because their feet sank into the sand. The servant remarked that they could not climb the hill because of the rich food and chocolate that they ate back home—a symptom of urban decadence as opposed to the rustic vigor of the Aztatlánians.

Right: Statue of Coatlicue, "She of the Serpent Skirt," mother of Huitzilopochtli, National Museum of Anthropology, Mexico City.

Below: Huitzilopochtli as a god, Codex Borbonicus.

When Coatlicue finally appeared and looked down on the sorcerers at the base of the hill, they found her to be a filthy, despicable woman who looked like she never washed, changed her clothes, or combed her hair. She was, in fact, still mourning the departure of her son Huitzilopochtli, who had promised years ago to return but had failed to do so.[16]

Huitzilopochtli, or "Hummingbird on the Left (South)," was the principal deity of the tribe later known as the Aztec. He was known as "Lord of Created Things" and "the Almighty." His martial character was symbolized by a lightning-snake spear. This was tempered, however, with a hummingbird panache. His overt dual nature of sky and earth may have been a precursor of the plumed serpent Quetzalcoatl. Warriors who died in battlefield were supposedly reincarnated as hummingbirds.

Diego Durán describes Huitzilopochtli's temple, Templo Mayor, in Tenochtitlán, which was actually a pair of adjacent chambers atop his pyramid. (The rain god Tlaloc was in the adjacent chamber, signifying his secondary importance in the Aztecan pantheon.) The idol of Huitzilopochtli was a wooden statue seated on a blue wooden bench—blue representing the sky. On each corner of the litter that held the bench was a serpent-headed pole. Durán believed that the litter with his likeness was carried around the country after he and the ancestors left on their migrations, in much the same manner that the Ark of the Covenant was transported across the Sinai wilderness.

Huitzilopochtli's helmet was shaped like a hummingbird's beak made of gold, and he had the bird's feathers on his left leg—hence his name. He was apparently conceptualized as facing west, the direction of the sun's path, underscoring his role as sun god. The idol wore a green mantle the color of the bird's feathers. His apron, which nearly reached his feet, was covered with green feathers adorned with gold.

His left hand held a white shield made of reeds, upon which five tufts of white feathers were arranged in a quincunx, which represented the Fifth Sun and fire. From the top of the shield a golden banner rose. From the shield's handle four arrows were extended. In his left hand he held a blue, undulating serpent.

From his belt rose another golden banner against his back. He wore bracelets and blue sandals.[17] The mid-20th century American explorer and prolific archaeological historian Victor W. von Hagen describes the cult of Huitzilopochtli.

> "Who were the Aztec and from whence—it is answered in their mythico-histories. Like all other such origin myths, these differ in detail, not in basic content. The Inca came out of caves; Greeks were given divine guidance by an *autologos* in a darkened sanctuary; Christian myths over-flow with heavenly-inspired grottoes. And so, the Aztec. They found in a cave the Hummingbird Wizard, the famous Huitzilopochtli (a name the conquerors never mastered, calling it *Huichilobos*, 'Witchy Wolves'). The idol gave them advice. It sounded well: wander, look for lands, avoid any large-scale fighting, send pioneers ahead, have them plant maize, when the harvest is ready move up to it; keep me, Huitzilopochtli, always with you, carrying me like a banner, feed me on human hearts torn from the recently sacrificed. . . . All of which the Aztec did."[18]

The following hymn to Huitzilopochtli was translated from Nahuatl. Note the turquoise that he wears, probably imported from the north. An alternate name for the figure was Xiuhpilli, "Turquoise Prince."

> "Huitzilopochtli, / Only a subject, / Only a mortal was. / A magician, / A terror, / A stirrer of strife, / A deceiver, / A maker of war, / An arranger of battles, / A lord of battles; / And of him it was said / That he hurled / His flaming serpent, / His fire stick; / Which means war, / Blood and burning; / And when his festival was celebrated, / Captives were slain, / Washed slaves were slain, / The merchants washed them. / And thus he was arrayed: / With head-dress of green feathers, / Holding his serpent torch, / Girded with a belt, / Bracelets upon his arms, / Wearing turquoises, / As a master of messengers."[19]

This poem identifies Huitzilopochtli as a bellicose mortal but not a deity. That being the case, I wonder if the conquistadors really had trouble pronouncing his name, or whether the canine reference was intentionally descriptive. For the Pueblo people of the north, dogs are generally associated with sorcery and death. I am also puzzled by the similarity between the Spanish designation for the Aztec god (*Huichilobos*) and the tribe living in Nayarit and northern Jalisco commonly known as the Huichol, but who call themselves the Wixáritari.

Franciscan missionary Bernardino de Sahagún (1499 – 1590) writes in his book *General History of the Things of New Spain* that the ancient Nahuas who left their primitive home Chicomoztoc, the land of the Seven Caves, worshipped only one god, Mixcoatl, or "Cloud Serpent." (Again, the sky-earth dichotomy.) He was recognized as god of the hunt and identified with the Milky Way. As fire god, he additionally invented a cosmic fire drill out of the heavens revolving around their polar axis; thereby he brought fire to humankind.

> "I come forth from Chicomoztoc, only to you, my friends,
>   to you, honored ones.
> I come forth from Tziuactitlan, only to you my friends,
>   only to you honored ones.
> I sought, I sought, in all directions I sought with my pack;
>   in all directions
> I sought with my pack. I sought, I sought, in all directions
> I sought with my traveling net.
> I took them in hand, I took them in hand;
>   yes, I took them in hand;
> yes, I took them in hand. In the ball ground
> I sang well and strong, like to the quetzal bird;
> I answered back to the god."[20]

In this poem in which Mixcoatl is speaking, the quetzal is, of course, a brilliantly hued bird of the subtropical southern regions. The "pack" may be a reference to the main accouterment of the *pochteca* previously mentioned. We also hear a reference to Tziuactitlan, which is "the land of the *tzihuac* bushes," apparently a kind of maguey cactus "of a sacred character." Also known as the century plant (*Agave americana*), it was used to make thread, rope, or coarse cloth. The plant was also fermented to make the intoxicating beverage called *octli*. Modern Mexicans still imbibe this strongly alcoholic liquor, which they call *pulque*.

The early 20th century Scottish mythologist Donald A. MacKenzie comments on the connection between the humming-bird, the agave cactus, and certain Huitzilopochtli rituals.

> "The humming-bird, which thrusts its long beak into flowers and feeds on honey-devouring insects and carries honey to its young, nests in the agave plant. It is not surprising, therefore, to find traces of belief in the honey elixir of life in connection with Huitzilopochtli rites…. In Mexico images of Huitzilopochtli were made of dough prepared from seeds and edible plants, or from maize, and mixed with honey and blood. The images were ceremonially eaten."[21]

Durán was horrified, by the way, that this pagan ritual of consuming Huitzilopochtli's flesh was so close to the Christian Eucharist. He thought it even might be Satan's perversion of the Holy Communion.

The maguey was in fact considered by the ancient Mexicans to be a sort of cosmic Tree of Life. At the base of the plant at the center of four conventionalized leaves (representing the cardinal directions) is a bulb storing the milky liquid—the womb of the Great Mother, or a type of "cave" that holds the elixir of life. In East Indian mythology it is akin to the pot containing *soma* (Amrita), the fluid of the primal sea. This brings to mind the legend of the Churning of the Milky Ocean, which, as the classic tome *Hamlet's Mill* has shown us, is a mytho-cosmic representation of the *axis mundi*.

Mixcoatl with regalia,
Codex Telleriano-Remensis, 16th century.

Icons of the Eight Nahua Tribes

1. Matlatzinca
People of the Fishnet
2. Tepaneca
People of the Stone Walls
3. Chichimeca
People of the Dog
4. Malinalca
People of the Braided Grass
5. Colhuaca
People of the Ancestors
6. Xochimilca
People of the Flower Fields
7. Chalca
People of the Jadeite
8. Huexotzinca
People of the Willows

At any rate, Sahagún refers to the migrating group not as the Nahuas but as the Chichimec, or "Sons of the Dog." (Again, a canine reference. I discuss this tribe extensively in my previous books. I believe they came from the north and probably not only lived at Chaco Canyon but dominated the region, determining its essential socio-economic character.) Also, the placename *Chichiman* itself means "Area of Milk," which may refer to the milky liquid of the maguey cactus of Aztatlán. This further reinforces the meaning of Culiacán as the "Place of Whiteness."

The Chichimec may as well have been called the "Sons of the Bow," for it was they who introduced this formidable weapon to Mesoamerica. Gordon Brotherston, British translator of Latin American texts, observes: "Along with the spear-thrower [atlatl] came the bow and arrow. As developed by peoples north of Mexico, it was brought south by the Nahua-speaking Chichimec and played a big role in Mesoamerica in the centuries immediately prior to the Spanish conquest. Because of its range and accuracies, this weapon was frequently related to the very notion of restless ambition and military expansion, and to what the Aztecs called the 'acquisitions of the hunt'."[22]

When the Chichimec empire began, the center of power was established at the "Wild Agave House," and the cardinal directions were determined by ceremonially shooting an arrow into each quarter, with a color assigned to each direction (north = red; west = yellow; south = white; east = green).[23]

The basic character of the Aztec, ruthless and obdurate as obsidian, was forged in the Chichimec heart. It was this fierce attitude that drove this barbarian race down from the north to institute a grand but brutal civilization. Inside the cave beneath the Crooked Hill, Huitzilopochtli himself spoke about the glorious rewards of the conquerors and their obligatory spoils of war. These included lavish goods, a life of ease, the choicest foods, the most beautiful women, the costliest equipment — any luxury desired. Their birthright demanded such things.

From a Nahuatl history written at the turn of the 17th century by an Aztec with the adopted Spanish name Cristóbal de Castillo , we hear the words of Huitzilopochtli:

"This is the first quality with which you will enhance yourself: Eagle & Jaguar; Fire & Water; Arrow & Shield. This will be your indispensable food, this you will live by, so that you proceed striking terror. The payment for your breast and heart will be your conquests, your overrunning and destroying the common people, the dwellers in all the places you reach, and when you take captives you will cut open their chests with a Flint on the sacrificial stone and you will offer their hearts to the brilliant Movement in the sky."[24]

The Chichimecs and their constellation of "barbaric" northern gods apparently brought with them an astral theology that reinforced the north-south meridian. The 20th century French anthropologist Jacques Soustelle describes this celestial religion.

"As the god of a tribe of hunters and warriors from the north, Uitzilopochtli [Huitzilopochtli] belonged to a group of stellar and celestial gods who had been brought down by the northern nations that had invaded Mexico— gods such as Tezcalipoca, the god of the Great Bear, of the night sky, the protean wizard who sees all in his obsidian mirror, the 'young man', Telpochtli, who protects young warriors; and Mixcoatl, the god of the Milky Way, the protector of hunters and, under the name of Camaxtli, the national god of Tlaxcala. It may be that the nomads of the steppes knew only a small number of deities and that *their religion was essentially, if not entirely, astral* [italics added]."[25]

The Seven Caves of Aztlán

Among the Aztecs "...there was an almost universal belief that the goddess Citlalicue [Coatlicue] gave birth to a *tecpatl* which fell from the sky to the earth at a place called Chicomoztoc (Seven Caverns) : that from the *tecpatl* came sixteen hundred gods and goddesses : and that, after a complaint to

Citlalicue that there was no one to worship them, mankind was created for their service."[26] A *tecpatl* was a stone knife used for human sacrifice. It was also a glyph indicating one of the days of the month.

In another parturition legend involving Coatlicue, a ball of brilliantly colored feathers fell from the sky upon the goddess, thus impregnating her with Huitzilopochtli. This sort of "immaculate conception" seemed unnatural to Huitzilopochtli's sister, a beautiful sorceress named Coyolxauhqui. She was so enraged that she gathered her 400 brothers and devised a plot to kill Coatlicue and child *in utero*. At the last moment, however, Huitzilopochtli leapt fully-grown from his mother's womb and slew his sister. He then cut off her head and threw it in the sky, where it became the moon. He also killed most of his brothers and hurled them into the heavens, where they became the southern stars.

Some of the names of the ancient homeland were transferred to Mesa Central once the Aztec tribe was finally settled. For instance, the Hill of Colhuacán, now known as Cerro de la Estrella (Hill of the Star), is located on the edge of Mexico City. On the summit of this volcanic prominence, ruins can still be seen of a temple dedicated to Mixcoatl, father of Ce Acatl Tolpiltzin (Quetzalcoatl). This latter king, incidentally, was identified by his fair skin, thick black beard, and long hair.[27]

After Huitzilopochtli and the ancestors departed southward to eventually morph into the Aztecs of Anahuac, the place they had left became infested with dense, thorny bushes and brambles—much as we see Culiacán today.

A final semantic variation of the name Colhuacán (Culiacán) is "Place Where Roads Turn." The trade route from the south ran north-northwest along the coast of Culiacán, the last stop before one headed off into what was then known as Terra Incognita. The geographer Carl Sauer was puzzled by the fact that at Culiacán, the Guzmán expedition had veered due north, trying to find a passage through the Sierra Madre Occidental. It would have been much easier just to follow the coast up through Sonora in order to attain their objective of Cibola, the reputed

Seven Cities of Gold, which are now generally recognized as being the Zuni area of western New Mexico. Carl Sauer comments:

"From the densely peopled lands of central Mexico a road led by way of the coastal lowlands of the Mexican Northwest to the northern land of the Pueblo Indians, and, at the last, to California. It is here called the Road to Cibola, since the search for the legendary Seven Cities was the main reason for its opening by the Spaniards. Initially the road was a well-used series of Indian trails. Turquoise was carried south over it; the plumage of parrots and other brightly colored birds of subtropical lowlands furnished the most important articles taken north. Buffalo skins, shells and pearls, metals, obsidian were other trade items of more or less importance. Maize appears also to have been an item of barter when there was a local crop failure."[28]

Another Carl, the late 19th century Norwegian explorer and ethnographer Carl Lumholtz, said that his native guide referred to the south-to-north road across the mountains as *el camino de los antiguos* ("road of the ancient ones").[29] This may be a reference to the Colhuaca, or the People of the Ancestors. It was basically a footpath rather than an equestrian trail, which makes Guzmán's unsuccessful attempt in the 16th century to head for the region located due north even more of a mystery. Guzmán was apparently acting on information of his own native guide, "...whose father traded into the back country, exchanging fine feathers for ornaments, by a forty days' journey northward, and one that involved passage of a wilderness."[30]

The narrative continues: "...once or twice he himself had accompanied his father, and had seen towns so large that he could compare them in size to Mexico [City] and its suburbs. There were seven of these towns, and there were whole rows of streets inhabited by gold and silver workers. He said besides, that in order to reach these seven towns it was necessary to cross a desert for forty days, where there was no vegetation except short grass about five inches in height, and that the direction was to the north between both oceans."[31] Thus, in the fervid minds of the gold seekers, the Seven Cities of Cibola were conflated with the Seven Caves of the ancestral Aztecs.

What great city of substantial wealth lies due north of Culiacán? Across some of the most rugged and impassible *sierras* and *barrancas* in the world we find –at a distance of 388 miles– the ancient urban center of Paquimé (or Casas Grandes—see previous chapter). A trek of 40 days would mean that indigenous traders would make nearly 10 miles per day. The accepted average distance for prehistoric foot travel under normal conditions is 22 miles per day.[32] But these were not normal conditions, far from it; so a little less than half the average daily walking distance sounds plausible.

However, if the traders did manage 20 or so miles per day, in 40 days they would have reached the equally impressive prehistoric metropolis in Chaco Canyon. (Culiacán due north to Chaco Canyon = 780 miles.) Some tribes in the region, such as the Tarahumara, are renowned for their ability to run great distances at great speed. One problem with our early 16th century narrator, however, is that Chaco Canyon by that time had been abandoned for over three centuries. Perhaps the *camino* really did live up to its name, and the narrator's distant ancestors had routinely used the route.

Long before the final Aztec migration east to the Valley of Mexico, the south-north route had been well established. Even though the journey was arduous, the incredible riches at the road's destination would have been worth it. The slogan, then, might have been: "Go north, young man." North, the migratory path of hummingbird and heron. North, the road the sun makes along the horizon during the new year's youth. Not north by northwest, but simply north.

Despite its well established trade relations, the empire of Aztlán was lost not due to drought and starvation but primarily to disease and massacre. The beginning of the end came in August 13th, 1521 at Tenochtitlán with Cuahtémoc's surrender. It took only a decade-and-a-half for the conquistadores to finish the job at Aztlán, thereby achieving the conquest of Mexico.

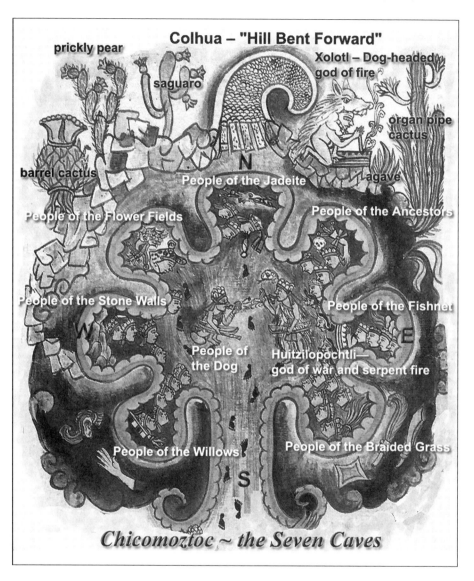

Colhua – "Hill Bent Forward"

prickly pear

saguaro

Xolotl – Dog-headed god of fire

organ pipe cactus

barrel cactus

N

People of the Jadeite

agave

People of the Flower Fields

People of the Ancestors

People of the Stone Walls

W

E

People of the Fishnet

People of the Dog

Huitzilopochtli— god of war and serpent fire

People of the Willows

S

People of the Braided Grass

Chicomoztoc ~ the Seven Caves

Historia Tolteca-Chichimeca, 16th century.

Chicomoztoc, the Nahua's primordial Seven Caves (or perhaps a single, seven-lobed cave) inside the bent hill Colhua, contained the original eight tribes. At the center we see the Chichimeca leader in a colloquy with Huitzilopochtli. At the far end of the cavern is the glyph 1 Flint, which symbolizes the North but also refers specifically to 1168 AD, the date on which the tribes departed from Aztlán to journey to their ultimate home in the Valley of Mexico, arriving around 1248. On top of the cave are the native cacti of this arid region. Xolotl is the dog-headed deity of fire, lightning, the underworld, and death. (See the eight tribes' icons on p. 257.)

Detail of the lower portion of a painting from Historia Tolteca-Chichimeca. Note the black beards of the two figures on the right talking (see "speech-scrolls") with the Chichimeca on the left. Also on the right: a bow-and-arrow, a bag of water breaking open (birth?), and a sacred bundle made of jaguar skin, known as a *tlquimilolli*.

Facing pages from the Codex Boturini, 16th century.

Note: the glyph of the Ancestors, the Colhuaca, atop the pyramid on the island. A paddler departs from the island and reaches the shore at the 1 Flint glyph, representing 1168 AD. The figure goes to a grotto inside of the bent hill Colhua, where Huitzilopochtli is declaiming. The migration, depicted by footprints going west to east, continues past the ancestors' glyph. This shows the route of four priests ("god-bearers") with backpacks on their way to Tenochtitlán. The first part of this vignette resembles the Hopi legend regarding the migration from the previous Third World to the current Fourth World. The ancestral Hopi were inhabitants of an island that was ultimately destroyed by a global flood. They fled on reed boats, sailing eastward across the Pacific, stopping for a time on various islands ("stepping stones") and then moving on. "Leaving their boats, they traveled by foot eastward across the island to the water's edge. Here they found growing some more of the hollow plants like reeds or bamboo, which they cut down. Directed by Spider Woman, they laid some of these in a row with another row on top of them in the opposite direction and tied them all together with vines and leaves. This made a raft big enough for one family or more. When enough rafts were made for all, Spider Woman directed them to make paddles."[33] The people continued onward, "...traveling, still east and a little north." They made their way to the mouth of the Colorado River, and then paddled upstream ("uphill") until a wall of steep mountains rose. At last they arrived at the "Place of Emergence" in Grand Canyon, which is called the *Sipapuni*. From there the ancestors of the Hopi spread out to populate the Colorado Plateau.

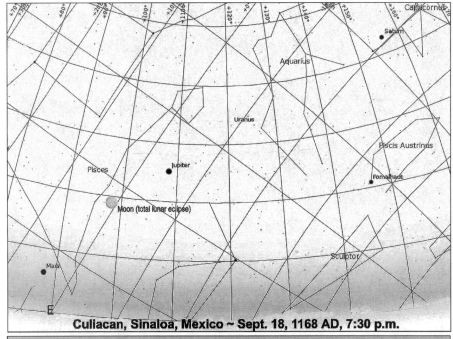

Culiacan, Sinaloa, Mexico ~ Sept. 18, 1168 AD, 7:30 p.m.

Early 20th century art historian Herbert J. Spinden specifies the exact date of the new era. "The Toltec Era was established by Quetzalcoatl, after a simplified model of the Mayan calendar, on August 6, 1168 A.D., this day corresponding to a day 1 Tecpatl (1 Flint) in the first position of a month Toxcatl."[34] The first 52-year cycle began in 1168 and the 13th and last began in 1844.

The Aztecs reputedly departed from Aztlán during 1 Flint, which corresponds to 1168 AD. What prompted their migration? On the evening of September 18th of that year, a total lunar eclipse occurred, when the Moon turned to blood. Not only that, there was also a stunning alignment of planets: Mars hovering above the horizon, the eclipsed Moon, Jupiter, Uranus (barely visible to the naked eye), and Saturn. This planetary line-up had been arranging itself since the spring of that year. At 4:40 a.m. on June 5th, for instance, a grouping of celestial bodies were aligned from left to right on an oblique angle with the horizon: the heliacal rising of Mercury just above the horizon, Aldebaran in Taurus above and to the right of Mercury, a crescent Moon just below the Pleiades, Venus as the morning star, the triad of Jupiter-Mars-Uranus very close together, and finally Saturn at the far upper-right (south). (Archaeoastronomer Robert Dragon has also found a Mogollon star map rock near Linden, Arizona showing this unusual arrangement.[35]) Was this celestial display an omen signifying that the proto-Aztecs should begin their final journey? As previously mentioned, the Chichimeca brought with them from their homeland in the north an astral theology that would have found divine meaning in such planetary and stellar configurations.

Chapter 11
ABCs of Orion —
Ants, Bulls, Bird-Men, & Copper

Orion and Etymology

We all inherit the words we use, while remaining unaware of what might be called their linguistic genealogy. This is necessary because the multiple processes of verbal and written communication are extremely complex. Most of us recognize Orion's magnificent fiery presence in the winter sky, for instance, yet have no idea where his name comes from. Since my books deal so heavily with this particular constellation, I'd like to explore the bloodlines of this name—that is, its philological associations.

Orion cognates, or related words, include: **origin** (source of all being), **orifice** (mouth, entryway, or stargate), **orient** (east, where the sun, Orion and the other stars are born), **orrery** (mechanical device representing the heavens), **orison** (a prayer), **oracle** (a divine utterance), **oragious** (stormy, tempestuous—rare usage), **orrest** (battle, contest, obsolete word), **ora** (either a Danish/Anglo-Saxon form of money or a margin, border, or coast), **oriole** (a golden bird), and **oryx** (a large African antelope, or gemsbok—sacred to the San Bushmen of the Kalahari Desert), as well as **oribi** (a small African antelope). The Latin root **auri-** (gold) may be substituted for **ori-**, thus evoking a solar connotation. **Aurochs**, or **urus** and **ür** (extinct European wild ox, ancestor of domestic cattle, *Bos primigenius*, **Bos taurus**), suggests the close relationship between Orion and Taurus.

Premier researcher of stellar names Richard Hinckley Allen

believes that the word "Orion" is derived from the Akkadian *Uru-anna*, which means "Light of Heaven" and refers to the sun.[1] This curious stellar-solar connection perhaps points to Orion's universal potency that is reflected in a number of cultures. According to the Nigerian scholar Dr. Catherine Acholonu-Olumba, the original source of the constellation's name was the Igbo word *Ora-ana* or *Ora-ani*, which means "the Sun in the Duat [underworld]."

In ancient Egypt, Osiris/Orion descended to the Duat for 70 days—the same period as the mummification process. In late spring the constellation became invisible in the early evening sky, only to return at its heliacal rising in mid-summer. Perhaps this star pattern possessed a numinosity in the underworld equal to the luminosity of our daily solar presence.

For the Igbo of Western Africa *Ora-iyi-enu* means "The Sun in the midst of the Waters of the Firmament." This may refer to the sun on the ecliptic passing through the Milky Way, which was conceptualized in ancient times as a river of stars—in this context the Niger River. (In Egypt it was, of course, the Nile.) One tributary of the Niger River contains the **or-** phoneme as well. Professor Acholonu comments:

> "*Orashi* is a river in Orlu zone - the place of Ele (El) - the god of the autochthons, who is also Atum-Ra/*Atu-Ora* (Word of God/Christ). Ora-shi literally means Ora-Eshi 'People of *Eshi*'/ 'People of the Sun'/ 'Eshi-Sun'– 'The Central Sun'. *Eshi* is derived from, or is, the origin of the word *Sirius*, while *Ora* is the origin of *Orion*. Thus *Ora-shi* implies *Orion-Sirius*. In my analyses I connect Orashi with the god-man Ele who was actually my first ancestor. He was the god of agriculture in Sumer where he is also called *Orashi* – a river God. The name of my clan/town is derived from his name: *Orlu* is the anglicized form of Ele, whom we call (as in Hebrew El Elyon) 'He/God-man of the Heights' or *Okwa-ra Ugwu Ele*."

Thus, Orion-Sirius are paired here in the same way Osiris/Orion and Isis/Sirius were associated in ancient Egypt. Dr. Acholonu adds,

"**Ora** is the origin of **Ra**, and **Atum** is from **Atu**, which means in Igbo Shaman language (Afa) - 'The Word of God/Logos'. **Ora** means 'sun', but also 'Son of God'. It also means 'the people', i.e. all Igbos."[2]

The chief deity of the ancient Egyptian ceremonial city of Heliopolis (literally "sun city"), was Mnevis (alternately written *Mer-wer*), a black bull, also referred to as *Kemwer*, "great black one."[3] (See picture on p. 270.) We will see the importance of the bull-motif shortly.

Among the Yoruba of Nigeria, Ori represents the god of wisdom who guides souls through the celestial realm and determines mental abilities on the earth plane. The *ori* is also a specific spiritual aspect of a human that serves as the individual's guardian and is connected to one's life-plan or fate. The word *oriki* refers to a praise-song describing a person's physical attributes, deeds, and successes or failures. This same West African tribe calls heaven or sky Orun and recognizes the sky god Orisa-nla (also known as Obatala, i.e. Osiris), who created the earth and shaped all living things. He is associated with the color white; for instance, he wears white raiment and lives in a white palace.[4] In addition, the Yoruba see Orunmila (i.e. Thoth) as the deity of healing and divination or destiny.[5]

More negative connotations originate in both the Middle East and the Pacific region. Orotalt was a pre-Islamic Arabian tutelary god equated with Dionysus, and Oro was the Tahitian god of war.[6]

Most mythological figures have dual roles that sometime contradict each other. On the positive side, for instance, the Yoruba refer to any god or supernatural being or in fact anything holy as *orisha* (also spelled *orisa*).[7] This is reminiscent of the Iroquois word *orenda*, which refers to a non-personal, supernatural force present in varying degrees in natural objects, animals, or humans that confers sacred powers of accomplishment.[8]

On the negative side, the secret Ogboni cult of the Yoruba conceives of Oro as a plague god, possibly associated with Ora, the plague god of Babylon, or Erra, the Akkadian deity of pestilence and mayhem.[9] These deities were similar to the Canaanite god of war and plagues named Reseph, and the related Phoenician storm god Baal, who assumes the classic Orion stance.

Statuette of Baal, right arm raised in classic Orion stance. Bronze figurine, 14th – 12th centuries BC, Ras Shamra (Ugarit), Syria. Note long Phrygian headdress (elongated head?).

Mnevis, bull-headed god, bronze statue, 4th – 3rd century BC, Heliopolis. Note sun disk and uraeus on crest.

Right: Nearly 20 mi. north of Damascus on Younan Mt. (ele. 7,500 ft.), this bronze statue dedicated to Orion was found. Three ruins from the Roman/Byzantine eras contained a sacrifical altar, bronze coins, & iron/bronze spearheads. Local legends say this was Orion's birthplace.

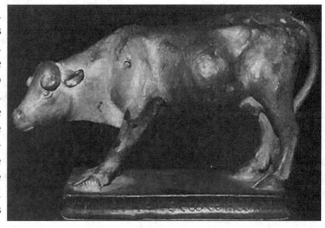

This stance consists of an upraised right arm holding a club and an extended left arm holding either a shield or lion's skin.[10] A sword hangs from his belt and waves lap his feet—in the case of the constellation, the river Eridanus (Eri-danus). Jim Bailey's book *Sailing to Paradise*[11] depicts a bronze sculpture made by the Mossi tribe in Burkina Faso. It shows a warrior with a javelin instead of a club in his upraised right hand and a shield with an engraved spiral in his left. The figure wears a pointed Phrygian cap (a kind of Phoenician headgear), and he has a short sword or dagger in his belt.

The same *Ora* phoneme mentioned above was also used in South America. A word referring to Orion is found on a cosmological drawing from around 1619 made by Pachacuti Yamqui, an Inca nobleman. His sketch describes the wall of a temple in Cusco, Peru. The word *orcorara* refers to the cross formed by the horizontal belt stars of Orion and the vertical staff of Betelgeuse and Rigel.[12]

Finally, there are all the **ari-** or **eri-** cognates. In Icelandic/Old Norse, it means "eagle"; in Hebrew, "lion"; in Sanskrit, either "enemy" or "small sword" (like Orion's). As noted in Chapter 2, the word aristocracy derives from the Greek *aristos*, which literally means "best" or "noblest." Ares was the Greek god of war, and *arete* was the aggregate qualities of good character. The French word *arete* denotes "mountain ridge" and comes from the Latin *arista*, an "ear of wheat." (We recall that the Greek *oros* means "mountain.")

The related Sanskrit word *arya*, as in Aryan, means "of high rank" or "noble." In her new book *Eden in Sumer on the Niger* (January 2013), Dr. Acholonu states: "Aryans emerged from the Indian arm of the Sumerian refugees from ancient Nigeria. The term **Arya/Aerie/Herie** from which is derived the German **Herr** ('Lord'), which [L. A.] Waddell says originated in Sumer, is a cognate of Igbo **Eri**. Robert Bauval in *Black Genesis: The Prehistoric Origins of Ancient Egypt* actually revealed that the Blacks who first populated Egypt by 3,000 – 4,000 B.C. were the Napta Playans, who migrated from the direction of Chad in West Africa—a people whose kings bore the title **Herri**!" (See Bauval quote on p. 66.)

Somewhere in the plexus of Orion phonemes –**ora / ore / ori / oro / ari / auri / auro / eri / uru**– we find our starry companion, contentious though he is.

Orion and Ants

Orion's actual Indo-European root is somewhat surprising. The name Orion is formed by dropping the initial 'm' in the stem *morui*, which supposedly means "ant."[13] The constellation's narrow waist perhaps suggests this insect. I have previously written about Hopi legends from the American Southwest regarding "Ant People," and how they provided refuge in subterranean caverns, or "ant kivas," for the Hopi during the destruction of the first two Worlds (or Ages). (See pp. 130-7.) Suffice to say that the Hopi word *anu* means "ant," and the Hopi word *naki* or *naakwatsim* means "friend."[14] The *Anu-naki* = "ant-friend" —the Sumerian Annunaki, or the Watchers who came down from the heavens.

Anu (or Danu) was also the appellation of the Celtic mother goddess and patroness of the dead. In addition, Anu was another name for the Egyptian city of Heliopolis, where the *benben* stone of meteoric iron was kept. Furthermore, the Egyptian word *anu* meant products, revenues, or something brought in as well as gifts, tributes, and offerings. This refers to both the ants' ability to store provisions and the reverence given to the Ant People.

The Hopi word for Orion's belt is *Hotòmqam*, which literally means "to string up," "beads on a string," or "trey."[15] This might refer to the three shiny, bead-like sections of an ant's body: head, thorax, and abdomen.

One of the oldest Hopi villages was named Oraibi, so the *Ora-* prefix also influenced these Amerindians. *Orai* means "place of the rock" or "round rock." This village is located atop one of the three primary Mesas where the Hopi had finally settled circa 1100 AD after centuries of migration. Discussed in the first chapter, the Arizona Star Correlation posits that these three Mesas correspond to the belt stars of Orion, similar to the three major pyramids on the Giza plateau.

Morui, which is the root-word of Orion associated with ants, in southern Africa means "one who is rich in cattle."

"In the Sesotho language of Lesotho, a person who is wealthy is called a 'morui.' However, not all forms of wealth

are equally respected. One who is rich in cattle is more highly respected than one who keeps his wealth in a bank
account or household property. The reason for this is that
cattle can benefit not only the owner but the whole community. The true morui will place some of his cattle in the care
of others in the village so they, too, can benefit from them,
loan them to others for use during the plowing season and
sell them to those in need, with the price depending on the
circumstances of the one in need. Money in the bank or
household property is considered a selfish form of wealth,
whereas cattle can help transform the whole community. A
man with money 'only helps himself'; a true morui 'knows
the poor.' A morui is a vital part of village life and produc-
tivity, not someone detached and separated from it."[16]

Orion and Bulls

In this context we may recall the Greek myth of Orion's birth
(mentioned on p. 76). Zeus, Hermes, and Poseidon were traveling
on Earth, when they encountered Hyrieus, King of Boeotia, which
was the oldest city in Greece. This childless widower desired to
have a son. The gods then urinated on the hide of a bull (the constellation Taurus?) and buried it in the ground. Nine months later
Orion emerged. His name thus also derives from *urina*, or "urine."

Picking up the theme of ants again, we note one particular
type of this insect. The name "pissant" comes from the urine-like
stench produced by formic acid (venom) that ants secrete in
their nesting materials. *Formica rufa* is one such variety of ant,
but others with similar characteristics exist. The word pissant
may be derived from the term pismire, literally "urinating ant."[17]

One version of the Greek myth says that an ox hide rather
than a bull hide was used, so this might be related to the hide-
shaped copper ingots that were smelted during the Bronze Age.
One Cypriot incense burner from circa 1200 BC shows a member
of the so-called Sea People carrying a large copper ingot ox hide
across his shoulders. Some scholars claim that this group, which

ruled the Mediterranean and perhaps the world during this time, was actually comprised of mariner-invader Anatolians in alliance with the mariner-trader Phoenicians.[18]

Author Frank Joseph, however, believes that the Sea People were from Atlantis, though his interpretation of the myth uses a much later time-frame than do most. "According to Plato, the Atlanteans were the foremost copper barons of the Bronze Age."[19] More importantly, the six-sided ingots resemble the morphology of the Orion constellation, with their narrower portion in the middle. Copper ingots formed like an hourglass have been found in as diverse regions as Crete and Zimbabwe. I have personally observed ancient, ox hide-shaped petroglyphs in the Northern Cape province of South Africa.[20]

Considering the connotations of gold and wealth, one wonders where the term "bullion" derives. In fact, it comes from the Latin *bullio*, which means "boiling," referring to the melted mass of ore. But maybe "boiling mad" as well, like the oragious starry Bull that ushers in the stormy weather of autumn.

Pashupati, "Lord of all Animals,"alternately known as Prajapati, "Lord of Creatures." Tilak identifies the latter as Orion, who was killed by Rudra, storm god and "Lord of Cattle." This proto-Shiva clay seal was found at Mohenjodaro, dated c. 2900 – 1900 BC. The tri-faced, ichthyphallic, horned yogi is surrounded by water buffalo, rhinoceros, elephant, tiger, and deer.

Copper ingot, hide-shaped, Crete.

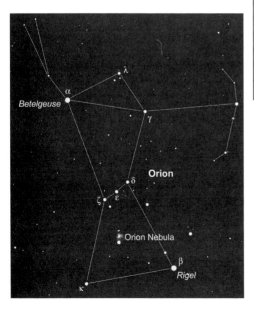

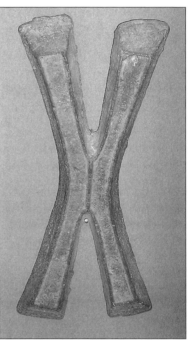

Orion-shaped copper ingot
from Zimbabwe.
National Museum,
Bloemfontein, South Africa.

Orion and Copper

In addition to the "urine" etymology, the name Orion might possibly derive from the Greek word *oros*, or "mountain." The English word "ore" comes from a conflation of a number of older words meaning brass, copper, bronze, or brazen. Orichalcum (Greek *Orei-chalkos*, or "mountain copper") was a copper-gold alloy that Plato said covered the walls of Atlantis.

Orion was also known as a skilled smith, or worker in metals. "It is said that Orion was an excellent workman in iron; and that he fabricated a subterranean palace for Vulcan."[21] During the Bronze Age, Orion may have excelled in the forging of copper and tin as well. This world era corresponds in Hopi legends to Kuskurza, the Third World, which, like Atlantis, was destroyed by a deluge. This age was symbolized by the color red and the metal copper—in Hopi called *palasiva*.[22] (Hopi elders say we are now at the end of the Fourth World.)

In southern Arizona the Akimel O'odham (Pima) and the Tohono O'odham (Papago) refer to the ancestral Hohokam as *Sivanyi*, literally "Metal Ones."[23] This name comes from the fact that either they or their neighbors to the south in Aztlán had forged a great quantity of tinklers and small bells from copper mined locally. Many historic copper mines are also located in Arizona, some still in production. "The state ...is the hub of copper mining in the United States, contributing more than 60 percent of the copper mined in the nation. In fact, the amount of copper in Arizona is so unusual that it has been called a planetary resource."[24]

As we saw in Chapter 6, the Hokokam had inhabited the Phoenix Basin (i.e. Valley of the Sun) for about a thousand years beginning in 300 BC and had built the major villages of Pueblo Grande, Snaketown, and Casa Grande (not to be confused with Casas Grandes, or Paquimé)—all located near the modern metropolis of Phoenix. Inhabitants of this city, by the way, are called Phoenicians.

The Hindu god Siva once assumed the form of a hunter and shot one of Brahman's heads with an arrow, thus creating Orion. Siva (or Shiva) was a less violent aspect of the ruddy Rudra, lord of storms and cattle. Siva's Third Eye chakra, or pineal gland, is

276

reputedly made of copper, and is represented on his phallic-stone shrine called a *lingam*.

Following up on metallurgic aspects of the *ur-* prefix, we find that *urruru* is the Sumerian word for "to smelt," and Oruru was an ancient mining center in Bolivia near Tiawanaku.[25] In addition, *uradu* is the Sumerian word for "copper," and Eridu was the oldest and most sacred city in Sumer.[26] In turn, Eri was the name of the Igbo (Nigerian) equivalent of the Egyptian Thoth, who taught the science and art of metallurgy.[27]

Again, the *eri-* prefix reminds us of the river at the foot of Orion: Eridanus, as discussed in Chapter 2. However, the "Dan" in Eri*dan*us may refer to one of the twelve tribes of Israel. This impetuous, war-like tribe had been compared in the Bible to biting serpents or adders (Genesis: 49: 16-17) and were said to "remain in ships" (Judges: 5:17)—i.e. mariners.

Diffusionist American scholar Cyrus H. Gordon calls them "Danite desperadoes" (not a reference to the Mormon vigilante group, of course). This is due to the fact that prior to being admitted to the Hebrew tribal confederation, they could not inherit land. Thus, they were forced to sail the high seas, where conquest and acquisition of booty became a way of life.[28] The Danites were, in fact, one of the factions of the heretofore mentioned Sea People. In Sanskrit, the word *danu* variously denotes "conqueror," "class of demons," "prosperity," and "fluid" or "water."[29] The Dan were also known as Danaus, Danuna, Danaids, Danaoi, Danai, and Denyen.[30] They may have originated in Adana, a city in south-central Anatolia.

In his two epic poems, Homer identified the earliest Greeks as the Danaans or Danaeans. The recovery in 1960 of a Bronze Age ship off the coast of southwestern Turkey proves that a Syro-Palestinian contingent was indeed plying the waters of the Mediterranean during the time of Homer, about 1200 BC. As part of the expedition, photojournalist Peter Throckmorton describes the quantity of artifacts manufactured by an advanced degree of metallurgy that indeed had made the Bronze Age possible. It was, he said. "...the largest hoard of pre-classical copper and bronze implements ever found in the Aegean area." This included "four-handled copper ingots" weighing 55 pounds each, as well as bronze axes, adzes, spearheads, knives, chisels, pins, picks, hoes, and bowls.[31]

It is interesting to note that in the Nahuatl language of the Aztecs, the world *atl* means "water," whereas in the Peruvian Quechua language, the word *antis* means "copper." *Atl-antis*, that is, Atlantis, perhaps because the legendary city's walls were reputedly covered with orichalcum, a copper-gold alloy.

Orion and Bird-Men (From West Africa to India to Easter Island)

Like the Mediterranean Danites, the Dan tribe that inhabited Côte d'Ivoire was associated with boats—reed rafts in particular. However, its members were therianthropically conceptualized as bird-men. These beings with human bodies and birds-of-prey heads reputedly bequeathed all the arts and sciences of civilization to the native people of West Africa. Scholar Andrew Collins speculates that the Danite bird-men may actually have been the biblical Watchers, or fallen angels.

"The idea of bird-men acting as bringers of knowledge and wisdom to mortal kind is not unique to the Middle East. An African tribe called Dan, who live close to the village of Man on the Ivory Coast, say that at the beginning of time, in the days of their first ancestors, a race of 'attractive human birds appeared, possessing all the sciences which they handed on to mankind'. Even today the tribal artists make *copper* [italics added] representations of these bird-men, who are shown with human bodies and heads supporting long beaks, like those of birds of prey."[32]

In addition, the Idanre (I-dan-re) community of the Yoruba claims that Noah's ark landed at their village, and that they even still possess pieces of it![33]

The Danite bird-men are also reminiscent of the Hindu mythical entity called, Garuda—half-eagle, half man. With the head and wings of a bird and the body of a human, he was king of the feathered tribes and adversary of the serpent race.[34]

So, on one hand, the Danites were biblically associated with serpents; in other cultures they were affiliated with birds. Thus, they assume the potent shamanic aspects of both ophidian and avian, of Snake People and Bird People—the merging of which finds it quintessential manifestation in the Mesoamerican plumed serpent named Kukulkan or Quetzalcoatl.

A similar creature with bird-head and human frame was worshipped by the bird cult on Easter Island (Rapa Nui). Atop a high precipice at the lip of the Rano Kao volcanic crater on the southwestern tip of the island, hundreds of petroglyphs of the-rianthropes depicted in profile with arched backs and curved beaks have been carved in bas-relief into the rocks. (See p. 281.)

Between 50 and 75 semi-subterranean, mostly oval-shaped chambers had been constructed of horizontal stone slabs that formed thick walls arching upward to corbel-vaulted ceilings. These kiva-like chambers were used to house the bird-men, who were called *tangata-manu* (literally, "man-bird"; note tan-/dan similarity) as they waited for the return of the sooty tern (*Sterna fuscata*) to a tiny island of Motu Nui a short distance off the coast.

The Easter Island name for the sooty tern is *manu-tara*, liter-ally "bird-sun," suggesting the primordial egg of the phoenix or *Benu* bird in Heliopolis. Graham Hancock states that the word *tangata-manu* actually means *"learned* man of the sacred bird" and refers to ibis-headed Thoth with his long, curved beak.[35]

The Easter Island word *raa* means "sun." There are indeed many variations of "Ra," the Egyptian sun god, in the names of geographic and geological features on the island—for instance, the three main volcanic craters: Rano Kao, Rano Aroi, and Rano Raraku. Incidentally, the name of the site where the bird cult per-formed its ceremonies is Orongo—another **oro** word-variation similar to those we explored in the first section of this chapter.[36] One source gives "round" as the meaning of *orongo*, perhaps referring to the adjacent Rano Kao caldera, which measures about a mile in diameter and is 700 feet deep. Four small holes bored into an *ahu* (rock platform) at the site were apparently used as alignments to solstice and equinox points on the horizon.

The summer solstice ceremony (December 21st in the southern hemisphere) called *paina*, when the dead were honored, paradoxically depended on the positioning of Orion's belt.[37] British traveler Katherine Routledge, who visited the island between 1914 and 1915, found on an eastern headland a spiral petroglyph that the natives called "rock-for-seeing-stars." Nearby was a star map consisting of ten cupules carved in stone.

She also relates the "only nature myth" she encountered there, which was told only during the summer season. A married woman who went down to bathe was abducted and raped by a stranger. This blameless occurrence nonetheless enraged her husband, who in anger killed her. She fled to the sky where she became a star. The husband followed, carrying their two children, who together with their mother became Orion's belt.[38] The motifs of violence and rape seem to follow Orion around the world.

It is a significant fact that the Rapa Nui bird-man who gains his esteemed position for a period of one year does not actually accomplish this through his own efforts. On the contrary, in late July or August the *tangata-manu* is sequestered in his chamber on the lofty cliffs overlooking the sea at Orongo, while his *hopu-manu*, or servant of the bird, plunges into the furious currents below with a little food and a tiny bundle of bound reeds, or *pora*. He swims to the islet of Moto Nui, there to wait with other competitors in a cave (sometimes for weeks) for the return of the sacred tern. The swim is obviously fraught with dangers, such as being attacked by sharks or dashed against the rocks and drowned.

When the birds finally return with their deafening cries, the first *hopu* to retrieve the "Mystery Egg" (see Chapter 13) yells up to his master on the precipice: "Shave your head, you have got the egg!" Routledge describes this portion of the ceremony:

> "The defeated hopu started at once to swim from the island to the shore, while the winner, who was obliged to fast while the egg was in his possession, put it in a little basket, and going down to the landing-rock, dipped it into the sea. One meaning of the word hopu is 'washed.'

  quote continued on p. 282

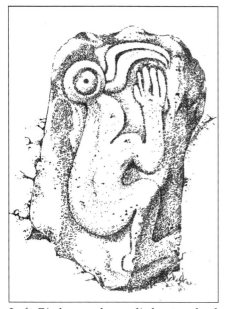

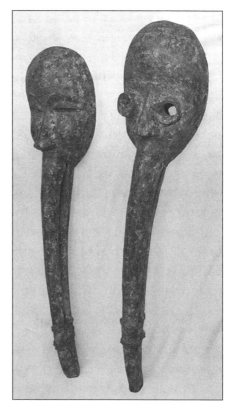

Left: Bird-man, bas-relief petroglyph at Orongo, Rapa Nui.
Right: Wooden masks of bird-man, Dan tribe, Poro Society, Ivory Coast, left-female/right-male, 8″ x 33″.
Below: Bird-men chambers.

He then tied the basket round his forehead and was able to swim quickly, as the gods were with him."[39]

On reaching the main island, the *hopu-manu* climbs the dizzying cliffs to hand over the holy egg to the *tangata-manu*, who assumes his regal office as bird-man. During the next year the latter is considered the keeper of that period's *mana*, or vital force. He lives in solitary abstinence in a hut near the previously mentioned caldera called Rano Raraku, near the quarry where are obtained many *moai*, or the iconic statues for which Easter Island is famous. (In fact, the logo for Adventures Unlimited Press, the publisher of this book, is a *moai*.) His servant, *hopu-manu*, also lives alone for twelve moons in an adjacent hut.[40] This area, which contains *moai*, an *ahu* (ceremonial platform), and the burial grounds of the bird-men, is called *Orohié*—yet another **oro** word.[41]

Readers may have noticed the similarity between the "servants" of the bird-men, namely the *hopu*, and the tribe from northern Arizona, the Hopi. This may be more than merely a linguistic coincidence. In the Polynesian language, the word *hopu* means "to dive under water," or "to bathe," which makes sense, given the duties of the *hopu-manu*. However, the homonym *hopu* also means "to sue for peace." The Hopi tribe is known as the "People of Peace"—the name "Hopi" being a contraction of *Hópitu*, or "peaceful ones." The Polynesian word *hopu* additionally refers to "a certain prayer at the end of a ceremony," indicating its ritual nature.[42]

The Polynesian term *hopupu* refers to "a species of the *totara*," or the reed (*Schoenoplectus californicus ssp. tatora*). This giant bulrush sedge is used to make the floating *pora* used by the *hopu*. The pre-Incan Uros of the Lake Titicaca region of Peru use this same reed to construct their boats called *caballitos de totora*. *Schoenoplectus californicus* (also genus *Scirpus*) is the giant reed that also grows along the lower Colorado River.

Another term for "reed" used on Rapa Nui is *nga'atu*.[43] The similar Hopi word *nga'at* means "medicine root," and the Hopi term *ngat'a* refers to "tumpline, head or shoulder strap for carrying a burden on the back."[44] The Polyneisan word *hopoi* mean "to carry or convey a burden,"[45] such as the *hopu-manu* might have done for the *tangata-manu*, or "bird-men."

Part of this ritual involves the victorious *hopu-manu* tying a small basket to his forehead in which the prized sacred egg rests during his hazardous swim back to Rapa Nui. The Hopi word *ho'apu* means "wicker basket," used as a burden basket.[46]

In my book *Eye of the Phoenix*, I state that the reed is the hallmark of high civilization and culture wherever it is found: Mesoamerica, South America, Egypt, Sumer. The major village of Shungopovi (Songòopavi), the so-called the "mother-village" on Second Mesa, is known as "the place by the spring where the tall reeds grow." (In the Arizona Orion Correlation, this village corresponds to the star Alnilam. See Chapter 1.) The Third Mesa village of Bacavi (Paaqavi) is "the place of the jointed reed." The Hopi word *hopaqa* means "a species of large reed," or bamboo.[47] The Hopi Bamboo (Reed) Clan is called *Wukopaqavi*, literally "giant reed."

The social stratification between *tangata* ("man") and *hopu* ("servant") may be the remnant of the two basic groups that once coexisted, sometimes uneasily, on Rapa Nui. This vertical caste system consisted of the rulers named the *Hanau eepe* ("Long Ears, or "stout people") and the workers named *Hanau momoko* ("Short Ears," or "thin people"). In Hopi, the word *èepew* means "in opposition to, opposing, counter to, adversely."[48] The Hopi term *mómoki* means to "be dying," and the near homophone *momoki* means "bundle."[49] The Spanish called the Hopi tribe the Moqui, or Moki, which connotes snivel or runny noses, perhaps reflecting the general state of health when the Spanish encountered them in the mid-16th century.

The Long Ears were said to be tall (averaging six-and-a-half feet in height), light-skinned (dare I say Caucasian?) with red hair and ear lobes stretched by wooden plugs (sometimes extending them to their shoulders). Some of the enigmatic *moai* statues have a red topknot and elongated ear lobes, perhaps emulating these bizarre men. The Short Ears possessed typical Polynesian physical characteristics and did not lengthen their ear lobes. By most accounts the Long Ears are considered to have been seafarers, perhaps even the Sea People previously mentioned. After they arrived on Easter Island, they began to govern the land and its people, while the Short Ears were forced to toil on their masters' projects.

Finally the Short Ears had had enough of this severe servitude imposed by Long Ears' imperious rule, and they rebelled. All the Long Ears but one were trapped in a two-mile-long ditch and burned to death in an "earth oven." The only surviving Long Ear was named Ororoina –yet another **oro** word– from which all the Long Ears on Rapa Nui today are descended.[50]

Early legends of Easter Island involve a King Hotu-Matua, who lived in a country called Maori (New Zealand?) on a continent named Hiva. Finding that his island was sinking into the ocean, he and his tribe migrated to Rapa Nui.[51] This, of course, sounds very familiar, with myths of the lost continent of Lemuria or Mu echoing through the ages. (See next chapter.)

Explorer, archaeologist, and author Thor Heyerdahl describes a possible submerged road system at Rapa Nui.

"In many parts of the island we had seen wide paved roads which disappeared straight down into the sea. These mysterious constructions had in the course of time stimulated a great number of vivid speculations. They have been one of the main supports for all who believe that Easter Island is the remains of a sunken continent. The paved roads, it has been said, undoubtedly continued along the ocean floor, and if one could follow them, the ruins of the sunken continent of Mu could be reached."[52]

The Polynesian *hiva* means "a clan, the company in a canoe," indicating the sea voyage, and *hivahiva* means "abundance," perhaps referring to the paradisiacal plenitude of Hotu-Matua's former homeland.[53]

It is interesting to note, though, that the Hopi word *kiva* refers to a subterranean prayer-chamber; when one descends into the structure, one is essentially going back to the previous Third World (or Age) in antediluvian times. As we will see in the next chapter, the Hopi believe they escaped a tremendous deluge that destroyed the Third World by sailing eastward across the ocean on reed rafts.

One additional note of interest in the context of our **oro** words involves a rival of Hotu-Matua named Oroi, who was a nobleman (*ariki*—recall the discussion of *ari-* at the end of the first section of this chapter). Warfare between the tribe of Hotu-Matua and the tribe of Oroi started on Hiva and continued on Rapa Nui, until the former finally managed to kill the latter but refrained from consuming his flesh out of deference to his rank.[54] The Polynesian word *oroi* means either "to alter the course, as a ship" or "dark, dismal, as a place." Perhaps Oroi was basically evil, or at least not quite on the level, to which another Polyneisan definition of *oroi* attests: "out of perpendicular, as a wall, or a house." The name Oro is "the god of war, the great national god of Tahiti," and *orooro* is "an ornament of feathers used for religious purposes, and also worn by warriors."[55]

What is the actual time-frame for the populating of the island that these legends talk about? Is there any archaeological evidence? Thor Heyerdahl claims that the fire in the fortification trench where most of the Long Ears perished was radiocarbon-dated to about the mid-17th century, though the earliest charcoal he found at a lower level dated to approximately 400 AD.[56] David Hatcher Childress cites a few results from Heyerdahl's 1987 excavations, which found a buried structure made of vertical stonework and a buried pavement with the C-14 dates of 800 AD and 1100 AD.[57] This latter date almost exactly concurs with the period when the first pueblo villages were being built on the Hopi Mesas. Other radiocarbon-dating done by William S. Ayers of Tulane University suggests that Easter Island was inhabited for almost twelve hundred years. "The time range for use of the site as a ceremonial centre was from A.D. 690 ± 130 to the late 1800s."[58]

British archaeologist Paul Bahn and New Zealand botanist John Flenley published an analysis of the decline in tree pollen found in the bogs of the calderas, which indicate rapid deforestation. Their findings suggest "...that the earliest partial decline of the tree pollen may occur as early as AD 690 [again] or even AD 100, and that it took many centuries for the decline to spread from the original settlement in the south east to the rest of the island. The statue building they say began in earnest around AD 900, and that the ecological crash came around 1500."[59]

Heyerdahl witnessed one nocturnal ceremony in which a group

of Long Ear descendants wearing paper bird-masks with long beaks struck the ground with war clubs, oars, and stone picks while singing the stone cutters' song in preparation for the sculpting of a *moai*.

> "They were all deeply serious, and the singing went on and on till one of our fellows came out of the tent with a lamp. Then the chorus stopped abruptly, and they all murmured 'no,' and hid their faces in their hands. When the light disappeared, the song began again; one man started, and then the rest joined in, the old woman last. I felt far away from the South Sea Islands: strangely enough there was something to the music which reminded me of visits with the Pueblo Indians in New Mexico, and the archaeologists said the same."[60]

Is this merely a subjective association or is there an actual connection between the *hopu* of Easter Island and the Hopi of Arizona? Perhaps it is simply a coincidence that the two locations are exactly on the same meridian. Orongo (109° 25′ 30″ W) is 4,355 miles south of White House Ruin (109° 28′ 10″ W), located near the Arizona-New Mexico border in Canyon de Chelly, but is only 2.3 miles west of it.

Childress briefly summarizes Heyerdahl's overall theory of a global maritime culture: "Heyerdahl believes that a race of seafarers that used reed boats and worshipped the sun once ranged the entire world. He cites such reed boat centers as Tiahuanaco and Chan Chan in South America, Easter Island, Lothal and the coastal cities of the Indus Valley Civilization, Mesopotamia, Egypt and Morocco as centers for this world-wide trading culture."[61]

The clan of the bird-man was named *ao*, which was also the dance path from Mataveri to Orongo. The word *ao* additionally referred to a ceremonial oar about five feet long, carved and painted with a human head.[62] The Polynesian word *ao* means "Heaven; blessedness, happiness; the state of the blessed."[63] The Hopi word *á'ove* is a postposition meaning "above," as in "sky above."[64] Did long-eared bird-men take their short-eared servants with them on their many sea voyages? The next chapter will explore the link, through both legends and genetics, between the South Pacific and the Desert Southwest.

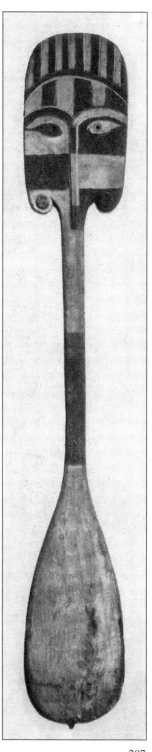

Above: Wooden statue of bird-man, 10.3″ tall,
British Museum.
Right: *ao* , ceremonial paddle.

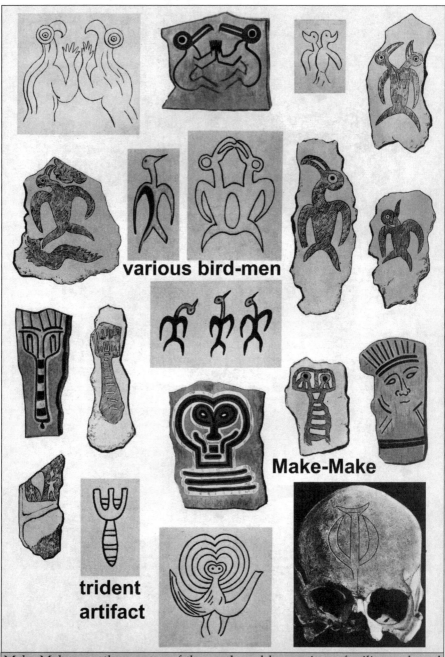

various bird-men

Make-Make

trident artifact

Make-Make was the creator of the earth and humanity, a fertility god, and the major deity of the bird-men cult. This god resembles the Hopi death god Masau'u and the Aztec rain god Tlaloc. A trident was carried by the Greek sea god Poseidon, the Roman underworld god Pluto, the Hindu destroyer god Shiva, and perhaps Make-Make as well.

Dolichocephalic skull found on Rapa Nui, Lafaille Museum, La Rochelle, France. Francis Maziére, who explored the island in the early 1960s, writes: "We were fascinated by the idea of seeing one of these king's skulls at last. After we had turned and twisted a great while among the lava boulders our friend showed us a hidden cave, and in a recess within it, the ancient, secret skull. We were very much moved, but apart from that there were two things

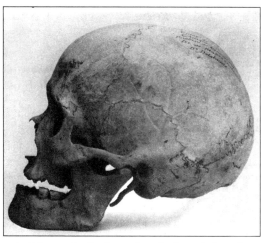

that struck us at once: the skull was dolichocephalic (long-headed) and therefore out of the ordinary run, and that it had a perfect set of teeth, which is extremely rare among the Polynesians of today. Thanks to this native friend doors now open to us, as though this skull did indeed possess mana, as he asserted."[65]

Two Long Ears wooden statues with beards and Phoenician hooked noses. At left, bird-men carved on bald head, accentuated backbone and rib cage.

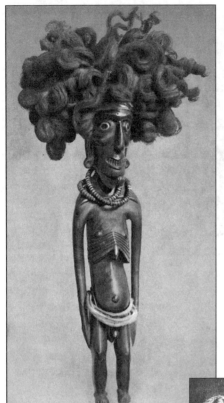

Upper-left: Wooden statue, Long Ear with human hair (red?), 13.75" tall, Trocadéro Museum, Paris.

Upper-right: Wooden head, Long Ear carved with bird-men, obsidian left eye, right eye missing. At foot of Rano Kao crater is an obsidian quarry named Orito—another **oro** word.

Lower-right: Long Ear with beard, light-colored eyes, and feather-headdress. Picture drawn during Captain Cook's voyage to Easter Island, 1774.

Facing page: upper-left, wooden statue with ET Grey-like eyes; middle, female Long Ear, right hand on heart, left hand pointing to vulva; right, Oro war god, Tahiti, 18" tall, Metropolitan Museum of Art, New York, wooden core bound with woven coconut fiber, venerated by the Arioi (**Ari**-oi, p. 271), a secret society of nobility; lower: canoes and *ao* paddle. Checkerboard may represent the Milky Way.

HOMME DE L'ISLE DE PÁQUES.

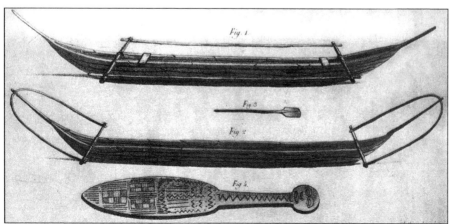

Back of *Hoa Hakananai'a*, "Master Wave-Breaker" *moai* statue, Orongo, 2.42 meters tall, 4 tons, basalt, British Museum. Carved tern, 3 *ao* oars, 4 vulvas, bird-men (the one on left has 6 toes), sun above band, and "M."

Chapter 12
Epic Sea Voyages
of the Ancestral Hopi

Dual Legends of the Emergence

The end of Chapter 10 briefly describes Hopi legends of a monumental journey across the ocean on reed rafts. However, the Hopi apparently have a dual explanation for their transition from the previous Third World to the current Fourth World. On one hand, they tell stories of the minority of their ancestors who lived righteously in the former epoch and still followed the ways of the Creator, while the majority were mired in spiritual decadence and social chaos.

These chosen few finally ascended from the underworld through a giant reed that poked through a hole in the sky. This reed was called either the *Paaqavi* or the *Soongwuka*, the latter term literally meaning "reed-big" but actually denoting the Milky Way (and perhaps signifying a sidereal journey).[1] The end of the reed led to the hole in the dome-shaped Sipàapuni (see Chapter 1), thus bringing them into the Grand Canyon. From there, they spread out across the Desert Southwest in order to populate various sites, building pueblo villages and leaving rock art, thereby marking the boundaries of their territory over the course of centuries of perpetual migration that ultimately ended with the settling of the three Hopi Mesas at the *Tuuwanasavi*, or the "Center of the World."

An alternate mythological explanation for the shift in world-ages involves a trans-oceanic migration on reed rafts. Harold

Courlander, scholar of Hopi culture, comments: "The myth of the arrival by an ocean voyage persists in various clan traditions. The name Water Clan in Hopi is Patkinyamu, literally meaning Dwelling-on-Water (that is, Houseboat) Clan. The belief is that before these people arrived at ancient Palatkwapi they reached the present world after a long water crossing."[2] The great reed legend is more frequent on First Mesa, whereas the ocean voyage story is more common on Third Mesa.

Palatkwapi refers to the "Red City of the South." A. M. Stephen, an early ethnographer of the Hopi, briefly describes the clan's place of origin. "The Patki clan came from Pala'tkwabi [Palatkwapi]. No one knows just where that Red land is, but it is somewhere in the far *southwest* [italics added]."[3] He furthermore states that this clan transported various religious artifacts from the Red City as well as significant Hopi rituals, such as the winter solstice ceremony.

Water Clan, or Patki, is one of the main Hopi clans that made the maritime journey. Also called the Water-House (or Houseboat) Clan, it is related to a number of other clans associated in one way or another with water: Rain-Cloud Clan, Lightning Clan, Rainbow Clan, Water Bird Clan (viz. snipe), Wild Duck Clan, Water Snake Clan, Frog Clan, Sprouting Corn Clan, and a few others. Whiting also associates the Water Clan with the Reed Clan.[4]

Albert Yava, a Hopi-Tewa of Arizona, describes the Patki Clan's journey over the ocean.

"…sometime after they left the place of emergence they made a long journey across a large expanse of water in boats with dwellings constructed on them. The body of water is believed to be the ocean, but just what part of the ocean it was we do not know. It seems that the Water Clan had a big village somewhere before Palatkwa [Palatkwapi], but corruption and evil set in and they had to leave. That is when they made the ocean voyage. Palatkwa was their next big village. One thing you hear from the Patki people is that in ancient times they were white, not Indian color. They say, 'My ancestors had white skins, but because of evil things that happened, we lost all that.' They also say,

'The Patki people are the ones who are supposed to teach the Hopis good moral values, how to lead good lives.'"[5]

Despite its politically incorrect tone, Yava's statement implies that white people shared the journey with those who would become the Pueblo people. In the context of the previous chapter, the Long Ears may have accompanied the Short Ears to the North American continent. Yava also claims that the Patki Clan possessed moral authority and righteousness, such as that possessed by the people who ascended through the big reed in the first version of the migration myth.

The Tewa are a Pueblo group that lives in New Mexico, but some of its members also live in a village called Hano on First Mesa in Arizona. The Hopi name for spiritual chief is *kikmongwi*, but the similar Tewa term is *poa'atoyong*, which literally means "leader-after-the-flood."[6] Directly adjacent to Hano is the Hopi village of Sichomovi (Sitsom'ovi), which was established by the Patki Clan.[7]

Today the Patki Clan is in charge of sky watching in order to regulate the agricultural and ceremonial calendar. In particular, the *taawa mongwimu'yta* ("sun-chiefs") calibrate sunrise and sunset points on the horizon for the purpose of determining the summer and winter solstices. Perhaps these skills crucial in navigating upon the ocean were eventually adapted to an agrarian existence in the desert after the Hopi made it to their final homeland.

The common factor of these dual legends is, of course, the reed. As previously mentioned, the Reed Clan is named *Wukopaqavi*, and the reed plays a huge role in the cultural life of the Hopi. For instance, a reed mat contains a bride's wedding blanket, which is worn at the naming of her first child but also at last becomes her shroud.

In 1970 a Hopi named Homer Cooyama from the village of Kykotsmovi claimed that the giant reed legend was merely a "cover-story" for uninitiated children. The actual legend, he said, involved the destruction of the Third World by a deluge and that the Hopi sailed across the sea to escape it. Referring to those already initiated into the kiva societies, Cooyama stated: "But these Hopi people know that they came from across the ocean and migrated here. And they never forgot their religion."8 Others, such as the previously mentioned Don C. Talayesva, believed much the same thing.9

The "underworld" may simply be the world to the south, perhaps even south of the equator. Again, A. M. Stephen from his *Hopi Journal*: "On the [sun-chief's] altar the nadir is represented in the south. Inferably Pala'tkwabi is the Underworld, i.e. the world before the Emergence."10 From this we may assume that the Red City had an antediluvian existence. Stephen's writing also states: "Two elders are making Pa'lülükoñ [Water Serpent] prayer sticks, blue-green prayer sticks, some to be deposited at sun spring, others at the *southwest* [italics added] for Pala'tkwabi."11 Hence, the Hopi even have a local shrine representing this distant land. Incidentally, blue-green is the symbolic color of the southwest.

The Hopi word *pala* means both "moisture" and "red," the latter being symbolic of the *southeastern* direction. The Hopi word *paatala* means "be gleaming, shining with water, as after a rain," and *palatala* means "diffused red light from a meteorological condition such as at sunrise, sunset, or after rain."12 The Sanskrit word *patala* has at least three denotations: (1) "pale red or pink"(2) "one of the regions under the earth, the abode of serpents or demons" and (3) "one of the lower regions of the world."13 In Greek mythology, Pallas was a Titan associated with war who was slain by Athena, goddess of wisdom, civilization, law, and just warfare.

Augustus Le Plongeon, about whom I will soon say a bit more, claimed that the Hindus painted red their god Ganesha, the elephant-headed deity of prudence, intellect, literature, and science. "By this they perhaps wished to indicate that men of that color, coming from Pátâla, the antipodes, imported to India, with civilization, the knowledge of letters, arts, and sciences. In Polynesia, red is still regarded by the natives of the islands as a favorite color with the gods."14

A couple of other terms from India are relevant in this context. My friend and colleague Shree Subash Bose says that the name of the ancient American Indians in his native Tamil language is *Sigappu*, which is similar to the Hopi term for their

Place of Emergence from the underworld, *Sipapu*.[15] The Sanskrit word *zona* means the following: "red, crimson, purple, fire, blood."[16] The same word in Greek and Latin refers, coincidentally, to the "belt stars of Orion," as noted in Chapter 2.

Considering the two explanations for the Hopi emergence into the Fourth World, it is possible that the "underworld" of the first legend is a reference to the watery place on the other side of the globe, the antipodes, or the Land Down Under—that is, Australia or the South Pacific in general.

> "Do you come from a land down under?
> Where women glow and men plunder?
> Can't you hear, can't you hear the thunder?
> You better run, you better take cover."
> —Men at Work

The Time of the Ancient Mariners

Were the Hopi once a seafaring people? Is it really possible that these die-hard denizens of the desert who now engage in dry farming, supplicating the kachinas with prayers for rain, were once a maritime culture? At least British-born Colonel James Churchward thought so. During the early 20th century he was the main proponent of the theory of the lost (i.e. submerged) continent of Mu, or Lemuria (referred to in the previous chapter.)

This reputed continent once measured 5,000 miles in length from east to west and 3,000 miles in width from north to south. Its northern boundary was the Hawaiian Islands; its southern boundary was a line roughly between Easter Island and Fiji. Mu supposedly possessed an enlightened and highly civilized society with a population of sixty-four million. Until about 12,000 years ago it functioned as the world's center for education, trade, and commerce. At that time cataclysmic earthquakes, tsunamis, and volcanoes destroyed this great continent, leaving only the remnants of those archipelagos we see today—or so goes the myth.

Churchward believed that the so-called Cliff Dwellers were

the last wave of colonizers from Mu, their gateway to the region being the mouth of the Colorado River. "Cliff Dwellers," of course, is a reference to the Ancestral Puebloans (formerly called the Anasazi), who lived at places like Betatakin and Keet Seel in northern Arizona (mentioned in Chapter 1), as well as at Mesa Verde in southwestern Colorado. Churchward also claimed that the Hopi and the Zuni among all the Pueblo people were the most clearly linked to the Mu traditions.

> "That the Cliff Dwellers came from Mu is certain, for every one of their pictures that are used as guide-posts contains a reference to Mu. In fact, rock writings and pictures of the Cliff Dwellers, except those drawn for artistic effect, are permeated with references to Mu, both before and after her submersion. In addition to this, they invariably use the symbols that were in vogue in the Motherland."[17]

Incidentally, the Hopi term *yúmu* (or *yúmu'yta*) means "to have mothers "—that is, a mother, a ceremonial mother, or maternal aunts.[18] Although Churchward says that ascribing an exact date to the migration from Mu to the Desert Southwest is "problematical," he speculates that the first of the immigrants may have arrived about 12,500 years ago.[19] This date, coincidentally, is the same as the Egyptian golden age of *Zep Tepi*, the First Time (see p. 236), when the three major pyramids on the Giza Plateau were aligned to the belt stars of Orion—if not the actual structures, then at least the layout of the future pyramids.

In the early 1930s Churchward made a brief visit to Arizona and New Mexico, where he saw many similarities between the symbols of the pueblo people and those of Mu. "At a ceremonial dance I was astonished to see that the blanket of the Chief was covered with the Sacred Symbols of the Motherland, Mu. One symbol in particular attracted my attention, as it was identically like the central figure of the Hindu Cosmic Diagram, the Sri Santara. In the Motherland's Diagram the Twelve Gates to the World Beyond was symbolized by twelve scallops. The Pueblos like the Hindus have symbolized theirs by twelve triangle points."[20]

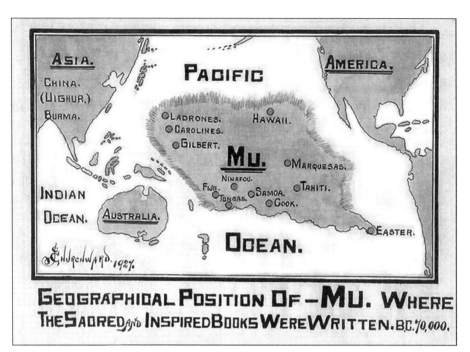

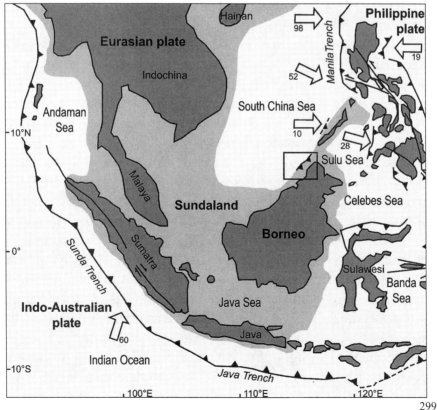

It is interesting to note that Churchward claimed that the icon of three parallel bars, usually vertical, was Mu's numerical symbol.[21] This may represent either the triadic belt stars of Orion or Poseidon's trident. These three lines also resemble the Egyptian hieroglyphic for *Sah*, the stars of Orion. Three upright feathers on the "Crown of Mu" symbolize the continent as well. "Three feathers were the ornament on the head piece of Ra Mu, the King High Priest of Mu."[22]

In addition, the six-sided geometric form –either an hourglass shape or two equilateral triangles with their apexes touching– represents Mu's alphabetical symbol.[23] As we saw in the previous chapter, copper ingots were customarily forged in an ox hide shape, which also symbolizes the shape of Orion's torso. Rock art expert LaVan Martineau says that this shape represents two arrowheads pointing at each other, thus indicating warfare.[24]

Another name for Mu was *Kui* or the Land of Kui. "The birthplace of the sacred mysteries. Mu—the Land of the West. *That land of Kui. The motherland of the gods.*" Churchward also claims that Mu was the Motherland of Man, since a god originally was not a deity to be worshipped but simply a departed soul. Thus, Kui was the land of departed souls located in the underworld.[25] (According to Churchward, *Kui* was a Mayan word related to the ancient Egyptian concept of *Ka*, an etheric double that was something like a guardian angel. (An entire chapter in my book *The Eye of the Phoenix* is devoted to global variations of *ka*, which is the first syllable of the Hopi kachina, also spelled *katsina*.)

Possibly related to Kui, the Hopi word *atkya* or *atkye'* means "down, down there, down below" but it also generally refers to any place southwest of the Hopi Mesas.[26] This harkens back to the discussion in the preceding section of this chapter about the duality of "underworld" and the "land down under," which is to the southwest or west. In addition, variations of the Hopi syllable *kuy* are related to "drawing water"—the element that destroyed Mu.[27]

Churchward claimed that the "...cliff writings of North America all support the fact that the first religion was pure Monotheism, that the Creator created all things and today is controlling the Universe with all the life throughout it."[28] The Hopi similarly believe in a universal Creator, although they also conceptualize secondary deities.

From *Sacred Mysteries Among the Mayas And the Quiches* by Augustus LePlongeon

...the generic name of *"Lands of the West"* and represented by the character ▨▨ which is an image of the crown worn by some of the high chiefs in Mayax.

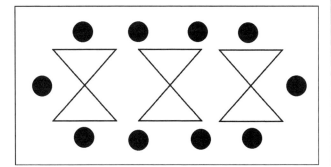

Upper-left: Glyph for "Lands to the West" and triadic vertical feathers on the Crown of Mu. Upper-right: Letter M, Mu's alphabetical symbol. Middle-left: Symbol of Ten Tribes of Mu. Middle-right: Egyptian hieroglyphic for *Sah*, Orion. Lower-right: flat kachina doll of Masau'u, Hopi god of the underworld. Note the opposed-triangle icon on chest and three vertical bars below.

He also believed that vestiges of the temples or megalithic structures of Mu could be found on many South Sea Islands, including Rapa Nui, Mangaia (one of the more southerly of the Cook Islands), Tongatapu, and Pohnpei (one of the Caroline Islands farther west).[29]

Edgar Cayce and the Cliff Dwellers

Mu was also frequently mentioned, oddly enough, in the life readings of Edgar Cayce, the so-called "sleeping prophet," who was renowned for his abilities to find physical cures for his clients, describe past lives in Atlantis, Egypt, or other places, and prognosticate about future world-events. For instance, one woman in a former life apparently migrated from Mu to the American Southwest during the beginning of the deluge. "...we find the entity was in that land now known as American, during those periods when changes that had brought about the sinking of Mu or Lemuria, or those peoples in the periods who had changed to what is now a portion of the Rocky Mountain area; Arizona, New Mexico, portions of Nevada and Utah."[30]

In one life reading, Cayce even mentions the cliff dwellers by name. "The entity was among the first that have become known as the cave or cliff dwellers, in the portions now known as Utah, Arizona, Colorado and New Mexico. In those environs and places did the entity make for its activities, in the name, Uramm."[31] Another past life reading describes the role that the person played in the development of the Pueblo culture. "The entity was in that land now known as the American during the periods when there were sojournings of those from the Land of Mu, or Lemuria. The entity was then among the first of those that were born in what is now portions of Arizona and Utah, and among those who established the lands there for the building up or growing of that civilization in those experiences; and was in the name Uuluoou. The entity led many to a greater understanding of how there might be made the closer relationships with the material things and the spiritual thoughts of the people."[32]

Cayce in yet another reading refers to the "Lost Tribes" and gives a specific migration date from Mu that is much earlier than the conventional 8th century BC date for the Ten Lost Tribes of Israel.

"With the injection of those of greater power in their activity in the land, during that period as would be called 3,000 years before the Prince of Peace came, those peoples that were of the Lost Tribes, a portion came into the land; infusing their activities upon the peoples from Mu in the southernmost portion of that called America or United States, and then moved on to the activities in Mexico, Yucatan, centralizing that now about the spots where the central [portion] of Mexico now stands, or Mexico City. Hence there arose through the age a different civilization, a *mixture* again."[33]

Despite his idiosyncratic mode of expression, Cayce presents a picture of a migration from Mu to the Desert Southwest and a subsequent movement southward into Mexico and Maya territory—again, much earlier than the actual Chichimec migration into the Valley of Mexico (mentioned in Chapter 7 and discussed in Chapter 9).

Churchward also talks about the Ten Lost Tribes, ascribing a Lemurian origin. "At the time when Mu was submerged records say: Man on Mu had developed into ten distinct tribes and types of men."[34] He provides a symbol of ten dots surrounding three double-equilateral triangles described above—perhaps again signifying Orion in its rising, meridian, and setting positions. (See middle-left diagram on p. 301.)

Returning to the Cayce readings, we see that one woman migrated from India to Arizona, there becoming an important individual. "The entity among those, then, that set up this combination of cults that built in the land the temples and the dwellings in the rocks. The entity then gained much through that experience, becoming the priestess to those peoples... and giving much to the aborigines of the land, and understanding, and of [the] same came those that made of the land, or of the metals and the clays, much of that that was later taken in the

Yucatan land, in the Mexico land, into the southern land, being driven down by the heavy men from the north."[35] The entity apparently migrated to Arizona, bringing her knowledge of metallurgy and pottery production, which was taught to the people and later exported to Mesoamerica. Archaeologists have found evidence in southern Arizona and northern Mexico of the smelting of copper artifacts, including tiny bells. Ceramic production, of course, was a cultural epitome in the American Southwest—see Chapter 8 and Chapter 10, for instance.

The "heavy men of the north" is possibly a reference to the Chichimecs, the barbaric "Sons of the Dog," which were probably part of the Hopi Bow Clan. Cayce's time-frame, however, is again much earlier than the 12th century AD historical migration.

Although the name "Mu" originated from an 1864 mistranslation by Charles Étienne Brasseur de Bourbourg (1814 – 1874) of the *Codex Troano*, Churchward actually got the concept from his archaeologist-friend and Freemason Augustus Le Plongeon (1826 – 1908), quoted above. The latter scholar actually did bona fide archaeological work in Yucatan, such as unearthing the Chac Mool statue at Chichen Itza. Le Plongeon speculated that the Land of Mu was actually Atlantis and not a Pacific continent. "The Lands to the West," in his estimation, referred to the area west of Egypt.

Le Plongeon also believed a Queen Móo ruled Chichen Itza along with her husband and brother Prince Coh. Her totem was the macaw while his was the serpent. The co-regents also supposedly founded the Egyptian civilization, as the pair is an archetypal reflection of Osiris and Isis.[36]

Le Plongeon, Churchward, and Cayce all allowed for the possibility of a sunken continent in the Pacific. In academia, of course, Mu is moot—much like the "A-word," Atlantis.

The Lost Continent of Sundaland

The basic question remains: Did any continent even remotely resembling Mu or Lemuria ever actually exist in the Pacific? In a word, yes. Geologist Robert Schoch describes a landmass that once could be found in the area of Malaysia.

> "In 18,000 B.C., when sea level was much lower, a continent-sized expanse of land in Southeast Asia lay where the southern reach of the South China Sea, the Gulf of Thailand, and the Java Sea are now. When the sea rose, a land area equal in extent to the Indian subcontinent sank slowly beneath the waves, leaving only the relative highlands of the Malay Archipelago, Indochina, Borneo, and the many islands of Indonesia protruding above them. Geologists call this expanse of drowned land the Sunda Shelf or Sundaland."[37]

Glacial maximum was about 18,000 BC, and three major floods occurred since then: in 11,500 BC, 9500 BC, and 6000 BC. This last date is when Schoch believes that Sundaland finally succumbed to the waves.[38] (See map at the bottom of p. 299.) Author Graham Hancock points out that between 15,000 and 7,000 years ago, a huge amount of agriculturally rich land was lost when it was submerged by post-glacial flooding. The Ice Age continent now lies beneath more than 300 feet of water. "Prior to its final inundation of about 8,000 years ago, this consisted of more than 3 million square kilometers of prime antediluvian real estate extending from the Malaysian peninsula through what are now the Indonesian islands and the Philippines."[39]

So where did the people of Sundaland (or Mu) flee to during this last and perhaps worst of the the post-ice age floods? According to pediatrician, geneticist, and author Stephen Oppenheimer in his book *Eden In the East*, the refugees sailed to all points of the compass.

> "...when the final dramatic rise in water-level occurred between 8000 and 7500 years ago, the last of a series of emigrations from the sinking Sunda shelf began. Migrations routes went south toward Australia, east toward the Pacific, west into the Indian Ocean and north into the Asian Mainland. Today's descendants of the eastern refugees in the Pacific, inhabiting the many islands of

Melanesia, Polynesia and Micronesia, speak languages of the Austronesian family, which they share with island Southeast Asians. In their flight they carried their domestic animals and food plants with them in large ocean-going canoes."[40]

They brought with them the knowledge and skills that allowed civilization to flower in Mesopotamia, India, Egypt, Greece, and China. One piece of evidence that illustrates this cultural dispersal from a common source is 4th millennium bronze making, which occurred concurrently in both Thailand and Mesopotamia. In addition, a bronze mask found in Sichuan, China, closely resembles the Tiki carvings of Polynesia.[41] The obvious origin, claims Oppenheimer, was Sundaland.

Surprisingly, the theosophist Helena P. Blavatsky said much the same thing in the late 19th century regarding the submerged continent of Lemuria. "Three great nations claimed in antiquity a direct descent from the kingdom of Saturn or Lemuria (confused already several thousands of years before our era with Atlantis) : and these were the Egyptians, the Phoenicians (*vide* Sanchoniathon), and the old Greek (*vide* Diodorus, after Plato). But the oldest civilized country of Asia—India—can be shown to claim the same descent likewise. Sub-races by Karmic law or destiny repeat unconsciously the first steps of their respective mother-races."[42] Incidentally, Saturn, or the Roman god Saturnus, as I have shown in my book *The Kivas of Heaven*, is indirectly associated with the Orion, which relates to my previous discussion of the Lemurian tripartite icon and the constellation.

If the Sundalanders migrated westward, it is equally probable that another group of them also sailed eastward, island-hopping along the way. As evidence for a migration toward the sunrise, Schoch points to the spread of the Austronesian language family of Southeast Asia, fanning out across the Pacific. "Austronesian (the name means 'southern islands') includes the indigenous tongues spoken from Madagascar through the Malay Peninsula and Archipelago and into Polynesia as far as Hawaii and Easter Island, with the exception of the Australian, Papuan, and Negrito languages. The spread of Austronesian languages across such a great expanse of earth, much of which is covered by water, shows the nautical abilities of Austronesian speakers."[43]

In this context it is interesting to note that the Hopi word for "boat" or "ship" is *paaki*, whereas the Polynesian word for "boat" is the near-homophone *pahi*.[44] We are perhaps seeing evidence of the farthest extent of this post-flood migration.

If the concept of dual migration (both westward and eastward) from the Source (i.e. Sundaland) is valid, then similar tales containing both linguistic and thematic congruities should be apparent. Indeed, the biblical legend of God creating humans is mirrored in a Tahitian myth. Again, Blavatsky comments:

"The rib is bone, and when we read in Genesis that Eve was made out of the rib, it only means that the *Race with bones* was produced out of a previous Race and Races, who were 'boneless.' This is an esoteric tenet spread far and wide, as it is almost universal under its various forms. A Tahitian tradition states that man was created out of *Aræa*, 'red Earth.' Taaroa, the creative power, the chief god, 'put man to sleep for long years, for several lives,' which means racial periods, and is a reference to his *mental sleep*, as shown elsewhere. During that time the deity pulled an *Ivi* (bone) out of man and she became a woman."

Madame Blavatky's footnote on this quote is as follows: "Missionaries seem to have pounced on this name *Ivi* and made of it *Eve*. But, as shown by Professor Max Müller, Eve is not a Hebrew name but an European transformation of [Jewish letters], chavah, 'life,' or mother of all living ; while the Tahitian *Ivi* and the Maori *Wheva* meant bone and bone only."[45]

Churchward also notices a similarity between the Creation as described in the Bible and a Polynesian cosmogonic legend. He writes, "The Polynesians say: 'In the beginning there was no light, life or sound in the world. A boundless night called Po enveloped everything, over which Tanaoa (darkness) and Mutu-Hei (silence) reigned supreme. Then the god of light separated from Tanaoa (darkness), fought him and drove him away, and confined him to the night.'"[46] The Hopi word *pa* means both "water" and "wonder." And *pu'* in the same language means "now, today, at the present time, currently."[47]

Frank Waters in his book *Mexico Mystique* talks about the recurrent cycles of time as a universal archetype in both the East and the West.

> "The mythological creation and destruction of four previous worlds is not a unique conception of the ancient Nuhuas and Mayas, or of contemporary Pueblos and Navahos. The belief was common to Hindu and Tibetan Buddhism; to Zoroasterism, the religion of Persia; to the Chinese; and it is found in the myths of Iceland and the Polynesian islands. Heraclitus and Aristarchus both taught that the earth was destroyed periodically; and Hesiod, the Greek historian, recounted the destruction of four previous worlds."[48]

The number of world-ages differ according to the culture. The Aztecs counted four previous worlds, whereas the Hopi and the Maya still count three. And most Mayan and Hopi elders say we are at the end of the Fourth World.

The time of the ancient mariners probably began circa 6000 BC with the final inundation of Sundaland or Mu. (The appellation probably depends on whether or not you are a tenured professor.) At any rate, this deluge was the end of the Hopi Third World, which had been host to a high civilization. The Hopi believe that the people of the Third World had constructed large metropolises in different countries. With their complex and technologically advanced society, they even built aerial vehicles with which they made war on each other. These are akin to the *vimanas* of Hindu lore. The Hopi call them *paatuwvota*, which means "magic flying shield," or, etymologically, either "wonder-shield" or "water-shield."[49] Some theorists of lost continents speculate that Mu and Atlantis even engaged in warfare against each other. As described at the beginning of this chapter, the Hopi escaped the global deluge on low-tech reed rafts to the New World.

The Voyages of the Starship Nephilim

"He's gone off the deep end into the wild blue yonder." Perhaps you are thinking along those lines due to my suggestion that the aerial disks of the Hopi Third World may have been real. Nevertheless, their legends report that these flying saucers were piloted by kachinas, spirit-beings who sometimes descended to earth and took Hopi brides, just like the Nephilim reputedly did. In my defense, I present a couple of Melanesian legends that also talk about extraterrestrial visitation.

Once upon a time a winged serpent named Hatuibwari came from the sky and landed on the summit of a mountain, where she created humans, animals, and plants. She had female breasts but a man's face. "Winged serpent" may actually be the aircraft flown by this androgynous woman, who supposedly created all beings and the vegetable food they eat.[50] In another story "...the first chief and his light-skinned wife came down from the sky, and a sanctuary of stone walls was built round them, and some of the other chiefs were light-haired. The analogy of our stone-using culture heroes Qat-Ambat-Tigaro, etc. is beyond doubt. We have repeatedly found the culture heroes associated with the sky, or living in the sky, and many of the culture heroes were light-skinned, as were also the sky-beings associated with them..."[51]

So, not only do we have legendary culture heroes –in this case, those tall, light-skinned, bearded argonauts with long ear lobes who plied the high seas for plunder ("Where women glow and men plunder...")– we also see that the lighter color of the skin extends to interlopers from the heavens. Recall the quote in the first section of this chapter made by Albert Yava, the Hopi-Tewa from Arizona. He believed that members the Water Clan were originally light-skinned, the way all his people were before they became corrupted at the end of the Third World.

In fact, even today the Tewa of New Mexico recognize a red-bearded, long-haired kachina called *Pala Sowichme Angak'*. Of course, Native Americans are not genetically disposed to have thick beards, especially red ones, such as is worn by this kachina. At Hopi-land his name is *Sio Angak'china* (or *Angaktsin*), and the

Zuni equivalent called *Kokkokshi* is considered that pueblo's first kachina.[52] His hair falls loose down his back to resemble rain. Beloved for his melodic songs, he is a bringer of gentle moisture and flowers.[53] Many times he appears with a white mask.

An interesting resonance exists between the Hopi word *Angak'*, and a people in the Bible named Anakim. One passage describes a confrontation between the Hebrews and an evil land where "...all the people that we saw in it are men of a great stature. And there we saw the giants, the sons of Anak, which come of the giants: and we were in our own sight as grasshoppers, and so we were in their sight." Instead of "giants," the New International Version of the Bible states: "We saw the Nephilim there (the descendants of Anak come from the Nephilim)." (Numbers 13:32-33) Because of their intimidating height and warlike nature, the Anakim must have been simply terrifying to the Hebrews.

Author Andrew Collins comments on this race that some believe was actually the Phoenicians, or Canaanites. "The word Anak is generally taken by Jewish scholars to mean 'long-necked', or 'men with necklaces', conjuring an immediate image of the ring collars worn even today by certain tribes of central Africa."[54] Incidentally, the Kayan women of Burma are known to wear similar brass collars to give the appearance of stretched necks, perhaps in imitation of the ancient Long Necks. In this context it is interesting to note that the beach on the north coast of Easter Island where the Long Ears first landed was called *Anakena*.

Did the red-haired Long Ears with beards (discussed in the previous chapter) attain their great height partly because of their long necks? If so, they might have been the proto-Phoenicians, or "red men" —not because of their skin color or the purple dye they traditionally produced but because of their hair color. The Greek historian Heraclitus claims that the Phoenicians originated in the Red Sea area and later moved to Palestine. However, this was not the gulf between the northeastern coast of Africa and Saudi Arabia, as we know the name today; instead the Red Sea of yore was the Indian Ocean and its gulfs.[55]

A more disturbing question to ask is: Was the amalgam known variously as the Anakim/Phoenician/Long Ears actually the biblical Nephilim, or the Watchers, who originally came down from the skies—perhaps in aerial vehicles? The Bible, of course, couches these entities in terms of "fallen angels." According to the Book of Genesis, the Nephilim were the "sons of God" who mated with the "daughters of men," thereby spawning the rebellious "giants in the earth." (Genesis 6:2, 6: 4).

Masonic researchers Christopher Knight and Robert Lomas have provided the semantic derivation of Nephilim. "The word 'Nephilim' is of uncertain origin, but it has been observed by specialist scholars that the root Aramaic word *nephîlâ* is the name of the constellation Orion, and therefore, Nephilim would seem to mean 'those that are of Orion'."[56] The Hebrews knew the constellation by the name of the *cesîl*, and his terrestrial counterpart was Nimrod, the giant and mighty hunter whose Mesopotamian empire included the city of Babel (or *bab-el*, literally "god-gate.")[57] We recall that the word *zona*, referring to "the belt stars of Orion," is also the Sanskrit word meaning *red*.

Perhaps at this point you are seeing red and starting to discount the current discussion as mere supernatural (i.e. superstitious) nonsense. But as we shall see in the next section, the Hopi *naturally* have their fair share of light-skinned people.

Gene Flow and Counter Current

To the layperson genetics can seem like a foreign language. Phylogenetic trees look somewhat like schematics for electronic circuit boards. I can read neither. However, if one can manage to decipher the academic literature, certain clues about population migration become apparent.

Gene flow is defined as the transference of genetic variation, or alleles, from one population to another. When we map similar genetic traits at different places on Earth, we can reasonably trace migration patterns of different groups of people during various historical time periods. It is a complex science, and much speculation can accompany the data. However, using a few genetic indicators, I believe that certain definitive statements can be made about Hopi migration myths that describe an epic journey from the South Pacific to the American Southwest.

One consistent genetic marker that is distributed over a hypothetical migration route from west to east (i.e. from Polynesia to North America) is manifested by the disorder of albinism. In the abstract to a 2010 article published in *Journal of Human Genetics*, Helene C. Johanson describes her study of the very high numbers of albino people found in the South Pacific. "Oculocutaneous albinism type 2 (OCA2) is a human autosomal-recessive hypopigmentation disorder associated with pathological mutations of the OCA2 gene. In this study, we investigated a form of OCA in a Polynesian population with an observed phenotype characterized by fair skin, some brown nevi [birthmarks] present in the sun-exposed areas and green or blue eyes. Hair presented with a unique red coloration since birth, with tones ranging across individuals from Yellow-Red to Brown-Red, or Auburn."

Translating the scientific jargon, we can generally say that albinism occurs when both parents carry a mutated OCA2 gene that causes reduced pigmentation in both the skin and the eyes. This results in light-colored skin, sometimes in otherwise darker colored populations, and in white, yellow, or red hair, even when black hair predominates. Albinos also have pink or bluish-green eyes, depending on the level of ocular pigmentation. This holds true even among mostly brown-eyed populations.[58]

Johanson's research focused on the Tuvalu Islands, formerly the Ellice Islands, where she found an exceedingly high rate of albinism. "I found that in Tuvalu 1 in 669 people are born with albinism. This is one of the highest recorded rates of Oculocutaneous Albinism Type 2 in the World. Especially when you compare this with the general figure of 1 in 17,000 quoted for all types of albinism in America. I found anecdotally that *the general trend across the Pacific Island nations was reported to be at similarly high levels to that in Tuvalu.* [italics added]"[59]

Although not genetically related to albinism (or achromatosis), the condition of colorblindness (or achromatopsia) is endemic to two of the Caroline Islands, namely Pohnpei and Pingelap—the latter an atoll a little over 165 miles east of the former. In fact,

10% of the population on both islands has the disorder—a rate among the highest in the world. In 1995 British neurologist Oliver Sacks traveled to Micronesia in order to study the condition, thus the title of his popular book *The Island of the Colorblind*.[60]

However, both conditions –albinism and colorblindness– exhibit photosensitivity (or even photophobia), poor visual acuity, and nystagmus, or involuntary eye movements. Consequently, the existence of either disorder in a given population is not readily apparent because those affected tend to stay indoors away from harsh sunlight—either in the tropics or the desert. Albinos also have increased rates of both myopia and melanoma. On these islands colorblindness is known by the term *maskun*, which literally means "not see."[61] Coincidentally, the Hopi word *mas* literally means "gray." This word is also the root of the name Masau'u, god of the underworld.[62]

Johanson stated that 1 in 669 people of Tuvalu have albinism. However, the Hopi and other Southwestern tribes have substantially higher rates of the disorder. Studies done by Charles M. Woolf in 1962 and 1964 found the following: Hopi, 1 in 227; Zuni, 1 in 247; San Juan, 1 in 500. A earlier study of the Hopi done in 1900 had obtained an even higher rate: 1 in 182. Woolf found the highest rate of all was among the Jemez: 1 in 140. The Navajo, on the other hand, showed a relatively decreased rate of 1 in 3,750.[63] Still, all of these figures are very much higher than the European rate for albinism: 1 in 20,000.[64] The Navajo statistic is probably the result of interbreeding with the Puebloans.

In the Southwest no stigma seems to be attached to albinism, except perhaps marriage desirability. Between about 1850 and 1865, the village chief of Oraibi named Nakwaiyamptiwa of the Bear Clan was a Hopi albino whose nickname was Qötctaka, or "white man." Anthropologist Mischa Titiev describes the effective leader: "He is supposed to have been a good chief and a good rain-maker. During a plague of prairie dogs one fall he is said to have called for a Masau Katcina [Masau'u Kachina] dance, which caused a veritable cloudburst that drowned all the prairie dogs. Nakwaiyamptiwa never married, because in those days 'ladies' did not like albinos."[65]

Another ethnic group, the Kuna of the San Blas Islands on the Caribbean coast of Panama, also have a high rate of albinism. Two different studies in 1925 and 1940 obtained the following rates: 1 in 146, and 1 in 213, respectively.[66] The Kuna believe that albinos belong to a highly intelligent, elite shamanic group called the "Children of the Moon." Their supernatural powers include the ability to heal snakebites, cure headaches, remove fish bones stuck in the throat, and foretell the future. "Kuna mythology puts albinos –who have pale skin and white or ginger hair due to pigment deficiency– at the heart of creation, teaching that God sent his albino son to Earth to teach humans how to live."[67] This is very similar to the previously quoted statement by Albert Yava about the Hopi Water Clan.

There appears to be a genetic link between the Hopi and the Kuna. Sheldon C. Reed writes in *The Journal of Heredity*: "Some thousands of years ago, though not long in terms of generations, all these Indians probably had some ancestors in common and it is quite possible that one of these 'Founding Fathers' was a carrier of the gene for albinism."[68] The Kuna word *sipu* means "albino," whereas the the Hopi word *sipyuk* means "metalwork, especially silver."[69] Silver is, of course, a whitish metal.

Returning briefly to a theme dealt with in Chapter 2, we see that the Kuna believe that the "whirlpool of God" is located beneath the roots of the *Palluwalla* tree, or Saltwater-Tree. It was created when the sun-god in the form of a cosmic tapir chopped down the tree, causing saltwater to gush out and form the oceans.[70] Salt, of course, implies whiteness. In Hopi, *pala* has connotations of both "water" and "red," while *wala* means "splashing, sloshing."[71]

One quintessential question remains: Is there a physical mechanism between these three geographic pockets of albinism –the Tuvalu Islands, Panama, and the American Southwest– that would link them and thus allow for migration?

Between Oceania and the western coast of South America, the equatorial counter currents produce a steady stream flowing west to east. Located approximately 5° north and south of the equator, these surface currents would have provided ocean-going outrigger canoes or reed rafts an easy eastward ride, much like the horizontal conveyor belts in airports. These north and south equatorial counter currents are in turn sandwiched between the north and south equatorial currents, which flow in the opposite direction, east to west, and are located between 10° and 20° north and south of the equator. Hence, round trips as well could have theoretically been made by boat.

The ancient mariners could have conceivably sailed the vast distances across the Pacific to northwestern South America, followed the currents' loop northward up the western coast to Panama, Central America, and finally southwestern Mexico. From there they could have trekked northward on foot along the western coast of Mexico to the mouth of the Colorado River, then fanned out across the American Southwest to arrive at their ultimate homeland. A monumental journey, for sure, but it did not necessarily have to be made all at once. It could have taken decades, centuries, or even millennia.

Except for statements such as the Patki Clan members once had white skin, the modern Puebloans seem to have forgotten in the long intervening period the origin of their high levels of albinism. Some attribute the condition to the fact that the mother may have had sexual relations with a white man.[72] Others claim ceremonial faux pas. "Albinism is said by Hopi to be caused by making white prayer-sticks during a wife's pregnancy."[73] Regardless of its actual cause, albinism is in fact pervasive in three main regions: Oceania, Panama, and the American Southwest.

A Few Other Genetic Migration-Markers

One major distinguishing genetic marker is mitochrondrial DNA (mtDNA). The mitochondrion is basically a nuclear organelle, supplying most of a cell's energy—sort of like a battery. Unlike nuclear DNA, it does not recombine and thus has nothing to do with the male Y-chromosome. It is instead maternally inherited, passing strictly from mother to daughter. This, incidentally, mirrors both the Polynesian and the Hopi matrilineal societies.[74]

Photo of albino boy, Zuni Pueblo, 1873, by George V. Allen, Smithsonian.

EXPEDITION OF 1873.

1st Lieut. GEO. M. WHEELER, Corps of Eng'rs, Com'dg.

No. 54—Albino Boy and Zuni Indian Boy, Zuni Pueblos, New Mexico.

Albino Hopi Flute Priest, second from the right.

The world's populations are designated by five major mitochrondrial types called haplogroups, or clades: A, B, C, D, and X. Geneticists call the founding of such a certain group as its "coalescence time." Particularly important to note is that an early pre-Columbian founding can be determined and distinguished from one that is post-Columbian. In addition, it is important to understand that haplogroup distribution among modern Puebloans is not significantly different from that of their ancestors, the Anasazi or the Hohokam.[75]

In the American Southwest, haplogroup B unequivocally predominates, with a maximum frequency of 89% found at Jemez Pueblo,[76] which, as we recall, also had the highest level of albinism. On the other hand, in eastern Siberia, haplogroup B is –curiously and conspicuously– absent. In this area where, so to speak, tons of B should be present, we instead find only haplogroups A, C, and D.[77] After all, this was supposedly the staging point for trans-Beringia migration. One explanation is that haplogroup B once existed in eastern Siberia but for some reason became extinct; this, however, seems unlikely.

Where in the western Pacific does haplogroup B predominant? Well, we find high frequencies of it in Mongolia and South China.[78] However, "B-Central" would most likely be identified as Polynesia. Haplogroup B is found in 93% of males and females living today who report their maternal line as Polynesian.[79]

Stephen Oppenheimer, whom I quoted earlier in this chapter, discusses a key Asian deletion in the mtDNA called the nine-base pair (9-bp) deletion.

"A date no less than 6000-7250 BC, possibly much greater, has been suggested for the American wing of spread of this deletion. A recent study in Alaska suggests that the 9-bp deletion reached the Americas well before the arrival of the present circum-Arctic populations of Eskimos, Aleuts and Athapascans, none of whom possess the 9-bp deletion. There is currently a debate about whether the trans-Pacific island populations represent evidence for Thor Heyerdahl's South American-Pacific connection."[80]

The particular segment of the gene where the 9-bp deletion occurs is designated as region V. "The region V deletion has been observed mainly in individuals from East Asian populations or populations that are derived from East Asia, such as Native Americans. The frequency of deletion in Asia varies from 100% in some Polynesian groups (Samoans, Maoris, and Niuean) to 0% among Highland New Guinea and Australian Aborigine groups. The region V deletion is absent in modern northeastern Siberian populations..." This study indicates that the rate for the base pair deletion among speakers of Uto-Aztecan (e.g. Hopi), Zuni, Tanoan (viz. Tewa, Tiwa, and Towa—the latter from the afore-mentioned Jemez Pueblo) is 46.5%—the highest in North America.[81] Again, the Siberian-Alaskan land bridge shows signs of crumbling, at least as the sole means of access to the New World.

The geographic distribution of human genetic material is designated by a number of other specific markers, one of which is called human lymphocyte antigens (HLAs). These alleles are basically proteins on white blood cells that produce antibodies. An allele is an alternative form of a gene –one member of a pair– that is located at a specific position on a specific chromosome. The distribution of HLAs differs among world populations and may thus be used in tracing ancient migrations.

According to physical anthropologist James L. Guthrie, a number of different HLAs occur in populations where one wouldn't expect them to be.

"...certain indigenous American populations have HLA alleles that are rare in America but common in parts of the world not usually associated with American Indian origins, and many of the unexpected HLAs are characteristic of populations sometimes claimed, on the basis of other kinds of evidence, to have had ancient contacts with Americans. In other words, there seems to be genetic support for the idea of ancient interhemispheric mobility. I propose that the 'non-Indian' HLAs were introduced from the outside at various times between the initial colonizations of the hemisphere [via Beringia] and the late fifteenth century A.D. [Columbian]."[82]

The numbers for the HLA called B*16, one of the typical "American" alleles, suggest a possible trans-Pacific influence. For instance, the frequency rate for the Papago (Tohono O'odham) is 17.3% while that for the Philippines is 17.6%. The Pima (Akimel O'odham) and the Navajo both have a rate of 12.0% for this allele, while the Cook Islanders have a frequency rate of 12.8%.[83]

Another monograph suggests a link between the Pima of Arizona and the Maori of New Zealand. "The phylogenetic relationships for the HLA system show the Pima population of North American to have the closest relationship with the Maori, suggesting that, even though the main movement of Polynesians was from east to west, some minor Native American influence could not be excluded."[84]

A few genetic markers other than HLAs provide additional evidence for cultural diffusionism.[85] Transferrins, for instance, are proteins that react with iron, transferring them to bone marrow. Over 97% of the world's populations are characterized by type C (TFC). However, two significant variants exist: type B and type D. TFB is found in Polynesia, India, Africa, and at least 23 American Indian groups, although information on these types is limited. The presence of Tranferrin B was found among the Papago and Pima, which implies that a genetic intermingling occurred with groups from Polynesia, India, or even Africa.[86]

In our Journey to the East we have seen Lemurian theories, psychic past-life recollections, and genetic mapping—three prongs of the trident we raise high in salute to the ancient mariners who ultimately became desert farmers.

In this chapter, I have discussed the Hopi migration from the Third World to the Fourth. The next chapter will deal with the transition from the Fourth World to the Fifth.

The Pillar of Heaven

Many island cultures of Oceania once understood the astronomical fact that if a particular star passes directly or nearly directly overhead as it reaches its meridian (highest point in the sky), the observer's terrestrial latitude will be equivalent to the star's declination, or celestial latitude. (Some natives still remember this knowledge.) On Tonga this type of asterism is known as a *fanakenga*, "the star that points down to an island, its overhead star."[87] In Tahiti this star-island connection is called the "pillar of heaven"; in Maori it is known as a "prop of heaven."[88] One hymn found written on an Easter Island *rongorongo* board invokes not only the first-born son of the earth but also the "prop of heaven."[89]

Sky pillars greatly assist navigators in determining how far north or south in a relative sense their location is at any given time. For instance, the island of Pohnpei in the Caroline Islands is located at 6.5° north latitude. Arno Atoll in the Marshall Islands is very close to 6.5° north latitude, but it is 920 miles to the east. Palmyra Atoll and Kingman Reef in the Line Islands are both less than one degree south of 6.5° north latitude, but they are located about 2,700 miles to the east of Pohnpei.

The star that served as the "prop of heaven" for these three locations is the giant red star Betelgeuse, the right shoulder of Orion. At 4:10 a.m. on December 21st, 1150 AD (winter solstice), this star was directly overhead. (See star chart to the right.) If a mariner from Pohnpei, for instance, sailed eastward, always keeping this star directly overhead each night, he or she would eventually reach the Marshall Islands.

Pohnpei lies over a thousand miles northeast of New Guinea and is only 18 miles across. As previously mentioned, James Churchward believed that on Pohnpei "...there stand vestiges of old stone temples and other lithic remains that take us back to the time of Mu."[90]

On the southeast side of the island is its most famous attraction: the megalithic city of Nan Madol. In a shallow lagoon of a steamy mangrove swamp, the Nan Madolians (whoever they were) constructed an artificial island from massive *dull-red* and black basalt "logs"quarried from the other side of the island. Measuring 10 to 25 feet long, some of these hexagonal columns weighed 20 tons. The massive, crude walls rose up to 30 feet high. The people also carved canals out of the coral 30 feet wide and five feet deep. Tunnels connected a number of larger islands in the vicinity. The entire city encompassed 11 square miles. A 1963 Smithsonian Institution survey of the site resulted in radiocarbon dates as early as 1180 AD.[91] In the harbor, scuba divers have found evidence of a submerged city that legends say is a mirror image of Nan Madol.[92]

Pohn-pei literally means "upon a stone altar." The Hopi word *pongya* means "to display ceremonial objects on an altar."[93] Nan Modal means "space between canals." The Hopi word *nani'i* means "in two separate places or groups."[94] The island's native name is Panapé. The Hopi word *panaptsa* means "mirror."[95] This may reflect (no pun intended) the concept of Nan Madol mirroring the legendary city submerged in the harbor 100 feet down.

On p. 294, I quoted the Hopi-Tewa Albert Yava as saying that the Water Clan had built a city "somewhere" before they made their ocean voyage and subsequently built Palatkwapi, "Red City of the South." Was Pohnpei actually Palatkwapi I, whose stellar-pillar was Betelgeuse?

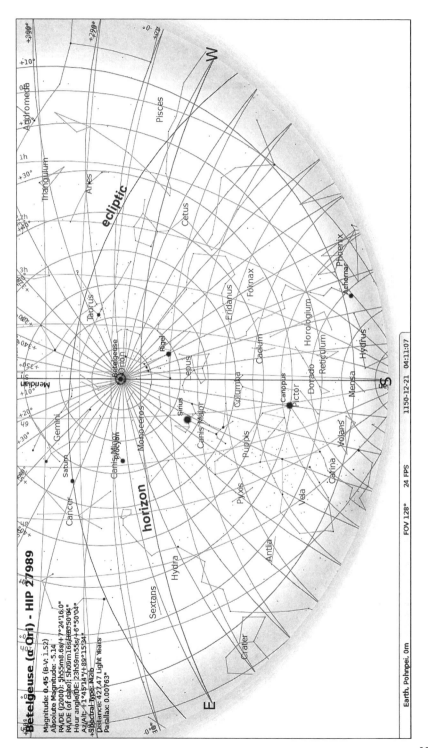

Betelgeuse (α-Ori) - HIP 27989

Magnitude: 0.45 (B-v: 1.52)
Absolute Magnitude: -5.14
RA/DE (J2000): 5h55m8.66/+7°24'16.0"
RA/DE (of date): 5h09m16s/+6°50'04"
Hour angle/DE: 23h59m55s/+6°50'04"
Az/Alt: +1°45'14"/+89°15'34"
Spectral Type: M2Ib
Distance: 427,47 Light Years
Parallax: 0.00763"

Earth, Pohnpei, 0m   FOV 128°   24 FPS   1150-12-21 04:11:07

The huge complex of Nan Madol is located at 6° 5' 40" N terrestrial latitude. In 1150 AD, the approximate period of habitation, Betelgeuse was at 6° 50' 04"celestial latitude (declination). (It is currently at 7° 24' 16".) Thus, this red star in Orion was a "pillar of heaven" planted on Pohnpei. Nan Madol may have been the original Palatkwapi, the Red City of the South, which was reconstructed somewhere in the New World after the ocean voyage.

The Gulf of Panama, where perhaps the ancestral albino Kuna landed, is only one-half degree of latitude north of Pohnpei—and 8,300 miles to the east.

Lower-right: dull-red exterior wall of Nan Madol.

Chapter 13
Hopi Mystery Egg
and Prophecies of the Fifth World

Legacy of Prophecy

The Hopi of Arizona, more than most other tribes of North America, have developed as a people according to the dictates and demands of what may be called a legacy of prophecy. The predictions of the life to come do not merely pertain to the Hopi themselves but deal with impending events on a global scale. Because the Hopi are basically an aggregation of clans and villages rather than a monolithic tribe, the sources of the prophecies, which began to come to light in the mid-20th century, are fragmentary and multifarious. The lack of narrative clarity has to do in part with the secretive nature of the Hopi. These isolated, sedentary farmers living in simple stone pueblos on the high desert of the American Southwest have looked into the future from their underground kivas (communal prayer-chambers) and have seen some rather disturbing scenarios. Many times they do not wish to share these with the outside world.

Like the Maya among whom the Hopi once lived and with whom they later traded, the Hopi conceptualize the cycles of time as world-ages. Unlike the Maya, however, the Hopi are rarely specific about the dates for the shifting of ages. It has been said that the Maya were masters of time, whereas the Hopi are masters of space. (The verb tenses here are deliberate, given that the Maya no longer follow the Long Count calendar of 394-year cycles, but instead use the Tzolk'in calender of 260 days—an amazingly complex system nonetheless.) The Hopi, on the other hand, still perform sacred rituals within an annual ceremonial cycle upon their three primary mesas in order to keep the whole world in balance.

As time goes by, this task is increasingly difficult because our contemporary lifestyle, with its concomitant technological gadgetry and unseemly allures, continues to erode traditional ways of life and ancestral Hopi values. Fewer and fewer young Hopis are learning their indigenous language, customs, and ceremonies. More youth are leaving Hopi-land to seek employment in urban areas. Those that do stay on the reservation are confronted with intratribal squabbles and, much worse, with high rates of alcoholism and increasingly available destructive street drugs. The dire signs of a Native American version of the "End Times" are everywhere.

Many Hopi spiritual elders (singular, *kikmongwi*) claim that we are living in the final days of the Fourth World. During the past 60 or so years, different Hopis have predicted various earth changes as signals that the current age is ending and the Fifth World is beginning. In 1970, Dan Katchongva, Sun Clan leader from the village of Hotevilla, who died at age 112, spoke about deteriorating conditions of our time:

"We have teachings and prophecies informing us that we must be alert for the signs and omens which will come about to give us courage and strength to stand on our beliefs. Blood will flow. Our hair and our clothing will be scattered upon the earth. Nature will speak to us with its mighty breath of wind. There will be earthquakes and floods causing great disasters, changes in the seasons and in the weather, disappearance of wildlife, and famine in different forms. There will be gradual corruption and confusion among the leaders and the people all over the world, and wars will come about like powerful winds. All of this has been planned from the beginning of creation."[1]

Hopi (Moqui) Indians Snake Kiva Oraibi Pueblo. 6x8 533

Drawing of petroglyphs on Prophecy Rock, Third Mesa, Arizona.

Another spiritual elder from the same village, David Monongye, who may have lived even longer than Grandfather Dan, had warned: "When earthquakes, floods, hailstorms, drought, and famine will be the life of every day, the time will have then come for the return to the true path, or going the zig-zag way."[2]

The "zig-zag way" refers to a line carved on Prophecy Rock in Hopi-land (bottom of p. 325). It is the upper of two parallel lines and represents the path of the Two-Hearts who are wreaking havoc on our Earth Mother and living contrary to the laws of nature and ecological principles. The lower line, on the other hand, is the path of the One-Hearts, close to soil and the growth of corn, beans, squash—that is, adhering to the true Hopi way. The upper path is divorced from the natural world and totally immersed in a synthetic, manufactured reality of iPhones and Xbox 360s. The lower way, rooted in earth-based rhythms, finds sustenance and solace from corn pollen, sunlight, soaking rains, and vast desert vistas—a life in accordance with the Creator.

One author who chooses to remains anonymous has expressed this dichotomy beautifully and artfully in a recent monograph.

"Regarding the Original Instructions, there are two Hopi words which must be clearly understood; **navoti** and *koyaanisqatsi*. Navoti [*nah-vo-tee*] essentially means 'life in balance.' Koyaanisqatsi [*koy-ah-neh-skot-see*] translates as 'life out of balance.' When Massau'u revealed the Original Instructions, he also created the image carved on Prophecy Rock, which shows the two paths possible for humankind to take on this journey through the Fourth World. The True Path in life, *navoti*, is indicated by the lower line, and the path of *koyaanisqatsi* is represented by the upper line."[3]

The Hopi term *navoti* also means "teachings, traditions, body of knowledge, cultural beliefs."[4] This sounds very similar to the Tibetan Buddhist concept of Dharma, or spiritual teachings and obligations as well as the harmony and divinely ordained natural order of the universe. *Navoti* can also be compared with the Hopi word *wukwlavayi*, which means "words of elders containing wise counsel or prophetic opinions, oral tradition."[5] That is, eternal visions from the past that impinge upon the future world.

Grandfather Martin Gashweseoma, of the Fire Clan and also from Hotevilla, stated to a group of us in front of Prophecy Rock during the summer of 2011 that this lower line represented "everlasting life" and the rising sun. Indeed, I did a quick compass-check of the extended lower line (see upper-right of bottom the graphic on p. 325) and found that if one stood at that point with his/her back to the rock, one would face the 60° azimuth—the spot on the horizon where the sun rises on the summer solstice (in Hopi, *susawupatawa*). The Hopi say that at this time Taawa, the sun god, is the strongest and resides in his *Taawaki*, or "summer house."[6]

The petroglyphs are carved on the vertical surface of a sandstone boulder. Before I give some *possible* interpretations, let me say that these are my personal views and are in *no* way the official Hopi interpretation of Prophecy Rock. A monolithic, codified explanation off these prophetic symbols does not exist anyway.

That said, a few of my own observations follow: The figure at the lower-left is Masau'u, the Hopi god of death, fire, and the earthly plane. He carries a bow with his arrow pointing to the underworld (or the previous Third World). His left hand holds the path to the current Fourth World.

The circle to the right represents the Earth or rim of the horizon. The Christian cross signifies the Spanish (Catholic) incursion of Hopi-land. The square represents a village, pueblo, plaza, or the Hopi territory.

The two parallel lines, which are obliquely positioned, refer to the two paths humankind may take at the end of the Fourth World. The upper line is the path of the Two-Hearts. On this line are four figures holding hands, the last figure appearing to have two heads (hearts?). This line ends in a zig-zag up in the air. The lower line is the path of the One-Hearts. Resting on this line from left to right are three circles, which represent three world shakings or three world wars. To the right of the last circle is a corn stalk and a Hopi man tending corn. This line extends to the right across another section of the rock, whereas the upper line is not extended. Note that the line on the right that is between the two parallel lines and perpendicular to them represents the last chance the Two-Hearts have to descend to the true path on the lower line before the current age is destroyed.

Various Hopi predictions of the Fourth World's denouement have also included an increasingly erratic climate and a few specific signals of social and political imbalance:

· A "gourd of ashes" would fall on the Earth (e.g. nuclear explosions, first at Trinity Site in New Mexico; then the dual holocausts at Hiroshima and Nagasaki, death toll: conservatively, 225,000; and finally the other hydrogen bomb tests on Pacific atolls and in the American Southwest, with their carcinogenic effects on the "down-winders"). These nuclear detonations first prompted the Hopi spiritual elders to "go public" with their previously secret prophecies and share them with the rest of the world.

· Earthquakes (e.g. the January 2010 temblor in Haiti, death toll: 225,000; the March 2011 Japanese earthquake, death toll: nearly 19,000, with many more exposed to fatal doses of radioactivity after leakage from the Fukushima Power Plant).

· Epidemics (e.g. the cholera epidemic that followed the Haitian quake; and the 2009 H1N1-swine flu, death toll: 17,000 globally in just six months).

· Tsunamis (e.g. the Indonesian disaster of December 2004, death toll: 280,000; and the Japanese earth-trauma of 2011).

· Various record floods (e.g. U.S. Midwest, spring 2011; New England, August 2011 from Hurricane Irene); and famines (e.g. Horn of Africa, 2011).

· Droughts (e.g. U.S. Midwest, summer 2012) and wildfires (e.g. Arizona, Texas, 2011; Colorado, New Mexico, Oregon, summer, 2012); violent earth changes worldwide.

· Tornadoes (e.g. U.S., spring 2011, death toll: 550 — as many as the last ten years combined).

· More erratic and severe weather patterns, such as hurricanes (e.g. Katrina in 2005 that decimated New Orleans, death toll: 1,836).

· "Roads in the heavens" that vehicles will travel on (e.g. either benign contrails or deleterious chemtrails).

· People will be living in the sky (e.g. International Space Station).

· Women will wear men's clothing (e.g. Women's Liberation Movement, etc.).

· Hopi delegates will travel to the "House of Mica" (e.g. Four times the Hopi journeyed to the U.N. building in New York, but their pleas for peace were ignored).

Grandfather Martin Gashweseoma, Fire Clan, Hotevilla, Arizona, 2010, at Prophecy Rock, Third Mesa, Hopi Reservation.

White Feather Prophecies

In the summer of 1958 a minister named David Young was driving across the Four Corners region when he picked up an old Hopi man named White Feather by the side of the road. This spiritual elder of the Bear Clan confessed that all his sons were dead and that the Hopi ceremonial cycle was slowly becoming extinct. After sensing Reverend Young was trustworthy, he decided to pass along nine primary Hopi prophecies that together would herald the destruction of the Fourth World.

White Feather stated that his ancestors had foretold of the coming of beasts huge as buffalo except with long horns (cattle), and white-skinned people with thunder-sticks (guns)—all long before they arrived. White Feather also said his elders had talked about the appearance of "snakes of iron" (railroads) and "rivers of stone that make pictures in the sun" spreading across the land (concrete highways with their water mirages). Spinning wheels with voices in them would also come (either the settlers' wagon wheels or the whining tires of today's speeding cars). He said his grandfathers had predicted as well that a "giant spider web" would entangle the Earth prior to the end of the Fourth World (telegraph, telephone, power lines, and now the Internet).

One of the last signs would be when young people with long hair come to Hopi-land to learn Native ways (the counterculture revolution of the late 60s and early 70s). Another one of the final signs would be when the sea turns black and all living things in it died (the Gulf oil spill in the summer of 2010). The ninth and final sign describes a "dwelling place in the heavens" that crashes to earth, thereby producing a brilliant blue star (*Sakwa Sohu*). Directly following that, the Hopi ceremonies would altogether cease.

The entheogen investigator and cultural commentator Daniel Pinchbeck draws the comparison between the Blue Star and the Norway Spiral, which erupted in the early morning sky over northern Norway on December 9th, 2009. (See top of p. 333.) "The Norway spiral has resonance with the Hopi prophecies of the Blue Star Kachina, which appears at the end of the Fourth World—if not that signifying event itself, perhaps a foreshadowing or retro-causal echo of it. The spiral seems like a message, invitation, or indication that the earth and its inhabitants are on the threshold of a deep transformation."[7]

White Feather furthermore said that the conclusion of the Fourth World would be accompanied by great wars and mass destruction. He believed this will especially occur in the land where the "first light of wisdom" appeared (perhaps the Middle East). Fiery columns of smoke would rise, which may remind us of the surrealistic scene of Sadam Hussein setting Kuwait oil wells on fire during the first Gulf War. This is also reminiscent of the "Shock and Awe" campaign that started the subsequent, disastrous Iraq War. Remember, this humble Hopi man was talking in 1958.

> "These are the Signs that great destruction is coming. The world shall rock to and fro. The white man will battle against other people in other lands—with those who possessed the first light of wisdom. There will be many columns of smoke and fire such as White Feather has seen the white man make in the deserts not far from here. Only those which come will cause disease and a great dying. Many of my people, understanding the prophecies, shall be safe. Those who stay and live in the places of my people also shall be safe."[8]

This account is corroborated by a passage in Frank Waters' classic *Book of the Hopi*, published in 1963. "World War III will be started by those peoples who first received the light [the divine wisdom or intelligence] in the other old countries [India, China, Egypt, Palestine, Africa]. The United States will be destroyed, land and people, by atomic bombs and radioactivity. Only the Hopis and their homeland will be preserved as an oasis to which refugees will flee."[9]

We need not be reminded of the early 2011 turmoil in the Middle East known as the "Arab Spring." Mass protests and unrest continue, even at the time of this writing, resulting now in the deaths of thousands of innocent people in Syria who are seeking to throw off the yoke of dictatorship and military rule. Tunisia, Egypt, Bahrain, Yemen, Libya, and Syria may be the lands possessing the "first light of wisdom," to which the Hopi elder referred more than a half-century ago.

In my book *Eye of the Phoenix*, I quoted from a 1955 meeting of Hopi people with the Bureau of Indian Affairs at Keams Canyon, Arizona. Many elders surprisingly described apocalyptic scenes leading up to the Day of Purification, which included world wars, a scorched earth, rivers of blood, boiling oceans, and bombs raining down like hailstones. Scary stuff! The urgency of prophecy must have outweighed the intended purpose of the meeting, which was initially supposed to be about simply mundane matters such as livestock management, forced boarding school attendance, and the introduction of alcohol on the reservation. In the Hopi cosmos, it's all connected.

Ovum Mysterium

Another of the prophetic grandfathers from Hotevilla, Dan Evehema, who was also well over a hundred when he died, spoke of the ultimate phase of the Fourth World.

> "The final stage, called 'The Great Day of Purification,' has been described as a 'Mystery Egg' in which the forces of the swastika and the Sun plus a third force symbolized by the color 'red' culminate either in total rebirth or total annihilation—we don't know which. But the choice is yours, war and natural catastrophe may be involved. The degree of violence will be determined by the degree of inequity caused among the peoples of the world and in the balance of nature. In this crisis rich and poor will be forced to struggle as equals in order to survive."[10]

Above: Norway Spiral, December 9th, 2009.
Below: Spiral petroglyph from the V-Bar-V Heritage Site, northern Arizona.

The standard explanation for what produced this spiral involves the failure of a Russian Bulava ballistic missile launched from a submarine in the White Sea. (The Russian word *bulava* literally means "mace"—the kind, incidentally, that Orion holds.) This ICBM with a range of 5,000 miles can carry up to 10 hypersonic individually guided, maneuverable reentry vehicles—i.e. MIRVs or nuclear warheads yielding 100-150 kilotons each.

Although not a "dwelling place" per se, this test rocket's crash did essentially coincide with the formation of a blue star spiral, a geometric figure depicted by Hopi petroglyphs all over the American Southwest. These rock carvings generally signify cosmic portals or interdimensional gateways.

Whether the missile's failure and the spiral were causally related or that some other force affected the atmospheric conditions has been endlessly debated on the Internet. (Some claim, for example, that EISCAT, Norway's version of HAARP, was responsible. The Norway spiral died after a few minutes, collapsing into what appeared to be a black hole.

Again we see a rather grim assessment of the global state of affairs, but at least our sense of justice is satisfied by the last sentence of Evehema's quotation, in which those who caused untold misery and deprivation across the world by their immoral financial dealings that triggered the Great Recession (Depression?) of 2008 will not ultimately escape the consequences of their actions, no matter the extent of their assets or stock portfolios.

So, what exactly is the "Mystery Egg," which in Hopi is called *Nöhu Na'uyi'yta*? Many cultures around the world use this archetype to symbolize an extended cycle of time, an era, or a world age. In his book *Mystery Religions in the Ancient World*, Joscelyn Godwin states that... "The world-egg represents the entirety, in potentia, of one cosmic cycle, and its sundering symbolizes the polarity of positive and negative forces without which no world could unfold in time and space."[11]

Inside the Mystery Egg is one of its three potencies: the Sun, represented by the yolk. We recall that the Aztecs referred to a world-age as a "Sun," and that we are soon to enter the Sixth Sun. Also hidden inside the shell is the masculine swastika—the four-armed cross representing either the four cardinal directions or the four forces of nature (air, fire, water, earth). Working in tandem with the swastika is the feminine Maltese cross, which may represent menstrual blood.[12]

Ancient Egyptian cosmogony describes the divine spirit coming into existence as a circle in the primeval waters of the abyss. Certain texts speak of his initial state as a "dweller in his egg" and "master of yesterday." This latter designation emphasizes the previous age, but he was probably master of the world to come as well. "Here and there one comes upon traces of an old myth that the sun had burst out as a bird from the great egg which the Primeval Being, a goose, had laid in the waters of the Abyss."[13] In addition to the goose, other avian connotations include Horus in his capacity as falcon god of the sky (with his right eye manifesting the solar emblem called a *Wadjet*—see pp. 76-77), and the phoenix in its connection with the recurring cycles of time.

The Egyptian account of the Creation is paralleled in the

Hindu *Rigveda*. A deity known as Hiranyagarbha, later referred to as either Brahma or Prajapati (i.e. the constellation Orion), is the prime generative force manifested as a golden egg.

"In the beginning rose Haranyagarbha,
    born Only Lord of all created beings.
He fixeth and holdeth up this earth and heaven...
What time the mighty waters came, containing
    the universal germ,
producing Agni [god of fire].
Thence sprang the Gods' one spirit into being...
He in his might surveyed the floods
containing productive force and generating Worship.
He is the God of gods, and none beside him.
What God shall we adore with our oblation?"[14]

The genesis of monotheism is apparent in these early Hindu verses that pay homage to the golden egg, golden fetus, or golden womb. This occult symbol was also acknowledged by both the Pythagorean and Orphic mystery schools. "The golden egg from which Brahma burst forth is equivalent to the Pythagorean circle with its a central point (or hole)."[15] The latter figure is technically called a circumpunct, the ancient image that Dan Brown recently recycled in his novel *The Lost Symbol*. (See Chapter 1 in the current book.)

In the Greek religion of Orphism, Protogonus ("first-born") was the initial creation of the Cosmic Egg, which sometimes is depicted with a serpent spiraling around it. (Our spiral motif redux. See the top of p. 337.) He was also known as Phanes (literally, "I bring to light"), an androgenous sun god with golden wings. In the former case, we are reminded that snakes as well as birds are hatched from eggs, and that the Hopi perform a biannual Snake Dance in August, when they handle venomous rattlesnakes in order to honor these emissaries of the aqueous underworld.

In Chapter 1, I discussed the supreme importance in Hopi tradition of what they call the Sipàapuni, which is a naturally formed travertine dome located on the north bank of the Little Colorado River in Grand Canyon. As the legendary Place of Emergence, it is perhaps the most important spot in the Hopi cosmology. In a universal sense, the Sipàapuni may be conceptualized as an *omphalos*, or one of many "navels" in the world that are used to mark a cosmic center. Indeed the Hopi word *sipna* literally means the "navel" of a person but sometimes also carries a geodetic connotation.[16]

An *omphalos*, a type of ovoid stone such as the one found at Delphi in Greece, is frequently carved with a knotted net covering it to symbolize the longitude and latitude grid. The Grand Canyon Sipàapuni located along a serpentine river of turquoise water resembles a partially buried egg, with the dot in the center signifying its fertilization. Incidentally, the word *omphalos* resonates with another name for Osiris (Orion). Robert Temple, renowned especially for his scholarly work on Dogon cosmology and the star Sirius, remarks: "Before leaving Plutarch behind, we might note also that in 'Isis and Osiris', he tells us that a name for Osiris is *Omphis*. An interesting tie-in with the oracles, attested by Plutarch as current in Egypt in his day."[17]

The ovum is also a crucial factor in the cosmogony of the Dogon, who live in cliff dwellings along the Bandiagara Escarpment in Mali. (These domiciles coincidentally remind one of the pueblo cliff dwellings of the ancestral Hopi in the American Southwest.) Author Laird Scranton comments on the Dogon creator-god Amma: "Dogon cosmology begins with the god Amma, who was the creator of the universe and said to have housed all the potential seeds and signs of future creation. We know from tribal drawings and other physical renderings that Amma's egg looks like an inverted cone."[18]

The Dogon god may be related to the Egyptian creator-god Amun (also Amon, Amen, and later, Amun-Ra), and the former's egg corresponds to the cone-shaped *benben* stone found atop the obelisk in the Temple of the Phoenix at Heliopolis ("sun-city").[19] This stone consisted of meteoric iron that was shaped during its descent to earth.

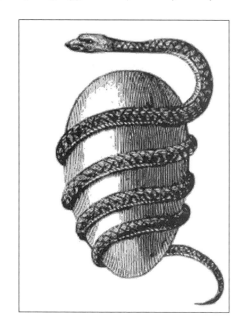

Above-left : Circumpunct, the universal symbol of the sun, gold, the heart, the sacred center, or the divine spark of consciousness.
Above-right: Cosmic Egg of Orphism.   Middle left: Dogon *kanaga* mask.
Below-left: *Omphalos*, with geodetic net, Delphi Museum.
Below-right: Delphi *omphalos*, cone.

Once every 60 years the Dogon perform their Sigui ceremony, whose purpose is the "renovation of the world." In the village-center a *kanaga* symbol is painted in red ochre on a rock, below which a hole is dug.[20] With his egg buried in the earth, Amma thus reveals himself in the form of the whirling potency of the *kanaga* in order to revitalize the world.

Marcel Griaule and Germaine Dieterlen, whose anthropological research on the Dogon and their cultural connection to the star Sirius is renowned, describe the transformative process: "According to all the initiates, the *kanaga* mask represents on the one hand the static gesture of the god, and on the other hand the *swastika* [italics added], through the repetition of the same gesture at an angle of 90° to the first. The second figure represents the god whirling round as he comes down to earth to reorganize the world in chaos."[21]

Hence, we see three primary elements in this cyclic festival of world renewal: the swastika-like *kanaga* symbol, red ochre (symbolizing menstrual blood), and Amma's solar egg. This same triad is contained in the Hopi Mystery Egg. The Hopi word *aama*, incidentally, means "to bury, cover (with earth or any particular matter)."[22] When the sun is buried in the ground, it journeys somnambulantly through the underworld toward its awakening at the next sunrise.

The cone-shaped head-piece above the eye-holes on the *kanaga* mask perhaps represents Amma's egg buried in the earth, whereas the wooden extensions signify the hands of Amma in the kinetic process of re-creation of the Earth. One hand points downward to the ground, while the other points toward heaven. This geometric shape resembles the Knights Templar Cross of Lorraine carried during the Crusades, and manifests the hermetic maxim "As above, so below." The distinctive icon also appears as the *vajra* (thunderbolt) of the Hindu storm god Indra, the double-trident of the Sumerian earth god Ninurta, and the monitor lizard associated with the Phoenician sky god Baal-Shamin.[23] As previously mentioned, Baal also assumes the classic stance of the Orion constellation, with a weapon in his upraised right hand.

The Hopi Mystery Egg is thought to contain two stark alternatives: either total annihilation and death or purification and rebirth. Dan Katchongva describes in greater detail the three elements inside this egg.

"We will have three people standing behind us, ready to fulfill our prophecies when we get into hopeless difficulties: The Meha Symbol (which refers to a plant that has a long root, milky sap, grows back when cut off, and has a flower shaped like a swastika, symbolizing the four great forces of nature in motion), the Sun Symbol, and the Red Symbol. Bahanna's [Pahana's, White Man's] intrusion into the Hopi way of life will set the Meha Symbol in motion, so that certain people will work for the four great forces of nature (the four directions, the controlling forces, the original force) which will rock the world into war. When this happens we will know that our prophecies are coming true. We will gather strength and stand firm."[24]

The yolk, of course, metaphorically refers to the Sun. The Meha, also spelled *möha*, is known as the Largeflower Skeletonplant (*Lygodesmia grandiflora*). The albumen might refer to the milky substance of its root, which is used as a salve for sunburn. Its leaves are chewed to to increase mother's milk, and they are also used as greens boiled with meat.[25] The Red Symbol might refer to the spot of blood sometimes found inside an egg and corresponds to the Maltese cross.

Grandfather Katchongva continues his description of the progression that the three world shakings will take.

"This great movement will fall, but because its subsistence is milk, and because it is controlled by the four forces of nature, it will rise again to put the world in motion, creating another war, in which both the Meha and the Sun Symbol will be at work. Then it will rest in order to rise a third time. Our prophecy foretells that the third event will be the decisive one. Our road plan foretells the outcome. This sacred writing [of the Prophecy Rock petroglyphs] speaks the word of the Great Spirit. It could mean the mysterious life seed with two principles of tomorrow, indicating one, inside of which is two. The third and last, which will it bring forth, purification or destruction? This third event will depend upon the Red Symbol, which will take command, setting the four forces of nature (Meha) in motion for the benefit of the Sun. When he sets these forces in motion the whole world will shake and turn red and turn against the people who are hindering the Hopi cultural life. To all these people Purification Day will come."[26]

The Fiery Egg of Hildegard von Bingen

The language of prophecy is frequently puzzling, and this is not restricted to merely the Hopi. In the mid-12th century, at about the same time that the Hopi were constructing villages on three Hopi Mesas that would ultimately become the heart of their final homeland, the mother superior of a convent on the banks of the Rhine River in Germany was experiencing regular holy visions. In addition to being a nun, Hildegard von Bingen was a mystic, prophet, political and social moralist, musical composer, poet, naturalist, herbalist, gemologist, author of medicinal and botanical texts, and playwright (penning the earliest morality play). Sequestered in her kiva-like meditation cell, she began to receive a series of bizarre psychic tableaus that she sketched on wax, which were subsequently turned into paintings. Her accompanying interpretations of these visions were also later transcribed. In an illuminated manuscript called *Scivias* ("Know the Way"), she presents these 26 visions, each with a Biblical exegesis. One vision in particular concerns us here.

From Vision Three:

"After this I saw a vast instrument, round and shadowed, in the *shape of an egg* [italics added], small at the top, large in the middle and narrowed at the bottom; outside it, surrounding its circumference, there was bright fire with, as it were, a shadowy zone under it... But from the fire that surrounded the instrument issued a blast with whirlwinds, and from the zone beneath it rushed forth another blast with its own whirlwinds, which diffused themselves hither and thither throughout the instrument. In that zone too there was a dark fire of such great horror that I could not look at it, whose force shook the whole zone, full of thunder, tempest, and exceedingly sharp stones both large and small. And while it made its thunders heard, the bright fire and the winds and the air were in commotion, so that lightning preceded those thunders; for the fire felt within itself the turbulence of those thunders."

Exegesis:

"The firmament in the likeness of an egg and what it signifies:

For this vast instrument, round and shadowed, in the shape of an egg, small at the top, large in the middle and narrowed at the bottom, faithfully shows Omnipotent God, incomprehensible in His majesty and inestimable in His mysteries and the hope of all the faithful; for humanity at first was rude and rough and simple in its actions, but was enlarged through the Old and New Testaments, and finally at the end of the world is destined to be beset with many tribulations."[27]

Surrounded by a field of blue ether, this egg-shaped "instrument" is engulfed in flames. At the top of the teardrop-shaped figure is the blazing Sun, along with three vertical red stars—probably the outer planets of Mars, Jupiter, and Saturn, but they could instead represent the belt stars of Orion as they appear on the eastern horizon. The next darker layer inward shows heaps of hailstones from which issue red tongues of lightning. The figure inside of this resembles a blue *vesica piscis* filled with the golden fixed stars, the Moon, and two vertical red stars, which perhaps represent the inner planets of Mercury and Venus, or alternately, the Hyades of Taurus.

Going inward, we find ten light-green humps surrounding a violet layer of nested lines, as well as a blue-white layer that may correspond to the moist atmosphere. At the very center of this mandala we see what Hildegard called the "sandy globe of great magnitude," which is the Earth itself, with what appears to be a river streaming through it. Each layer has its corresponding source of air ("whirlwinds"), depicted by a curious tri-visaged form. The top of the picture is oriented to the East, the bottom to the West, the right to the South, and the left to the North.

Some commentators have noticed that the overall shape basically resembles the female genitalia, which may be the unconscious impulse for this particular vision. "Hildegard the theologian compared God to a Cosmic Egg that surges flames into the universe, emptying and filling itself like a womb—creative, beneficial, and nurturing to all life within. She spoke of this sacred feminine as Divine Love, the essence of the universe—the highest fiery power that shines in water, burns in the sun, moon, and stars, stirring everything into existence, and causing all life to glisten with this light."[28]

Perhaps more important for the purpose of this chapter, though, is the fact that Hildegard associated egg iconography with a temporal progression which is eschatological, culminating in the "end of the world" with its accompanying hardships and suffering—much like the Hopi scenarios that we have seen. In many cases the details found in the Book of Revelation resonate with those of Hopi prophecy. However, we should be reminded that the Hopi, out of all the tribes in the Southwest, were the least affected by the conversion attempts of Catholic missionaries or the evangelism of Protestant preachers.

"The Universe," Hildegard von Bingen, 1151 AD.

Teardrop Egg

Three centuries later than Hildegard on the other side of the globe lived an Aztec ruler of Texcoco, Mexico, named Nezahualcoatl, or "Hungry Coyote." He was a philosopher, engineer, poet, and, as the painting shows, warrior. However, he encouraged the sacrifice of flowers rather than humans, at least in one of his temples. Living in the mid-15th century, he foretold the destruction of the Aztec empire less than a century later.

"Let me not be angry that the grandeur of Mexico
    is to be destroyed.
The smoking stars gather against it:
    the one who cares for flowers
is about to be destroyed.
    He who cared for books wept, he wept
for the beginning of the destruction."[29]

Notice that on his fringed shield is the red Mystery Egg floating in a sea of blue. Does the ovum rest in the waters of creation, or does it burn in the sky of destruction?

If we go back to the mid-2nd millennium BC, we find yet another egg-shape in Egypt, the land that was itself created by a primeval Egg. Senmut (also spelled Senenmut) was Queen Hatshepsut's steward and chief architect, who erected the twin obelisks at the entrance to the Temple of Karnak and designed the mortuary temple at Deir el-Bahari. On the ceiling of his tomb we find a number of astronomical references. These include Osiris/Orion standing in a barque below three vertical stars representing Orion's belt on the eastern horizon. To the right of the belt we see the Mystery Egg comprised of three nested teardrop shapes. The egg contains one star at its center, one at its tip, and two flanking it.

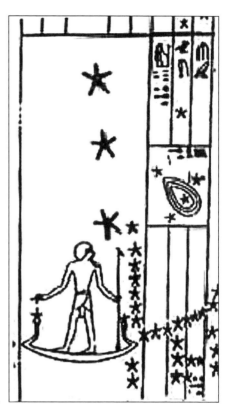

Left: Painting of Nezahualcoatl,
Codex Ixtlilxochitl, early 17th century.
He is assuming classic Orion stance.
Right: Ceiling of Senmut's tomb,
c. 1500 BC, Osiris/Orion in star-barque.

An egg-shaped
symbol carved on
the doorstep of the
eastern side-gate
of Thiruvannaika
Temple at
Tiruchirapalli,
Tamil Nadu, India.
Courtesy Shree
Subash Bose.

Another egg icon is found in a temple in southern India. It is described by my colleague Shree T. L. Subash Chandira Bose. (See bottom of previous page.) "The symbol consists of lines and some geometrical shapes. There is a point known as Bindu at the centre. Then there are ten lines that form a bird symbol having sixteen parts. Then five circles, one on each cardinal direction, such as east, south, west and north, and the fifth one is hidden at the centre in the form of divine light within light. Finally there are ten numbers of lights within lights all around this symbol."[30]

The temple represents one of the five natural elements, water—the other four being earth, wind, fire, and space. Inside is a Siva *lingam* (or Shiva phallic stone) idol with water oozing nearby it. The goddess of the temple is called Akilandiswari, which means "ruler-goddess of the universe."[31]

In regard to the essential meaning of the icon, Brother Shree Subash quotes another authority: "Sri Sakthi Sthothiram says: 'Oh Mother [goddess]! You are the one, the glorious bright light hidden within the shape having a head, two wings, a tail and body, and which is covered with five sheaths, such as Food Sheath, Breath Sheath, Mind Sheath, Intelligence Sheath, and Bliss Sheath. Those who realize and understand the above shall became a Brahma Gyani, the knower of the Absolute or ultimate reality.'"[32]

The Bindu is the point of pure awareness in which time and space collapse into a single point. This may be analogous to the center of the circumpunct previously mentioned. It may also be the doorway into the Hopi Fifth World, accessible to each and every one of us regardless of race.

I write this in July, 2012. The Mystery Egg may or may not have cracked open on December 21st, 2012, the end-date of the current cycle of the Mayan calendar, unleashing the combined forces of the Sun, the whirling four-armed swastika (Earth-quarters), and the commanding blood-red symbol. These elements may instead manifest themselves gradually over the "2012 era," as Maya scholar John Major Jenkins likes to put it, with the Fifth World arriving at an unspecified time—or just "soon," as Hopi spiritual elders like to say.

One way or another, it shall be revealed. The Hopi word *màatak-* means "be displayed, be shown, be revealed" and *maat-ap-* means "release."³³ Perhaps the definition of a similar word from ancient Egypt is more than a coincidence: *Maat*, "a goddess, the personification of law, order, rule, truth, right, righteousness, canon, justice, straightness, integrity, uprightness, and of the highest conception of physical and moral law known to the Egyptians."³⁴

In the afterlife Judgement Scene of the underworld, *Maat* was literally the feather of truth against which the heart of the deceased was weighed on the scales of justice. In essence, one's true heart was revealed. The avian emblem of *Maat* applied to both the microcosm and the macrocosm—that is, to the individual's character and composite deeds as well as to the rules by which the entire universe functioned. Both the ancient Egyptians and the Hopi must have valued this concept of balance immensely. For instance, the Hopi term *maa'at* means "hand," and *masa'at* refers to "wing" or "feathers" (the hand of the bird).³⁵ In order to fly, a bird must be balanced, or in other words, possess two wings.

Further synchronicities (psychologist C. G. Jung's term for "meaningful coincidences") may be found in a few Sanskrit words. For instance, *maata* means "mother," *mata* refers to "religion," and *mati* denotes both "intellect" and "prescience."³⁶ We are not surprised, then, to also learn that the Classic Mayan word *mat* means "cormorant," a water bird associated with fertility, and that the word *matz* refers to "sage" or "learned man."³⁷ In addition, the *K'iche* Mayan dialect's proper noun Ma't refers to "Magdelena" (Mary Magdalene?), and the adjective *ma'tam* means "late."³⁸

We hope it is not too late to make it back to the correct path leading to the Fifth World. Grandfather Katchongva describes the safe passage to the next cycle.

"The Purifier, commanded by the Red Symbol, with the help of the Sun and the Meha [*möha*], will weed out the wicked who have disturbed the way of life of the Hopi,

the true way of life on Earth. The wicked will be behead-
ed and will speak no more. This will be the Purification
for all righteous people, the Earth, and all living things on
the Earth. The ills of the Earth will be cured. Mother Earth
will bloom again and all people will unite into peace and
harmony for a long time to come."[39]

In harmony with the theme of rebirth rather than annihilation, Grandfather Monongye describes the Purification and its
ultimate outcome.

"It will then open our hearts and minds when a new age
is about to be, with people renewed and purified through
fire. It will be like the pure gold of a new day. But fire is
red, and when it takes command, it will set the forces of
nature in motion. We will then know purification day has
come. We all are the caretakers of life. The balance of
nature depends on us. The world will be what we want it
to be."[40]

It is totally in our hands—raised, both palms open, in praise
of life and light.

Judgement Scene from the Egyptian *Book of the Dead*. Jackal-headed Anubis weighs the heart of the deceased against the *Maat* feather. Note the human-headed bird perched on a pylon, which represents *Ba*, or the soul.

Petroglyph of the Creator in prayer stance, upraised palms, northern AZ. Superimposed cloud symbols, snake, and graffiti—the sacred & the profane.

349

Endnotes and Bibliography

Chapter 1: Star Correlations and Earth Chakras

1. Robert Bauval and Adrian Gilbert, *The Orion Mystery: Unlocking the Secrets of the Pyramids* (New York: Crown Publishers, Inc., 1994), p. 125 ff.
Note: The discussion of the Egyptian master plan by Bauval, Gilbert, and, later, Graham Hancock is much more complex than described in this chapter. Their opus involves precession of the equinoxes, star-targeted shafts in the Great Pyramid, and other topics not directly relevant to my discussion. Their compelling work, however, has generally challenged many orthodox ideas in Egyptology and has generated heated debates both on the amateur and the professional levels.
2. Graham Hancock and Robert Bauval, *The Message of the Sphinx: A Quest for the Hidden Legacy of Mankind* (New York: Three Rivers Press, 1996), pp. 152-3.
3. E. A. Wallis Budge, *An Egyptian Hieroglyphic Dictionary*, Vol. II (New York: Dover Publications, Inc., 1978, 1920), p. 638b.
4. *Hopi-English Dictionary of the Third Mesa Dialect*, edited by Kenneth C. Hill, Emory Sekaquaptewa, Mary E. Black, and Ekkehart Malotki (Tucson: University of Arizona Press, 1998), p. 521.
5. *Hopi-English Dictionary*, ibid., p. 683.
6. Steve Renshaw and Saori Ihara, "Star Shrines in Japan," January 1996, www2.gol.com/users/stever/starshrn.htm.
7. Jefferson Reid and Stephanie Whittlesey, *The Archaeology of Ancient Arizona* (Tucson, Arizona: The University of Arizona Press, 1997), p. 112.
8. J. McKim Malville, Claudia Putnam, *Prehistoric Astronomy in the Southwest* (Boulder Colorado: Johnson Books, 1993, 1989), p. 23.
Note: Azimuth is defined as the arc of the horizon measured in degrees clockwise from the true north point. The Sipàapuni (or Sipapuni) is the name for the Hopi entrance to the underworld in Grand Canyon, located near the confluence of the Little Colorado River and the Colorado River. The San Francisco Peaks near the town of Flagstaff are the highest mountains in Arizona and are considered sacred to both the Hopi and the Navajo.
9. As previously mentioned, the Hopi kachinas (also spelled *katsinam*, plural of *katsina*) are somewhat like angels. That is, they are basically benevolent

supernatural beings that act as spiritual messengers. The Hopi have many different types of kachinas that they honor with masked dances during the spring and early summer in the village plazas. However, the kachinas travel from the San Francisco Peaks to the Mesas after the winter solstice and stay until well into the agricultural season. Thus, they assist the Hopi in the sowing and tending of the corn. They depart for their mountainous home shortly after the summer solstice when the monsoon rains arrive in July.

10. Frank Waters and Oswald White Bear Fredericks, *Book of the Hopi* (New York: Penguin Books, 1987, 1963, p. 9.

11. All light-year distances cited from http://www.daviddarling.info.

12. Jacqueline Mitton, *The Penguin Dictionary of Astronomy* (London: Penguin Books Ltd, 1993, 1991), pp. 354-6, p. 369.

13. www.seti.org/page.aspx?pid=685.

14. personal email communication, 29 August, 2002.

15. http://planetquest.jpl.nasa.gov/TPF/tpf_index.cfm.

16. www.solstation.com/stars/pi3ori2.htm.

17. Jim Kaler, http://stars.astro.illinois.edu/sow/pi5ori.html.

18. personal Facebook communication, Dr. Edward Gleason, October 17, 2011.

19. Joel Stebbins, "The Ellipsoidal Variable Star, Pi 5 Orionis," *The Astrophysical Journal: An International Review of Spectroscopy and Astronomical Physics*, ed. George E. Hale, Vol. 51, American Astronomical Society, University of Chicago Press, 1920; S. L. Morris, "The Ellipsoidal Variable Stars,"*The Astrophysical Journal*, Vol. 295, August 1, 1985.

20. Paul A. LaViolette's book *Decoding the Message of the Pulsars* is discussed in Gary A. David, *The Kivas of Heaven: Ancient Hopi Starlore* (Kempton, Illinois: Adventures Unlimited Press, 2010), pp. 118-20.

21. Gary A. David, *Eye of the Phoenix: Mysterious Visions and Secrets of the American Southwest* (Kempton, Illinois: Adventures Unlimited Press, 2008), p. 130.

22. Alex Patterson, *Hopi Pottery Symbols* (Boulder Colorado: Johnson Books, 1994), pp. 28-9.

23. Mischa Titiev, "A Hopi Salt Expedition," *American Anthropologist*, Vol. 39, Issue 2, April-June 1937, p. 251.

24. Don Talayesva, edited by Leo W. Simmons, *Sun Chief: An Autobiography of a Hopi Indian* (New Haven: Yale University Press, 1974, 1942), p. 241, p. 236.

25. J. H. Butchert, "The Lower Gorge of the Little Colorado River," May 1956, www.hkhinc.com/hikes/littlecolorado/butchartnotes.htm.

26. Dan Brown, *The Lost Symbol* (New York: Doubleday, 2009), p. 459.

27. Richard C. Hoagland and Michael Bara, *Dark Mission: The Secret History of NASA* (Los Angeles: Feral House, 2007), p. 70.

Chapter 2: OZ (Orion Zone) Rising

1. Lokmanya Bal Gangadhar Tilak, *Orion: A Search Into the Ancientness of Aryan-Vedic Culture* (Delhi: Vijay Goel, 2005, 1893), p. 63, p. 128, p. 133; http://spokensanskrit.de.
2. William Smith, LL. D., *Smith's Bible Dictionary* (New York: Family Library, 1973), p. 49; see "Zone," definition 3.c., *The Oxford English Dictionary*, and Richard Hinckley Allen, *Star Names: Their Lore and Meaning* (New York: Dover Publications, Inc., 1963, reprint 1899), p. 315.
3. Will C. Barnes, *Arizona Place Names*, introduction by Bernard L. Fontana (Tucson: The University of Arizona Press, 1997, 1988), p. 27.
4. Allen, *Star Names*, op. cit., p. 304.
5. Waters and Fredericks, *Book of the Hopi*, op. cit., p. 343; Harold Courlander, *The Fourth World of the Hopis: the Epic Story of the Hopi Indians As Preserved In Their Legends and Traditions* (Albuquerque, New Mexico: University of New Mexico Press, 1991, 1971), p. 236; *Hopi-English Dictionary*, op. cit., p. 515, p. 521, p. 639.
6. Charlotte A. Black Elk quoted in Ronald Goodman, *Lakota Star Knowledge: Studies In Lakota Stellar Theology* (Rosebud, South Dakota: Sinte Gleska College, 1990), p. 51.
7. The American bison was the mainstay of Lakota diet and the source of most of the tribe's clothing, footwear, adornments, robes, bedding, tools, utensils, ropes, saddles, bridles, cradles, carrying cases, drums, drum sticks, and, of course, domiciles—namely, the tipi. It would not be an overstatement to say that the hunting, killing, and culinary preparation of the buffalo assumed an overall spiritual dimension. *Tatanka* (buffalo) was, in fact, included in the pantheon of Lakota deities.
8. See Chapter 3 of John G. Niehardt, *Black Elk Speaks: Being the Life Story of a Holy Man of the Oglala Sioux* (Albany: State University of New York Press, 2008, 1932).
9. A. Waller Hastings, Northern State University, Aberdeen, South Dakota, "L. Frank Baum's Editorials on the Sioux Nation," www.history.ox.ac.uk/hsmt/courses_reading/undergraduate/ authority_of_nature/week_7/baum.pdf
10. Mircea Eliade, *The Sacred and the Profane: The Nature of Religion*, translated from the French by Willard R. Trask (New York: A Harvest Book/ Harcourt, Brace, & World, Inc., 1959, 1957), pp. 128-9.
11. Mircea Eliade, *Cosmos and History: The Myth of the Eternal Return*, translated from the French by Willard R. Trask (New York: Harper Torchbooks/Harper & Brothers, 1959, 1954), p. 12, p. 13.
12. Black Elk quoted in Goodman, *Lakota Star Knowledge*, op. cit., p. 50.
13. *Hopi-English Dictionary*, op. cit., p. 693.
14. R. T. Rundle Clark, *Myth and Symbol in Ancient Egypt* (London: Thames and Hudson, Ltd., 1978, 1959), pp. 39-41.

15. Clark, *Myth and Symbol...*, ibid., pp. 245-8.
16. *Hopi-English Dictionary*, op. cit., p. 76.
17. Budge, *An Egyptian Hieroglyphic Dictionary*, Vol. I, op. cit., p. 218a.
18. *Hopi-English Dictionary*, op. cit., p. 104.
19. www.daviddarling.info/encyclopedia/O/Ozma.html.
20. Robert Burnham, Jr., *Celestial Handbook: An Observer's Guide to the Universe Beyond the Solar System*, Vol. II (New York: Dover Publications, Inc., 1978, 1966), p. 889; www.solstation.com/stars/eps-erid.htm.
21. Robert Sanders, "UC Berkeley astronomers find magnetic Slinky in constellation of Orion," January 12, 2006, University of California, Berkeley, www.eurekalert.org/pub_releases/2006-01/uoc--uba010906.php.
22. Giorgio Santillana and Hertha Von Dechend, *Hamlet's Mill: An Essay Investigating the Origins of Human Knowledge and Its Transmission Through Myth* (Boston: David R. Godine, Publisher, Inc., 1998, 1969), p. 210. The Greek word *zalos*, also spelled *salos*, means "tossing of the sea in a tempest; agitation, rolling" —a swelling, swirling, or roaring of waves, i.e. a maelstrom. However, the same word also carries the sense of either "fool" or "holy folly." The Hebrew name for Orion is *Kesil* (or *cesîl*), which signifies "'Foolish,' 'Impious,' 'Inconstant,' or 'Self-confident.'" http://concordances.org/greek/4535.htm; Derek Krueger, *Symeon the Holy Fool: Leontius' Life and the Late Antique City* (Berkeley: University of California Press, 1996), http://publishing.cdlib.org/ucpressebooks; Allen, *Star Names*, op. cit., p. 308.
23. Page Bryant, *Terravision: A Traveler's Guide to the Living Planet Earth* (New York: Ballantine Books, 1991), pp. 38-9, p. 89, p. 91.
24. J. E. Cirlot, *A Dictionary of Symbols* (New York: Philosophical Library, 1971, 1962), p. 306.
25. Joseph Campbell, *The Inner Reaches of Outer Space: Metaphor as Myth and as Religion* (New York: Harper & Row, Publishers, 1988, 1986), p. 89-90.
26. Howard Carter, *The Tomb of Tutankhamen* (Ex Calibur Books/E.P. Dutton, 1972, 1954), p. 142, p. 144.
27. Arthur Avalon (Sir John Woodroffe), *The Serpent Power: the Secrets of Tantric and Shaktic Yoga* (New York: Dover Publications, Inc. 1974, 1919), pp. 1-3.
28. Dennis Tedlock, translator and commentator, *Popol Vuh: The Mayan Book of the Dawn of Life* (New York: Touchstone Books, Simon & Schuster, Inc., 1986, 1985), p. 341.
29. Garrick Mallery, *Picture Writing of the American Indians*, Vol. 2 (New York, Dover Publications, Inc. 1972, 1893), pp. 701-2.
30. Alex Patterson, *Hopi Pottery Symbols* (Boulder: Johnson Books, 1994), pp. 28-9. See chapter on spirals in David, *Eye of the Phoenix*, op. cit.
31. *Hisatsinom* refers to the ancestral Hopi. They are frequently misnamed the Anasazi, which is a Diné (Navajo) word meaning "Ancient One" or "Ancient Enemy."
32. http://descendantofgods.tripod.com/id151.html
33. www.jnanadana.org/hopi/techqua_ikachi_i.html

34. *Hopi-English Dictionary*, op. cit., p. 362.

35. *Hopi-English Dictionary*, op. cit., p. 232, p. 234.

36. Cooper quoted by Michael E. Salla, PhD, "A Report on the Motivations and Activities of Extraterrestrial Races," www.bibliotecapleyades.net/vida_alien/alien_zetareticuli02.htm. Also, see a chapter in my book *The Kivas of Heaven*, op. cit., about the imminent possibility of Betelgeuse going supernova.

37. www.exopaedia.org/Greys.

38. George Andrews, "The Greys, Rigel, and Procyon," www.bibliotecapleyades.net/vida_alien/esp_vida_alien_18zb.htm.

39. Jim Kaler, "Stars," http://stars.astro.illinois.edu/sow/cursa.html.

40. Graham Hancock, *Fingerprints of the Gods* (New York: Crown Trade Paperbacks, 1995), p. 235. Chapters 28-30 of this book provide a lucid and lively description of the phenomenon of precession of the equinoxes as well as of de Santillana's and von Dechend's work in general.

41. Santillana and Dechend, *Hamlet's Mill*, op. cit., p. 233, p. 306.

42. Ovid, *The Metamorphoses*, translated by Horace Gregory, Book II (New York: A Mentor Book/New American Library, 1960, 1958), p. 59.

43. Plato, *Timaeus*, translated by Benjamin Jowett, http://classics.mit.edu/Plato/timaeus.html.

44. Santillana and Dechend, *Hamlet's Mill*, op. cit., pp. 258-9.

45. Bernadette Brady, *Brady's Book of Fixed Stars* (York Beach, Maine: Samuel Weiser, Inc., 1998), pp. 138-140. "**colure** A great circle on the celestial sphere, passing through the celestial poles and either the equinoxes (equinoctial colure) or the solstices (solsticial colure)." Jacqueline Mitton, *The Penguin Dictionary of Astronomy* (London: Penguin Books, 1993, 1991), pp. 79-80.

46. Santillana and Dechend, *Hamlet's Mill*, op. cit., p. 87, p. 91.

47. Snorri Sturluson, *The Prose Edda: Tales From Norse Mythology*, translated by Jean I. Young (Berkeley: University of California Press, 1954), p. 118.

48. *Hopi-English Dictionary*, op. cit., p. 662, p. 237.

49. Santillana and Dechend, *Hamlet's Mill*, op. cit., p. 166.

50. Snorri Sturluson, *The Prose Edda*, op. cit., p. 118.

51. Santillana and Dechend, *Hamlet's Mill*, op. cit., p. 148.

52. Francis Huxley, *The Way of the Sacred: The Rites and Symbols, Beliefs and Tabus, That Men Have Held in Awe and Wonder Through the Ages* (New York: Dell Publishing Co., Inc., Laurel Edition, 1976, reprint 1974), pp. 199-200.

53. Santillana and Dechend, *Hamlet's Mill*, op. cit., p. 188.

54. *Dictionary of Greek and Roman Antiquities*, edited by William George Smith, Charles Anthon, (New York: Harper & Brothers, Publishers, 1870, p. 429, http://books.goggle.com.

55. Tariq Malik, "The World's Tallest Rockets: How They Stack Up," September 14, 2011, www.space.com/12944-worlds-tallest-rockets-comparison.html; www.nasa.gov/exploration/systems/mpcv/index.html.

Chapter 3: Egyptian Orion—Psychedelic Barley God

1. Allen, *Star Names*, op. cit., p. 308.
2. Budge, *An Egyptian Hieroglyphic Dictionary*, Vol. II, op. cit., p. 668a.
3. Budge, *An Egyptian Hieroglyphic Dictionary*, Vol. II, op. cit., p. 672b, p. 673a.
4. Robert Bauval and Thomas Brophy, Ph.D., *Black Genesis: The Prehistoric Origins of Ancient Egypt* (Rochester, Vermont: Bear & Company, 2011), p. 210.
5. Santillana and Dechend, *Hamlet's Mill*, op. cit., pp. 31-2.
6. Justin W., "Dionysus and the Origin of Wine," www.environmentalgraffiti.com/news-dionysus-and-origin-divine-wine.
7. Robert Graves, *The Greek Myths* (Mt. Kisco, New York: Moyer Bell Limited, 1988, 1960, 1955), p. 108; Herodotus, *The History*, 2.42, 2.156, 2.171, translated by David Grene, (Chicago: University of Chicago Press, 1987).
8. Budge, *An Egyptian Hieroglyphic Dictionary*, Vol. I, op. cit., p. 514a.
9. Budge, *An Egyptian Hieroglyphic Dictionary*, Vol. I, op. cit., p. 401a, p. 408a, p. 407b.
10. Budge, *An Egyptian Hieroglyphic Dictionary*, Vol. I, op. cit., p. 401a, p. 408b.
11. Budge, *An Egyptian Hieroglyphic Dictionary*, Vol. II, op. cit., p. 821b; Budge, *An Egyptian Hieroglyphic Dictionary*, Vol. I, op. cit., p. 403a.
12. E. A. Wallis Budge, *Osiris and the Egyptian Resurrection*, Vol. I (New York: Dover Publications, Inc., 1973, 1911), p. 80.
13. Budge, *Osiris*, Vol. I, ibid., p. 58.
14. Jeff Nisbet, "The Pyramids of Scotland Revisited," www.mythomorph.com/mm/content/2009/1018the_pyramids_of_scotland_revisited.php#more.
15. Donald A. MacKenzie, *Egyptian Myth and Legend* (New York: Bell Publishing Company, 1978, 1907), pp. 27-8.
16. Budge, *An Egyptian Hieroglyphic Dictionary*, Vol. I, op. cit., p. 219b.
17. David, *The Kivas of Heaven*, op. cit., pp. 27-32.
18. http://facts.randomhistory.com/interesting-facts-about-egypt.html.
19. Sir James George Frazier, *The Golden Bough: A Study in Magic and Religion*, Vol. I, abridged edition (New York: MacMillan Company, 1940, 1922), p. 399.
20. E. A. Wallis Budge, *The Gods of the Egyptians*, Vol. I (New York: Dover Publications, Inc., 1969, 1904), pp. 38-9.
21. Budge, *Osiris*, Vol. I, op. cit., p. 220.
22. A. E. Wallis Budge, *The Dwellers On the Nile: The Life, History, Religion and Literature of the Ancient Egyptians* (New York: Dover Publications. Inc., 1977, 1926), pp. 282-3.
23. Frazier, *The Golden Bough*, op. cit., p. 443.
24. *Encyclopaedia Britannica*, 15th Edition (Chicago: Encyclopaedia Britannica, Inc., 1979), Vol. III, p. 847; Vol. 14, p. 201.

25. R. Gordon Wasson, Carl A. P. Ruck, Albert Hofmann, *The Road to Eleusis: Unveiling the Secret of the Mysteries* (New York: A Harvest/HBJ Book, 1978), p. 32.

26. John Major Jenkins, *Galactic Alignment: The Transformation of Consciousness According to Mayan, Egyptian, and Vedic Traditions* (Rochester, Vermont: Bear & Company, 2002), pp. 170-1.

27. Herodotus, *The History*, op. cit., p. 205.

28. Budge, *An Egyptian Hieroglyphic Dictionary*, op. cit., Vol. II, p. 890a-b; Vol. I, p. 523a.

29. Stephen R. Berlant, "The entheomycological origin of Egyptian crowns and the esoteric underpinnings of Egyptian religion," *Journal of Ethnopharmacology*, Vol. 102, Issue 2, November 2005, pp. 275-288.

30. *The Pyramid Texts*, translated by Samuel A. B. Mercer, Utterance 273-274 (New York: Longmans, Green & Co, 1952), www.sacred-texts.com/egy/pyt/pyt13.htm.

31. Wasson, Ruck, and Hofmann, *The Road to Eleusis*, op. cit., caption on Plate 9.

32. William Kelly Simpson, editor, *The Literature of Ancient Egypt: An Anthology of Stories, Instructions, and Poetry*, translated by R. O. Faulkner, E. F. Wente, Jr., and W. K. Simpson (New Haven, Connecticut: Yale University Press, 1973), pp. 26-30.

33. www.erowid.org/archive/rhodium/pdf/claviceps.identification.pdf.

34. Robert Hewitt Brown, *Stellar Theology and Masonic Astronomy* (Kessinger Publishing, rare reprints, no publication date), p. 86; http://www.theoi.com/Titan/TitanisRhea.html.

35. *The Pyramid Texts*, op. cit., Utterance 46, http://www.sacred-texts.com/egy/pyt/pyt13.htm.

36. Budge, *The Gods of the Egyptians*, Vol. I, op. cit., p. 164.

37. William Henry, *Starwalkers and the Dimension of the Blessed* (Kempton, Illinois: Adventures Unlimited Press, 2007), p. 236.

38. Joscelyn Godwin, *Mystery Religions In the Ancient World* (San Francisco: Harper & Row, Publishers, 1981), p. 35.

39. Adrian Gilbert, *Signs In the Sky* (London: Bantam Press, 2000), p. 214.

40. Lucie Lamy, *Egyptian Mysteries: New Light On Ancient Spiritual Knowledge* (New York: Crossroad Publishing Company, 1981), p. 14.

41. Clark, *Myth and Symbol in Ancient Egypt*, op. cit., p. 227; *Budge, An Egyptian Hieroglyphic Dictionary*, op. cit., Vol. I, p. 8b.

42. www.per-aset.org/coffin_texts_referencing_aset.htm.

43. Budge, *An Egyptian Hieroglyphic Dictionary*, op. cit., Vol. I, p. 8b; *Hopi-English Dictionary*, op. cit., p. 8.

44. Philip Gardiner and Gary Osborn, *The Serpent Grail: The Truth Behind the Holy Grail, the Philosopher's Stone and the Elixir of Life* (London: Watkins Publishing, 2005), p. 29.

45. Budge, *An Egyptian Hieroglyphic Dictionary*, op. cit., Vol. I, p. 9a, p. 24a.

46. Hancock and Bauval, *The Message of the Sphinx*, op. cit., p. 209.

47. Hancock and Bauval, *The Message of the Sphinx*, ibid., p. 210.
48. Allen, *Star Names*, op. cit., p. 318-9; www.astrology-central.com/stars/Meissa.htm.
49. www.constellationsofwords.com/stars/Meissa.html.
50. www.nasa.gov/mission_pages/WISE/multimedia/gallery/pia14040.html.

Chapter 4: Grand Canyon and the Hopi Underworld

1. John Muir, "The Grand Canon of the Colorado," *Writing the Western Landscape*, edited by Ann H. Zwinger (Boston: Beacon Press, 1994), pp. 97-8.
2. www.grandcanyontreks.org/place.htm; www.allhikers.com/Allhikers/Other/Grand-Canyon-Place-Names.htm
3. Robert C. Euler, "The Archaeology of Canyon Country," *John Wesley Powell and the Anthropology of the Canyon Country*, Geological Survey Professional Paper 670 (Washington: United States Government Printing Office, 1969, reprinted by Grand Canyon Natural History Association, 1981, 1977), p. 8.
4. T. H. Watkins et al., *The Grand Colorado: The Story of a River and Its Canyons* (Palo Alto, California: American West Publishing Company), p. 19.
5. Douglas W. Swartz, *On the Edge of Splendor: Exploring Grand Canyon's Human Past* (Santa Fe, New Mexico: The School of American Research, 1996), pp. 49-59; http://grandcanyonhistory.clas.asu.edu/sites_coloradorivercorridor_unkardelta.html.
6. David Hatcher Childress, *Lost Cities and Ancient Mysteries of the Southwest* (Kempton, Illinois: Adventures Unlimited Press, 2009), p. 419.
7. J. W. Powell, *The Exploration of the Colorado River and Its Canyons* (New York: Dover Publications, Inc., 1961, reprint of *Canyons of the Colorado*, 1895), pp. 241-2.
8. T. L. Subash Chandira Bose, "Were there close links between ancient America and India?," unpublished manuscript.
9. George Wharton James, *In and Around the Grand Canyon: the Grand Canyon of the Colorado River in Arizona* (Boston: Little Brown & Co., 1900), p. 330.
10. Swartz, *On the Edge of Splendor*, op. cit., pp. 65-6.
11. Colin Fletcher, *The Man Who Walked Through Time* (New York: Vintage Books/Random House, Inc., 1989, 1967), pp. 215-6.
12. Titiev, "A Hopi Salt Expedition,"op. cit., p. 250.
13. Edmund Nequatewa, *Truth of a Hopi: Stories Relating to the Origin, Myths, and Clan Histories of the Hopi* (Flagstaff, Arizona: Museum of Northern Arizona, 1967, 1936, pp. 121-2.
14. Jesse Walter Fewkes, *Hopi Katchinas* (New York: Dover Publications, Inc., 1985. 1903), p. 32.
15. Walt Whitman, "Song of Myself," Section 51, *Leaves of Grass*, 1855, 1881.
17. Virginia Morell, "The Unexpected Canyon," *National Geographic*, Vol. 209, No. 1, January 2008, p. 43.

17. Fred Eggan, "The Hopi Cosmology or World-View," *Kachinas in the Pueblo World*, edited by Polly Schaafsma (Salt Lake City: The University of Utah Press, 2000), p. 14.

18. Ekkehart Malotki and Michael Lomatuway'ma, *Maasaw: Profile of a Hopi God* (Lincoln: University of Nebraska Press, 1987), pp. 259-261.

19. Jon Manchip White, *A World Elsewhere: Life in the American Southwest* (College Station: Texas A&M University Press, 1975), p. 15.

20. Talayesva, *Sun Chief*, op. cit., p. 124.

21. Mischa Titiev, *Old Oraibi: A Study of the Hopi Indians of Third Mesa* (Albuquerque: University of New Mexico Press, 1992, 1944), pp. 171-7.

22. Maria D. Glowacka, "*Hikwsi* in Traditional Hopi Philosophy,"*American Indian Culture and Research Journal*, Vol. 23, No. 2, 1999, pp. 137-143.

23. John D. Loftin, *Religion and Hopi Life In the Twentieth Century* (Bloomington: University of Indiana Press, 1994, 1991), pp. 14-5.

24. David Lewis-Williams, *The Mind In the Cave: Consciousness and the Origins of Art* (London: Thames & Hudson, Ltd., 2002), pp. 144-7.

25. Titiev, *Old Oraibi*, op. cit., p. 175, p. 176.

26. H. R. Voth, *The Traditions of the Hopi* (Chicago, Illinois: Field Columbian Museum, Pub. 96, Anthropological Series, Vol. VIII, March 1905; *Hopi-English Dictionary*, op. cit., p. 115.

27. Sven Gronemeyer, "Tortuguero, Tabasco, Mexico," p. 25, http://www.sven-gronemeyer.de/download/acta-mesoamericana_17.pdf. In June of 2012, Maya scholar David Stuart announced the discovery at the La Corona site in Guatemala of a second Mayan monument with a reference to the 12.21.12-date. www.utexas.edu/know/2012/06/28/la-corona.

28. David, *The Kivas of Heaven*, op. cit., pp. 67-9.

29. *Hopi Dictionary*, op. cit., p. 587.

30. Jesse Walter Fewkes, *Tusayan Katcinas and Hopi Altars* (Albuquerque, New Mexico: Awanyu Publishing, Inc., 1990, 1897, p. 257.

31. John Nakagawa, "Grandfather Martin Gashweseoma, Hotevilla, Hopi, July 5, 2010, April 25, 2009," www.youtube.com/watch?v=3pOOOdNxPZQ.

32. Loftin, *Religion and Hopi Life*, op. cit., pp. xvi-xvii.

33. Barton Wright, *Hopi Kachinas: The Complete Guide to Collecting Kachina Dolls* (Flagstaff, Arizona: Northland Publishing, 1988, 1977), pp. 110-2.

34. Budge, *The Gods of the Egyptians*, Vol. II, op. cit., p. 153, p. 154.

35. *Hopi Dictionary*, op. cit., p. 36; Glowacka, "*Hikwsi* in Traditional Hopi Philosophy," op. cit.

36. Clark, *Myth and Symbol in Ancient Egypt*, op. cit., p. 153.

37. Murray Hope, *The Sirius Connection: Unlocking the Secrets of Ancient Egypt* (Shaftesbury, Dorset, England: Element Books Limited, 1996), p. 194.

38. G. M. Mullett, *Spider Woman Stories: Legends of the Hopi Indians* (Tucson, Arizona: The University of Arizona Press, 1991, 1979), pp. 20-1; *Hopi Dictionary*, op. cit., p. 287.

39. Budge, *An Egyptian Hieroglyphic Dictionary*, Vol. I, op. cit., p. 233a; Vol. II,

p. 778b.

40. *Hopi Dictionary*, op. cit., p. 153.

41. Charles F. Lummis, *The Land of Poco Tiempo* (Albuquerque: The University of New Mexico Press, 1975, 1952, 1921, 1893, p. 106.

Chapter 5: Grand Canyon Cave Enigma

1. The entire article has been republished in Childress, *Lost Cities and Ancient Mysteries of the Southwest*, op. cit., pp. 383-91. The first republication after the initial newspaper article was probably in a book called *Arizona Cavalcade*, edited by Joseph Miller. (New York: Hasting House, Publishers, 1962), pp. 280-6. Numerous websites have also published the same article, though some contain minor variations or deletions that may significantly alter certain facts.

2. Frank Joseph, "Underground City of the Grand Canyon, Fact or Fable?" *Ancient American*, Vol. 5, No. 36, December 2000, p. 23.

3. Childress, *Lost Cities and Ancient Mysteries of the Southwest*, op. cit., p. 383.

4. http://mysteriousarizona.com. Scroll down to the link on the left: "Lost City of the Dead at the Grand Canyon."

5. David Hatcher Childrees, *Lost Cities of North & Central America* (Stelle, Illinois: Adventures Unlimited Press, 1992), p. 322; Jack Andrews' letter to the Smithsonian, May 17th, 1999 and their reply a month later: http://mysteriousarizona.com/smithsonianletter.html.

6. Keir Brooks Sterling et al., *Biographical Dictionary of American and Canadian Naturalists and Environmentalists* (Westport, Connecticut: Greenwood Publishing Group, Inc., 1997), pp. 411-14, http://books.goggle.com; www.davidstarrjordan.org/lifetimes.html.

7. http://en.wikipedia.org/wiki/Human_Betterment_Foundation; http://en.wikipedia.org/wiki/Compulsory_sterilization.

8. *Encyclopaedia Brittanica*, Micropaedia, Vol. V (Chicago: Encyclopaedia Brittanica, Inc., 1979), p. 608.

9. http://freepages.genealogy.rootsweb.ancestry.com/~npmelton/sr25stan.htm.

10. President Richard M. Nixon, a member beginning in 1953, remarked homophobically on the Watergate Tapes re. the club's mid-July bash: "The Bohemian Grove, that I attend from time to time—the Easterners and the others come there—but it is the most faggy goddamn thing you could ever imagine, that San Francisco crowd that goes in there; it's just terrible! I mean I won't shake hands with anybody from San Francisco." http://en.wikipedia.org/wiki/Bohemian_Grove.

11. http://vertebrates.si.edu/fishes/ichthyology_history/ichs_colls/jordan_david.html.

12. Mark Thompson, *American Character: The Curious Life of Charles Fletcher*

Lummis and the Rediscovery of the Southwest (New York: Skyhorse Publishing, Inc./Arcade Publishing, 2001), p. 3.

13. Charles F. Lummis, *Some Strange Corners of Our Country: The Wonderland of the Southwest* (New York: The Century Co., 1892), p. 8.

14. David Starr Jordan, *The Days of a Man: Being Memories of a Naturalist, Teacher, and Minor Prophet of Democracy*, Vol. I, 1851-1899 (New York: World Book Company, 1922), pp. 620-624.

15. David Starr Jordan, *The Days of a Man: Being Memories of a Naturalist, Teacher, and Minor Prophet of Democracy*, Vol. II, 1900-1922 (New York: World Book Company, 1922), p. 252, pp. 255-8.

According to one source, Samuel Torel Bastedo, former Ontario Deputy Commissioner of Fisheries, who was working with Jordan, resigned from the survey in December, 1908, in order to fill another post in the Canadian government. Margaret Beattie Bogue, *Fishing the Great Lakes: An Environmental History, 1783-1933* (Madison: University of Wisconsin Press, 2000), p. 313.

16. Smithsonian Institution Archives, Charles D. Walcott Collection, 1851 - 1940 and undated, http://siarchives.si.edu/collections/siris_arc_217204.

17. Stephen Jay Gould, *Wonderful Life: The Burgess Shale and the Nature of History* (New York: W. W. Norton & Company, Inc., 1989), p. 242, http://books.goggle.com.

18. http://siarchives.si.edu/history/charles-doolittle-walcott; www.burgess-shale.bc.ca/discover-burgess-shale/charles-doolittle-walcott; www.strangescience.net/walcott.htm.

19. Ellis Leon Yochelson, *Charles Doolittle Walcott, Paleontologist* (Kent, Ohio: Kent State University Press, 1998), p. 148.

20. J. W. Powell, "The Scientific Explorer," *Grand Canyon of Arizona: Being a Book of Words From Many Pens, About the Grand Canyon of the Colorado River in Arizona* (Chicago: Poole Brothers/Passenger Department of the Santa Fe, 1902), pp. 19-20.

21. Ellis L. Yochelson, "Charles Doolittle Walcott: A Biographical Memoir, 1850-1927" (Washington, D.C.: National Academy of Sciences, 1967), p. 477.

22. *An Illustrated History of North Idaho: Embracing Nez Perces, Idaho, Latah, Kootenai and Shoshone Counties, State of Idaho* (Western Historical Publishing Company, 1903), p. 577, http://archive.org/details/illustratedhisto00slwerich; Victoria E. Mitchell "History of the Dewey Mine, Idaho County, Idaho," Idaho Geological Survey, Main Office at Moscow, University of Idaho, Moscow, undated.

23. "Descendants of Joseph Kinkaid," http://idaho.idgenweb.org/PDF/Kinkaid_private.pdf.

24. Barry Fell, *Saga America* (New York: Times Books, 1980), p. 78.

25. George H. Billingsley, Earle E. Spanner, Dove Menkes, *Quest For the Pillar of Gold: The Mines & Miners of the Grand Canyon* (Grand Canyon, Arizona: Grand Canyon Association, 1997), pp. 69-70,

26. Billingsley et al., *Quest For the Pillar of Gold*, ibid., p. 85-6.

27. Billingsley et al., *Quest For the Pillar of Gold,* ibid., p. 73-5.

28. William H. Calvin, *The River That Flows Uphill: A Journey From the Big Bang to the Big Brain* (San Francisco: Sierra Club Books, 1986), p. 90.

29. Halka Chronic, *Roadside Geology of Arizona* (Missoula, Montana: Mountain Press Publishing Company, 2003, 1983), p. 283.

30. J. D. Sartor, "Meteorological Investigation of the Wupatki Blowhole System,"*Plateau,* Vol. 37, No. 1, Summer 1964, pp. 26-34.

31. D. L. Lamar, "Geology of the Wupatki Blowhole System, ibid., pp. 35-40.

32. Bret D. Tobin and David J. Weary, "U.S. Geological Survey Open-File Report 2004-1352," http://pubs.usgs.gov/of/2004/1352/data/USA_karst.pdf.

33. Waters and Fredericks, *Book of the Hopi,* op. cit., pp. 13-14.

34. Gene D. Matlock, B.A., M.A., "Is the Hopi Deity Kokopelli an Ancient Hindu God?", www.viewzone.com/kokopeli.html.

35. *Hopi Dictionary,* op. cit., p. 2. To read more about the Ant People, see David, *Eye of the Phoenix,* op. cit.

36. Jefferson Reid and Stephanie Whittlesey, *The Archaeology of Ancient Arizona,* (Tucson, Arizona: The University of Arizona Press, 1997), p. 112.

37. http://archive.org/details/outwestland25archrich.

38. Stephen Mehler, "The Search for Kinnaman's Entrance," *Atlantis Rising,* Issue No. 10, Winter 1997.

39. Jim Bailey, *Sailing to Paradise: The Discovery of the Americas By 7000 B.C.* (New York: Simon & Schuster, 1994), pp. 38-9.

40. Bailey, *Sailing to Paradise,* ibid, pp. 40-1.

41. Salim George Khalaf, "Phoenician Trade and Ships," http://phoenicia.org/trade.html.

42. *Hieroglyphics of Horapollo,* translated Alexander Turner Cory, 1840, pp. 73, http://www.sacred-texts.com/egy/hh/hh054.htm.

43. Gerald Massey, *Ancient Egypt: The Light of the World, A Work of Reclamation and Restitution in Twelve Books* (London: T. Fisher Unwin/Adelphi Terrace, 1907, www.theosophical.ca/books/ AncientEgyptTheLightOfTheWorld_GMassey.pdf.

44. David Hatcher Childress and Brian Foerster, *The Enigma of Cranial Deformation* (Kempton, Illinois: Adventures Unlimited Press, 2012), p. 142.

45. Helen Fairley, *Boatsman Quarterly Review: the Journal of Grand Canyon River Guides, Inc.,* Vol. 10, No. 4, Fall 1997, www.gcrg.org/ bqr/10-4/kwagunt.html.

46. *Hopi Dictionary,* op. cit., p. 167.

47. Nequatewa, *Truth of a Hopi,* op. cit., p. 126.

48. J. Walter Fewkes, "The New-Fire Ceremony," *American Anthropologist,* Vol. 2, 1900 (New York: Kraus Reprint Corp., 1963), pp. 117-8.

49. *Hopi Dictionary,* op. cit. p. 600.

50. Bradfield, *An Interpretation of Hopi Culture,* op. cit., p. 295-6.

51. Bradfield, ibid, p. 322, n. 12. "I use this word, rather than the more familiar *cosmography*, to indicate that the Hopi approach to the world, while it makes use of much clear-sighted empirical observations, is primarily intuitive: and that the body of knowledge consequent on this approach is more akin to a work of imagination that to a scientific construct. Like any work of the imagination, it is internally consistent, follows its own logic, and does not depend for its verity on an appeal to fact – nor can it be overturned by such an appeal."
52. www.burlingtonnews.net/arizona.html.
53. John Rhodes, "The Reptilian-Human Connection," 1994, www.reptoids.com/Vault/ArticleClassics/1994RepHuConn.htm.
Another incredible claim on related matters was issued by the late Robert Ghost Wolf, who said he was of mixed Hopi, Iroquois, and Lakota descent. "I have touched the carvings of ancient Egyptians in the New Mexico and Arizona Deserts in Colorado, and in Illinois. I stood in awe of statues of Horus and RA that towered over me carved in the fire pink stone of the desert caves, those who carved these effigies, perhaps they were the Native Americans? I have seen with my own eyes bodies that were ten and twelve feet in height buried in crypts wearing armor, draped in silk and cotton cloth, and carrying huge broad swords, were these the Native Americans? Conventional history says they could not be, but there are things that historians have neglected to include in the books we were taught from back in school."
www.wolflodge.org/stargate/Colorado/Destiny%20Images/starnations.htm.
54. Cindy Yurth and Duane Beyal, "Targeting the Confluence," *Navajo Times*, June 14, 2012, http://navajotimes.com/news/2012/0612/061412con.php.
55. http://thathideousman.blogspot.com/2011/08/wisdom-of-theodore-roosevelt-grand.html.
56. Harvey Butchart, *Butchart Grand Canyon Treks: 12,000 Miles Through the Grand Canyon* (Bishop, California: Spotted Dog Press, 200, 1997), p. 103.
57. Lee Siegel, "Anasazi Mummified Some of Their Dead, Anthropologist Contends," April 5, 1998, *Los Angeles Times*, http://articles.latimes.com/1998/apr/05/local/me-36099.

Chapter 6: Pyramids and Canals—Earthworks of the Hohokam

1. Ross Hamilton, *Star Mounds: Legacy of a Native American Mystery* (Berkeley: North Atlantic Books, 2012).
2. See the chapter in my book *Eye of the Phoenix*, op. cit., about the global mystery circle at 33 degrees north latitude.
3. Rose Houk, *Hohokam* (Tucson, Arizona: Southwest Park and Monument Association, 1992), p. 2.

4. Suzanne K. Fish and Paul R. Fish, editors, *The Hohokam Millennium* (Santa Fe, New Mexico: School For Advanced Research Press, 2007), p. 1.
5. Fish and Fish, *The Hohokam Millennium*, ibid, p. 5.
6. H. M. Wormington, *Prehistoric Indians of the Southwest* (Denver, Colorado: The Denver Museum of Natural History, 1973, 1947), p. 125.
7. David Grant Noble, *Ancient Ruins of the Southwest: An Archaeological Guide* (Flagstaff, Arizona: Northland Publishing, 1981), p. 15.
8. Linda S. Cordell, *Prehistory of the Southwest* (San Diego, California: Academic Press, Inc., Harcourt Brace Jovanovich, Publishers, 1984), p. 280.
9. Houk, *Hohokam*, op. cit., pp. 7-8.
10. David Hatcher Childress, *Lost Cities of North & Central America* (Stelle, Illinois: Adventures Unlimited Press, 1993, 1992), pp. 295-7.
11. Stephen H. Lekson, *A History of the Ancient Southwest* (Santa Fe: School For Advanced Research Press, 2008), p. 81.
12. Ernest E. Snyder, *Prehistoric Arizona* (Phoenix: Golden West Publishers, 1987), p. 54.
13. Stephen Plog, *Ancient Peoples of the American Southwest* (Thames and Hudson, Ltd., 1997), p. 136.
The population of London in 1200 AD was 20,000 - 25,000. www.cch.kcl.ac.uk/legacy/teaching/av1000/ numerical/problems/london/london-pop-table.html.
14. Plog, *Ancient Peoples of the American Southwest*, ibid, p. 73.
15. Reid and Whittlesey, *The Archaeology of Ancient Arizona*, op. cit., pp. 92-3.
16. John C. McGregor, *Southwestern Archaeology* (Urbana, Illinois: University of Illinois Press, 1977, 1941), p. 152.
17. Lekson, *A History of the Ancient Southwest*, op. cit., p. 120.
18. Houk, *Hohokam*, op. cit., p. 13.
19. Fish and Fish, *The Hohokam Millennium*, op. cit., p. 52.
20. Reid and Whittlesey, *The Archaeology of Ancient Arizona* op. cit., p. 92.
21. David R. Wilcox, "Hohokam Social Complexity," *Chaco & Hohokam: Prehistoric Regional Systems in the American Southwest*, edited by Patricia L. Crown and W. James Judge (Santa Fe, New Mexico: School of American Research Press, 1991), p. 266.
22. Wilcox, "Hohokam Social Complexity," *Chaco & Hohokam*, ibid., p. 262.
23. Gregory, "Form and Variation in Hohokam Settlement Patterns," *Chaco & Hohokam*, ibid., pp. 165-9.
24. Reid and Whittlesey, *The Archaeology of Ancient Arizona* op. cit., p. 97.
25. McGregor, *Southwestern Archaeology*, op. cit., p. 428.
26. Fish and Fish, *The Hohokam Millennium*, op. cit., p. 52-4.
27. Fish and Fish, *The Hohokam Millennium*, ibid., p. 54.
28. Lekson, *A History of the Ancient Southwest*, op. cit., p. 169.
29. David A. Gregory et al., *The 1982—1984 Excavations At Las Colinas, The Mound 8 Precinct*, Archaeological Series 162, Vol. 3, Arizona State Museum/University of Arizona, 1988, p. 70.

30. Plog, *Ancient Peoples of the American Southwest*, op. cit., p. 179.

31. Noble, *Ancient Ruins of the Southwest*, op. cit., p. 24.

32. Noble, *Ancient Ruins of the Southwest*, ibid., p. 19.

33. Lekson, *A History of the Ancient Southwest*, op. cit., pp. 205-6.

34. Arizona Museum of Natural History, www.azmnh.org/arch/mesagrande.aspx.

35. Owen Lindauer and John H. Blitz, "Higher Ground: The Archaeology of North American Platform Mounds," *Journal of Archaeological Research*, Vol. 5, No. 2, 1997, p. 185.
Living on the desert floor, the Hohokam must have been consummate sky waters. It is possible that Snaketown may have originally been oriented in relation to Gila Butte, which lies 3.5 miles to the southeast. At the base of this dual-crested peak, the Hohokam built their major irrigation canal and mined schist that was used in palettes and pottery temper. However, Gila Butte lies at 118° azimuth in relation to Snaketown. At this latitude the winter solstice sun rises at the same azimuthal degree, so the sun-god would have risen through the notch between the two parts of the butte on the shortest day of the year. Perhaps like the Hopi, the Hohokam may have performed a solstice ceremony to bring back the sun from his southward journey along the horizon. As Stephanie M. Whittlesey has observed, "Gila Butte was myth given substance and place, a fusion of the vital and the sacred. It might have been the Hohokam creation story set in stone." Fish and Fish, *The Hohokam Millennium*, op. cit., pp. 71-2.

Chapter 7: All Roads Lead to... Chaco

1. J. McKim Malville, *A Guide to Prehistoric Astronomy in the Southwest* (Boulder, Colorado: Johnson Books, 2008), pp. 74-9; www.angelfire.com/indie/anna_jones1/fajada_butte.html.

2. Ferguson, William M., and Arthur H. Rohn, *Anasazi Ruins of the Southwest In Color* (Albuquerque, New Mexico: University of New Mexico Press, 1987), p. 198.

3. Robert P. Powers, "Outliers and Roads in the Chaco System," *New Light On Chaco Canyon*, edited by David Grant Noble (Santa Fe, New Mexico; School of American Research Press, 1984), pp. 52-3.

4. Kathryn Gabriel, *Road to Center Place: A Cultural Atlas of Chaco Canyon and the Anasazi* (Boulder, Colorado: Johnson Publishing Company, 1991), p. 6.

5. Michael P. Marshall, "The Chacoan Roads: A Cosmological Interpretation," *Anasazi: Architecture and American Design*, Baker H. Morrow, Vincent Barrett Price, editors (Albuquerque: University of New Mexico Press), p. 69.

6. Anna Sofaer, Michael P. Marshall, Rolf M. Sinclair, "The Great North Road: a Cosmographic Expression of the Chaco Culture of New Mexico,"

www.solsticeproject.org/greanort.htm.

7. Sofaer et al.,ibid., www.solsticeproject.org/greanort.htm.

8. William H. Calvin, "Leapfrogging Gnomons: A method for surveying a very long north-south line without modern instruments," http://williamcalvin.com/1990s/1997gnomon.htm.

9. *Hopi Dictionary*, op. cit., p. 93.

10. Anna Sofaer, "The Primary Architecture of the Chacoan Culture," *Anasazi Architecture and American Design*, op. cit., pp. 88-132.

11. Leigh Kuwanwisiwman, "Yupköyvi: The Hopi Story of Chaco Canyon," *In Search of Chaco: New Approaches to an Archaeological Enigma*, edited by David Grant Noble (Santa Fe, New Mexico: School of American Research Press, 2004), pp. 41-7; *Hopi Dictionary*, op. cit., p. 802.

12. Anna Sofaer, "Pueblo Bonito Petroglyph On Fajada Butte: Solar Aspects," *Celestial Seasonings: Connotations of Rock Art*, Papers of the 1994 International Rock Art Congress, edited by E.C. Krupp, 1994, www.solsticeproject.org/celeseas.htm.

13. Anna, Sofaer, "Pueblo Bonito Petroglyph On Fajada Butte: Solar Aspects," www.solsticeproject.org/pueblobonito.pdf.

14. Kendrick Frazier, *People of Chaco: A Canyon and Its Culture* (New York: W. W. Norton & Co., 2005, 1986), p. 234.

15. Lekson, *A History of the Ancient Southwest*, op. cit., pp. 65-6.

16. Stephen Plog and Carrie Heiten, "Hierarchy and Social Inequity in the American Southwest, A.D. 800-1200," November 8, 2010, National Academy of Sciences, www.pnas.org/content/107/46/19619.full#ref-42.

17. Plog and Heiten, ibid.

18. Plog and Heiten, ibid.

19. David R. Wilcox, Phil C. Wiegand, J. Scott Wood and Jerry B. Howard, "Ancient Cultural Interplay of the American Southwest in the Mexican Northwest," *Journal of the Southwest*, Vol. 50, No. 2, Summer 2008, p. 116; http://jsw.arizona.edu/sites/jsw.arizona.edu/files/ JSW%20Summer%202008.pdf.

20. Stephen C. McCluskey, "Calendars and Symbolism: Functions of Observations in Hopi Astronomy," *Archaeoastronomy, (Journal for the History of Astronomy)*, No. 15, 1990, p. S2.

21. Stuart A. Northrop, *Minerals of New Mexico* (Albuquerque: University of New Mexico, 1944, 1959), p. 520, pp. 528-30.

22. Washington Matthews, *Navaho Legends* (Salt Lake City: University of Utah Press, 1994), pp. 81-87.

23. Stephen Lekson, *The Chaco Meridian: Centers of Political Power in the Ancient Southwest* (Walnut Creek, California: Altamira Press, 1999), p. 149.

24. Robert S. McPherson, *Sacred Land Sacred View* (Salt Lake City: Brigham Young University, 1992), p. 87.

25. www.firerocknavajocasino.com.

26. www.indianvillage.com/turqspiritual.htm.

27. James Q. Jacobs, "The Chaco Meridian," www.jqjacobs.net/southwest/chaco_meridian.html.

28. Lekson, *The Chaco Meridian,* op. cit., p. 50.

29. Lekson, *The Chaco Meridian,* ibid., p. 158.

30. Mary Austin, *The Land of Little Rain* (New York: The American Museum of Natural History, Anchor Books/Doubleday & Company., Inc, Garden City, , 1962), p. 13-4.

31. http://en.wikipedia.org/wiki/Chichimeca.

32. *Hopi Dictionary,* op. cit., p. 425; Waters and Fredericks, *Book of the Hopi,* op. cit., p. 150.

33. *Hopi Dictionary,* op. cit., p. 343.

34. *Hopi Dictionary,* ibid., p. 383.

35. *Hopi Dictionary,* ibid., p. 102.

36. *Hopi Dictionary,* ibid., p. 420.

37. Leslie Marmon Silko, *Ceremony* (New York: Penguin Books USA Inc., 1986, 1977), pp. 133-4, p. 136.

38. Charles C. Kolb, " The American Southwest Revisited: Violence and Cannibalism, and the Anasazi and Toltecs of Mesoamerica," www.hnet.org/reviews/showrev.php?id=3512.

39. George H. Pepper, *Pueblo Bonito* (Albuquerque: University of New Mexico Press, 1996), p. 378.

40. Stephen H. Lekson, *Great Pueblo Architecture of Chaco Canyon, New Mexico* (Albuquerque, New Mexico: University of New Mexico, 1984), p. 104.

41. Lekson, *Great Pueblo Architecture...,* ibid., p. 79.

42. Christy G. Turner, II, and Jacqueline A. Turner, *Man Corn: Cannibalism and Violence in the Prehistoric American Southwest* (Salt Lake City: The University of Utah Press, 199), pp. 263-9.

43. Peter J. McKenna, *The Architecture and Material Culture of 29SJ1360, Chaco Canyon, New Mexico* (Albuquerque, New Mexico: U.S. Department of the Interior/National Park Service, 1984), p. 321, p. 314, p. 101.

Chapter 8: Mimbres—A Pre-Columbian Counterculture In New Mexico

1. Norman T. Oppelt, *Guide to Prehistoric Ruins of the Southwest* (Boulder, Colorado: Pruett Publishing Company, 1989, 1981), p. 51.

2. John Kanter, *Ancient Puebloan Southwest* (Cambridge, UK: Cambridge University Press, 2004), pp. 146-7; Steven A. LeBlanc, *The Mimbres People: Ancient Pueblo Painters of the American Southwest* (London: Thames and Hudson, 1983), pp. 47-71.

3. Lekson, *The Chaco Meridian,* op. cit., p. 55.

4. Jesse Walter Fewkes, "Designs On Prehistoric Pottery From the Mimbres Valley, New Mexico," *The Mimbres Art and Archaeology* (Albuquerque, New Mexico: Avanyu Publishing, Inc., 1993, 1989, reprint of three essays published by The Smithsonian Institution between 1914 and 1924), pp. 1-2.
5. J. J. Brody, *Mimbres Painted Pottery*, (Santa Fe, New Mexico: School of American Research Press, 2005), p. 2.
6. Stephen C. Jett, Peter B. Moyle, "The Exotic Origins of Fishes Depicted on Prehistoric Pottery from New Mexico," *American Antiquity*, Vol. 51, No. 4, pp. 688-720.
7. Rose Houck, *Mogollon: Prehistoric Cultures of the Southwest* (Tucson, Arizona: Southwest Parks and Monuments Association, 1992), p. 11.
8. Kanter, *Ancient Puebloan Southwest*, op. cit., p. 120.
9. Valli S. Powell-Marti and Patricia A. Gilman, *Mimbres Society* (Tucson, Arizona: University of Arizona Press, 2006), p. 139, p. 142.
10. William N. Morgan, *Ancient Architecture of the Southwest* (Austin: University of Texas Press, 1994), p. 34.
11. Powell-Marti and Gilman, *Mimbres Society*, op. cit., p. 25.
12. Powell-Marti and Gilman, ibid., p. 27.
13. Powell-Marti and Gilman, ibid., p. 142.
14. Kanter, *Ancient Puebloan Southwest*, op. cit., p. 122.
15. Waters and Fredericks, *Book of the Hopi*, op. cit., p. 10, p. 13.
16. W. Y. Evans-Wentz, *The Tibetan Book of the Dead* (London: Oxford University Press, 1980, 1960), p. xiii.
17. Ray Urbaniak, www.naturalfrequency.net/Ray/mimbres.htm.
18. Marc Thompson, "The Evolution of Mimbres Iconography," *Kachinas In the Pueblo World*, op. cit., p. 104.
19. Fewkes, "Additional Designs On Prehistoric Mimbres Pottery," *The Mimbres Art and Archaeology*, op. cit., p. 6.
20. An alternate Hopi spelling is *tuu'awta*, which literally means "message." The word *tuu'awt* means "have a vision, have a mystical experience of seeing something extraordinary in nature or of déjà vu." *Hopi Dictionary*, op. cit., p. 683; *Tua-t*, "a very ancient name for the land of the dead, and of the Other World," Budge, *An Egyptian Hieroglyphic Dictionary*, Vol. II, op. cit., p. 871b-72a.
21. Ben A. Nelson, "Aggregation, Warfare, and the Spread of the Mesoamerican Tradition," *The Archaeology of Regional Interaction: Religion, Warfare, and Exchange*, edited by Michelle Hegmon (Boulder: University of Colorado Press, 2008), p. 327.
22. J. J. Brody, Catherine J. Scott, Steven A. LeBlanc, *Mimbres Pottery: Ancient Art of the American Southwest* (New York: The American Federation of the Arts, 1983), p. 13.
23. Steven A. LeBlanc and Katherine E. Register, *Constant Battles: Why We Fight* (New York: St. Martin's Griffin/Macmillan, 2004), p. 56.
Incidentally, Leblanc is the archaeologist who is probably most responsible for exposing the stereotype of the "peaceful Anasazi."

24. David, *The Kivas of Heaven*, op. cit.
25. Bob Cox, "The Entheogenic Tradition Of The Mogollon Mimbres Culture," http://web.archive.org/web/20041217235531/www.mimbres.com/Entheo/blcon.htm.
26. Cox, ibid.

Chapter 9: Paquimé—Mummies, a Meteorite, and the Macaw Constellation

1. Lekson, *The Chaco Meridian*, op. cit., p. 160.
2. Lekson, *A History of the Ancient Southwest*, op. cit., p. 213.
3. Lekson, *A History of the Ancient Southwest*, ibid., p. 210.
4. Stephen H. Lekson, "Was Casas a Pueblo?", *The Casas Grandes World*, edited by Curtis F. Schaafsma and Carroll L. Riley (Salt Lake: University of Utah, 1999), p. 85.
5. See a chapter on the Tau icon in my book *Eye of the Phoenix*, op. cit.
6. Christine S. VanPool, Todd L. VanPool, *Signs of the Casas Grandes Shamans* (Salt Lake: University of Utah Press, 2007), p. 30, p. 113.
7. *The Mineralogical Magazine and Journal of the Mineralogical Society*, Vol. IX, No. 41, April 1890 (London: Simpkin, Marshall, Hamilton, Kent & Co.), pp. 120-121, http://books.goggle.com; Wirt Tassin, "The Casas Grandes Meteorite," *Proceedings of the National Museum*, Washington, D.C., 1902, Vol. XXV, No. 1277, p. 69-74, http://biostor.org/reference/78971.
8. Oliver Cummings Farrington, *Catalogue of the Meteorites of North America, To January 1, 1909* (Washington, D.C.: Memoirs of the National Academy of Sciences, Volume XIII, 1915), p. 111.
9. http://curiousexpeditions.org/?p=547. See my book *Eye of the Phoenix*, op. cit., for a look at the meteorite trade network in the American Southwest.
10. Lekson, *A History of the Ancient Southwest*, op. cit., p. 336.
11. Gordon F. M. Rakita, "Ancestors and Elites: Emergent Complexity, Ritual Practice, and Mortuary Behavior at Paquimé, Chihuahua, Mexico," *Religion in the Prehistoric Southwest*, edited by Christine S. VanPool, Todd, L. VanPool, and David A. Philips, Jr. (Lanham, Maryland: Altamira Press, 2006), p. 230.
12. Renee Opperman, *Astronomical Implications of the Architecture at Casa Grande, Arizona* (Greeley, Colorado: Museum of Anthropology, University of Northern Colorado, 1980), pp. 51-2.
13. Di Peso quoted in Christy G. Turner, II, "The Dentition of Casas Grandes with Suggestions On Epigenetic Relationships among Mexican and Southwestern U.S. Populations," *The Casas Grandes World*, op. cit., p. 234.
14. VanPool and VanPool, *Signs of the Casas Grandes Shamans*, op. cit., p. 127.
15. VanPool and VanPool, *Signs of the Casas Grandes Shamans*, ibid., p. 126.
16. Paul Devereaux, "Acculturated Topographical Effects of Shamanic Trance Consciousness in Archaic and Medieval Landscapes," *Journal of*

Scientific Exploration, Vol. 7, No. 1, 1993, pp. 23-7.

17. Hamilton A. Tyler, *Pueblo Birds and Myths* (Flagstaff, Arizona: Northland Publishing, 1991), pp. 13-4.

18. H. R. Voth, *The Traditions of the Hopi*, 1905, pp. 157-9, www.sacred-texts.com/nam/hopi/toth/toth051.htm.

19. Andrew D. Somerville, Ben A. Nelson, and Kelly J. Knudson, "Isotopic Investigation of Pre-Hispanic Macaw Breeding in Northwest Mexico," *Journal of Anthropological Archaeology*, Vol. 29, 2010, p. 126.

20. Bradfield, *An Interpretation of Hopi Culture*, op. cit., pp. 239-40, p. 312.

21. Charmion R. McKusik, "Casas Grandes Macaws," *Archaeology Southwest*, Vol. 21, No. 1, Winter 2007, p. 5.

22. Ferguson and Rohn, *Anasazi Ruins of the Southwest In Color*, op. cit., p. 211.

23. Kathy Roler Durand and Stephen R. Durand, "Animal Bones from Salmon Pueblo," *Archaeology Southwest*, Vol. 20, No. 3, Summer 2006, p. 12.

24. Lekson, *The Chaco Meridian*, op. cit., p. 100.

25. www.alltribes.info/index.php/Arizona_Turquoise_Mines.

26. www.desertusa.com/ind1/ind_new/ind13.html.

27. Turner, "The Dentition of Casas Grandes... ," *The Casas Grandes World*, op. cit., pp. 229-33.

28. Richard D. Fisher, "The Great Anasazi Mystery ~ A Cold Case File Reopened," unpublished manuscript.

29. Allen, *Star Names*, op. cit., p. 256.

30. William Tyler Olcott, *Star Lore: Myths, Legends, and Facts* (Mineola, New York: Dover Publications, Inc., 2004), pp. 233-4.

31. Brady, *Brady's Book of Fixed Stars*, op. cit., p. 261, p. 263.

32. Somerville et al., "Isotopic Investigation...," op. cit., pp. 126-7.

33. Richard D. Fisher, "Paquime: the Anasazi Rosetta Stone," June 2004, www.canyonsworldwide.com/fisher/site.htm.

34. VanPool and VanPool, *Signs of the Casas Grandes Shamans*, op. cit., p. 101.

35. G. P. Können and J. van Maanen, "Planetary Occultations of Bright Stars," *Journal of the British Astronomical Association*, Vol. 91, No. 2, 1981, p. 152, p. 154, http://s3.amazonaws.com/guntherkonnen/documents/55/1981_OccStarPlan_JBAA.pdf?1292778579.

36. Opperman, *Astronomical Implications...*, op. cit., pp. 46-7.

37. VanPool and VanPool, *Signs of the Casas Grandes Shamans*, op. cit., pp. 131-132.

38. VanPool and VanPool, *Signs of the Casas Grandes Shamans*, ibid., pp. 131-2.

39. VanPool and VanPool, *Signs of the Casas Grandes Shamans*, ibid., p. 131.

40. Hancock and Bauval, *The Message of the Sphinx*, op. cit., pp. 247-67.

41. Hancock, *Fingerprints of the Gods*, op. cit., p. 381.

42. www.zodiacal.com/tools/lat_table.php.

43. T. Alan Pitezel, "The Hilltop Site of El Pueblito," *Archaeology Southwest*,

Vol. 17, No. 2, Spring 2003, Center for Desert Archaeology.

44. VanPool and VanPool, *Signs of the Casas Grandes Shamans*, op. cit., p. 32, p. 132.

45. Craig Childs, *House of Rain: Tracking a Vanished Civilization Across the American Southwest* (New York: Little, Brown and Company, 2006), pp. 385-6.

46. T. J. Ferguson and E. Richard Hart, *A Zuni Atlas* (Norman: University of Oklahoma Press, 1985), p. 22.

47. Cordell, *Prehistory of the Southwest*, op. cit., pp. 275-6.

48. Waters and Fredericks, *Book of the Hopi*, op. cit., p. 68.

49. Voth, *The Traditions of the Hopi*, op. cit., p. 53.

50. Adrian Ricinos, *Popol Vuh: Sacred Book of the Ancient Quiché*, Spanish version of the original Maya translated by S. G. Morley and D. Goetz (Norman, Oklahoma: University of Oklahoma Press, 1950).

51. Rakita, "Ancestors and Elites," *Religion in the Prehistoric Southwest*, op. cit., pp. 230-1.

Chapter 10: The Lost Empire of Aztlán

1. Lekson, *The Chaco Meridian*, op. cit., p. 185.

2. Carl Sauer, Donald Brand, *Aztatlán: Prehistoric Mexican Frontier*, Ibero-Americana, No. 1, Berkeley, California: University of California Press, 1932, p. 29.

3. Sauer and Brand, *Aztatlán*, ibid., pp. 41-9.

4. Sauer and Brand, *Aztatlán*, ibid., pp. 43-4.

5. Sauer and Brand, *Aztatlán*, ibid., p. 7.

6. Sauer and Brand, *Aztatlán*, ibid., p. 47.

7. Sauer and Brand, *Aztatlán*, ibid., p. 45.

8. Sauer and Brand, *Aztatlán*, ibid., p. 32.

9. Isabel Kelly, *Excavations At Culiacan, Sinaloa*, Ibero-Americana 25, Berkeley, California: University of California Press, 1945, p. 23.

10. Sauer and Brand, *Aztatlán*, op. cit., p. 41.

11. Sauer and Brand, *Aztatlán*, ibid., p. 61.

12. Kelly, *Excavations At Culiacan*, op. cit., p. 4-5.

13. Sauer and Brand, *Aztatlán*, op. cit., p. 31.

14. F. S. Hulse, "Skeletal Material," Appendix III, Kelly, *Excavations At Culiacan*, op. cit., p. 198.

Basketmakers were the predecessors of the Pueblo people in the American Southwest. They made wicker basketry as well as coiled pottery, and used dry farming methods.

15. Frederick Starr, *Aztec Place-Names: Their Meaning and Mode of Composition*, Chicago: privately printed, 1920. www.columbia.edu/cu/lweb/digital/collections/cul/texts/ldpd_6072319_000/ldpd_6072319_000.pdf.

16. Fray Diego Durán, *The History of the Indies of New Spain*, translated by Doris Heyden (Norman, Oklahoma: University of Oklahoma Press, 1994),

pp. 212-22.

17. Fray Diego Durán, *Book of the Gods and Rites and The Ancient Calendar*, translated by Fernando Horcasitas and Doris Heyden (Norman, Oklahoma: University of Oklahoma Press, 1971, 1977), pp. 72-3.

18. Victor W. von Hagen, *The Aztec: Man and Tribe* (New York: Mentor Ancient Civilizations/The New American Library, 1958), p. 50.

19. Daniel G. Brinton, *Rig Veda Americanus. Sacred Songs of the Ancient Mexicans, With a Gloss in Nahuatl*, 1890, www.gutenberg.org/files/14993/14993-h/14993-h.htm.

20. Brinton, *Rig Veda Americanus*, ibid.

21. Donald Mackenzie, *Myths of Pre-Columbian America* (Mineola, New York: Dover Publications, Inc., 1996, 1923), p. 289-90.

22. Gordon Brotherston and Ed Dorn, *Image of the New World* (London: Thames and Hudson, 1979), p. 188.

23. Brotherston and Dorn, *Image of the New World*, ibid., p. 196-7.

24. Brotherston and Dorn, *Image of the New World*, ibid., p. 201.

25. Jacques Soustelle, *The Daily Life of the Aztecs On the Eve of the Spanish Conquest*, translated by Patrick O'Brien, New York: The Macmillan Company, 1962), pp. 102-3.

26. *The Mineralogical Magazine and Journal of the Mineralogical Society*, Vol. IX, No 41, April 1890 (London: Simpkin, Marshall, Hamilton, Kent & Co.), p. 101, http://books.goggle.com.

27. Michael D. Coe, *Mexico* (New York: Praeger Publishers, 1977, 1962), p. 116.

28. Carl Sauer, "The Road to Cibola," *Land and Life: A Selection From the Writings of Carl Ortwin Sauer*, edited by John Leighly (Berkeley, California: University of California Press, 1974, 1963), pp. 53-4.

29. Lekson, *The Chaco Meridian*, op. cit., pp. 183-4.

30. Sauer, "The Road to Cibola," *Land and Life*, op. cit., p. 61.

31. A. F. Bandelier, "Hemenway Southwestern Archaeological Expedition," *Papers of the Archaeological Institute of America* (Cambridge: John Wilson & Son, 1890), pp. 11-12.

32. Lekson, *The Chaco Meridian*, op. cit., p. 186.

33. Waters and Fredericks, *Book of the Hopi*, op. cit., pp. 18-20.

34. Herbert J. Spinden, *Civilizations of Mexico and Central America* (Mineola, New York: Dover Publications, Inc.), 1999, 1928), p. 172.

35. Robert Dragon, "The Winter Sky Petroglyph at Roundy Crossing," Conference on Archaeoastronomy of the American Southwest, 2009, www.caasw.org/2009Conference.html.

Chapter 11: ABCs of Orion—Ants, Bulls, Bird-Men, & Copper

1. Allen, *Star Names*, op. cit., p. 304.

2. Catherine Acholonu-Olumba, personal email communications, April 21,

April 28, 2011; see www.carcafriculture.org.

3. http://en.wikipedia.org/wiki/Mnevis.

4. E. Thomas Lawson, *Religions of Africa: Traditions in Transformation* (Prospect Heights, Illinois: Waveland Press, Inc., 1998, 1985), pp. 54-69.

5. Prof. Catherine Acholonu, "Osiris and Isis - God and Goddess of Nubia: Matching the Testimony of Edgar Cayce with ancient Nigerian mythology," www.migration-diffusion.info/article.php?id=197.

6. Michael Jordan, *Encyclopedia of Gods: Over 2,500 Deities of the World* (New York: Facts on File, Inc, 1993), pp. 194-5.

7. E. A. Wallis Budge, *Osiris and the Egyptian Resurrection*, Vol. I , op. cit., p. 372.

8. http://dictionary.reference.com/browse/orenda.

9. Jim Bailey, *Sailing to Paradise*, op. cit., p. 223.

10. See Greg Taylor's excellent essay "The God with the Upraised Arm," www.dailygrail.com/features/god-with-the-upraised-arm.

11. Bailey, *Sailing to Paradise*, op. cit., p. 223.

12. William Sullivan, *The Secret of the Incas: Myth, Astronomy, and the War Against Time* (New York: Three Rivers Press, 1996), pp. 103-4; www.earthinstitute.columbia.edu/news/aboutStory/about1_4c.html.

13. Joseph T. Shipley, *Origin of English Words: A Discursive Dictionary of Indo-European Roots*, (Baltimore: Johns Hopkins University Press, 1984), pp.256-8.

14. *Hopi Dictionary*, op. cit., p. 31, p. 271.

15. *Hopi Dictionary*, ibid., p. 104.

16. Rethabile, "Morui," *On Sesotho*, http://sesotho.blogspot.com/2005/01/morui.html.

17. http://en.wikipedia.org/wiki/Pissant.

18. Sanford Holst, "Sea Peoples and the Phoenicians: a Critical Turning Point in History," www.phoenician.org/sea_peoples.htm#_ednref17.

19. Frank Joseph, *Survivors of Atlantis: Their Impact on World Culture* (Rochester, Vermont: Bear & Co., 2004), p. 5.

20. See my book *The Kivas of Heaven*, op. cit, p. 175, p. 289.

21. John Lemprière, *A Classical Dictionary: Containing a Copious Account of All the Proper Names Mentioned in Ancient Authors*, (New York: Evert Duyckinck, & Co., 1825), p. 500, http://books.goggle.com.

22. Waters and Frederick, *Book of the Hopi*, op. cit., pp. 17-20; *Hopi Dictionary*, op. cit., p. 383.

23. Noble, *Ancient Ruins of the Southwest*, op. cit., p. 22.

24. David M. Hendricks, *Arizona Soils* (Tucson: University of Arizona, College of Agriculture, 1985), p. 16, http://southwest.library.arizona.edu/azso/front.1_div.1.html.

25. Hugh Fox, *Home of the Gods* (Lakeville, Minnesota: Galde Press, Inc.), p. 70.

26. Bailey, *Sailing to Paradise*, op. cit., p. 284.

27. Catherine Acholonu-Olumba, *The Lost Testament of the Ancestors of Adam:*

Unearthing Heliopolis /Igbo Ukwu – The Celestial City of the Gods of Egypt and India (Wuse Abuja, Nigeria: CARC Publications, 2010).

28. Cyrus H. Gordon, *The Ancient Near East* (New York: W. W. Norton & Co., Inc., 1965, 1953), p. 156.

29. http://spokensanskrit.de.

30. Andrea Salimbeti, "The Greek Age of Bronze: Sea Peoples," www.salimbeti.com/micenei/sea.htm.

31. John Philip Cohane, *The Key* (New York: Schocken Books, 1976, 1969), pp. 43-6, p. 104; http://en.wikipedia.org/wiki/Cape_Gelidonya.

32. Andrew Collins, *From the Ashes of Angels: The Forbidden Legacy of a Fallen Race* (Rochester, Vermont: Bear & Company, 2001, 1996), p. 58. Collins quotes James Bailey, *The God-Kings and the Titans: New World Ascendancy in Ancient Times* (New York: St. Martin's Press, 1973), p. 186.

33. Bailey, *Sailing to Paradise*, op. cit., p. 307.

34. W. J. Wilkins, *Hindu Mythology* (New Delhi: Rupa & Co., 1991, 1882), pp. 449-56.

35. Graham Hancock, *Heaven's Mirror: Quest For the Lost Civilization* (New York: Crown Publishers, Inc., 1998), pp. 243-4.

36. Stéphen-Charles Chauvet, *Easter Island and Its Mysteries*, translated by Ann M. Altman, edited by Shawn McLaughlin, 2005, 1935, www.chauvet-translation.com/religion.htm.

37. David Pratt, "Easter Island: land of mystery," November 2004, Part 3, http://davidpratt.info/easter3.htm.

38. Katherine Routledge, *The Mystery of Easter Island* (Kempton, Illinois: Adventures Unlimited Press, 1998, 1919), p. 235.

39. Routledge, *The Mystery of Easter Island*, ibid., pp. 261-2.

40. Francis Maziére, *Mysteries of Easter Island* (New York: Tower Publications, Inc./W. W. Norton & Company, Inc., 1968, 1965), pp. 74-9.

41. Routledge, *The Mystery of Easter Island*, op. cit., p. 264.

42. Herbert John Davies, *A Tahitian and English dictionary, with introductory remarks on the Polynesian language, and a short grammar of the Tahitian dialect: with an appendix containing a list of foreign words used in the Tahitian Bible, in commerce, etc., with the sources from whence they have been derived* (Tahiti: The London Missionary Society's Press, 1851), p. 109, http://archive.org/details/tahitianenglishd00davirich.

43. http://en.wikipedia.org/wiki/Totora_(plant).

44. *Hopi Dictionary*, op. cit., p. 317.

45. Davies, *A Tahitian and English dictionary*, op. cit., p. 109.

46. *Hopi Dictionary*, op. cit., p. 88.

47. *Hopi Dictionary*, op. cit., p. 99.

48. *Hopi Dictionary*, op. cit., p. 46.

49. *Hopi Dictionary*, op. cit., p. 244.

50. Thor Heyerdahl, *Aku-Aku: The Secret of Easter Island* (Chicago: Rand

McNally & Company, 1958). pp. 123-6.

51. Maziére, *Mysteries of Easter Island,* op. cit., pp. 35-7.

52. Heyerdahl, *Aku-Aku,* op. cit., p. 190.

53. Davies, *A Tahitian and English dictionary,* op. cit., p. 106.

54. L. Sprague de Camp and Catherine C. de Camp, *Citadels of Mystery* (New York: Ballantine Books, 1964, 1946), pp. 246-7.

55. Davies, *A Tahitian and English dictionary,* op. cit., p. 173, p. 172.

56. Heyerdahl, *Aku-Aku,* op. cit., p. 128.

57. David Hatcher Childress, *Lost Cities of Ancient Lemuria & the Pacific* (Kempton, Illinois: Adventures Unlimited Press, 2002, 1988), p. 290.

58. William S. Ayres, "Radiocarbon dates from Easter Island," *Journal of Polynesian Society,* Vol. 80, No. 4, 1971, pp. 497-504, http://www.jps.auckland.ac.nz/document//Volume_80_1971/Volume_80,_No._4/ Radiocarbon_dates_from_Easter_Island,_by_William_S._Ayres,_p_497_-_504/p1.

59. www.hilites.org.uk/easter-island/the-dating-of-easter-island.

60. Heyerdahl, *Aku-Aku,* op. cit., p. 134.

61. Childress, *Lost Cities of Ancient Lemuria & the Pacific,* op. cit., p. 315.

62. Chauvet, *Easter Island and Its Mysteries,* op. cit., www.chauvet-translation.com/religion.htm.

63. Davies, *A Tahitian and English dictionary,* op. cit., p. 24.

64. *Hopi Dictionary,* op. cit. p. 2.

65. Maziére, *Mysteries of Easter Island.* op. cit., p. 82-3.
An old man, who was "a descendant"of the royal line " (in other words, a Long Ear) had shown Maziére this cave on the north coast that held the skull. "Mana" is spiritual power.

Chapter 12: Epic Sea Voyages of the Ancestral Hopi

1. *Hopi Dictionary,* op. cit., p. 372, p. 571.

2. Courlander, *The Fourth World of the Hopis,* op. cit., p. 204.

3. Alexander M. Stephen, and Elsie Clew Parsons, editor, *Hopi Journal,* Vol. II (New York: AMS Press, Inc., 1969, reprint 1936), p. 849.

4. Alfred F. Whiting, *Ethnobotany of the Hopi* (Flagstaff, Arizona: Museum of Northern Arizona Bulletin Series: No 15, 1939.

5. Albert Yava, *Big Snow Falling: A Tewa-Hopi Indian's Life and Times and the History and Traditions of His People,* edited by Harold Courlander (Albuquerque: University of New Mexico Press, 1978), p. 61-2.

6. Yava, *Big Snow Falling,* ibid., p. 46.

7. Yava, *Big Snow Falling,* ibid., p. 70.

8. Harold Courlander, *Hopi Voices: Recollections, Traditions, and Narratives of the Hopi Indians* (Albuquerque: University of New Mexico Press, 1982), p. 37.

9. Courlander, *Hopi Voices,* ibid., p. 12.

10. Stephen, *Hopi Journal,* Vol. I, op. cit., p. 54.

11. Stephen, *Hopi Journal*, Vol. II, ibid., p. 311.
12. *Hopi Dictionary*, op. cit., p. 382, p. 375, p. 370.
13. http://spokensanskrit.de.
14. Augustus Le Plongeon, M.D., *Maya/Atlantis, Queen Móo and the Egyptian Sphinx* (Blauvelt, New York: Rudolf Steiner Publications, 1973), pp. 99-100.
15. Bose, "Were there close links between ancient America and India?", op. cit., p. 4.
16. http://spokensanskrit.de.
17. James Churchward, *The Lost Continent of Mu*, introduction by David Hatcher Childress (Kempton, Illinois: Adventures Unlimited Press, 2007, 1926), pp 226-7.
18. *Hopi Dictionary*, op. cit., p. 791.
19. Churchward, *The Lost Continent of Mu*, op. cit., p. 212.
20. Colonel James Churchward, *The Sacred Symbols of Mu* (New York: Ives Washburn, Publisher, 1933), p. 202.
21. James Churchward, *The Children of Mu* (Albuquerque: Be Books/The C. W. Daniel Company Ltd., 1988, 1959), p. 240.
22. Churchward, *The Sacred Symbols of Mu*, op. cit., p. 141.
23. Churchward, *The Children of Mu*, op. cit., p. 240.
24. LaVan Martineau, *The Rocks Begin To Speak* (Las Vegas, Nevada: KC Publications, Inc. 1994, 1973), p. 97.
25. Churchward, *The Lost Continent of Mu*, op. cit., p. 77-8.
26. *Hopi Dictionary*, op. cit., p. 36.
27. *Hopi Dictionary*, ibid., p. 163.
28. Churchward, *The Sacred Symbols of Mu*, op. cit., p. 116.
29. Churchward, *The Lost Continent of Mu*, op. cit., p. 45.
30. Vada F. Carlson, *The Great Migration: Emergence of the Americas As Indicated in the Readings of Edgar Cayce*, (851-2) (Virginia Beach, Virginia: A.R.E. Press, 1970), p. 51.
31. Carlson, *The Great Migration*, ibid., (1252-1), p. 53.
32. Carlson, *The Great Migration*, ibid., (691-1), p. 52.
33. Carolyn Hatt, *The Maya, Based on the Edgar Cayce Readings*, (5750-1) (Virginia Beach, Virginia: A.R.E. Press, 1972), p. 42.
34. Churchward, *The Children of Mu*, op. cit., p. 48.
35. "Edgar Cayce – The Empire of Og," www.esoterism.ro/english/edgar-cayce-og.php.
36. Augustus Le Plongeon, *Sacred Mysteries Among the Mayas and the Quiches* (Minneapolis, Minnesota: Wizards Bookshelf, 1973).
37. Robert Schoch, Ph.D., with Robert Aquinas McNally, *Voyages of the Pyramid Builders: The True Origins of the Pyramids from Lost Egypt to Ancient America* (New York: Tarcher/Penguin Books, 2004, 2003), p. 244.
38. Schoch, *Voyage of the Pyramid Builders*, ibid., p. 261.
39. Graham Hancock, *Underworld: The Mysterious Origins of Civilization*

(New York: Three Rivers Press, 2002), p. 269.

40. Stephen Oppenheimer, *Eden In the East: The Drowned Continent of Southeast Asia* (London: Weidenfeld and Nicolson, 1998), p. 10.

41. Oppenheimer, *Eden In the East*, ibid., pp.11-2, p. 434.

42. H. P. Blavatsky, *The Secret Doctrine: The Synthesis of Science, Religion, and Philosophy*, Vol. II (London: The Theosophical Publishing Company, Limited, 1988, 1888), p. 768.

43. Schoch, *Voyage of the Pyramid Builders*, op. cit., pp. 247-8.

44. *Hopi Dictionary*, op. cit., p. 369; David Lewis, *We, the Navigators: The Ancient Art of Landfinding in the Pacific* (Honolulu: The University Press of Hawaii, 1979, 1972), p. 256; Davies, *A Tahitian and English dictionary*, op. cit., p. 180.

45. Blavatsky, *The Secret Doctrine*, Vol. II, op. cit., pp. 193-4.

46. Churchward, *The Sacred Symbols of Mu*, op. cit., pp. 270-1.

47. *Hopi Dictionary*, op. cit., p. 366, p. 444.

48. Frank Waters, *Mexico Mystique: The Coming Sixth World Consciousness* (Chicago: Sage Books/The Swallow Press Incorporated, 1975), p. 104.

49. *Hopi Dictionary*, op. cit., p. 376.
See a chapter on Hopi flying shields in each of my two my previous books: *Eye of the Phoenix*, op. cit, and *The Kivas of Heaven*, op. cit.

50. Alphonse Riesenfeld, *The Megalithic Culture of Melanesia* (Leiden, Holland: E. J. Brill, 1950), p. 150, http://books.goggle.com.

51. Riesenfeld, *The Megalithic Culture of Melanesia*, ibid., p. 165.

52. Schaafsma, *Kachinas In the Pueblo World*, op. cit., pp. 144-5.

53. Wright, *Hopi Kachinas*, op. cit., p. 86.

54. Collins, *From the Ashes of Angels*, op. cit., p. 64.

55. Heraclitus, *The History*, 1:1, op. cit, p. 33, and note 1.

56. Christopher Knight and Robert Lomas, *Uriel's Machine: Uncovering the Secrets of Stonehenge, Noah's Flood, and the Dawn of Civilization* (Gloucester, Massachusetts: Fair Winds Press, 2001, 1999), p. 137.

57. Smith, *Smith's Bible Dictionary*, op, cit, p. 474.

58. Helene C. Johanson, "Inheritance of a novel mutated allele of the OCA2 gene associated with high incidence of oculocutaneous albinism in a Polynesian community," *Journal of Human Genetics*, Vol. 55, 2010, pp. 103-11, www.nature.com/jhg/journal/v55/n2/abs/jhg2009130a.html.

59. Helene C. Johanson, Pacific Islands Stories: Pacific Albinism Project, February 26, 2012, http://blog.spevi.net/2012/02/ pacific-islands-stories-pacific.html.

60. Oliver Sacks, *The Island of the Colorblind* (New York: Alfred A. Knopf, 1997).

61. Sacks, *The Island of the Colorblind*, ibid., pp. 53-4.

62. *Hopi Dictionary*, op. cit., p. 232.

63. Charles M. Woolf, "Albinism Among Indians in Arizona and New

Mexico," *American Journal of Human Genetics*, Vol. 17, No. 1, January, 1965, p. 24, p. 23.

64. Charles M. Woolf and Robert B. Grant, "Albinism Among the Hopi in Arizona," presented at a meeting of the American Society of Human Genetics, Corvalis, Oregon, August 31, 1962, p. 391.

65. Titiev, *Old Oraibi*, op. cit., p. 72.

66. Woolf and Grant, "Albinism Among the Hopi in Arizona," op. cit., p. 391.

67. Mike Powers, "Panama's Indian albinos a revered elite," Isla Tigre, Panama, Reuters.

68. Sheldon C. Reed, "Speculations About Human Albinism," *Journal of Heredity*, Vol. 56, No. 2, 1965, p. 64.

69. http://en.wikipedia.org/wiki/Kuna_people; *Hopi Dictionary*, op. cit, p. 506.

70. Santillana and Dechend, *Hamlet's Mill*, op. cit., p. 213.

71. *Hopi Dictionary*, op. cit., p. 382, p. 728.

72. Woolf, "Albinism Among Indians...," op. cit., p. 29.

73. Elsie Worthington Clews Parsons, *Pueblo Indian Religion*, Vol. 1, (Lincoln: University of Nebraska Press, 1996), pp. 90-1.

74. Per Hage, "Was Proto-Oceanic Society Matrilineal?", *The Journal of the Polynesian Society*, Vol. 107, No. 4, December 1998, p. 365, www.jstor.org/discover/10.2307/20706828?uid=3739256&uid=2129&uid=2&uid=70&uid=4&sid=21100950077193; Titiev, *Old Oraibi*, op. cit., p. 7.

75. Malhi RS, Mortensen HM, Eshleman JA, Kemp BM, Lorenz JG, Kaestle FA, Johnson JR, Gorodezky C, Smith DG, "Native American mtDNA Prehistory in the American Southwest," *American Journal of Physical Anthropology*, Vol. 120, No. 2, p. 111, p. 119.

76. Malhi et al., "Native American mtDNA Prehistory...," ibid., p. 112.

77. Jason A. Eschleman, Ripan S. Malhi, and David Glenn Smith, "Mitochondrial DNA Studies of Native Americans: Conceptions and Misconceptions of the Population Prehistory of the Americas," *Evolutionary Anthropology*, Vol. 12, 2003, p. 9.

78. Malhi et al., "Native American mtDNA Prehistory...," op. cit., p. 119.

79. http://freepages.genealogy.rootsweb.ancestry.com/~gkbopp/DNA/HAWAII%20DNA.

80. Oppenheimer, *Eden In the East*, op. cit., p. 197.

81. Joseph G. Lorentz, and David G. Smith, "Distribution of the 9-bp mitochondrial DNA region V deletion among North American Indians, " *Human Biology*, Vol. 66, No. 5, October 1994.

82. James L. Guthrie, "Human Lymphocyte Antigens: Apparent Afro-Asiatic, Southern Asian, & European HLAs in Indigenous American Populations," *Pre-Columbiana: A Journal of Long-Distance Contacts*, Vol. 2, No. 2 & 3, December 2000/June 2001, pp. 90-1, www.neara.org/Guthrie/lymphocyteantigens01.htm.

83. Guthrie, "Human Lymphocyte Antigens...,"ibid., p. 119.

84. Behe Fahey, "The Asiatic Neolithic, the Southern Mongoloid Dispersal, and Their Possible Significance for the Americas," *Pre-Columbiana: A Journal of Long-Distance Contacts*, Vol. 2, No. 2 & 3, December 2000/June 2001, p. 181.

85. Put simply, cultural diffusionism proposes that ancient people got around on foot or by boat a lot more than commonly assumed—around the world, in fact. This theory posits that a free flow of trade goods and cultural motifs existed globally, perhaps as early as the Neolithic period.

During the 20th century, anthropologists and archaeologists, many of them tenured or supported by universities, had suggested that the diffusionist theory, which prevailed in the last part of the previous century, was inherently racist. The theory, they said, implies that Caucasians had bestowed the benefits of civilization on the "darker" races in order to bring them toward the light.

Proposing an alternative isolationist theory, this Columbus-was-first crowd described a scenario of scattered, provincial tribes of Native Americans going it alone the best way they could on a sparsely populated continent. In our current age when racial equality is at least an ideal, the notion of a group of white, patriarchal benefactors influencing the "benighted" aboriginal cultures is repugnant and retrograde—if it were in fact true.

But in some ways the isolationist theory is the racist one because it assumes that the native peoples of North and South America were not intelligent or skilled enough to accomplish long distance travel by land or sea—other than the initial trudge from Siberia to Alaska and Canada via the Bering Straits' "land bridge."

86. Guthrie, "Human Lymphocyte Antigens....", op. cit., p. 129.

87. Lewis, *We, the Navigators*, op. cit., p. 236.

88. Robert D. Craig, *Dictionary of Polynesian Mythology* (New York: Greenwood Press, Inc.1989), p. 57.

89. Camp and Camp, *Citadels of Mystery*, op. cit., p. 256.

90. Churchward, *The Lost Continent of Mu*, op. cit., p. 45.

91. David D. Zink, *The Ancient Stones Speak: A Journey To the World's Most Mysterious Megalithic Sites* (New York: E. P. Dutton, 1979), p. 159.

92. Childress, *Lost Cities of Ancient Lemuria & the Pacific*, op. cit., p. 211-27.

93. *Hopi Dictionary*, op. cit., p. 423.

94. *Hopi Dictionary*, ibid., p. 296.

95. *Hopi Dictionary*, ibid., p. 386.

Chapter 13: Hopi Mystery Egg and Prophecies of the Fifth World

1. Dan Katchongva, "Hopi Prophecies From the Beginning of Life to the Day of Purification," January 29, 1970, Hotevilla, Arizona,

www.bibliotecapleyades.net/esp_leyenda_hopi1.htm.
2. Robert Boissiere, *Meditations With The Hopi* (Santa Fe: Bear & Co., 1986), www.hopiland.net/index.php?pg=47&body=prock-01.
3. Anon., *Hopi-Tibetan Prophecy: Return of Elder Brother*, unpublished manuscript, 2011.
4. *Hopi Dictionary*, op. cit., p. 309.
5. *Hopi Dictionary*, ibid., p. 748.
6. *Hopi Dictionary*, ibid., p. 567.
7. www.realitysandwich.com/thoughts_norway_spiral.
8. www.crystalinks.com/hopi2.html.
9. Waters and Fredericks, *Book of The Hopi*, op. cit., p. 334. Brackets in the quote were included by Waters.
10. Dan Evehema quoted in Thomas E. Mails, *The Hopi Survival Kit* (New York: Stewart, Tabori, and Chang, 1997), pp. 209-10.
11. Joscelyn Godwin, *Mystery Religions in the Ancient World* (San Francisco: Harper & Row, Publishers, Inc., 1981), p. 100.
12. See David, *Eye of the Phoenix,* op. cit., for a discussion of positive swastika symbolism that antedates the horrors of Nazism, as well as the worldwide, pre-WWI use of the Maltese cross.
13. Clark, *Myth and Symbol In Ancient Egypt,* op. cit., p. 74, p. 56, p. 213.
14. *The Hymns of the Rgveda*, Vol. II, translated by Ralph T. H. Griffith, Book X, Hymn CXXI, Verses 1, 7, and 8 (Varanasi, India: The Chowkhamba Sanskrit Series Office, 1971), pp. 566-7.
15. J. E. Cirlot, *A Dictionary of Symbols*, op. cit., p. 90.
16. *Hopi Dictionary*, op. cit., p. 506.
17. Robert Temple, *The Sirius Mystery: New Scientific Evidence of Alien Contact 5,000 Years Ago* (Rochester, Vermont: Destiny Books/Inner Traditions, 1998), p. 254.
18. Laird Scranton, *Sacred Symbols of the Dogon: The Key to Advanced Science In the Ancient Egyptian Hieroglyphs* (Rochester, Vermont: Inner Traditions, 2007), p. 31.
19. Laird Scranton, *The Science of the Dogon: Decoding the African Mystery Tradition* (Rochester, Vermont: Inner Traditions, 2006, 2002), pp. 111-2.
20. In David, *The Kivas of Heaven,* op. cit., the comparison is drawn between the *kanaga* ("hand of god") mask worn by the Dogon and the headdress worn by Apache *gan* spirits in Arizona. The complex Dogon cosmology includes Sirius A, which Sumerian and Babylonian sources refer to as the Bow Star, along with the invisible white dwarf Sirius B (discovered in 1862) and Sirius C (discovered recently by scientists).
D. Benest and J. L. Duvent, "Is Sirius a triple star?", *Astronomy and Astrophysics*, No. 299, 1995, pp. 621-8, www.bibliotecapleyades.net/archivos_pdf/sirius_triple_star.pdf.
The Awa Society performs the Sigui ceremony, briefly discussed on p. 324. Perhaps it is more than a coincidence that the Hopi word *awat* means "bow"

(weapon). *Hopi Dictionary*, op. cit., p. 41.

21. Marcel Griaule and Germaine Dieterlen, "A Sudanese Sirius System," quoted from Appendix I, Temple, *The Sirius Mystery*, op. cit., p. 319, p. 333.

22. *Hopi Dictionary*, op. cit., p. 5.

23. Bailey, *Sailing to Paradise*, op. cit., p. 197.

24. Katchongva, "Hopi Prophecies...," op. cit.

25. http://herb.umd.umich.edu/herb/
search.pl?searchstring=Lygodesmia+grandiflora.

26. Katchongva, "Hopi Prophecies...," op. cit.

27. Hildegard of Bingen, *Scivias*, translated by Columba Hart and Jane Bishop (Mahwah, New Jersey: Paulist Press, 1990), pp. 93-4.

28. Dianna Elizabeth Conner, "Hildegard von Bingen's Visions of the Divine Feminine," www.empowerment-for-the-soul.com/article_visionsdivine.pdf.

29. www.carnaval.com/dead/aztec_poetry.htm.

30. T. L. Subash Chandira Bose, "A Unique Sacred Symbol Found In a Temple In Tamil Nadu," 2004, Atma jothi Kureedum Adu Puli villaiyaatum (in Tamil), Lalitha Publication, Coimbatote, Tamil Nadu, India.

31. http://thiruvanaikavaltemple.org.

32. Bose, "A Unique Sacred Symbol...," op. cit.

33. *Hopi Dictionary*, op. cit., p. 220.

34. Budge, *An Egyptian Hieroglyphic Dictionary*, Vol. I, p. 271b.

35. *Hopi Dictionary*, op. cit., p. 217, p. 232.

36. www.dictionary.tamilcube.com/, http://spokensanskrit.de.

37. www.mesoweb.com/resources/vocabulary/Vocabulary.pdf, p. 57, p. 58.

38. Allen J. Christenson,"K'iche-English Dictionary and Guide To Pronunciation of the K'iche-Maya Alphabet," www.famsi.org/mayawriting/dictionary/christenson/quidic_complete.pdf.

39. Katchongva, "Hopi Prophecies...," op. cit.

40. Boissiere, *Meditations With The Hopi*, op. cit.

Gary A. David has been an independent researcher of Southwestern archaeological ruins and rock art for nearly twenty-five years. His books about the ancestral Pueblo cultures of Arizona and New Mexico include: *The Orion Zone–Ancient Star Cities of the American Southwest, Eye of the Phoenix–Mysterious Visions and Secrets of the American Southwest,* and *The Kivas of Heaven–Ancient Hopi Starlore. Star Shrines and Earthworks of the Desert Southwest* is his fourth nonfiction book. These are all available from Adventures Unlimited Press.

Mr. David earned a master's degree from the University of Colorado and is a former college professor. He is also a poet, with numerous volumes published, and a professional lead guitarist/vocalist.

His articles or interviews have appeared in many magazines, including *Ancient American, Atlantis Rising, Fate, Fenix* (Italy), *Mysteries* (Greece), *Sagenhafte Zeiten* (Switzerland, Erich von Däniken's "Legendary Times"), *UFO,* and *World Explorer,* as well as in anthologies such as *Lost Knowledge of the Ancients: A Graham Hancock Reader* and *Underground: The Disinformation Guide to Ancient Civilizations.* Gary continues to give lectures and international radio interviews. He recently appeared on the History Channel's TV series "Decoded" and "Ancient Aliens." His website is: www.theorionzone.com.

Gary, his wife, and an aging cat live together in rural northern Arizona, where the skies are still relatively pristine.

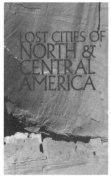

ANCIENT ALIENS ON THE MOON
By Mike Bara
What did NASA find in their explorations of the solar system that they may have kept from the general public? How ancient really are these ruins on the Moon? Using official NASA and Russian photos of the Moon, Bara looks at vast cityscapes and domes in the Sinus Medii region as well as glass domes in the Crisium region. Bara also takes a detailed look at the mission of Apollo 17 and the case that this was a salvage mission, primarily concerned with investigating an opening into a massive hexagonal ruin near the landing site. Chapters include: The History of Lunar Anomalies; The Early 20th Century; Sinus Medii; To the Moon Alice!; Mare Crisium; Yes, Virginia, We Really Went to the Moon; Apollo 17; more. Tons of photos of the Moon examined for possible structures and other anomalies.
348 Pages. 6x9 Paperback. Illustrated.. $19.95. Code: AAOM

ANCIENT TECHNOLOGY IN PERU & BOLIVIA
By David Hatcher Childress
Childress speculates on the existence of a sunken city in Lake Titicaca and reveals new evidence that the Sumerians may have arrived in South America 4,000 years ago. He demonstrates that the use of "keystone cuts" with metal clamps poured into them to secure megalithic construction was an advanced technology used all over the world, from the Andes to Egypt, Greece and Southeast Asia. He maintains that only power tools could have made the intricate articulation and drill holes found in extremely hard granite and basalt blocks in Bolivia and Peru, and that the megalith builders had to have had advanced methods for moving and stacking gigantic blocks of stone, some weighing over 100 tons.
340 Pages. 6x9 Paperback. Illustrated.. $19.95 Code: ATP

THE ILLUSTRATED DOOM SURVIVAL GUIDE
Don't Panic!
By Matt "DoomGuy" Victor
With over 500 very detailed and easy-to-understand illustrations, this book literally shows you how to do things like build a fire with whatever is at hand, perform field surgeries, identify and test foodstuffs, and form twine, snares and fishhooks. In any doomsday scenario, being able to provide things of real value—such as clothing, tools, medical supplies, labor, food and water—will be of the utmost importance. This book gives you the particulars to help you survive in any environment with little to no equipment, and make it through the first critical junctures after a disaster. Beyond any disaster you will have the knowledge to rebuild shelter, farm from seed to seed, raise animals, treat medical problems, predict the weather and protect your loved ones.
356 Pages. 6x9 Paperback. Illustrated. $20.00. Code: IDSG

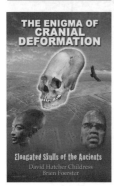

THE ENIGMA OF CRANIAL DEFORMATION
Elongated Skulls of the Ancients
By David Hatcher Childress and Brien Foerster
In a book filled with over a hundred astonishing photos and a color photo section, Childress and Foerster take us to Peru, Bolivia, Egypt, Malta, China, Mexico and other places in search of strange elongated skulls and other cranial deformation. The puzzle of why diverse ancient people—even on remote Pacific Islands—would use head-binding to create elongated heads is mystifying. Where did they even get this idea? Did some people naturally look this way—with long narrow heads? Were they some alien race? Were they an elite race that roamed the entire planet? Why do anthropologists rarely talk about cranial deformation and know so little about it?
250 Pages. 6x9 Paperback. Illustrated. $19.95. Code: ECD

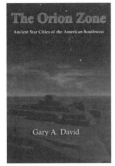

THE ORION ZONE
Ancient Star Cities of the American Southwest
by Gary A. David

This book on ancient star lore explores the mysterious location of Pueblos in the American Southwest, circa 1100 AD, that appear to be a mirror image of the major stars of the Orion constellation. Packed with maps, diagrams, astronomical charts, and photos of ruins and rock art, *The Orion Zone* explores this terrestrial-celestial relationship and its astounding global significance. Chapters include: Leaving Many Footprints—The Emergence and Migrations of the Anazazi; The Sky Over the Hopi Villages; Orion Rising in the Dark Crystal; The Cosmo-Magical Cities of the Anazazi; Windows Onto the Cosmos; To Calibrate the March of Time; They Came from Across the Ocean—The Patki (Water) Clan and the Snake Clan of the Hopi; Ancient and Mysterious Monuments; Beyond That Fiery Day; more.

346 pages. 6x9 Paperback. Illustrated. $19.95. Code: OZON

EYE OF THE PHOENIX
Mysterious Visions &
Secrets of the American Southwest
by Gary A. David

Contents includes: The Great Pyramids of Arizona; Chaco Canyon—Ancient City of the Dog Star; Phoenix—Masonic Metropolis in the Valley of the Sun; Along the 33rd Parallel—A Global Mystery Circle; The Flying Shields of the Hopi Katsinam; Is the Starchild a Hopi God?; The Ant People of Orion—Ancient Star Beings of the Hopi; Serpent Knights of the Round Temple; The Nagas—Origin of the Hopi Snake Clan?; The Tau (or T-shaped) Cross—Hopi/Maya/Egyptian Connections; The Hopi Stone Tablets of Techqua Ikachi; The Four Arms of Destiny—Swastikas in the Hopi World of the End Times; and more.

348 pages. 6x9 Paperback. Illustrated. $16.95. Code: EOPX

THE KIVAS OF HEAVEN
Ancient Hopi Starlore
By Gary A. David

Orion dominates the winter sky, flanked by Taurus the Bull on one side and Canis the Great Dog on the other—three key constellations for the Hopi and prehistoric Pueblo People of the American Southwest. When these stars appear in the entryway of the kiva roof, they synchronize the sacred rituals being performed below. Chapters include: What *is* a Kiva?; Stargates in Antiquity; New Mexico's Orion Kivas; Colorado's Orion Temple; Hopi Flying Saucers; Book of Revelation and 2012; Indian Mothman and Sacred Datura; Tales of Giants and Cannibals; Chaco Canyon: Mirror of Sirius; Dog Stars in the Land of Enchantment; The Chaco-Chakra Meridian; Seven Spiritual Cities of Gold; Orion's Global Legacy; more.

386 Pages. 6x9 Paperback. $19.95. Code: KOH

MAPS OF THE ANCIENT SEA KINGS
Evidence of Advanced Civilization in the Ice Age
by Charles H. Hapgood

Charles Hapgood has found the evidence in the Piri Reis Map that shows Antarctica, the Hadji Ahmed map, the Oronteus Finaeus and other amazing maps. Hapgood concluded that these maps were made from more ancient maps from the various ancient archives around the world, now lost. Not only were these unknown people more advanced in mapmaking than any people prior to the 18th century, it appears they mapped all the continents. The Americas were mapped thousands of years before Columbus. Antarctica was mapped when its coasts were free of ice!

316 PAGES. 7x10 PAPERBACK. ILLUSTRATED. $19.95. CODE: MASK

PIRATES & THE LOST TEMPLAR FLEET
The Secret Naval War Between the Templars & the Vatican
by David Hatcher Childress

Childress takes us into the fascinating world of maverick sea captains who were Knights Templar (and later Scottish Rite Free Masons) who battled the ships that sailed for the Pope. The lost Templar fleet was originally based at La Rochelle in southern France, but fled to the deep fiords of Scotland upon the dissolution of the Order by King Phillip. This banned fleet of ships was later commanded by the St. Clair family of Rosslyn Chapel (birthplace of Free Masonry). St. Clair and his Templars made a voyage to Canada in the year 1298 AD, nearly 100 years before Columbus! Later, this fleet of ships and new ones to come, flew the Skull and Crossbones, the symbol of the Knights Templar.

320 PAGES. 6x9 PAPERBACK. ILLUSTRATED. $16.95. CODE: PLTF

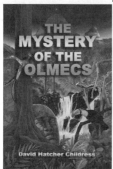

THE MYSTERY OF THE OLMECS
by David Hatcher Childress

The Olmecs were not acknowledged to have existed as a civilization until an international archeological meeting in Mexico City in 1942. Now, the Olmecs are slowly being recognized as the Mother Culture of Mesoamerica, having invented writing, the ball game and the "Mayan" Calendar. But who were the Olmecs? Where did they come from? What happened to them? How sophisticated was their culture? Why are many Olmec statues and figurines seemingly of foreign peoples such as Africans, Europeans and Chinese? Is there a link with Atlantis? In this heavily illustrated book, join Childress in search of the lost cities of the Olmecs! Chapters include: The Mystery of Quizuo; The Mystery of Transoceanic Trade; The Mystery of Cranial Deformation; more.

296 PAGES. 6x9 PAPERBACK. ILLUSTRATED. BIBLIOGRAPHY. COLOR SECTION. $20.00. CODE: MOLM

THE LAND OF OSIRIS
An Introduction to Khemitology
by Stephen S. Mehler

Was there an advanced prehistoric civilization in ancient Egypt who built the great pyramids and carved the Great Sphinx? Did the pyramids serve as energy devices and not as tombs for kings? Mehler has uncovered an indigenous oral tradition that still exists in Egypt, and has been fortunate to have studied with a living master of this tradition, Abd'El Hakim Awyan. Mehler has also been given permission to present these teachings to the Western world, teachings that unfold a whole new understanding of ancient Egypt. Chapters include: Egyptology and Its Paradigms; Asgat Nefer—The Harmony of Water; Khemit and the Myth of Atlantis; The Extraterrestrial Question; more.

272 PAGES. 6x9 PAPERBACK. ILLUSTRATED. COLOR SECTION. BIBLIOGRAPHY. $18.00 CODE: LOOS

SUNKEN REALMS
A Survey of Underwater Ruins Around the World
By Karen Mutton

Australian researcher Mutton starts with the underwater cities in the Mediterranean, and then moves into Europe and the Atlantic. She continues with chapters on the Caribbean and then moves through the extensive sites in the Pacific and Indian Oceans. Places covered in this book include: Tartessos; Cadiz; Morocco; Alexandria; Cyprus; Malta; Thule & Hyperborea; Celtic Realms Lyonesse, Ys, and Hy Brasil; Canary and Azore Islands; Bahamas; Cuba; Bermuda; Mexico; Peru; Micronesia; California; Japan; Indian Ocean; Sri Lanka Land Bridge; India; Sumer; Lake Titicaca; more.

320 Pages. 6x9 Paperback. $20.00. Code: SRLM

LOST CITIES & ANCIENT MYSTERIES OF THE SOUTHWEST
By David Hatcher Childress

Join David as he searches for the lost mines and stumbles upon a hollow mountain with a billion dollars of gold bars hidden deep inside it! In Arizona he investigates tales of Egyptian catacombs in the Grand Canyon, cruises along the Devil's Highway, and tackles the century-old mystery of the Lost Dutchman mine. In Nevada and California Childress checks out the rumors of mummified giants and weird tunnels in Death Valley, plus the mysterious remains of ancient dwellers alongside lakes that dried up tens of thousands of years ago.

486 Pages. 6x9 Paperback. Illustrated. $19.95. Code: LCSW

PATH OF THE POLE
Cataclysmic Pole Shift Geology
by Charles H. Hapgood

Maps of the Ancient Sea Kings author Hapgood's classic book *Path of the Pole* is back in print! Hapgood researched Antarctica, ancient maps and the geological record to conclude that the Earth's crust has slipped on the inner core many times in the past, changing the position of the pole. *Path of the Pole* discusses the various "pole shifts" in Earth's past, giving evidence for each one, and moves on to possible future pole shifts.

356 PAGES. 6x9 PAPERBACK. ILLUSTRATED. $16.95. CODE: POP

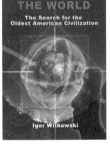

AXIS OF THE WORLD
The Search for the Oldest American Civilization
by Igor Witkowski

Polish author Witkowski's research reveals remnants of a high civilization that was able to exert its influence on almost the entire planet, and did so with full consciousness. Sites around South America show that this was not just one of the places influenced by this culture, but a place where they built their crowning achievements. Easter Island, in the southeastern Pacific, constitutes one of them. The Rongo-Rongo language that developed there points westward to the Indus Valley. Taken together, the facts presented by Witkowski provide a fresh, new proof that an antediluvian, great civilization flourished several millennia ago.

220 pages. 6x9 Paperback. Illustrated. References. $18.95. Code: AXOW

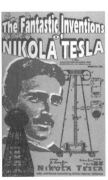

THE FANTASTIC INVENTIONS OF NIKOLA TESLA
by Nikola Tesla with additional material by
David Hatcher Childress

This book is a readable compendium of patents, diagrams, photos and explanations of the many incredible inventions of the originator of the modern era of electrification. In Tesla's own words are such topics as wireless transmission of power, death rays, and radio-controlled airships. In addition, rare material on a secret city built at a remote jungle site in South America by one of Tesla's students, Guglielmo Marconi. Marconi's secret group claims to have built flying saucers in the 1940s and to have gone to Mars in the early 1950s! Incredible photos of these Tesla craft are included. •His plan to transmit free electricity into the atmosphere. •How electrical devices would work using only small antennas. •Why unlimited power could be utilized anywhere on earth. •How radio and radar technology can be used as death-ray weapons in Star Wars.

342 PAGES. 6x9 PAPERBACK. ILLUSTRATED. $16.95. CODE: FINT

ORDER FORM

10% Discount When You Order 3 or More Items!

One Adventure Place
P.O. Box 74
Kempton, Illinois 60946
United States of America
Tel.: 815-253-6390 • Fax: 815-253-6300
Email: auphq@frontiernet.net
http://www.adventuresunlimitedpress.com

ORDERING INSTRUCTIONS

✓ Remit by USD$ Check, Money Order or Credit Card

✓ Visa, Master Card, Discover & AmEx Accepted

✓ Paypal Payments Can Be Made To:
   info@wexclub.com

✓ Prices May Change Without Notice

✓ 10% Discount for 3 or more Items

SHIPPING CHARGES

United States

✓ Postal Book Rate { $4.00 First Item
                     50¢ Each Additional Item

✓ POSTAL BOOK RATE Cannot Be Tracked!

✓ Priority Mail { $5.00 First Item
                  $2.00 Each Additional Item

✓ UPS { $6.00 First Item
        $1.50 Each Additional Item

NOTE: UPS Delivery Available to Mainland USA Only

Canada

✓ Postal Air Mail { $10.00 First Item
                    $2.50 Each Additional Item

✓ Personal Checks or Bank Drafts MUST BE
  US$ and Drawn on a US Bank

✓ Canadian Postal Money Orders OK

✓ Payment MUST BE US$

All Other Countries

✓ Sorry, No Surface Delivery!

✓ Postal Air Mail { $16.00 First Item
                    $6.00 Each Additional Item

✓ Checks and Money Orders MUST BE US$
  and Drawn on a US Bank or branch.

✓ Paypal Payments Can Be Made in US$ To:
  info@wexclub.com

SPECIAL NOTES

✓ RETAILERS: Standard Discounts Available

✓ BACKORDERS: We Backorder all Out-of-
  Stock Items Unless Otherwise Requested

✓ PRO FORMA INVOICES: Available on Request

ORDER ONLINE AT: www.adventuresunlimitedpress.com

Please check: ☑

☐ This is my first order   ☐ I have ordered before

Name

Address

City

State/Province   Postal Code

Country

Phone day   Evening

Fax   Email

Item Code	Item Description	Qty	Total

Subtotal ▶	

Please check: ☑   Less Discount-10% for 3 or more items ▶

☐ Postal-Surface   Balance ▶

☐ Postal-Air Mail   Illinois Residents 6.25% Sales Tax ▶
   (Priority in USA)   Previous Credit ▶

☐ UPS   Shipping ▶
   (Mainland USA only) Total (check/MO in USD$ only) ▶

☐ Visa/MasterCard/Discover/American Express

Card Number

Expiration Date

10% Discount When You Order 3 or More Items!